D1604299

MR. RUTLEDGE
OF SOUTH CAROLINA

JOHN RUTLEDGE (1791)
From the miniature by John Trumbull
Used with permission of Yale University Art Gallery

Mr. Rutledge

OF SOUTH CAROLINA

RICHARD BARRY

BOOKS FOR LIBRARIES PRESS
A Division of Arno Press, Inc.
New York, New York

INTERNATIONAL STANDARD BOOK NUMBER:
0-8369-5618-4

LIBRARY OF CONGRESS CATALOG CARD NUMBER:
71-146851

PRINTED IN THE UNITED STATES OF AMERICA

To His Elizabeth

and

To Mine

ACKNOWLEDGMENTS

The author wishes to thank all those in South Carolina, North Carolina, and elsewhere, who, because they possessed records, were their custodians, or had access to source material concerning John Rutledge, helped to make this volume possible. The many kindnesses extended to him he attributes to the character and the importance of the subject.

Thanks are due to the present members of the Rutledge family: Mr. Archibald Rutledge, Mr. Pinckney Rutledge, Miss Marie Rutledge, Miss Caroline Rutledge, Miss Anna Rutledge, and the late Mrs. Edmund Felder—all of whom were generous in showing the author their relics and in contributing their special knowledge.

The author's thanks are also due to the specialists in southern history: Professor Robert Meriwether of the University of South Carolina, author of the article on John Rutledge in the *American Dictionary of Biography;* Professor J. H. Easterby of the College of Charleston, author of the article on Charles Pinckney in the same volume. The author is indebted for creative criticism to Professor Archibald Henderson, Professor J. G. deRoulhac Hamilton, and Professor George Coffin Taylor all of the University of North Carolina; and, to the historian of South Carolina, Professor David Duncan Wallace, of Wofford College, Spartanburg, S. C.

Mr. A. S. Salley, the State Historian of South Carolina, offered every facility at his command. Colonel Aiken Simmons, president of the Historical Commission of the city of Charleston, gave generously of his time and attention. Mr. Langdon Cheves searched his memory and his records to supply data otherwise unobtainable. Mr. O. T. Wallace, Clerk of the Court, in Charleston, patiently and courteously assisted in the successful probe of the pre-Revolutionary files in the County Court House.

Mr. Solon J. Buck, chief archivist of the Government of the United States, and his predecessor, now Professor of American History, in the University of North Carolina, Dr. Robert D. W. Connor, kindly pointed the way to source material with which they are familiar.

Mr. William W. Ball, the justly celebrated editor of the Charleston *News and Courier*, assisted most generously and in practical ways that only a newspaperman can command.

Mr. Arnoldus Vanderhorst, namesake and lineal descendant of the Governor to whom Rutledge resigned his commission as Chief Justice of the state, permitted study of the Rutledge manuscripts in his private collection.

Mr. Theodore Jervey, president of the South Carolina Historical Society, and author of *The Slave Trade*, extended his interest, special knowledge, and advice.

Mr. S. Osgood Freeman, vestryman and treasurer of Christ Church, made it possible to study the records of Rutledge's membership.

To the authors in Charleston, whose intellectual hospitality made the path of research so pleasant, the author's gratitude can hardly be overstated. These include Mrs. Harriet Leiding, Miss Alice Huger Smith, Miss Josephine Pinckney, Mr. Herbert Ravenel Sass, and Mr. Charles Bennett.

Mr. E. Miltby Burton, curator of the Charleston Museum, assisted in re-creating the atmosphere of the time.

The present owners of 116 Broad Street, Dr. and Mrs. Harley Lindsey, graciously extended hospitality to an understanding of John Rutledge's "palace."

Miss Mabel Webber, genealogist, the chief authority on the origins of South Carolina's principal families, gave liberally of her time and material.

Mr. William C. Wolfe, of Orangeburg, and members of his family who are the present owners of the house in which Governor Rutledge lived at times during the Revolution, generously cooperated.

The author is deeply indebted to the sympathetic and intelligent services of the many librarians who assisted: in particular Miss Ellen Fitzsimmons of the Charleston Library Society, Mrs. Lyman A. Cotton, curator of the Southern Collection at Chapel Hill, N. C., Miss Ellen H. Jervey of the Genealogical Society, Charleston, Miss Belle da Costa Greene of the J. P. Morgan Library in New York, Mr. Martin of the Manuscript Room of the Library of Congress, and Mr. William Reitzel, director of the Historical Society of Pennsylvania.

To Mr. W. Adolphe Roberts, of Jamaica, author of *The Caribbean, Admiral Raphael Semmes, The French in the West Indies,* and other works, for resignation of material.

To Mr. Glenn N. W. McNaughton, of New York, for his substantial assistance in the original research and for his encouragement in "the dark days of early discovery."

To the staffs of the Congressional Library in Washington, the library of the Daughters of the American Revolution in Washington, the Carnegie Library in Washington, the library of the Historical Society of Pennsylvania in Philadelphia, the library of the University of North Carolina in Chapel Hill, the library of the University of South Carolina in Columbia, the state library in the statehouse at Columbia, the library of the Charleston Library Society, the library of the College of Charleston, the public library in Charleston, the library of the S. C. Historical and Genealogical Society, the library of the University of Georgia in Athens, Ga., the New York Public Library, the library of the New York Historical Society, the library of the American-Irish Historical Society, the library of the Museum of the City of New York, and to Mr. Charles Jenkins of Philadelphia.

However, the writer has not secured the approval of any of these authorities for any portion of his completed manuscript. Through them he secured the opportunity to peruse above seven thousand manuscripts, more than two thousand old newspapers, above three hundred books of original records, and the volumes listed in the bibliography. The responsibility for his interpretations and conclusions is entirely his own.

—RICHARD BARRY

CONTENTS

MR. RUTLEDGE

OF SOUTH CAROLINA

I.

ANDREW RUTLEDGE came penniless to the New World, with the degree of LL.B. from Trinity College, Dublin, and some knowledge not contained in books. He was under thirty, lanky, with impressive dignity and discreetly silent as to his origin.

Arriving in Charles Town the young barrister found South Carolina in its third generation. Soldiers had pushed out the frontiers hundreds of miles. Ecclesiastics and physicians were firmly established. The legal profession was coming into its second generation.

This was in 1730.

The King's Council, the local ruling oligarchy, shortly granted Andrew, for no stated consideration and rent free, a thousand acres in Kingston. The land, however, was uncultivated and cultivation of the soil was no part of the young emigrant's purpose, though to get into "government" the law required that one "be a Christian communicant" and own land.

Andrew, therefore, traded his thousand wild acres for a hundred and fifty acres, partly cultivated, only twenty miles from the state house, in Christ Church Parish. There he joined the Episcopal church; shortly he was elected to the Assembly.

This all occurred within two years. It was a comparatively fresh settlement in a virgin land, to be sure, but even so the quick rise of Andrew Rutledge could hardly be explained solely on the basis of his charming personality and his Dublin degree. Here was unwonted progress "without visible means," and people talked. Some said he was "a younger son"; others that "an eminent personage," unnamed but doubtless someone in London, favored him.

These were only legends. The facts were more prosaic. Andrew's father owned and operated a small farm in County Tyrone, Ireland.

1

The family was numerous and humble, being originally Norman and crossing to Ireland from France in the time of Edward III. This French-Irish peasant (with the Scotch blood indicated by the son's Christian name) could not have given his son the advantage of a college education were it not that on the edge of his farm he operated a tavern. From its proceeds he managed to send Andrew to the University of Dublin.

When the father died he left to Andrew the care of his younger brother, John, who wanted to be a doctor. Andrew turned over to John the patrimony, which proved to be slender, though enough to help the younger brother through two terms at Trinity. Andrew went to London to practice law, promising to send John enough out of his earnings to keep him at Dublin.

In London Andrew found it not so easy to get ahead, but he learned something that decided him to try his luck in America. In Charles Town one Nicholas Trott proved to be Andrew's oyster.

Trott is still an historic enigma. Only two facts about him are undisputed: namely, that for the first generation of the eighteenth century he was one of the chief figures in South Carolina and that he was a scoundrel. Otherwise it was said he was the illegitimate son of one of the Lords Proprietors; that he was the grandson of the Earl of Bedford; that his natural parent was Lord Shaftesbury, chief promoter of the Carolinas, and a potent figure at the English court; that he was the absconding Governor of the Bahamas whom no one dared apprehend. Which, if any, of these scandalous rumors was true is not established.

Andrew Rutledge either knew the facts or Nicholas Trott believed he knew them. This knowledge and Andrew Rutledge's use of it was the source of his quick rise. The grant of land to him, without consideration, was on recommendation of Nicholas Trott, King's Councillor. His legal practice prospered because of his favor with Trott, who was also Chief Justice.

South Carolina was already steeped in the legend that it was peopled by wastrel aristocrats and dissolute adventurers of noble English stock. In fact, however, none of the eight British lords who secured the original grant from Charles II in 1660, nor any recognized descendant, ever set foot in America. No one of noble birth, legitimate or illegitimate (unless one of the rumors about Nicholass Trott was true), ever lived in South Carolina.

However, the legend—the romantic illusion—never died. The reason it persisted more in the Carolinas than in the other colonies is that when the first proprietary grant was made to the eight lords, their agents induced settlers to migrate by representing that in the new province they would be governed, as they had been at home, by the established and authentic nobility. When it was found that the Lords Proprietors would not forsake the comforts of England for an unprofitable wilderness, colonization slowed down; whereupon the Lords Proprietors invented a set of titles (Cacique, Landgrave, and so on) which colonists could purchase. These were not popular. Anyone with money enough to buy such a title knew it was spurious—for it was illegal for anyone but the king to bestow a real title—and had no desire to flourish on obvious counterfeit. The colonists wanted authentic bearers of the titles to which they were accustomed and in their absence they imagined passable substitutes. They so dearly loved a lord that for any scion thereof no bar could be sinister.

These psychologic origins of the South Carolinians formed their only essential difference from the first settlers of New England. None of them came to America with an "escape complex," except the French Huguenots, who constituted a minority. The others did not run away from political or religious persecution. Without important exception, they were British, French, German, Belgian, and Swiss immigrants, of hard-working, thrifty, common stock.

The lure was cheap land, and, more often than otherwise, rents were not paid because the Lords Proprietors did not build forts or roads, supply soldiers, kill Indians, or suppress piracy. So South Carolina was populated by discontented Europeans, who were determined to get the worth of the money they hadn't paid in—and were willing to fight for it.

Yet the underlying complaint—the subtle, controlling nuance of the early generations—a period closed only technically in 1719—was the resentment against the Lords Proprietors for not keeping their promises and coming in person to their lands. The colonists had no one to look up to, to set the pace and style, to govern and exploit them —except at a distance and by proxy.

Thus was the stage set for such a man as Nicholas Trott, who was the closest South Carolina could get to actual court nobility, and, by the way of Trott, for Andrew Rutledge.

When questioned the young barrister said he was born in Ireland. None of his contemporaries and none of his descendants knew any more of the Rutledge origin. Though he had influence with Nicholas Trott he shrewdly avoided becoming too closely identified with a man whom many distrusted. He also held fast to others, like the Bulls and the Izards, who were believed to have court connections. He played one against another while the lord-loving and lord-starved colonists were hoist with their own petard.

Obviously Andrew was not the type of Irishman who was willing to labor for a shilling a day. It was believed that he was of the gentry; even of the landed nobility; perhaps an Irish nobleman; in any event, a favorite of the King's, formerly even as now, resident in a subject land. "A man may hold all sorts of posts if he will only hold his tongue."

While the glamour was still about him, and he was socially the new lion of Charles Town, he met, among others, Colonel Hugh Hext, "a man of worth, intelligence, of great position in the province, and owner of vast tracts of land." He undertook a law suit for Colonel Hext, won it, and dined at the Hext home.

Hext was an old man with a young wife, his second, and a single child, a daughter, who was the apple of his eye. He had come, in 1684, from Dorsetshire, England, though genealogists have found that there were Hexts in Wales a thousand years ago. Hugh Hext's capital in 1684 was one hundred pounds sterling, gained as prize money while he was a lieutenant in the English army, serving in Flanders. This capital and his native ability placed him in the forefront of the great landed proprietors of South Carolina.

Seven years before Andrew Rutledge arrived in Charles Town,

Colonel Hugh Hext, a widower then, in his early sixties, had married Sarah Boone of Christ Church Parish, less than half his age, niece of a former Acting Governor, English-born. He then moved permanently into the Town, employed a factor to manage his business and overseers to operate his plantations on the St. Helena and Edisto Islands and on the Waccamaw, the Stono, and the Wando Rivers.

In 1732, after a full and prosperous life, Colonel Hugh Hext died. In 1733, his attorney, Andrew Rutledge, married his widow. For Rutledge this was a major achievement. It provided him with the necessary background, for no man could have a ruling voice in government unless he possessed an estate and lived up to it. He moved into the Hext home and was accepted as a member of the inner group of thirty or more families who ruled His Majesty's Province of South Carolina.

They were home-made English lords, everyone of them, even when French Huguenots, or Irish or Scotch or Welsh, or Teutonic in origin. No one yet displayed a coat of arms; they knew each other too well. Yet, each owned a principality. Slavery perfected manual service as it had not been perfected since antiquity. The South Carolina "lords" basked in luxury and measured each other warily, for each was in heart and in fact a potential ruler.

The fly in the ointment for Andrew Rutledge was the will of Hugh Hext which had bequeathed the income from the great estate to "my beloved wife for her lifetime only, and then in perpetuity, in fee simple, to my beloved daughter, Sarah Hext." To complicate matters further, Thomas Hext, Hugh's brother, a widower without issue, died and left his entire estate also to his "beloved niece, Sarah Hext."

The Thomas Hext estate—eleven hundred acres on the Waccamaw with one hundred and fifty slaves—was a fair dot in itself. Another uncle, Francis, said he too would make the little girl his heiress. When her mother died the girl would come into five or six times as much as her mother already had. The mother was frail and bore no children to Andrew Rutledge; if she had they would have been cut off from the Hext fortune. Her daughter, however, was the chief heiress in South Carolina.

Sarah was nine years old, "a lively child, of à brunette color, with blue eyes, and wide fetching smile; most intelligent and, indeed, the darling of the entire Hext family."

Andrew wrote to Doctor John Rutledge, his brother, who was in the East India merchant service as a ship's surgeon. The letter went to London, to Malta, to Aden and missed John as he was departing from Calcutta. He received it on his next trip out. He started at once for Charles Town.

It was two years before Doctor John arrived and went to live with his brother in the same house with little Sarah, now aged eleven. Shortly, he opened an office on Broad Street and put out a shingle: "Dr. John Rutledge, Master of Physick."

On Christmas Day, 1738, in Christ Church, across the Cooper River, Doctor John married Sarah Hext. The previous September she had been fourteen. He closed his office and never again practiced medicine.

The first-born of Dr. John Rutledge and Sarah Hext Rutledge was a boy. The date of his birth is unknown. It has been set as probably September, surely in the year 1739, when his mother was barely fifteen.

They named him John.

Except in his biologic urge and, perhaps, as a social entrepreneur, Doctor John revealed slight aptitude for being the head of a family. He was not interested in operating the paying plantation which Uncle Thomas had left the "beloved" Sarah and which automatically became his because of the act of the Assembly making a husband the possessor of his wife's estate. He took a cash offer for the Waccamaw lands and all the slaves except about twenty—enough to keep up a town house. Thus the usufruct of the lifework of a prosperous planter, representing thirty years of battle with malaria, swamps, lusty Negroes, tides, rains, and the rice market went to purchase and maintain a big house on Tradd Street.

There the John Rutledges settled—with twenty domestics in the slave house. The fortunate doctor, with no profession to distract him and no business to annoy him, and with a good margin of·cash on call at the factor's, had fallen into the cream pot. He concentrated all his energies on what seemed to him the most desirable of achievements, establishing a proper social milieu for the Rutledge name, which no longer possessed merely a legendary background.

For a time—until Sarah became more intimate with the actual facts about his college education—Doctor John permitted himself one useful activity; he tutored his own children.

These arrived with the regularity of the seasons and no more than nine to twelve months apart. After John II came Andrew II, then Sarah III, and Hugh II. These were within four years. After she passed eighteen years the rest interval for the mother was increased. Eighteen months separated Hugh from Thomas, and Thomas from Mary, who became a great beauty and the model for one of Romney's masterpieces. Eighteen months also separated Mary from the last child, Edward, who signed the Declaration of Independence.

Though none realized it, there was a duel to the death between Sarah and Doctor John as to which would survive the other, and in this contest each was handicapped. Sarah suffered from the excessive child-bearing which was customary in that era. Many women died young and stepmothers were commonplace.

Doctor John had to pay the toll required of a retired physician who, accustomed to unlimited alcohol, becomes the light of society in a hot climate. While Sarah, only in her 'teens, was making her substantial contributions to the life of the colony, her husband, nearly twice her age, did his part by creating a mixed drink which found polite approval. He called it Officers' Punch; it was composed of cognac and an East Indian aperitif, with a touch of spice. Officers' Punch, with Madeira, Bordeaux, and rum at regular intervals, became the chief source of entertainment in Tradd Street. Formal dinners were served twice a week and the house was always "open."

In his early life Doctor John had known many ship's officers; in the second year of his Charles Town residence he had served a militia regiment as surgeon, going into the woods for a few months against Indians. Thus, the nucleus of the society which centered at the Tradd Street house was composed of mariners from all parts of the empire and of soldiers going to and from frontier assignments.

However, brother Andrew supplied most of the guests, selected from important assemblymen, members of the Council, the judges, even the Governor himself. Andrew saw the road leading to the speakership of the Commons House of Assembly, possibly—though a vain hope—to the Chief Justiceship, perhaps to the Governorship.

Andrew required a place in which to weave his ambitious web, for his wife died and he did not own sufficient slaves, nor did he have the income to maintain the proper drawing room and a sufficiently generous table. So he combined with brother John.

For all practical purposes the brothers—Andrew and John—were one Rutledge. One supplied the house, the entertainment, and the light conversation; the other brought in the ruling minds of the port, an instinctive knowledge of governance and a will to power. Through the decade of the 1740's the political affairs of the Carolinas were discussed and debated by the leaders of Charles Town in the Rutledge house.

In this atmosphere John Rutledge spent his formative period. He had barely learned to talk when the most celebrated legal complication of the generation was thrown right into the Rutledge household through the retention of Andrew Rutledge as advocate by the Reverend Dr. Whitefield in his trial for heresy, insubordination, and unseemly conduct while wearing the sacred frock.

Dr. Whitefield was the most popular orator of his time. No church could hold the throngs which assembled to hear him; in Charles Town he spoke in an open field—alas, without having before him the official printed copy of the prayer book. In his impromptu fervor he neglected to frame his prayers within the ordained phraseology—an unforgivable ecclesiastical offense.

Andrew Rutledge appeared before the High Commissioners of the Established Church of England and pleaded for the harried cleric to no avail. Dr. Whitefield was suspended. Andrew appealed to the bishops and archbishops in England, traveling to London to reveal his forensic art, which was then rated the equal of any in America. However, the effort was useless. Dr. Whitefield was barred—so completely that he had to stay in the fields; eventually he co-operated in forming what became the Methodist Church in the South.

For four or five years the Whitefield case was the chief topic of conversation in South Carolina. It was more important than the Indian wars, the discovery of indigo, the phenomenal advance in rice export, the repeated protests of the Commons over rising taxes, the arrival of the new Governor, Mr. Glenn, or even than the great fire which wiped out the old town and caused the building of the new.

As a social phenomenon the episode dramatizes the form of the civilization it enlivened. During the same period in New England, for instance, witch hunting had just ceased; the shadow of the Mathers was still long over the land. In the Deep South anyone would have resented an assertion that they did not take their religion straight, and there were, of course, all phases of its expression; yet the Whitefield case illustrates the essential difference in public expression of religion in South Carolina. There was an objectivity about it.

That Andrew Rutledge, though deeply involved, rode the storm, reveals his resource in political tact. He was quick to sense that he could build popularity by championing Dr. Whitefield, a man who could attract more persons to a field than a horse race could; yet he did not forget that the Church of England was linked by law with the state. He doubled his contributions to Christ Church, was elected a vestryman; he induced Doctor John to do likewise.

Thus Andrew upheld the primacy of the established church, while in his professional capacity he championed the freeborn Englishman's right to open trial and to have his cause freely heard, however deep his infamy. The result was a political as well as a social triumph.

One day when little John was about five years old his uncle, his father, and his mother came upon the children playing "court" in the garden. Andrew, Hugh, and Sarah were the jurors. John paced before them, haranguing them with a plea to oust the wicked preacher who used words too familiar in speaking of the devil.

A moment later the boy approached the "jury" from the opposite direction and pleaded in heartfelt accents that they spare the holy man whose heart was aflame with the white light of religion.

If was, of course, a childish imitation of the résumés of court pleas he had so often heard from the lips of Uncle Andrew. Yet he had been impartial. He had given an imitation both of Uncle Andrew himself and of Uncle Andrew's imitation of the opposition.

Andrew Rutledge told the parents the boy would be a barrister, and a good one; he could argue either side at will.

Sarah Rutledge eventually made what was to her a fearful discovery. Despite his father's tutoring John apparently knew neither Latin nor Greek. So Andrew was obliged to undeceive her about Doctor John's erudition. His curtailed studies at Trinity College had given short shrift to Latin and Greek.

Sarah at once came to terms with Dr. David Rhind, who had been employed in the Middleton and the Manigault homes and was the most talked-of tutor in the colony. Yet, after working for a term with his new pupil, Dr. Rhind sorrowfully informed the mother that Latin and Greek seemed too difficult for young John. Moreover, the boy was defiant about them; he refused to buckle down and, study.

There was a family conference. Confident that proficiency in Latin and Greek was the one sure mark of a gentleman, Sarah favored severe discipline. Doctor John seemed indifferent; he was not in favor of driving the child—or anything else. Uncle Andrew spoke the decisive word. Nothing must be done, he said, to break the boy's will; they must learn the subject in which he excelled and develop that. The mother agreed. The advice coincided with her instinct to make a ruler of her first-born son.

They questioned Dr. Rhind and the tutor revealed that John was proficient only in mathematics. He was instructed to specialize in that subject and, as a result, before he was ten years old John Rutledge was said to be a better mathematician than any other pupil twice his age.

For Christmas of 1750 Doctor John planned a great celebration. Since its founding, two years before, he had been a leading devotee of the Charles Town Library Society, whose avowed object was "to cultivate a knowledge of the literature and the arts." He had responded with a liberal subscription to its original appeal for funds:

"Think of the fate of Babylon, Greece and Egypt which had no public libraries; think how different Great Britain is now than when discovered by Julius Caesar; do not let your children sink to the gross level of the native Indian."

To prevent such a catastrophe Doctor John formed the habit of taking his son to the library each afternoon, where he exposed him to the array of books, maps, globes—"almost 1500 to begin with and speedily increased"—while he himself went across the street to the Coffee House.

Although the children's education had been taken from his guidance and placed in the hands of Dr. Rhind, Doctor John was still striving with good grace to do his part. That Christmas he made an effort to supply an intellectual atmosphere for the budding minds of the household by inviting the unattached bachelors of the library to dinner.

For such an event proper preparation was necessary and the festivities began two days in advance—at Shepheard's and the Coffee House. Officers' Punch sank the caissons on which, it was hoped, would be reared an imposing structure. At the celebration they served, with the terrapin, "a heavy West Indian sauce," stayed and garnished with many liquors.

That night Doctor John was taken ill and on the twenty-sixth he died—in the thirty-seventh year of his age, before he had reached his drinking prime. On the twenty-seventh he was buried in St. Philip's churchyard.

In the marital duel Sarah was the victor. At twenty-six she was a widow, with seven small children, and she was still the richest woman in South Carolina.

John, eleven years old, automatically became "Mr. Rutledge." His will never had been broken. He had always had his way, though he was a dutiful boy, reared with six younger brothers and sisters, and taught to be considerate of their desires. He also had been taught to revere "Dr." Rutledge as the exalted head of the family; he had shown no distaste for obeying his father's wishes, even to spending hours in the library whenever the Doctor left him there.

Now, however, "Mr." Rutledge gave his first demonstration of manhood. He announced he would go no more to the Library Society. Distressed, his mother turned to Uncle Andrew, who was coming into his own at last.

The uncle had no children; the Hext fortune had eluded his grasp; yet the fruit of his planning was now his to mold and enjoy. Though his stepdaughter and his brother had produced this child, he felt that "Mr." Rutledge was as his own son. He could realize in the boy, perhaps, some of those final achievements which had beckoned to him but which he had not carried out. He had a talk with John about the library.

Like any first-rate mathematician John was clear and definite. He told his uncle that a man of his age—he was in his twelfth year— should be particularly careful about his mental habits. Literature and the arts, he said, were debilitating. They tended to corrupt a man's mind and might destroy him altogether. The "bachelors of the library," he said, were idlers. He wanted nothing to do with them.

Uncle Andrew considered this gravely. Was it the boy's tactful way of saying he always had resented his father's ways? Or was it the biting comment of an original thinker? Or both ? He asked what John wanted to do. "Mr." Rutledge replied that the only books he cared for were law books and that he wanted to go into Uncle Andrew's office and study there. So a place was made in the entryway of the assemblyman's office and there John Rutledge began reading— Coke on Littleton, Fleta, Glanville, Britten, and the 'actes' of the Assembly of South Carolina; and there he drafted his first legal papers.

Though he shunned the Library Society, as a center of intellectual dissipation, John attended the theatre regularly, beginning with his twelfth year. The first play he saw was "Cato, by Mr. Addison with a prologue by Mr. Pope," at the Dock Street Theatre. He was enchanted. From then on he always said that attending the theatre was the only proper mode of studying history and manners. Among the plays he saw were "Douglas, the Recruiting Officer," "The London Apprentice, or George Barnwell," "The Mourning Bride," and seven or eight plays of Shakespeare's, including "Lear," "Hamlet," and "Romeo and Juliet."

The year after Doctor John's death Andrew Rutledge was elected Speaker of the Commons House of Assembly, a post both of honor and of flexible political power, for the occupant was chosen by the representatives of the people to deal with the Governor, who represented the King; it was a fine post for incipient statecraft.

From the Rutledge law office on Broad Street, where John was a student clerk, to the State House, where the Assembly met, was less than a thousand yards. The morning when Uncle Andrew first took the gavel there was barely a quorum present, for the planters lagged in attendance. He looked over the heads of the members and saw, in the tiny gallery which could hold only about twenty spectators, his absorbed nephew. Thereafter, whenever the Assembly sat, John was in the front row of the gallery. The daily sessions were of one sitting only, lasting from eight in the morning to a little before noon, so that the assemblymen could avoid the heat. Afterwards, the Speaker would go to his office for an hour and thence home to dinner. John was at his side from the moment he left the rostrum until the end of the day.

As the theatre had supplanted the library in the boy's allegiance so now the Assembly began to supplant the theatre. He did occasionally miss attendance at the Dock Street playhouse, which was open four nights a week, but he never missed a session of the Assembly. Often he was alone in the dim little gallery, crouching up there, absorbed. No other boy in Charles Town and very few of its citizens —except on some notable occasion—hung intent over that dusty railing, drinking in eagerly those stodgy and often halting and stupid harangues.

Between John's twelfth and sixteenth birthdays the Commons House of Assembly of the Province of South Carolina debated, among others, measures which brought forth the essence of the whole British constitutional system. Especially they considered the effort of the King's Council to orginate tax bills, which challenged the right of the direct representatives of the people to have first voice in raising the money they must pay. These bills were debated, in principle and *a priori,* just as if they had been brought to the mind of man for the first time in history, by Andrew Rutledge and his associates.

The youthful John Rutledge attended closely, not only the debates but also the underplay of parliamentary procedure which was seldom apparent to the ordinary spectator, and in this his devoted tutor was the astute Andrew, in truth, John's intellectual and spiritual father. The Speaker often said in conference with intimates, "Care not who reigns; think only of who rules." That was the only quotation that Mr. Rutledge in later life attributed to his mentor. It is the theme of both careers.

When John was sixteen Andrew Rutledge died. This was his first major calamity. However, the grooves of his life were established; his character was formed; his destiny integrated. As he himself said, "The cards were placed in my hands; I had only to play them."

John went on studying law in the office of James Parsons, later Speaker of the Assembly. In two years Parsons said the young man was ready to practice. Sarah disagreed. Why, she asked, were the boys of the Pinckney, the Ravenel, the Manigault, the Middleton, the Lynch, and the Laurens families better than the boys of other families? Because they had graduated from Oxford or Cambridge or studied at the Middle Temple. She doubted if any young man in South Carolina could hope to hold his head level with the best of his fellows if he were not educated in the old country. She concealed from "Mr." Rutledge that Doctor John's easy ways had involved the estate and that factors and overseers were stripping her of what was left. She wanted nothing to hinder him while he was studying in England.

The month after he was eighteen John Rutledge sailed for London.

I.

O N DECEMBER 24, 1760, "two ships and a brigantine, under convoy of His Majesty's Ship of War Dolphin, Benj. Marlow, esq., commanding," lay windbound off the sea end of Sullivan's Island at the entrance to Charles Town Harbor. They had just broken the record for transatlantic crossing and were only forty-one days from England.

As soon as the breeze lifted, the little fleet would proceed to the inner harbor, ten miles away, and anchor, thus officially concluding the lucky crossing, for they had not met—as all English ships feared they might—either a Spanish man o' war or a French privateer or any pirate vessel. They bore the royal mails, sixty-nine immigrants, and seven cabin passengers.

Two canoes, each formed of a single huge hollowed log, called by its Indian name of piragua and manned by black rowers, were off to greet the fleet shortly after dawn. One bore Mr. Peter Timothy, who each week published the four-page *South Carolina Gazette.*

The community was already established in the American way of life and the record of its activity was set down weekly by journalism (model early eighteenth century); that journalism was a going and forthright concern was shown by the editor's enterprise this Christmas Eve. His publication date was December 23 (the day before), but on that noon first sight of the convoyed fleet had been signaled in from the outer islands and he did not want his subscribers to wait a full week for the latest news from London, so he postponed publication for a day and left open half of the second column on the third page.

Mr. Peter Timothy was the son of Louis Timothée, a French Protestant who had married a Dutch woman. Thirty years before the elder Timothée, "language master," had been fellow tenant in Phila-

15

delphia of the Junta, the brotherhood society organized by Benjamin Franklin. He was chosen to be the Literary Society's librarian; then, being a printer, he became journeyman in Franklin's shop and when that first chain-newspaper proprietor of America was reaching out to extend his enterprises, he went to Charles Town in 1733 and revived the defunct *Gazette*. Franklin furnished a third of the capital. Timothée died shortly; but his thrifty widow bought out the Franklin interest and turned the property over to her son, who named his son Benjamin Franklin Timothy and conducted his business carefully on lines laid down by the author of *Poor Richard*. Ship-news reporting had to be a specialty in a town whose life was so largely maritime, and on this Christmas Eve the young editor pressed his rowers until they distanced the rival canoe.

Reaching the flagship, Mr. Timothy went on board quickly and remained there an astonishingly short time. He flung himself back into his canoe and the Negroes paddled him furiously to the wharf. He rushed to his office in Tradd Street, where he was publisher, editor, business manager, reporter, printer, and pressman. There his first act was to reverse the second-column rule on the third page; then, not stopping to write, he picked up the compositor's stick and composed and set:

POSTSCRIPT

The arrival Dec. 24 of His Majesty's convoy . . . brings the most deeply affecting piece of intelligence we ever yet published, viz.; an account of the death of one of the greatest princes and best of kings on this earth, no less than HIS LATE MOST SACRED MAJESTY KING GEORGE II, of glorious and blessed memory, who departed this life suddenly, on the 25th of October last; when all his faithful subjects sustained a loss they cannot enough deplore, but which is in some measure made up by the accession of His Illustrious Grandson, who was proclaimed with all the usual formalities on the 26th of October by the name of KING GEORGE III, and as a prince (born in England on the 4th of June, 1738) of such distinguished abilities and so amiable a disposition that Britons cannot fail to continue, under his auspices, a most respectable, happy and free people.

The last paragraph of the postscript stated, in nonpareil type: "Among the passengers were Mr. Thomas Smith, jun., Mr. ——— Smith, and Mr. Rutledge, etc."

Meanwhile the second canoe came in alongside the flagship. Over the gunwale clambered two boys and a number of male guests. The boys were Andrew and Edward Rutledge, sons of the Widow Rutledge of the Lexington, Phillips, and Patey-Boone plantations. They had come to welcome their elder brother, John.

Among the guests was one Walter Greenland, a carpenter formerly employed by Mrs. Rutledge; when the family greetings were over, he asked John Rutledge to be his attorney in a case which several of the attorneys in the Town had refused to undertake, though Walter did not reveal this. It seemed propitious to the young law student; had not a client come down the bay to seek him, before he actually had entered the port and before he was admitted to the South Carolina bar? Without asking too many questions and in the midst of the fervor of homecoming, John accepted his first case without retainer.

The sou'-sou'wester that usually can be relied on in Charles Town by the forenoon blew in that Christmas Eve. By tacking skillfully the two ships managed to make their way down the bay and to anchor near Broad Street wharf well before dark.

From Granville's Bastion seventy-one sail could be counted; the new arrivals made an even seventy-five. They came from or were bound to Liverpool, Antigua, Barbados, Baltimore, Philadelphia, Boston, Havana, and Savannah. The same day in the harbor of New York there were only twenty-three vessels; in Boston Harbor forty-seven; off Baltimore eighteen; and off Philadelphia—the leading rival —sixty-two.

Charles Town in 1760 was, all things considered, probably the first port of the hemisphere. It was second only to Philadelphia in annual value of imports and second only to Baltimore in exports. On both counts it topped New York and Boston.

In appearance it was unique. The place of his birth to which John Rutledge returned was described by an eighteenth-century world traveler as "the most picturesque city in America." Another declared it to be "the richest."

The spit between the rivers on which the town was built was originally barren sand, passed over by the discoverers and utilized eventually only because it was an obvious seaport. Here grew up the huts and shacks, then the houses, and then the triple-decked palaces, lifted in air because of the scarcity of essential building space. Around the palaces, in walled gardens, grew oranges, magnolias, palmettos, azaleas, ilang-ilang, jasmine, and other tropical plants.

These residences of the rich, served by black slaves, were not typically English or American, nor yet French or Spanish, though suggesting something of each. The semi-tropic climate, as well as the diverse origins of the inhabitants, influenced everything, for on this tongue of land where a constant southwest breeze tempered the equatorial heat of summer, though the winters often flirted with a light frost, a race of mingled origin, but in its ruling element northern, was working out its destiny.

The stamp of England was on it, as the flag of Britain flew over it, but the colorful topography with its exotic architecture supported a sociologic pot into which were poured the stark practicality of the frontier, exaggerated European fashions, man's primal urge for freedom, English legal forms, the Anglo-Saxon reliance on parliamentary government, the philosopher's dream of Utopia, an exacting social background, a basic ethnic conflict, Oriental mental habits (the freeman embracing the despot), the British gift for colonization, Celtic precision and intuition, Huguenot thrift and adaptability, the Swiss, Dutch, and German talent for home-making, the Viking instinct for attack, the Quaker genius for "accommodation."

All these—and more—mingled there. The forces that were to subdue a continent were being marshalled and refined by a people who had just come out of sweaty shirtsleeves into scented ruffles and powdered wigs. They liked others to believe they were idlers and this created about them and among them an atmosphere of affectation, which insider and outsider often mistook for reality.

They had the diplomacy prompted by their mingled blood streams, but at heart they were fighters. They had come up fighting. Great riches, as the world went then, had come to them, but luxury had not dulled the zest of the conqueror nor his pride. They were near enough to their origins to be willing to gamble their destiny for causes in which they believed.

The young barrister seeking to establish himself knew that as a residence for wealthy men Charles Town exceeded anything west of London. The same *Gazette,* which turned its column rule for the death of George II and gave part of a modest line to the return of Mr. Rutledge, noted in three adjoining lines the death on Dec. 23 of Thomas Elliott, "esteemed the richest citizen of our province."

However, in addition to the Elliott fortune there were three others —those of the Manigaults, the Mazycks, and the Laurenses—each of which was believed to exceed any single fortune held in the North. Nor were these unduly conspicuous. On the peninsula between the Cooper and the Ashley Rivers, and below the "neck," were the residences and walled gardens of more than two hundred planters and merchants—"every one a king." These were largely the town houses of estate owners, each estate consisting of many thousands of acres, usually stretching inland along the adjacent two hundred miles of seacoast, or along the many inflowing rivers.

To serve this concentration of wealth and colonial power in its litigious activities there was a bar of twenty members and a bench of three.

Of the members of the bar "all but a very few" went down to the wharf to meet John Rutledge when he came home. They were headed by James Parsons and Charles Pinckney. Parsons, in whose office the young man had 'read law' earlier, told everyone, "the boy has it in him."

Behind Parsons and Pinckney lay an historic shadow, professionally distressing to them all, though seldom mentioned and never openly. Either might have been—should have been—Chief Justice; neither was.

Parsons, born in Ireland, was as much an Englishman as Peter Timothy with his French father and Dutch mother; perhaps more so, for he was a former member of the Inns of Court in London, where he had practiced successfully. The majority of his colleagues, with similar antecedents, recognized in him their "eldest and most learned" and, if they had had anything to say about it, he would have been their Chief Magistrate.

Pinckney, nephew of his namesake Charles Pinckney, who had died two years before, had just been made "Colonel" and was in command of the fortifications, though he remained active in law practice. He was of the colateral line in the third Pinckney generation. His grandfather, the original Thomas Pinckney, of all-English stock, came as a planter in 1692, bringing with him for investment the money he had made as a privateer out of Bristol, in the old days when a mariner who converted defenseless shipping to his own use was a "privateer" if he flew your flag, and a "pirate" otherwise.

"Old Tom's' son, Charles (the second generation Pinckney), had been educated in London as a barrister, had returned home to practice and became, in due time, even as Parsons /was now, "the most learned and the eldest." The sudden death of the presiding Chief Justice nine years before had confronted the Governor with an apparent necessity of selecting a first magistrate, though the law of the colony, established by the Crown as the condition under which government had been taken over from the Lords Proprietors at the request of the rebellious colonials, provided that the Crown appoint the Chief Justice, while his two associates might be laymen appointed by the Governor, also a Crown appointee.

After consultation with members of the bar, and with their almost unanimous consent, the Governor had appointed Charles Pinckney Chief Justice. Pinckney served six months; then from England came Mr. Peter Leigh with an appointment from the Crown as Chief Justice. Pinckney had to step aside.

The *Gazette* never published the facts behind the Leigh appointment, nor were they mentioned in public for many years, but they became common knowledge—"a legal secret." As an officer in charge of returns during the late election in England Mr. Leigh, conveniently for the government, had counted in its candidate, but the opposition charged him with falsifying the returns. The dispute became so great that the government decided to sacrifice him. Mr. Leigh resigned, but he had to be given a post. So it happened that the native South Carolina Englishman of unimpeachable character was forced to give way to the Englishman who came to his high office with a charge behind him of improper conduct.

Leigh administered the office for seven years, but in all that time his colleagues addressed their own man as "Chief Justice Pinckney," and so did many others. Without otherwise articulating their protest the colonists were warning each other that, whatever their qualifications, none of them need aspire to the highest places in the government.

Chief Justice Pinckney had gone to England where he placed his two young sons, Charles Cotesworth and Thomas, in schools. There he heard of the excellent impression being made at the Inns of Court by the nephew of his former associate, Andrew Rutledge, and he brought back this word to Charles Town. Since he was counted as a man both generous and just, his words took root, especially after his death, as his nephew, Colonel Pinckney, repeated them. Others had brought back similar reports.

Charles Town was very close to London, though six weeks away. It was said that if a man who had been to England appeared on the streets of Boston or Philadelphia he would be pointed out and people would turn to look at him, whereas the only man people would turn to look at in Charles Town was one who had not been to England. It was not, therefore, merely because he was a traveler from overseas that John Rutledge was met at the wharf by most of the members of the bar.

They saw John in the stern-sheets of the flat-bottomed boat as he was being lightered in. They noted first that he was dressed in black cloth and that buttons were strangely missing from his sleeves and pockets. The hose were of black silk, the buckles on his shoes of black. Though the shoes themselves and his gloves were of shamoy, there was a hanging band of black crape around his hat, the conventional weeper.

Yet as he stepped to the wharf he smiled and greeted them lightly, until someone jokingly asked him who was dead. And so it was they got the news, for the *Gazette* had been taken to their homes and they had not seen it.

George II was dead. "Long live King George III!" John Rutledge explained that he was wearing the mourning prescribed "for all gentlemen" by the Court Chamberlain in the Court Order of October 26. It gave him at once an added distinction among them, for he alone was in the mode. On the morrow all of them were dressed as he was.

A room had been reserved at Shepheard's Tavern, at Broad and Church Streets. They escorted him the two blocks across the cobblestones that had been brought in ballast and which now paved the streets nearest the wharves. A long table had been cleared in the taproom and there they sat down, under tall candles, and were waited upon by soft-voiced, deft darkies.

Christmas Eve supper was waiting for them all at home, so they confined themselves to a punch made of lemons, sugar, hot water, and Irish peat 'whusskey,' known as 'the river of life.' This punch was served from silver pitchers. Long-handled pipes, with Virginia tobacco, were passed.

This was the only time, except when alone at his own fireside, that a South Carolina gentleman could smoke. When a man was seen on the street smoking one of the "long seegars from Havana," he was known at once as an uncouth stranger, probably the Yankee skipper of a slave ship. So, at Shepheard's, mellowed by the peat tang of the punch, John's future colleagues looked him over.

They saw a thin young man, not very tall, about five feet eight. The reddish tinge in his light brown hair was concealed by a copious dusting of powder. He wore no wig, but his own plentiful hair was tied in the back with a black silk ribbon. His nostrils were very highly arched and were excessively delicate, yet the bridge of the nose was high. His ears were small and leaned against his head.

Despite his youth his body seemed set; he seldom moved it, but his head moved swiftly and his eyes darted rapidly, and always inquiringly. His mouth was mobile; his chin square. The frontal lobes over his eyes protruded; his combed-up hair accentuated the naturally high brow.

The wide-set eyes were blue-gray—sharpshooter's eyes. They always held the eyes of the person to whom he talked. He had one quality, repeatedly remarked upon, which grew more noticeable later: he knew what one was saying before all was said (he seemed to read it with his eyes) and he would often answer before one was through speaking. This made some people say he was rude or abrupt.

However, he ignored no one and was punctilious. He seemed to notice everything, especially the little things others overlooked. When one talked to him it was like coming into a sunny room. One started in anew, not only because he was cheerful, but because he seemed to have light—light everywhere.

Led by James Parsons and Charles Pinckney the members of the bar of Charles Town that Christmas Eve drank alternately to the new King, George III, and to their new associate. George Hanover was twenty-two; John Rutledge twenty-one. Each was coming into a kingdom.

2.

Sarah Hext Rutledge still owned three houses in Charles Town. The least of these was on Dock Street, which was no longer fashionable, and was being given over to business, especially since the building of the theatre there six years before. It was a rather small house, of only six or seven rooms, and was kept by the widow as a *pied à terre* for her rare sojourns in the city.

In this house John Rutledge was greeted by his mother and spent his first night in South Carolina after three years abroad.

The slave quarters in the rear of the Dock Street house had only three rooms, indicating that probably no more than six adult slaves could live there, beside the individual body servants who were often permitted to sleep in the bedroom at the foot of the master's or mistress's bed.

The minimum of domestic slaves required in a town house by one of the first families was ten or eleven. Some had as many as twenty. More than twenty was ostentatious; less than ten a confession of poverty. Ostentation was a grievous sin for which there was no real pardon among the discriminating. Poverty was a calamity for which there was no cure except wealth. The unwritten law of the colony, infinitely stronger than the written law, was exact on both points. Society positively would not tolerate either poverty or parvenus.

Was it because the town with its recent origins was too close to both? This was the beginning of the fourth generation, and only the second generation of cultured gentlefolk. Ninety years before, the first whites had driven the Indians from the site of the city and had settled down to establish their civilization.

Despite the mixed national origin, politically and socially Charles Town was a part of England, but "more English than the English." So far they consciously imitated only the virtues and pretensions of the mother country, not her vices. And they had a greater homogeneity, greater autocracy; the unwritten laws were more powerful in South Carolina than in the homeland.

"A man's word must be *better* than his bond, because unguaranteed. A woman's name must never pass his lips except in respect; a promise, however foolish, must be kept. If he wrongs any man he must offer his life in expiation. He must always be ready to fight for the State or his lady."

This was the order of "chivalry" under which they lived. John Locke, idealistic philosopher, had written the original form of government laid out for the colony, and while it had been proved impracticable and had been vastly altered, still "here existed as near a real Utopia as the world had seen in over 2,000 years. One must go back to Attica to find on earth before South Carolina in the seventeenth century any social group which brought so near to realization exalted purpose in a pleasant way of life."

Perhaps the small size of this miniature empire accentuated the rigidity of its social customs. There were in Charles Town no more than four thousand white inhabitants, and of these less than a quarter were of the first families. No person could enter that charmed inner circle without being at once intimately appraised. And the stoutest rule was: "Outsiders not wanted."

This spirit of self-reliance and self-sufficiency was so intense, so fierce, that it governed subconsciously the social as well as the political caste. Had they not already proved their mettle in casting off one form of government (that of the Lords Proprietors) and assuming another (the royal)? Did they have a premonition of a greater struggle still ahead? Who could insure success in that struggle but their own tried leaders? They were skeptical of outsiders and they were skeptical of anyone among them who could not maintain the standards of living they had set as desirable.

John Rutledge felt all this keenly when he stepped inside the Dock Street town house that Christmas Eve and found that his mother had no butler in the drawing room, no game cook in the kitchen, and no coachman in the yard. It meant nothing at all—less than nothing at all—to the cultivated keenness of his pride that a competent meat and vegetable cook had prepared an excellent meal, that there was a Corromantee house boy to pull out his chair and serve the meal, and a dutiful wench to care for the chambers.

This was not what he had been accustomed to from the time of his birth to the death of his father, ten years before. He knew well it was not what James Parsons went home to that night, nor Charles Pinckney, nor Gabriel Manigault, nor Isaac Mazyck, nor Henry Laurens, nor Arthur Middleton, nor scores of others.

His mother tried to make light of it by explaining that the slave quarters were required to house the rowers for the night, that she had left the game cook, the butler, and the coachman on the plantation whence the family would go on the morrow.

That only accentuated the lack. Where was Pompey, his body servant, the black boy with whom he had been brought up, who had been his playmate and companion until he went to England? He, too, was waiting on the plantation. There had not been room in the canoe to bring him.

All this his mother passed over with attempted lightness. John accepted it and went on to tell them of the life in London. He had heard Pitt speak in the House of Commons again and again. His eyes dilated as he described the orator. He rose and walked up and down and gave them an imitation—he remembered the orations, nearly word for word. When he told them that he had met Pitt personally, they all gasped. Edward wanted to know how he had managed it.

John told them. It had not seemed possible to get into the House that day. The galleries were crowded when he applied for entrance; he had been told to move on; but he had persisted and had slipped a sovereign into the hands of a guard, who smuggled him in. Then he had gone down to the edge of the gallery and was no more than twenty feet from the orator as he spoke; he had managed adroitly to slip into the members' lounge, where the great man was surrounded by friends who were congratulating him. John edged in and presented himself, gave his name, and said he came from Charles Town. The mention of Charles Town had taken Pitt away from his supporters. He had asked John many questions. The mother, Andrew, and Edward listened awe-struck. The greatest man in the British empire—in the world, indeed—had talked to their John. It seemed incredible.

He told them about the theatre. He had gone twice every week. That accounted for some of the money his mother had been sending him—six hundred pounds every year. Had he seen Garrick? Yes, indeed. Many times. He had seen him play "Lear" the week before George II died. Garrick, he said, was as great a man as Pitt—in a different way, of course. Then he gave them an imitation of Garrick. He imitated him in "Lear" and in "Macbeth" and in "Sir Giles Overreach."

What about his trip to Ireland? How had it happened? He told them about that. He had always dreamed of going to the University of Dublin, where his father and his uncle had gone, and he had managed it—and stayed there for three months.

His mother was eager for the details. But what could he do at a university in only three months? He took a paper from his pocket and showed them a "citation." It proved that he had written a thesis and that it had been accepted—making him a member of the university.

The widow seemed unhappy. Alas, she had not been able to send him the money to stay and spend four years at Dublin. He was not graduated. John laughed away her regrets, saying he had had all he wanted. She insisted he should have stayed at least five years in England and four in Ireland. Arthur Middleton was seven years in England. The Pinckney boys were to stay fourteen. Gabriel Manigault had been there nine years, and the rest of his life would write after his name the word "barrister," though he was now the richest man in America. It seemed to her a cruel blow of fate that she could manage no more than three years abroad for her son.

John said she had nothing to regret, that he was a member of the best university in the world, had been admitted to practice at the Middle Temple in London, and had tried two cases there as a barrister and *won* them. Neither Arthur Middleton nor Gabriel Manigault had done *that*.

Mrs. Rutledge was somewhat appeased. After all, she knew Gabriel and she knew Arthur and she knew John. Perhaps three years *was* enough for *her* boy.

John next asked his mother to reveal the facts about the estate, which she had concealed from him before. She wanted to wait until after Christmas to talk business, but that did not suit him. He must know at once. He was gentle about it, but determined. He was now the head of the family; he had a right to know, he said, and it was her duty to tell him.

So it appeared that the reason they could not have a town house properly equipped, like other first families, with a full quota of servants both in town and on the plantation, was that the old residence on Tradd Street, where John had grown up, had been leased for a long term, to the Peronneaus, with option to purchase; she believed they would never give it up. It was Peronneau lease money which had paid for his last year in England. The other house, the one on Coming Street, nearly twice as large as this mere cottage on Dock

Street, was also leased to a new family—the Bakers, also with option to purchase.

Why, asked John, had she given options to purchase with the leases? The tenants insisted, the widow explained. John made no comment, but it was enough to make him realize how much a man was needed to take affairs in hand.

There was more bad news. The Chapin brothers, down on St. Helena Island, to whom Dr. John had leased the old Thomas Hext plantation of seven hundred and fifty acres, declared that it really had been sold to them and were demanding deeds without further compensation. The overseer of the Stono plantation (1090 acres) had left summarily two months ago because Mrs. Rutledge could not pay his year's stipend, and the rice crop was a total failure there. On the Lexington plantation, given over largely to indigo, a pest had come in the late spring and the crop promised very little. At Phillips, the home place, the indigo was poor because the overseer had been supplanted by John's brother Thomas, not yet eighteen, and he had been persuaded by Fortune, the old slave who formerly managed things so well, to experiment in a new method of caking, with mediocre results. The Edisto Island property was not even being worked; the problem of an overseer rendered any profit from it unlikely.

Still worse was the implication in the courteous but chilling letter she showed him from Henry Laurens—"It is regretted that our facilities of credit cannot be extended beyond the first of the month *ultimo*." That would be in January. She owed him a bill running back over three years, covering nearly all needed supplies. A year's credit was customary; two years not unusual; but three years meant that the next step would be a letter from a lawyer.

It was the more surprising, she said, in Mr. Laurens, for she had not bought anything of him in several months. She had been buying from the Mazycks. John was startled; he considered that a mistake, he said, and insisted she take back her business to Laurens, talk to him, and give collateral if necessary. "Never turn your back on a creditor," he said, "Always keep your face to him."

There were many other bills, a minor one from the carpenter,

Walter Greenland. So that was why Greenland had sought John for an attorney—to collect a bill. Very well, he would pay it that way.

Two of the creditors had secured lawyers, and she had letters from them, inquisitive, rather than menacing. However, John knew well how serious this was. People did not retain lawyers without putting down retainers. They could not begin suit without putting up fees in cash. Collection suits were not customary unless bankruptcy appeared to be inevitable. That the Widow Rutledge had these letters was fatal proof that the infallible appraisal of the community had been passed on her affairs. By opinion of the informed she was insolvent. The vultures were hovering.

She had seen Mr. Parsons. He had told her not to worry. He would hold them off at least during the spring and summer when court was not sitting. John listened to it all gravely, appraised the situation quickly, and told her she need give her financial affairs no further thought. He would take care of everything.

To see his self-confidence was pleasing. It warmed her mother's heart, but, after all, she was a woman of experience. She had managed her affairs, operated the plantations, cared for the slaves, marketed her commodities, educated her children. As tactfully as possible, she told him that though she would not question his ability, she felt she had a right to know *how* he would manage.

By opening an office and starting the practice of law, he told her. He would do it the first possible day—on the second of January.

She asked if he realized that no man could make money from the practice of law in sufficient amount to meet their needs until he had been at the bar for years? She reminded him that Mr. Parsons often had said that he nearly starved during his first years of practice. Even Charles Pinckney, she recalled, went three years before he earned a sizable fee, and he had begun with the prestige of his uncle, the "Chief Justice," right behind him, not years in the past as was that of John's Uncle Andrew.

None of this had any effect on John. He listened to it as to any old story and dismissed it with a wave of the hand.

Then Mrs. Rutledge presented her solutions. She had three. The first was to sell the Stono plantation. An overture had been made to her—one-tenth cash down, with security for full payment within two years. This would pay all their debts.

John asked who made the offer. It was the former overseer, whose inattention, she believed, had caused the failure of the rice crop. John said to tell him there would be no sale. And he insisted they would not sell another acre of Rutledge land. Already it had dwindled to a third of what it had been when he was born. That was small enough.

Sarah sighed and presented her second solution: why not sell off some of the slaves—say about fifty (they had more than two hundred), in parcels of families, of course, and only to selected new owners. That would realize enough money to meet their most pressing obligations.

John was silent. Another unwritten law of the community was never to part with a slave. The blacks constituted the most obvious form of wealth. All men bought as many as possible and always put their surplus money into slaves, but no man ever sold one except in dire necessity. To sell slaves in parcels was open confession that you were liquidating an estate or were on the verge of bankruptcy. He refused to consider any such proposal.

Then the widow got around to her third solution—marriage. There were several possibilities, all nice girls of excellent family, and any one of them—provided he followed her direction cautiously—would bring in a dot of from twenty thousand to fifty thousand pounds. That, also, would solve their problems.

John was cold. Mrs. Rutledge began talking excitedly about Miss Hörry—a charming girl, she said, nicely educated in France. Her people were devoted to her and had four prosperous plantations. She knew they would not think of letting her marry without a dot of at least thirty thousand pounds. Didn't John remember her? He said he remembered Miss Hörry.

Sarah felt encouraged. She thought perhaps it was time to let her son know the rest of her burden. So she talked frankly. For three years she had been sending every available pound of spare cash to him in London and now the other children were demanding as good an education as he had. Hugh was fifteen and he wanted to be a lawyer, too. Andrew had no desire for a professional career and was already at work in the Manigault warehouse as a shipping clerk, but he wanted to start in business for himself. He needed capital and—justly, she thought—asked to have his education money for that purpose. Then there was Sarah, nearly eighteen. Desirable young men were not giving her proper attention; apparently because they realized that her dot, if any, would be small. Thomas had not made his wishes known yet, but he was entitled to consideration, like the others. He was nineteen. As for Mary and Edward, they were only "babies," being thirteen and twelve, respectively, but she must plan for them. Each of them, she felt, should be entitled to as much as any of the others.

John waited respectfully for her to finish. Then he said he had a different plan which he proposed to put into effect. He would disclose nothing of it; she must trust him absolutely. It might be necessary for her to make over everything to him, just as it would have been if his father had died intestate, and the law of primogeniture had operated. As it was, Doctor John, by will, had bequeathed the estate so easily his to his wife. She would remain in ostensible possession, but Mr. Rutledge would have the option of full legal control.

In return for her stepping aside completely he promised to provide, in due time, a dot for Sarah, and also one for Mary when she grew up. He would find money to set up Andrew in business. He would talk with Thomas, learn what he wanted to do, and help him to do it. He would send Hugh to England for his legal education, possibly in the fall. She need worry no more about any of the bills. He would attend to all of them. He would take over the management of all the plantations.

She asked him where he would get the money. She must trust him to find the way for that, he said, but he would sell neither land nor slaves, nor did he intend to marry.

The widow felt thwarted. She was in the presence of something she never had contemplated, of something she could not define. She never before had known such a man—neither her father, nor his, nor his uncle, nor any of her uncles, the six Hext brothers, had been like this. Some of these men had been strong, far stronger than his father, Doctor John, but none of them had had this audacity, this secretive hardness, this soaring will. It stirred her pride, but what did it mean and where might it lead them? For ten years she had been the head of the family. She was widely praised, admired, and respected. She had been the greatest heiress of the colony; she was still one of its great matrons. It would not be easy to step aside so completely, and so abruptly. He was not consulting her; he was commanding her. There was no threat in what he said, yet its implication from anyone but the son she idolized would have been unbearable. She was like a hen who has been mothering a brood of barnyard chicks and suddenly finds among them an eaglet.

Andrew had long since gone out. Little Edward was by the fireplace, asleep, they thought, but they found he was weeping. He had heard everything and was crying because no provision had been made for him. John asked what he wanted to be. "A lawyer, just like you," said Edward. And John promised to provide the money to send him to England as soon as he was old enough, to the Inns of Court.

3.

Early the next morning Sarah and three of her sons went down to Queen Street wharf, where the canoe was tied, and embarked. The canoe was of the luxurious type afforded only by wealthy families. It was made of three enormous cypress logs, hollowed and cunningly jointed together. Over its rear third was erected an awning, with side curtains. There was even an arrangement for a partition so that there could be separate sleeping space when they went on long journeys.

Six rowers were there to speed them home. The tide was coming in, and with the tide they could row the twelve miles to the plantation in less than three hours. If the tide had been against them it would have taken more than twice as long.

It was the tide that had caused them to spend the night in town.

The widow had planned for John to sleep the first night at the plantation if he came in time; but his boat had docked six hours too late to catch the in tide.

Long before most people were up on Christmas morning, the Rutledges were off in their canoe. They went up the Cooper into the Wando River, east along the Wando to Holbreck's Creek, down Holbreck's to the south fork called Butler's Creek, and down Butler's to the wharf at the Phillips plantation, which was combined with Lexington plantation, and, also, with the Patey-Boone.

Thomas was there to meet them, with Hugh and Sarah and Mary. They crowded the tiny jetty of double boards that extended into the creek.

At the top of the bluff, chattering and bright-eyed, were the slaves. Most of them—the field hands, the mechanics, and the lesser domestics—stood far back, respectfully but joyously. In the front was the white-haired and proudly self-sufficient butler, a sort of field marshal overseeing them all. Beside him stood the stout middle-aged housekeeper and, almost equal in honor with her, the game cook. In the second rank were the meat and vegetable cook and the coachman, the poultry-minder, the dairyman, the farrier, the wagonwright, the fisherman, and the Negro preacher. With them—and only a grade lower—were the houseboys, the room wenches, and the stable boys.

A little to one side stood the body servants, a caste distinct from the others, headed by a beaming portly woman, Mauma. Each of the Rutledge children had nursed at her breast. It was about this time that Mrs. Pinckney wrote home from England about calling on the Crown Princess with her children; when she told that her children were always nursed by a Negro Mauma the Princess personally examined their skins and "cheerfully remarked it had not seemed to affect their color in the slightest."

John greeted his slaves one by one, by name, but when he came to Mauma he embraced her. Beside her stood a stripling of his own age, Pompey, his body servant, with whom he had spent eighteen years of his life. He shook hands with him in cordial affection.

As soon as the boys in the canoe could tie up and bring in his bundles, he unpacked and distributed the presents which he had brought from London—bright kerchiefs for the women, sashes for the men, toys for the children.

Now his amour propre was satisfied. Here was the plantation menage proper for a South Carolina gentleman. The satisfaction lay not in the mere fact of possession nor in the number of slaves. It was in the quality of the service, and especially in its origin. No man could go forth and *buy* a group of slaves to make up such a household. They were the product of cautious, slow selection over decades, generations. The choice was made only after many years and from among hundreds of slaves. Each of these domestics had some special talent, developed by training. If one died he was not replaced by purchase from outside, but by choice from among the likeliest of the slaves on the estate.

Thus the quality and also the loyalty of slave service was perfected. To degrade one of these house servants to a place in the fields was a punishment worse than imprisonment or the lash. The chance of rising from the field to the house was more alluring than any prospect of a change through running away.

All work was suspended for Christmas. In the town offices were closed, and only a few retail shops were open for a half day. That was why John had told his mother that the second of January was the first possible moment to open his office. Nothing important would be transacted before then.

Meanwhile the Rutledges exchanged hospitality with kinfolk and friends. Everyone was talking about the French and Indian War which was raging in the North. Major John Stuart had just come from Virginia, where he had had a narrow escape from a massacre. He dined with the Rutledges and told about his adventures.

It did not occur to John to fight the Indians. The military would look after that. His job was nearer home. Besides, his mother employed an Indian, a Yemasee, to supply the game for the table. John sent for him, had a consultation with him and gave him a new hatchet brought from England and a jacket of sequins. The Yemasee departed forthwith into the forest beyond the Wando.

John consulted his fisherman, one of his slaves, and told him what he wanted for a certain day about three weeks hence, the day against which the Indian was also to be prepared with his game. A great quantity of oysters must be provided. There must be "white-foots" obtained from the sea at the far end of the peninsula in Bull's Bay. There must be plenty of diamond-backed terrapin from the swamps; crayfish, shrimps, and deep-sea red snapper. As it was to be a special occasion the fisherman could have the large canoe, with necessary rowers, to take him far out and stay all day, and as many days as he found necessary.

The head woodcutter was also given a special job in preparation for the appointed day. He was to take the necessary gang of men into the swamps and bring in a great number of palmetto "cabbage." The "cabbage" was the heart of the palmetto tree and taking it out meant the death of the tree. When properly prepared over a long slow fire this marrow provided a dish resembling, in taste, a mixture of cauliflower, asparagus, and burr artichoke, with an added swamp tang of its own.

To those who called as well as to those on whom he called during Christmas week, John said casually, "I'm giving an oyster roast on Wednesday a fortnight. Will you come?"

Would they come? No doubt. Everyone knew what an "oyster roast" meant, for that was a very modest way of describing such a feast.

Meanwhile, he inspected the plantations. There were fourteen hundred acres at Phillips and the adjoining Lexington, which they owned, and another fourteen hundred leased acres at Boone Hall, which included the old Patey plantation. Sarah Hext was grand-daughter to a Boone, son of the early Acting Governor. Some of her children were born at Boone Hall.

The "money" crop was indigo. Now that the British govern-ment was paying a bounty, it paid better than rice. Moreover, rice culture was not possible at Phillips or Patey-Boone or Lexington, where the ground was high and the near-by water salt.

John's first concern was his slave quarters. Every plantation owner of sound vision thought first of the health of his live property. Sanitary conditions for the slaves were as necessary as social standing for his own family.

On the three plantations there were more than fifty separate cabins for slaves; they were of uniform architecture and construction, built of English brick with high pitched roofs of Spanish tile; and with broad fireplaces. There were three rooms in each, separated by brick partitions. Each would house a family; a man, his woman, his pickaninnies, and possibly an aged parent or two.

Thomas wanted to be a planter, so John went with him in the canoe up the Ashley River to the Stono, near Rintole's Ferry, and inspected the 1090-acre place, of which about four hundred acres was excellent land for rice. This was about fourteen miles northwest of Charles Town, just beyond the tidewater. It was decided that Thomas should live at Stono and have charge there as overseer for his brother.

The others were eager to learn John's decision as to where they should live. The girls wanted life in the town. The Dock Street theatre was giving four performances every week and a new French dancing master, M. deBourrone, had opened an academy on Church Street. Nearby was the hairdresser, Mlle. Penine. Invitations were out for the annual meeting of the St. Cecelia Society, which was already the most exclusive social organization in the new world, and there was talk that this year there might be dancing as well as the usual vocal and instrumental music. It was to be in the third week in January. Hugh and Edward also wanted to live in town. They talked about the advantages of the Charles Town Library Society to which Mr. Manigault had given the upper half of a fine mansion. It contained more than six thousand volumes.

John told them they could not live in town that winter; perhaps the next. They pleaded and protested; they said their mother had promised them they could "as soon as John comes home and there is no longer need to send away the cash." It was to no avail. He treated them indulgently and lightly, as if they were children, and his mother only the eldest of the lot.

The day after New Year's he was up before dawn, routing out the rowers. The tide was ebbing. The canoe landed him at Broad Street shortly after eight. He was at Mr. Parson's office when that elderly gentleman arrived at nine. He asked his former mentor if he would go before the court and "stand" for him, in application for admission to practice. Certainly, said Mr. Parsons, but court did not sit until April. What was the hurry?

John wanted it done at once, that day, that very hour. Mr. Parsons assented, but said it probably would be eleven o'clock before the proper magistrate could be summoned to the Court House. A messenger was sent around to his home. Meanwhile, John went across the street and asked Mr. Charles Pinckney to second him.

At eleven the acting Chief Justice, William Simpson, arrived at his chambers in the Court House. Ordinarily he would not have appeared so soon after a holiday, but a message from James Parsons was not easily ignored.

William Simpson was not an attorney. He was a lay justice, appointed by the Crown *ad interim*. He had been out from London only a year. He was a modest, obliging man who strove to do his best, who realized his inadequacy in the elaborate technique of the law, and who had great respect for Parsons's learning and Pinckney's ability. He tried to follow them and let himself be guided by them in all he did. If they agreed he was sure; if they disagreed he was distressed.

John Rutledge appeared in a new wig, deeply powdered in dead white. He wore a white muslin ruching and delicate cuffs of French lace under his brocaded black silk gown. This was the costume required for practitioners at the Temple and it had been made to his order, at a cost of fifty pounds, by the tailor in Regent Street who made the gowns and wigs for Lord Channing.

At it was not a court day neither the acting Chief Justice nor the other attorneys were wigged and gowned, but they were much interested in John's new outfit; they examined and admired it. Mr. Parsons told the Court his young friend had just come home to Charles Town and wanted to practice law. Justice Simpson looked at Mr. Pinckney and found assent from that quarter. He said that would be all right, that John Rutledge was welcome. No questions were asked; no papers submitted. John simply swore the oath.

Only the month before, however, Mr. Chief Justice Simpson had refused even to consider the application of Joshua Nogge, an attorney from Boston, though it was stated that he too was a member of the English bar.

Leaving his court costume at the Dock Street house, John, without a wig, went along Queen Street to the wharf, to the office of Austin, Laurens, and Appleby. He had to pass the slave-market quarters, which covered a whole block near the warehouses. A slaver from Havana was being unloaded of its living "merchandise," over two hundred slaves who would live there "on consignment" until sold by the firm.

There was great bustle, excitement, and stench. The fastidious young Rutledge forced his way to the office. At a distance he could hear the sharp, quick voice of Henry Laurens, dominating everything. Laurens had been at his desk since before dawn; it was known that he sometimes worked twenty hours a day. He not only attended to all his business in person; he also wrote all the letters, and he had hundreds of correspondents in all parts of the world. He was the most conspicuous, one of the wealthiest, and perhaps the most important man in South Carolina. The young barrister was starting at the top in picking Henry Laurens as the first nut he had to crack.

John was obliged to wait for others ahead of him and he noticed none was permitted to stay long. He had ample chance to inspect the man; until now he had seen Laurens only at a distance. He saw "a swarthy, well-knit man, below medium size, clearly a Huguenot, aggressive, very decided—the face that of a man very much the master of himself, his moods and his passions. Those lips, naturally so firm as not to need to be compressed, look suited to say sharp things if their owner chooses, and doubtless he sometimes will choose; eyes very watchful with a quizzical, twinkling humor, suggesting both fun and wit—a bit cock-sure—a keen, intelligent, melancholy countenance."

At length he was alone with the merchant and he introduced himself. Laurens received him cordially and asked many rapid-fire questions about London. John spoke with such intelligence about both the political and commercial situations that Laurens seemed to enjoy his conversation greatly.

John mentioned the family indebtedness; it was now his, and he would pay. Laurens changed his relaxed mood at once. "Good," he said. When would he pay? John said it would have to be later, after he had more time to "take hold." Then he quoted his mother as saying Mr. Laurens might have legal work for him.

The merchant reached in his desk, drew out a paper, and handed it to him. It was a bill against Andrew Guerin, planter, from another planter, Francis Bremar, deceased. The executors of the estate were Henry Laurens, James Laurens, Egerton Leigh, and Benjamin Gadsden.

This was queer. Egerton Leigh was an important attorney. Laurens divided his business largely between James Parsons and Egerton Leigh, the former for domestic, the latter for foreign actions. Why should Henry Laurens ask John to be his attorney, ostensibly for collection of a bad debt, when his co-executor in the affair was his own attorney? Was he being given a "dead" case so the merchant might be rid of him?

John said nothing of his thoughts. He thanked Laurens, pocketed the paper, said he would see to it, and then took from his own pocket a memorandum which he handed the merchant. It was a list of supplies he wanted. He said he would have his boys row around to the wharf and take them out that day.

Laurens read the list: "2 tuns Madeira, 4 cases schnapps, 4 cases Curacao cordial, 2 casks Bordeaux, 1 bbl. molasses," together with some hardware, muslins, and dried fruit.

The merchant started to hand back the memorandum, then paused and talked to John like a father. Did he not know that he already owed a bill more than three years old? Moreover, his mother had established other credit; why not call on that?

John said he preferred to do business with one firm.

Laurens pointed to the list and said that Mrs. Rutledge had not used half that wine in three years. He was sorry to learn John had fallen into such habits in England—if so, he could not be expected to supply indulgences for them—at least not on credit.

Then John frankly confided his plans. Henry Laurens listened and replied, with a quizzical grin, "All right—this time."

As Rutledge walked away he felt he had gained only a most doubtful legal assignment—a bone tossed from the rich man's table— and a final extension of credit.

That night the rowers took him back to the plantation with the tide. He announced to his mother, dramatically, that his career had begun. He was now a member of the South Carolina bar. He was attorney for the great Henry Laurens. He took from his pocket the few coins he had and tossed them to her.

"I start at the bottom," he said, "penniless."

There was, indeed, very little cash in the whole province. People, as a rule, did not pay cash. John might go for months without it. He needed no money for rent, labor, transportation, or food, most of which his servants grew or caught. Credit at a mercantile house supplied hardware, drygoods, and groceries. For his newspaper he paid once a year. His boy was his barber; the washerwoman did the laundry. He had brought back enough clothes from London for two or three years. The only times he might need cash would be at Shepheard's Tavern or the Coffee House in Elliott Street. His visits there would be in the late afternoon, for gentlemen of his intimacy did not go there in the evening. He thought of a way to avoid this without being obvious—and, at the same time, to make himself a marked man by establishing a new style.

He let it be known he would not sleep in town; that he preferred the plantation, not occasionally or once a week as others did, but every night. When the tide was right he rose before dawn and had his Negro boys row him to town. When the tide was against him he

rode horseback from Phillips to Mount Pleasant, and then had two
of his boys meet him with a canoe and row him the mile and half
across the Cooper estuary. He went back each night, part or all the
way by water, according to the tide.

This required him to leave town early—before the drinking
hour—and of course it solved the only remaining cash problem; it
also made him America's first daily commuter.

This tended to silence the tongues which speculated as to why
the Rutledges did not live in town that winter. John was not so old-
fashioned as that; he was living in the English manner, working at his
office in town each day, sleeping in the country every night.

Already, the word was spreading—the Rutledges were coming
back. This news gained strength when word also spread of the coming
feast.

The day of the oyster roast arrived.

At dawn the wagons were on the road, bringing supplies from
various parts of the plantation to the greensward in front of the
Great House, set at the end of its avenue of live oaks that stretched
a mile to the main highway. The oak trees were more than three
hundred feet apart.

The slaves brought utensils, dug pits, and set up a number of
ovens, in parallel lines, two hundred yards apart. The house wenches,
directed by the butler, set the long cypress tables which the carpenters
had erected midway between the ovens and just at the side of the
road. They used the ancestral napery, china, silverware, linen—some
of which had been brought by Hugh Hext from England in 1684
when he came with his original grant from the Lords Proprietors.

The feast was spread under a bright sky. It was shaded by the
Spanish moss which festooned in long spirals from the hoary oaks.
The brisk January air was pervaded by the tantalizing odors of the
cooking.

Before noon the guests began to arrive by buggy, by horseback,
or by canoe. The Hörrys came from St. Phillips' Parish, across two
rivers. They had to start at dawn, but Mrs. Rutledge had made sure

that Miss Hörry and her parents should be present. When she suggested guests who lived in other parishes, John had objected. She noted that he had asked, almost exclusively, their neighbors from Christ Church Parish, but he would not give her his reasons.

At noon John offered his arm to his mother and together they walked from the Great House down to the tables to inspect the service. After it was approved, to the proud satisfaction of the butler, the fine linen, silver, glass, china, and cutlery were removed to wicker baskets at the side.

The bare boards were then spread with individual linen mats, wooden oyster platters, oyster knives, and, for each guest, a protective arm-rest clamped to the table. There was also a large tumbler for each guest.

At noon the fires were started. Soon the pits on either side were glowing with hickory coals and the thin smoke was curling up into the tall fronds of the live oaks. Shortly after twelve more guests arrived. Everyone knew that promptness was important to the proper preparation of a roasted oyster, so all came before one o'clock.

In Christ Church there were sixty male communicants and about a hundred and fifty voters. More than half of these, with their wives and grown children, were present that day. The carpenters waited near-by with extra cypress lumber to add new tables if needed—and before long they were needed. The tables spread down the avenue for a quarter of a mile; but there was no crowding; everyone had plenty of elbow room. The effect was certainly baronial. The lord of the manor was "at home."

Precisely at one o'clock John blew a hunter's horn from the steps of the Great House. This was the signal for the "hands" to pour the oysters, by the barrelful, on the live coals. Simultaneously the guests were seated and the butler appeared, with his assistants, bearing silver pitchers of hot drinks—whiskey punch for the men, eggnog with a dash of nutmeg and a little Barbados rum for the women. The tumblers were filled.

No one tasted the punch, however, before John rose from the head of the first table, glass in hand, and offered the toast: "To our friends, neighbors and guests from Christ Church Parish—and else-where, welcome!" They all drank.

Instantly, a battalion of pickaninnies ran from the fires bearing platters of sputtering oysters straight from the hot coals. There fol-lowed a clatter of knives struggling with oysters. There was a picka-ninny for every two guests. They were trained to watch and keep everyone supplied with sizzling oysters, one at a time. The purpose was to get the freshly steamed oysters from the fire to the gullet with all the juices intact.

This went on for the better part of an hour. Then a male guest near the head of the table gave the signal—it was not thought seemly for the host to suggest any pause in the eating—and the men withdrew by stepping over the stationary benches.

When they had withdrawn, the women also rose. It was not so easy for them, especially the young ones who wore long bouffant skirts, to get out without confusion. They, too, had to get over the benches, and if a girl's or a woman's foot showed beyond the toe, her embarrassment was intense. The men chivalrously avoided the danger-ous chance of seeing a glint of hose above a shoe top. The matrons got themselves out, without help, and then assisted the girls.

The guests strolled along the creek or wandered over to the Negro cabins and watched the "picks" dance or otherwise rested for an hour, while the butler's assistants removed the rough tools of the oyster massacre and set the formal table.

About three o'clock they all came back from the creek or the cabins or the Great House, where some took their midday siesta, and sat down again at the long tables, now transformed to gleaming cascades of napery, crystal, china, and silver, with the early buds of January roses sprinkled down the middle.

Now it was apparent how ridiculous it was to call this an oyster roast. There were crayfish in aspic, shrimp and watercress salad, red snapper baked whole in Bordeaux sauce; there was a terrapin stew and venison patty, with a pudding made of palmetto hearts and yams baked so tenderly they fell into the mold of any hand they touched. There was Madeira for the men and schnapps for the women, or Bordeaux if they preferred. There were biscuit beaten hard and thin; each only a bite, but served plentifully. Everything was trundled to the tables in huge pannikins, which acted like fireless cookers to keep the food warm.

The eating went on for all of two hours. With the cardinals chattering above in the oak leaves, the winter sun sifting through, the Madeira softening any sense of haste, everyone felt free of time and space. Who wanted to hurry when confronted by a deep-sea red snapper baked in Bordeaux? Or a swamp terrapin who jumped from his diamond back so recently into the soup of beef stock set in rum? Or a plentiful helping of palmetto marrow?

The venison patty was the chef d'oeuvre. The women wanted to know what the game cook had put in it. The Indian had brought in the deer, but venison was only the base of a patty like this.

John Rutledge called his game cook, a wrinkled, dried-up old darky woman, black as coal, with kinky white hair. Her beady amber eyes glowed with suppressed excitement. She held herself aloof, proud, and dignified. She was not haughty, but she was equal to the best of them in personal distinction. The white folks—rulers of all the empire she ever knew—hung on her words, quizzing her in soft voices. What did she put in it? She shrugged her shoulders—"O, a little of this, a little of that." How long for the hanging, how long for the salting, how long for the boiling? "O, not too long—but long nuf." And where had she learned this momentous secret? From her "gran'maw, who'd it f'm 'er pappy," who got it "f'm Chicasaw— in part—an' part f'm a game cook who die sixty years afo'. She live Waccamaw plantation—she ol' 'oman afo' she wrastle deer patty— yel gotta be ol.'"

At last they gave it up and she went off to her kitchen—an empress with authority possessed by none other. She would not admit she felt herself better than anyone else on the plantation, but no one else approached her just the same.

Between John Rutledge and his game cook there was a strange bond. She never lived with anyone but Rutledges and Hexts. His father had chosen her and she was a possession that he cherished.

At last it was nearly sundown. The roast was almost over. John rose and told them, most casually, that he wanted to be a member of the Commons; and asked them to vote for him at the next election. What with the Madeira, the rum, the whiskey, and all the rest of the roast, there may have been confusion in grasping what he meant. Apparently he made no particular point of it. The guests agreed offhand that whatever he asked for he should have.

His mother was startled. As soon as the guests were gone she demanded to know what he meant. The two sitting members of the Assembly from Christ Church Parish, Mr. Carey and Mr. Bruton, had been there as his guests. How had he dared to speak that way? Besides, what was his hurry? If he wanted, indeed, to go to the Commons, it would be more seemly to wait another year, or two; to canvass the matter cautiously; to test the sense of the community.

John did not argue the matter with her. It was settled, he said.

The election was less than sixty days away. In that time John called personally on every voter in the parish, which was about six miles wide and about twenty-six miles long. He went to all the plantations on horseback.

The custom had been for the assemblymen who were sitting to be retained, if they desired or unless some upheaval threatened. As a rule men did not seek the office; the voters picked the most conspicuous among them for acumen and wealth to represent them. There was no political storm in sight. Carey had served eight years, Bruton four, without complaint. Why change?

The population of the colony was about eighty-seven thousand, less than half of whom were whites. Less than a quarter of the whites could qualify as voters, so there were no more than ten thousand potential voters in all the parishes of South Carolina. Practically, at times, there were only a few hundred regular voters in even the largest parish. Christ Church, numerically, was next to the smallest. There were eighteen parishes and thirty-six assemblymen.

These thirty-six men, however, held the actual ruling power of South Carolina. They held the veto power over the twelve councillors appointed by the Governor and they did not hesitate to exercise it.

No governor yet had successfully defied the Assembly. The present governor always consulted the Assembly cautiously.

To be a voter one had to be free, white, and twenty-one; to be Christian; and to have a freehold of at least fifty acres of land or to have been taxed the preceding year twenty shillings; and to have been resident one year.

The property qualifications for an assemblyman were higher. He must have at least five hundred acres of land in his own name, own ten slaves, or personal property to the extent of one thousand pounds. And *to have been a resident for at least one year*. There was no compensation.

Needless to say, there were no native professional politicians. The Commons (or Assembly) was made up of the men who had demonstrated their competence in amassing property and in caring for it. They all considered it a duty and a privilege to serve. Henry Laurens and Peter Manigault, declared by the Secretary of Trade and Plantations in London to be the two richest men in America, were both members, and were competing for the speakership.

As John Rutledge went about the parish asking for votes the question of his residence was raised. He argued that he had not forfeited residence by being in England for three years. The spirit of the law was to be regarded, he said, not the letter. His manner was ingratiating, and no one denied him.

He made no political arguments, except one, and that he did not insist upon. He told them he favored inoculation, and thought a law should be passed making it compulsory for public protection.

Inoculation against smallpox was a moot question. The rector of St. Michael's church in the Town had preached a most impressive sermon against the practice only six months before, following, it was said, a hint from London. He had declared it to be an invention of the devil, expressly made to persuade poor weak humans to pit their feeble wills against that of God. It was a mortal sin and a grievous heresy for a person to take into his hands the authority to fight a disease, apparently visited upon him by the Almighty. The Church would steadfastly oppose such brazen audacity. For one to be inoculated, or to declare himself in favor of it, was to make league with the powers of darkness. Let well enough alone! If God said you were to have smallpox you had smallpox, and there was the end of it.

Rutledge made no issue with the church; he did not refer to the rector's sermon. But he did tell his neighbors that he knew a Dr. John Martini in London, who formerly had been a resident of Charles Town, that Dr. Martini had inoculated him, and that he had been immune from the disease, which was a scourge to many. He reminded them that the year before six girls of good family threatened with the smallpox had been isolated on the edge of town while they were inoculated and had escaped the disease. For more than a year it had been the practice, he pointed out, for planters to inoculate their Negroes, and every one so treated had escaped the pox. Did they care more for their Negroes than for themselves?

Neither Mr. Carey nor Mr. Bruton condescended to discuss inoculation. It was too trivial a matter for the concern of statesmen.

The election came on March 11 and 12; it was held in the church, with the wardens as tellers. They handed the result to Mr. Timothy the day after election. On March 14, 1761, the *South Carolina Gazette* published the names of the members of the Assembly elected two days before. In the list appeared: "Christ Church Parish: Mr. James D. Carey, Mr. John Rutledge."

He was twenty-one and a half years old. His public career had begun. After his election was announced, John explained to his mother that an old custom of the colony, established for more than fifty years, exempted any member of the Assembly from being sent to jail *while the Assembly was sitting.*

There were two months of court session during which the Assembly did not meet, but it was hardly practicable to send a creditor to jail for what might be left of that short period after the preliminaries. While it was possible to seize real property to satisfy a judgment, imprisonment was considered the chief menace. Their incapacity to invoke it acted as a powerful deterrent on insistent creditors. There had been complaint about it, but the custom was stronger than the statute. As a result, practically, members of the Assembly enjoyed immunity from court action for debt.

John had been elected for three years. There was no salary but here was an agreeable perquisite. Mrs. Rutledge could see at last why it might be necessary to have everything in his name.

Within ninety days after stepping off the ship that brought him from England he had placed his family in safe harbor.

4·

The day after the spring election of 1761 John Rutledge opened his law office on the ground floor of a two-story building at the corner of Broad and Church Streets. A mechanic and family lived upstairs. At first Rutledge had only a single, small room in the rear. It is significant that he started alone and in a central location.

Across the street was a bare, level place. A few years earlier the bastion of the early fort, which was the outer wall of the first Town, had stood there. Several wooden benches were shaded by two enormous trees, a live oak and a magnolia.

This vacant lot was called The Corner. No woman ever stopped there, and no Negroes. Though it was in the middle of town, it was no ordinary loafing place. Even sailors learned not to use the benches, except on a Sunday or a holiday. It passed for the Town's stock exchange, bar association, gentlemen's club, planters' bourse, and political forum.

St. Michael's was a block away; the State House and the Court House the same distance; the Chambers used by the King's Council a block and a half down the street; the Governor's Mansion less than five minutes' walk; and all the lawyers' offices within three blocks.

The physical periphery of John Rutledge's life radiated from The Corner. Twelve hundred feet from it were the East Bay and the wharves. Always on the horizon a tangle of masts and spars could be seen. Ships were coming and going; some to London six weeks away; some to Boston, a fortnight's sail; and some to Baltimore or Philadelphia. The world was on the doorstep.

John Rutledge had his Negro body servant, Pompey, to shave

and dress him and to powder his hair; Negro messengers ran his errands, if only across the street. He would sooner have jumped in the bay than be seen carrying a parcel on the street. He had no stenographer or clerk; he wrote his own letters and he drew his own legal papers in a firm, easily legible long hand.

The Court sat in April, May, July, August, October, and November; generally from three to six in the afternoon. When the Assembly sat, which was at irregular times, it was from eight to eleven in the forenoon. John Rutledge attended every meeting of the Assembly and did not once address his fellow members. Some had heard, from London, that he had forensic skill. He was pressed to display it, but he refused, explaining that he thought it was better for a young man to listen to his elders. He seldom went to The Corner and when he was there he did not discuss public affairs. He did not frequent taverns or coffee houses. Young men of his own age felt there was something peculiar, something aloof about him; they did not know the burden of responsibility he carried or the worries he had. Though to some he seemed a favorite of fortune, with the chief riches of South Carolina at his command, in fact he was staggering under a weight whose measure he was only beginning to grasp.

The law business of Charles Town seemed to be as elusive as his mother had predicted. Though he went to his new office every day through the spring and summer, he received no clients. However, he had cases in Court.

The cash necessity which went with every court action engendered a horror of litigation in a community where cash was extremely scarce. Men could get credit in Charles Town for virtually everything except to "go to law." Other taxes were indirect and were not felt. Court taxes were direct and since they could be paid in cash only, they were serious matters.

Rutledge's principal client was Dr. John Martini, "practitioner of physick, residing now in the City of London, of His Majesty's principal dominion, late a resident of Charles Town." Dr. Martini was a colleague of his father's who had offered John an opportunity to collect a number of old, and apparently very bad, debts. John won five judgments in favor of Dr. Martini, and the money collected from one was used to pay the fees of the others suits, in all of which judgments were rendered in favor of John's client. He was not able to make further collections, however; the costs of the five judgments ate up the proceeds of the single successful collection. This fact could not have any immediate effect upon John's fortunes; Dr. Martini was six weeks away in London.

But in the Laurens case, the crumb he had grasped as it fell from the rich man's table, the situation was quite different. Officially the case was that of the Estate of Bremar vs Guerin; the costs were paid by the plaintiffs, of whom the chief was Henry Laurens, and amounted to 37 pounds, 14 shillings, 7½ pence. The court costs alone came to a sizable sum. These initial items, as recorded by Rutledge, were:

	pounds	shillings	pence
Attorney	3.	12.	
Judge		15.	10.
Clerk		19.	7½
	5.	7.	5½

In addition, other costs, for the judge's signature on the judgment and for entry in the docket and such items, came to more than two pounds. This was "law business" as Rutledge and his colleagues practiced it; the justice, the clerk, the attorney—all had to be paid in advance!

In the August term, judgment was handed down in favor of Rutledge's client and the papers were marked: "Judg't ordered, two hundred and thirty pounds, currency, with int. and costs." On the back of the judgment, Rutledge wrote, "Take good bail or bring the defendant to gaol." But below this, the bailiff noted, "Have been to the most notorious places of residence of the defendant." The defendant was not to be found; no satisfaction. No one ever escaped from the gaol at Logan and Queen Streets with its wall seven feet thick; Andrew Guerin, planter, neither paid nor went to gaol.

As a result of this unsuccessful effort Rutledge lost his credit with Henry Laurens, who, with more business at his call than any other person in the community, was widely respected as a precise, positive, and just man. If Laurens withdrew his credit how long could the Rutledges hold out?

In September, Mrs. Rutledge, needing supplies for the Great House, and Thomas, needing supplies for Stono, went back to the Mazycks for credit. The Mazycks filled the September order but served notice that without definite assurance of prompt payment it would be the last bit of credit extended to the Rutledges.

John's election to the Assembly was back-firing. His membership rendered him and his family immune, temporarily at least, from the severe processes of the law, but gave public notice of the immunity. To be devoid of cash was serious; but now he was without cash or credit.

Nor was this the worst. He was faced with a startling demand from the Chaplins (John and Benjamin, planters); they asked that his mother deed to them two farms on St. Helena Island, one of two hundred acres and one of a hundred and seventy acres, both of which had been in his father's estate. Of all the lands that had come down to Sarah these were the only continuously profitable pieces. This was due in large part to the skillful management of the Chaplins.

When the demand for the deeds came to John's attention, the harvest was in; the crops delivered to the Charles Town factors would produce more than a thousands pounds in cash—the only paying crops that year on all the Rutledge holdings.

The young attorney viewed the facts in the case. The St. Helena lands were part of an original grant of seven hundred and fifty acres from the Lords Proprietors to Edward Hext, his mother's uncle, who had bequeathed them to his niece, Sarah, from whom, at marriage, they went to Doctor John. The Chaplins claimed that Doctor John had sold them the lands, but of this they had no documentary proof. John Rutledge became convinced the Chaplins spoke truth; Doctor John had taken the money, with a verbal agreement to deliver deeds on request—a slipshod but not unusual proceeding for the period.

Here was a costly, if not a hard, decision. Legally John, for his mother, could seize the Chaplin crops, or he might bargain. He did neither. He hád taken over his father's obligations along with his father's assets. A given word was stronger than a written bond. So, on his advice, his mother deeded the two prime, paying parcels of land to the Chaplins for "five shillings" apiece.

On top of that came the Hörry case, on the outcome of which his mother was placing high hopes. The Hörrys were Huguenot planters, among the half dozen wealthiest and most influential families in the province, whose daughter Mrs. Rutledge favored as a wife for her son.

John did not know who would be the attorney for the defendant when he filed his plea for "trespass in the case, Daniel Hörry et ux vs Richard Moncrieff . . . damages to the land of said plaintiff in the sum of five hundred pounds, with the costs of this suit."

Charles Pinckney replied for Mr. Moncrieff, "denying all allegations of injury." This was Colonel Charles Pinckney, urbane leader of the bar of Charles Town, commandant of the fortifications, owner of the mansion occupied by the Governor, nephew of the former "Chief Justice." No opponent could have been more formidable.

There was a jury trial. John Hume, the foreman, wrote on the back of the plea, "Jury found for defendant, with costs." Nothing ever came of his mother's advice, or of John's relations with Miss Hörry.

A little later he took judgment for Thomas Crotty (a friend of his uncle's) against William Spikes for five hundred pounds—"trover" —"for craftily and subtlily converting possession of a Negro wench Dinah of a value of three hundred pounds in 1756, and of a full value of five hundred pounds in 1761"—"with costs"—and no satisfaction.

Then he got back, left-handedly, at Charles Pinckney in the case of Smith vs Gardner, where Pinckney appeared for the defendant and withdrew his plea. Thereupon Rutledge took a judgment by default and collected an attorney's fee—of one pound, ten shillings.

That was the record of the youthful attorney for his first two terms in Court, and up to the end of summer—nine default judgments and one jury case lost. The defeat was a social tragedy for his mother and the victories were Pyrrhic for him.

The bad collections entrusted to him by his father's and mother's friends had resulted only in his collecting attorneys' fees and court costs—from the friends. A few more successes of that kind and he would have to take down his shingle.

September is the hottest month of the year in Charles Town. During the September recess John went to the plantations. He felt desperate or he would not have chosen September for his inspection, but something had to be done and quickly. He knew that land was the basis of all wealth—land and slaves. While his mother owned both in abundance, they were without cash, without credit, and facing bankruptcy. Having industry and intelligence, he determined to apply them.

He spent a few days with Thomas at Stono and found his brother facing a failure in their only rice crop, because he planted the seed too late in April. The May birds had gobbled up the young shoots before they were firmly rooted. Neither intelligence nor industry could remedy the condition at Stono that season. Other elements were needed—experience and time. John made no criticism of Thomas, but left him and went to the Great House on the Wando.

His mother was overjoyed that he was going to spend a few weeks with her. It was her constant lament that he had had none of the flings of youth: no playtime. He was an old man young—the head of a family while others were in their adolescence. She often tried to make up for that, and this seemed to be a good chance. She planned social events. There were eligible debutantes besides Miss Hörry, and he must go about more with young people.

John would have none of it. He spent all his waking hours, afoot, on horseback, or with his rowers, covering the six thousand acres that composed the Phillips, Patey-Boone, and Lexington plantations, pushing up the creeks and into the swamps.

There were a thousand acres in indigo. If that crop was full it could more than save them, but the summer had been dry; a rust had settled on the plants; the indigo was rotting. John learned there might have been a way of saving it—in early summer. Artificial shade might have been provided by building plantain breaks over the rows. Why had this not been done? Because, said Old Fortune, who had been placed in charge, "Musses ent munney f'r twine." But there were many idle slaves. Why had they not improvised something? "No-buddy ent tole we." There was the trouble—no proper overseers.

John had one happy moment when he discovered there was an urgent cash offering at Gadsden's wharf for palmetto logs—if whole. In the swamps were many thousands of stand of palmetto, but inspection revealed that all the palmetto anywhere near the navigable waters had been ruthlessly de-hearted, in sapling, for the Rutledge table. He himself had ordered half a thousand "swamp cabbage" for the February oyster roast. The same thing had been going on, at his mother's order, and before that at his father's, for twenty years. The palmettos had not been conserved since the death of Hugh Hext. As a result he could not take advantage of the one cash market open.

Fortune, who was a horticulturist at heart, was experimenting with flax which might be worth something in five years.

The favorite slave had persuaded Mrs. Rutledge to plant oranges several years before. They were supposed to have their first bearing that year but the winter before, a heavy frost, the first in more than ten years, had ruined the crop. Fortune agreed they might as well root out the trees.

On all the plantations only a few spots were economically cultivated, chiefly the little truck gardens about the slave cabins, where the Negroes raised their own produce. Each black family had its own chickens, a pig or two, and plenty of fresh vegetables. And lucky for the Rutledges it was so, for that fall the family existed largely from the truck gardens of their slaves.

The slaves regarded "young Mausseh" with veneration. They would share their last turnip with him; they would do anything for him, except make the land pay without direction. Now John Rutledge realized that the South Carolina planters who wrung wealth from the soil lived on the land and gave themselves to it wholly. Making the land pay was a technical and full-time job.

He remembered what had happened to Mr. Pinckney, the late "Chief Justice," when he came back from England after a few years of neglecting his South Carolina estate. He had gone to his plantation on the Ashley for a few weeks, where he attempted to reorganize it personally and to make it more productive. The effort had killed him.

The strain was too much for John Rutledge too; and he finally collapsed. His mother called Dr. Moultrie who said it might be the fever. John should not have been so foolish as to go into the swamps in September. The best place for him was in Charles Town where there was always a breeze.

Mrs. Rutledge planned at once to move to the Town. Sick as he was, and unable to lift his head, John forbade any of them to go with him. Pompey carried him to the canoe and he was rowed down the Wando.

When they reached the Dock Street house they found the master bedroom did not get the prevailing western breezes. Pompey said the only room "fitten" for summer was his own, in the slave house.

So Pompey took John Rutledge to his own meagre quarters and nursed him. John's intense, repressed nature fell into acute melancholy. The "fever" was conquered, yet he was not well. Pompey reported that "young Mausseh" said he felt he was dying.

5.

When the Assembly convened for the fall term John Rutledge was not present; he was convalescing. Nor could he go to the Broad Street office, though he sent his boy each day to keep the place open in the hope that a client might appear.

On the second Monday Pompey came back to Dock Street in excitement. There was, he said, "a lady on law business," a Miss Mary Cooke, and she wanted an appointment. Rutledge made one for the next day, and then sent for information on Miss Cooke.

Pompey reported that she lived in the new part of town, on Anson Street, in St. Phillip's Parish. Her father, a widower, was a contractor who built warehouses and, sometimes, dwellings. She was his only child. At the moment her father was in a hospital.

The next day Rutledge went to his office, still pale and weak, and without Dr. Moultrie's approval. It was a great day; here was his first unsolicited client.

Mary Cooke insisted that Pompey leave the office before she would confide the nature of her "business." Finally, alone with the young attorney, she haltingly revealed that she had come to him because she had heard he knew how to handle deftly, and without scandal, "a claim against a recalcitrant male."

Another hope seemed to be exploded. He was desperately longing for real legal work to do. He wanted some case with a sure retainer, preferably with an imminent cash collection; or an estate to handle with probate fees in advance; or—wildest dream of all—an admiralty case with a fat cargo at stake, possibly with a quick auction in the offing and a cash percentage to be taken with the auctioneer's fee.

And all that was offered was an action in breach of promise. Miss Mary Cooke said he had done so well for Walter Greenland that she thought he could help her.

John Rutledge explained what had happened in the Greenland case, his first in Charles Town: he had appeared for the *defendant*, his mother's carpenter; the case had never come to Court because he had pointed out a flaw in the plea. The opposing attorney had made the mistake of addressing the Court as "Chief Justice" when, in fact, he was only an Acting Chief Justice. This error caused the action to be dismissed; then Rutledge had persuaded the carpenter to pay half the claim in settlement rather than face a possible new plea.

Miss Cooke was not to be thrust aside so easily. She could hardly listen to his explanation. How it was done did not concern her. Mr. Rutledge had brought about a settlement of a delicate situation without public discussion. That was all she wanted.

There never had been a breach of promise suit in any court in America. The young attorney said no.

Miss Mary Cooke then told Rutledge that the man in question was not a poor man. He was the rich William Lennox who, with his brother James, had just opened on Elliott Street the most pretentious general store ever seen in the port.

Rutledge told her to come back in a day or two after he had had time to look into the matter further. That afternoon he spent at The Corner inquiring about William Lennox.

Until the previous spring the chief merchants of Charles Town, wholesale and retail alike, had done business directly from their warehouses, built conveniently near the wharves. There were a number of small retail stores in 'smart' locations, along Tradd, Elliott, Dock, and Broad Streets and East Bay. These were one-commodity stores. One had shoes, another dry goods, another select groceries; they were specialty stores for the carriage trade. However, the bulk of supplies for households, as well as for plantations and ships, was sold from the warehouses, to which most thrifty shoppers went in person. There was no convenience for the buyer, who had to look at crude samples or order sight unseen, taking the reputation of a merchant as a guarantee. The warehouse merchants were the most substantial merchants west of London—Manigault, Legare, Laurens, Mazyck, Brewton. No buyer in Charles Town dared question their warranty or their empire.

The Lennox Brothers made a startling change in the state of affairs. They offered to the public, from their large retail shop in the most exclusive locality, readily reached by carriage without peril to soft shoes or delicate fabrics, every imaginable commodity, except "live property." That meant slaves alone were excepted. There was even a corner for cats and dogs.

The *Gazette* said that Lennox Brothers listed two hundred and eighty items that could be seen, "at least in sample," in their Elliott Street "emporium." They had everything from "carbines with bayonets, muslins, French napery, Sheffield cutlery, selected groceries and all manner of hardware, to shoemaker's wax, razors, haberdashery from London whence we especially represent in this province three exclusive purveyors of men's wear to His Majesty King George III; and, also, from Paris, for the Demoiselles and Matrons, gilt flacons of parfumerie of the Rhone in rose, in violette and in a distillation of a unique aroma hitherto quite unknown."

It was America's first department store. The Corner buzzed with an undertone of resentment against this challenge to the established order. If it succeeded, what would it mean to the Manigaults, the Brewtons, the Laurenses, and the others? They might become merely middlemen, or else be obliged to go into the buying or leasing of expensive locations in the heart of Town.

The Charles Town women, who did most of the buying, were gullible. (This was the consensus at The Corner.) They were flocking in droves to the Lennox store. New paint and the pavement in front and pleasant surroundings—far from the stench of slave quarters —seemed to be all they cared about. Established names, sound financial credits apparently meant little to them.

Two days later John Rutledge told Miss Cooke he would be her attorney on condition that she place herself absolutely in his hands. She was delighted and readily agreed. She paid the Court fees in advance.

John Rutledge called on the prosperous young merchant in his bustling "emporium," presented the claim of his client, Miss Cooke, and was ordered out. The next day, in his office, he explained to Miss Cooke that he could not get anything from William Lennox without a public airing of her complaint. He told her she must be prepared to offer herself before the altar of public scorn in an open court room. She would be the first woman in the colony, or in the New World, to bare her maidenly breast and reveal its sorrow and its shame.

She hesitated. But the banns were up for the marriage of William Lennox and another woman, and so she accepted the terms.

The young attorney did not have a book of forms or a digest of cases to guide him. In a way he was as much a pioneer as the new settler in the wilderness. He wrote his complaint and made up his order of specifications as he went along.

The plea read: "Mary Cooke, spinster, by her attorney, John Rutledge, complains that William Lennox, merchant, of Charles Town, being single and unmarried, in consideration that she, the said Mary, being then and yet unmarried . . . had promised faithfully, as she

had consented to receive him for her husband, when and as soon
as he should enter into the occupation of a merchant;—and afterward,
to-wit, December 1, 1760, the said William, being still sole and unmarried, and in consideration of the special instance that the said
Mary was still sole and unmarried at his special instance and request,
then and there *had agreed with him;*—and . . . the said Mary Cooke
in fact avers that after making all the promises and assumptions above
recorded, the said William did enter into the occupation of a merchant on the first day of September, 1761 . . . and that she is ready
to take and receive him to be her lawful wedded husband; and that
. . . the said William from her had notice and often there offered
so to do;—YET the said William, while he was sole, not regarding his
promises and assumptions aforesaid, whereby she had *agreed* with
him, contriving and fraudulently intending her the said Mary in this
behalf craftily and subtlily to deceive and totally to hinder her of her
preferment in marriage, did not take her the said Mary to wife according to the tenor of the said Promises and Assumptions; and, after
he had entered into the said occupation and business of a merchant,
and after six months, or on the 12th day of September, 1761, and often
before, was sued and requested by the said Mary to fulfill his many
obligations, and then and there entirely refused;—AND, on the 13th
day of September, 1761, caused to be announced before the altar of the
Episcopal Church of the parish of St. Phillip's in Charles Town, aforesaid, that within six weeks he would marry one Judith Gordin;—
and, THEREUPON, the said Mary saith she is worse and damage hath
sustained to the amount of seven thousand pounds.

—RUTLEDGE, *Plt'f's Atty.*

The *Gazette* did not mention the matter. The Lennox Brothers
were heavy advertisers. In any event, such a scandalous episode was
not worthy of public print.

The Corner, however, in December of 1761, was full of gossip
about it. How would John Rutledge prove his allegations? Had he
witnesses? How would the young lady describe her *agreement?*

Duels had been fought over this sort of thing, but no one had heard of a lawsuit like this. The community was shocked and every tongue was wagging. No man spoke of it at home, yet every woman knew more of it than any man. Had this Mary Cooke no *man* to challenge for her? Was John Rutledge mixed up with her? It seemed incredible, yet he stood forth for her, not with a pistol, but with a long legal document. What was there in it for him? Money? For shame! So wagged the tongues of the community.

At The Corner the elders of the Town admitted that at first glance the affair looked like a sad beginning for the nephew of the respected late Speaker Andrew; but there were arguments to be made for him. Curiously, they were made, softly but unctuously, by the proprietors of the great warehouses, and these were deftly led by their chiefs, Mr. Laurens and Mr. Mazyck. After all, these wise men observed, there was the majesty of the English law to be considered. While the affair was before the Court no man had a right to advance judgment. Besides, the merchants solemnly asserted, a contract was a contract. Why, they asked, should a marriage promise be different from any other?

Incidentally—and, of course, only incidentally—that upstart Lennox was the man involved. It was just like a man who advertised that he had everything for sale in stock, when he had only samples of more than half the things he mentioned in the *Gazette!* It was like such a man to take advantage of an unprotected spinster.

Action was prompt. Rutledge filed November 6. The writ was served November 9. The case came to trial December 1.

The jury drawn contained the names of leading citizens only. Among the twelve were Solomon Legaré, Miles Brewton, Richard Baker, Thomas Scott, Timothy Crosby, and Francis Lamons—all members of the Assembly and each a leader. Legaré and Brewton were merchants known from Amsterdam to Boston, from Savannah to Antigua, men whose lightest word in commerce was worth all the money then in circulation in America.

John Rutledge produced no evidence to bring a blush to any cheek. His master stroke was the cross-examination of the defendant, from whom he elicited the admission that he had promised, though only verbally, to marry Mary Cooke.

When the attorney for the plaintiff rose to address the jury the court room was packed to suffocation. He began in a low tone and he referred to his client only inferentially, conveying by tactful innuendo as an established fact, which the defendant had admitted, that Miss Mary Cooke was a virgin. She was, the orator asserted, with dignified reserve, inviolate though outraged. This, however, was but the framework for his picture and was uttered with a soft apology.

Rutledge's real subject was abstract—the inviolability of the given word. When he opened up, as Dr. David Ramsay said, "his eloquence astounded all." It came "like a tropic thunderstorm."

After only eleven minutes' consideration, the jury returned an immediate verdict—for twenty-five hundred pounds currency. Evidently the only thing in question had been the amount. Twenty-four hours later the verdict was marked—"satisfied." Rutledge's fee was one hundred guineas, which he took to his mother at once.

The next issue of the *Gazette*, December 5, 1761, ignored that disgraceful happening in the Court House which had attracted every idle male in Town. The principal item was this "intelligence" from London, dated September 10:

"Her Majesty alighted at the garden gate at Colchester, being handed out of her coach by His Royal Highness, the Prince of York, and upon her entrance into the garden sunk upon her knee to the King, in a most affectionate manner. He raised her up, saluted her, and then led her by the right hand into the palace, where she dined with His Majesty, the Princess Dowager and the Princess Augusta."

The Corner was a better news source. Henry Laurens was not present at the trial, but the next morning he sent for John Rutledge and gave him a "live" case to handle. The amount involved was three thousand pounds; the fee, four hundred and fifty pounds; retainer, one hundred pounds in cash.

Within two weeks Henry Middleton and Duval Peronneau also retained John Rutledge. Within the same period Miles Brewton told him he had a contract with Egerton Leigh for his services which had still a year to run, but that he would like Mr. Rutledge to submit an estimate for services for the year 1763.

It was not because he had won a breach of promise suit in the teeth of public disapproval; it was the way he did it. His technical moves, within the letter of the statute, had been utilized only as a setting for his basic plea, which was to the prevailing sense of contractual "morality." A rigid code bound together the elaborate commercial structures of the Town, and alone made them durable, for this code was obliged to operate within conflicting sets of written statutes, and in competition with Yankee rivals whose code was totally different. "Morality," with the South Carolina colonists, was, in effect, the cement which bound their commercial and domestic worlds. They respected the law, but they venerated "morality."

They recognized at once both the quality of the Rutledge cement and his deft wielding of his trowel. Perhaps they were well prepared to accept him, and this they did on his first "demonstration." He went to the top of the professional ladder in less than twelve months.

In all the legal history of the colony, now in its third generation, there had been nothing like it.

6.

The less informed, who looked upon the practice of the law as a black art and regarded it with aversion, heard how John Rutledge had handled those two breach of promise cases, and considered him an uncanny magician. Hearing how lucrative breach of promise might be if adroitly directed, several other prospective clients offered him cases; but he never took another of this type.

Rutledge confined himself, with a few notable exceptions, to important commercial causes for leading citizens. During 1761, his first year at the bar, the Court of Common Pleas (Court of Ordinary) of Charles Town heard one hundred and forty-two cases; in eleven of these John Rutledge appeared as attorney and he won ten. In his second year, 1762, the Court heard one hundred and seventy-three cases; Rutledge appeared as attorney in thirty-nine of them and lost none. In 1763 the Court heard one hundred and eighty-seven cases;

John Rutledge appeared in fifty-two and lost none. After the Hörry-Moncrieff suit he never lost a case in court.

It seems incredible, but he had his pick and he refused cases which did not conform to two standards: they must be right morally and right politically—that is, conforming to the established sense of propriety.

The two standards were separate facets of the same requirement. If a proffered case measured up to it he quickly found a legal way to win it. He had few law books and he never consulted them until he had learned the essential facts.

Shortly after the Cooke verdict he began altering his commuting habit. He no longer found it necessary to sleep each night in the country. He could be seen occasionally in the coffee houses at the punch hour. And The Corner saw him, regularly, five days a week. There was a bench under the magnolia tree, one end of which belonged, by common consent, to John Rutledge. Whenever he appeared anyone who occupied it rose at once and made way.

So, even from his twenty-third year, the essential life of the Town began to gravitate around John Rutledge. No man lifted an eye to him except with respect. Yet his attitude remained aloof; he was of them, but not one of them.

Perhaps Henry Laurens put his finger on the key to the mastery of this young man who had come up among them to surprise them all. "He fronts a fact more quickly than anyone I ever knew," wrote the merchant to an associate in explaining why he was trusting so young an attorney (Rutledge was barely twenty-four) with an involved case in admiralty law.

Though this was in the most sophisticated community of the new world; though the lawyers and judges wore the physical laces and robes and utilized the professional forms and symbols of far-off London; though fashionable ways of life seemed to be settled in established convention; and though the artificial accents of the eighteenth century limited the fresh, vigorous life of the new world—nevertheless, this was the *frontier*.

Only about a hundred miles away was the physical frontier

where men battled wild animals and savages while they held off a distant government and mastered a strange new land with means devised by themselves. Rutledge met problems in the Town in similar ways. In intellectual essence he was a frontiersman. He never fired a gun personally, but, mentally, he shot from the hip and with either hand. He never had an actual partner. Every problem he met was faced *a priori* and alone; and his decisions were most often made instantly. Yet all he did was according to established legal form.

The large proportion of the cases which fell to the youthful attorney, astounding as that is, is not so impressive as the fact that he tried such important cases for Middleton, Laurens, Brewton, Peronneau, and others—the chief men of their day.

The answer is partly found in Egerton Leigh. Egerton was the son of the late Chief Justice Peter Leigh, who, though he had been given his post as a reward for altering election returns, had proved an able judge. Egerton inherited his father's favor with the Crown, his ability, and also his lack of scruple.

At first and for a long time, Leigh's ability and his London connections seemed recommendation enough for Charles Town merchants seeking a lawyer. In the late 1750's and through 1761 he was, in fact, the most popular attorney in the province. He had the pick of the business. Though Charles Pinckney and James Parsons were his equals in a court room or on a brief neither had connections with the Ministry in London.

No wonder Egerton Leigh lorded it over the South Carolina bar. He was the attorney in fact, as well as at law, for Peter Manigault; he was the chief counsel for Miles Brewton and was closely associated with Henry Laurens. No person in ordinary walks of life approached him to discuss legal affairs; he required a retainer of one hundred pounds in advance "to look into a case."

However, toward the end of 1761, he committed an audacious rascality against a friend. He was so sure of his immunity he dared to flout even the code which ruled them all.

What it was, only The Corner knew. Henry Laurens eventually attacked Leigh in a political pamphlet, whereupon Leigh replied in kind. By then the Ministry in London was rallying to Leigh's defense and he became Sir Egerton Leigh, Baronet. On top of that he was appointed Judge in Admiralty. Leigh needed both title and judgeship. for his practice had quit him, quietly but decisively; that was the answer of Charles Town's leaders to the violator of its inner code.

"The law of life was the same then as it has been in all ages," as Guglielmo Ferrero said. "Great men are the play of what we call Destiny, though it is nothing more than the co-incidence of events, the emergence into action of hidden forces which no contemporary can be expected to discern."

It was John Rutledge's destiny to appear on the scene, to get that little shop window of the Cooke-Lennox case for the display of his abilities, at the moment when the most lucrative legal practice in America was looking for a new master.

And destiny was patiently waiting, for out of his handling of that opportunity came everything that followed. He established himself with Henry Laurens; he got the contract with Miles Brewton. He continued to represent Henry Middleton and Duval Peronneau. By the end of 1762 Egerton Leigh's practice was Rutledge's. Early in 1763 Rutledge announced he would require "a retainer of a hundred pounds to look into a case."

Other attorneys complained bitterly that there was no chance for them in Charles Town. All the important legal business was in the hands of James Parsons, Charles Pinckney, and John Rutledge. No other attorney could induce a leading man of property even to consider him professionally, except in those instances when the members of the triumvirate were unavailable.

Charles Town, perhaps, was not a great city, but it was fast becoming a type and symbol—a microcosm of all the cities that ever were at the threshold of an historical era. The Cherokees had been whipped and driven back and immigrants were pouring in with every ship; slaves were multiplying; unbelievable riches were beginning to pile up; all the luxuries of the known world were at hand; the El Dorado seen in mirage by the Spaniards two centuries before was now becoming a reality. The Town had twelve hundred houses and in them lived above six thousand whites with more than as many blacks, and a few leaders with the essentials of greatness.

These leaders were obliged to solve a compelling practical problem. They were extremely prosperous, yet the stream of South Carolina sovereignty was dammed up. Red tape was throttling the communal life; laws were conflicting and ill adapted to the current needs of the colony, while distance from the source retarded justice. The governors were unresponsive and lacking in actual authority. The judges were appointed by unseen agencies three thousand miles away.

The idea of complete political independence had not yet been openly expressed. That was sleeping in the womb of time. Yet something had to be done, and at once, for these men were not of the type to be easily thwarted.

The community was loyal to the British throne; it observed British laws with British forms; it accepted British social customs with an alacrity which deceived even those who observed them. It would have been shocked if anyone had said, or written, that it gave only lip service to the Crown. Practically, however, it solved its problems of governance in an ancient way.

Instinct guided this paramount communal necessity away from the agency of any single man. There was something almost equally repellent in a duumvirate. A triumvirate was the solution. Three trustworthy, competent men to watch each other, to cut the red tape; to settle things swiftly, silently, and at once; to keep the pool of justice as clear as possible; but, above all, to keep fresh water flowing through it constantly.

For several years this triumvirate had consisted of Parsons, Pinckney, and Leigh. Any one of them would have been the first to deny the allegation that they ruled Charles Town with almost autocratic power; but in that mercantile frontier, law business dominated all, and only one or another of the three could get an important piece of it for himself.

In the earlier triumvirate there was a serious flaw—Egerton Leigh. Leigh's fatal defect was in character; he could not be trusted. Triumvirs must be, like Caesar's wife, above suspicion. Then Leigh was replaced by the nephew of the late Andrew Rutledge. And from about the end of 1761, South Carolina was ruled for nearly fifteen years by Parsons, Pinckney, and Rutledge. When it began Parsons was forty-four, Pinckney thirty-seven, and Rutledge twenty-two.

The nature of this sovereignty was such that it had to be anonymous and had to operate anonymously; but it was real. The community, except for the members of the oligarchy at the top, realized only vaguely what was happening, and how it was happening. Nevertheless, the essential records—court reports, the journals of the Assembly, the annual messages of the Governor to the Crown—reveal it to have been the essence of the government of the colony.

Formally, there were three branches of government: the Governor, the courts, and the Assembly. While the Governor and the judges were appointed by the Crown, they were paid only by consent of the Assembly. Thus, whoever controlled the Assembly was in command.

About four-fifths of the members of the Assembly were planters and merchants, and one-fifth lawyers. The planters and merchants were jealous of their prerogatives as legislators, but were dilatory in attendance at the legislative sessions. When a South Carolina merchant or planter employed an attorney that man became his *alter ego*. Everything was entrusted to him. The habits formed in business followed automatically into legislation. The planters and merchants, eager for the honor but not the drudgery of legislation, only too willingly entrusted both to their chosen attorneys. So Parsons, Pinckney and Rutledge, never a firm, and each distinctively individual, got all the important law business, directed the Assembly, controlled the Governor, and dominated the Courts. They never importantly disagreed on fundamental policies. In public policy they were a unit. The least publicity, the slightest agitation might have ruined the triumvirate's hold, and certainly would have multiplied its difficulties. So it did nothing to attract attention to itself. All the triumvirate had— or wanted—was Power.

Occasionally they appeared against each other in Court, but only in minor litigation. The records show that in three years Rutledge faced Parsons twice and Pinckney five times. The fact that the youngest always won seems not to have altered the close bond of brotherly equality in which they worked.

The new member, Rutledge, took his place almost at once as the recognized public speaker of the triumvirate. After the episode of the Cooke trial the quality of his eloquence could not be doubted, though, strangely, he was parsimonious with it in Court and reserved it for use in the Assembly. He never spoke impromptu; at The Corner he listened, but did not argue; his punch at the coffee house was taken only at the polite hour before supper; he never appeared at the taverns in the evenings where political debates went on riotously through the night. The reason for this restraint was understood; he was the mouthpiece of the triumvirate; he could not talk promiscuously.

Thus, from the beginning, his oratory became almost a legend; it was not his for personal use, but a formal weapon to be reserved for certain occasions. Its quality was so different from the prevailing flamboyant style that the effect was electric. He used only short, sharp sentences without literary allusion or classical quotation, and with an intense emotional peroration. If word spread that John Rutledge was going to speak there was always a crowd, and yet his orations never involved personalities.

Attorneys in that place and period did not, as a rule, assault each other verbally, probably because of the prevalence of the duel, which was another unwritten code more potent than any proclamation of the King.

The full formalities were not always observed. Seconds were not always present to pace the distance, an umpire to give the word, a waiting surgeon, or a near-by carriage. An aggrieved party would send a message: "With my compliments, sir, will you kindly inform Mr. William Rawlings Randin that I will pass down the right side of Broad Street, going east, at three o'clock tomorrow afternoon, and that the clock in the steeple of St. Michael's Church will indicate the time." Mr. Randin might have called him a black-hearted fool. At the appointed hour, Broad Street, from Church to Bay, would be deserted; a gentleman would appear wearing a tricorn hat over powdered wig and lace ruffles, and there would be fresh buckles on his polished pumps. From across the street another similarly garbed person would approach; hands would slip in and out of shirt fronts; and pistols would bark. A neatly shaved, newly bathed, cleanly dressed cadaver might be ready for the undertaker.

That was the procedure. It was the seed from which sprang, by way of Tennessee and the Southwest border, the code of personal gun-play which in the next century dominated the Wild West. The duel on the streets of Charles Town occurred infrequently—there are records of only three in seven years—but that was enough. Men did not speak lightly of each other, any more than they did of women.

No member of the triumvirate ever fought a duel. They were not immune, but they guarded the approaches to insult so efficiently that they avoided danger of death from that direction, even in that hair-trigger climate. They avoided court action with similar discretion.

Nearly everything important was settled at the dinner table, between two and four in the afternoon. John Rutledge could readily send Pompey across the street to ask if Mr. Parsons, or Mr. Pinckney, would join him for dinner. Offices were opened again after four, but were sometimes occupied only by the clerks. Rutledge was at his desk from shortly after six in the morning until one in the afternoon. Seven hours was a business day for him in the office, but more business was transacted at The Corner, at his residence, and at the Court House.

Except for the theatre he had no city recreation. During the season the theatre was open four nights a week and he seldom failed to attend. He never played cards. He cared little for dancing. Until he was thirty-two years old he did not own a race horse, though horse-racing was the favorite sport of his colleagues.

He specialized, however, in developing the swiftest canoe in the colony. He kept his rowers in top condition. He found the family craft too cumbersome, and he had a new shell built of two spliced cypress logs, long and thin, with seats for six rowers and room for only one passenger, in the stern. He issued an open challenge to all comers. Only once was he outdistanced, and for that he put his rowers on bread and water for three days. Usually they had every possible indulgence.

Next he had to consider the matter of domicile, for a dining room was more important than an office. His first purchase of a lot was on Tradd Street, near the old Doctor 'Rutledge estate, now under lease to the Peronneaus. It had only a twenty-foot front, far too small for a town-house site. Before he could acquire the adjoining lot, he found to his liking a very large tract, nearly an acre, on the Broad Way which later became Meeting Street. This was the edge of the new fashionable residential district, near the site where Henry Laurens later built his substantial town house, and not far from the location of the Governor's Mansion belonging to Charles Pinckney.

However, he did not build on Meeting Street, because he persuaded the Peronneaus, whose attorney he had become, to give up the old Rutledge home. In the fall of 1762 his mother—and the seven children, with twenty slaves, moved back to the splendor which had been dimmed. Again the Rutledges were on top, for the first time since Uncle Andrew's death.

John kept all his promises. Hugh was sent to London and to the Middle Temple where John had lived for nearly three years. Andrew was established in a warehouse on East Bay and began a mercantile enterprise which, with the business John threw his way, prospered from the first. The attitude of suitors toward the girls changed at once. No one doubted now that each would have a substantial dot.

Meanwhile, Mrs. Rutledge had not transferred any of her property to John. None of the threatened suits was started. John took care of her obligations, took full responsibility for her property, succeeding Mr. Parsons as her attorney, and left her in actual ownership and control.

The widow was grateful. She absorbed readily all the adulation poured on her brilliant son. To be the mother of the new triumvir far transcended being the Hext heiress, or the wife of Dr. Rutledge. Here was a new life, more thrilling than any she ever had known.

However, she spent all the money she could get on the younger children. John had no need of it. He could look out for himself. Moreover, she devoted herself wholeheartedly to what she considered her principal duty, finding the proper wife for John. *Mariage de convenance* was the prevailing mode. The majority of the people she knew were mated in that way. She herself had been married thus, and it had turned out well. She could not doubt the wisdom of a marriage contract negotiated by parents.

A very likely prospect was Miss Henrietta Middleton, rather young as yet, barely thirteen; but Sarah herself had been married at fourteen, so she exerted herself in the retrieved Tradd Street residence to entertain the Middletons and others. Mr. Middleton's father had been Governor; the family ranked among the first in the province. She felt that a union of the Middletons and the Rutledges was indicated.

There was reason for Mrs. Rutledge to believe that if she could bring John to her way of thinking—though he seemed strangely indifferent to her desires in this matter—the Middletons would settle on their daughter a dot of sixty thousand pounds. This was double what had been expected from Miss Hörry.

Then, one Sunday, without the slightest warning, John Rutledge came home to supper with the new Mrs. John Rutledge. They had been married that evening, about six, by the Rector in St. Phillips Church, with two of the rector's servants as witnesses. No prior announcements and no guests. It was May 1, 1763.

The bride was Elizabeth Grimké, nineteen years old, "a brunette with blue eyes, of a small stature, reared exquisitely and of noted refinement." While not among the "first" families of merchants and planters, which included only those with really large holdings, the Grimkés were, nevertheless, well known and well-to-do. Elizabeth was born in Charles Town of the third generation resident in South Carolina. Certainly an "old" family.

The first immigrant, Elizabeth's grandfather, had spelled his name "Grimkey," evidently a concession to what he thought might be Anglican prejudices. He came from the border of Switzerland, a Huguenot, partly of Alsatian-Teutonic ancestry. He married a Frenchwoman named Faucheraud, prospered in Charles Town, and sent his sons and grandsons to England to be educated.

Elizabeth's father changed the name back to Grimké, which is evidence of the ascendancy of the Huguenots in the community, though the family became Episcopalian. Her brother, James, had been a student in the Middle Temple at the same time as John Rutledge. He was an intellectual. His chief interest was study; he was acquiring what became one of the chief private libraries in Charles Town; he was proficient in French and Spanish; and he had distinct aversions to both politics and business.

There was no political, professional, or financial relationship between John Rutledge and James Grimké, but they were lifelong intimate friends. Grimké was one of the library "idlers" whom John as a boy had condemned. John continued to disdain literary accomplishments; he made it a point not to read belles-lettres. History did not interest him, and he had no time for poetry or fiction.

Yet the Grimké residence was more a home to John than the Tradd Street house. There he had met and courted Elizabeth without any member of his family's knowing anything about it. When they decided to be married it was done abruptly. There was no marriage settlement.

Mrs. Sarah Rutledge had to accept the bride with what grace she could muster. Somehow John had cheated her out of what she felt to be her greatest prerogative, choosing a rich wife for him, and she could not even protest.

"John is a law unto himself," she said. "I wonder, sometimes, if he is my own flesh and blood."

In the fall of their marriage year the John Rutledges had a home of their own. John had been planning it all along, but it took him some time to find what he considered a correct permanent domicile. When he finally found it, he stayed there practically all his life.

He was making a great deal of ready money. For a man of his years it was an enormous income; and it is significant to note what he did with it after settling his mother's affairs, which ate up approximately half of what he made for several years.

The men of Charles Town continued to look upon two investments as of prime value, land and slaves. John Rutledge bought no slaves in the open market, a most significant fact in itself. For a time he bought no agricultural land, though two small parcels came to him as legal fees. Apparently, he wanted no more plantation "liability." He bought city property—piece after piece in rapid succession—as quickly as he got the cash and the parcels were available. Thus, among others, he acquired before his marriage the property at 116 Broad Street, and from time to time added to it the adjoining lots, together with a piece that carried him back to Queen Street in the rear. This was actually in the heart of Charles Town, a short walk from The Corner.

At 116 Broad Street he built his home, in the prevailing style, about six feet back from the street, with a driveway only wide enough for one carriage, with deep gardens in the rear and with a large slave house. The gardens extended back to Queen Street and contained an arbor and summer house. There were a carriage house and stable built of wood in the rear. The slave house and the master residence were made of brick and each had a slate roof.

A high stoop rose above a cellar which was only a few feet underground. The first floor—about six feet above the street—was given over to a very large dining room on the right, a small reception room on the left, and, in the rear, commodious kitchens, which had to accommodate stoves and all equipment in duplicate: one for the game cook and one for the meat and vegetable cook, each of whom had her own separate helpers.

The second floor, in its front half, was a drawing room, with a library only partly partitioned off. Thrown together, the two became, as required, a formal reception parlor, a ballroom, or, on occasion, a private rendezvous for councils of state. From the western windows of this room one could look down into the gardens of St. Andrews' Hall. At the front was Broad Street.

When they moved in, John had only two volumes for his library; these were Bacon's *Essays* and *Letters to His Son from Lord Chesterfield*. His law library was at the office. Elizabeth, with the aid of her brother, provided the mansion with an excellent library, though John seldom looked inside any of the books from one year's end to the other. He lived in an intellectual atmosphere; he knew about polite reading from what others said. John regarded books as proper furniture for a gentleman's home.

The Rutledge house had just two bedrooms and they were in the rear; provision for a family was only incidental. The house was deliberately planned, built, and maintained as a quasi-regal residence— the centre of formal and generous hospitality.

One of the most important rooms in the house was the wine cellar. It was located directly under the dining room, and had windows on the street. It was a space about thirty by twenty feet. Here could be accommodated two pipes of Madeira and two pipes of claret (a pipe being one hundred and ten gallons), in addition to plentiful casks and hampers of port, Lisbon, schnapps, sauterne, porter, and ale; and, also, demijohns of French brandy, West Indian rum, and Irish whiskey.

It was the butler's duty to see that at least one pipe each of claret and Madeira should be full to the brim at all times; while, from the other, he drew off quart bottles for daily use.

The drinking habits of the day reflected those of London; that is, sobriety in gentlemen was considered unimportant socially, but ladies seldom drank.

The most abstemious among the leaders of the port was Henry Laurens, now rapidly becoming Rutledge's chief client and one of his closest friends. He resolutely confined himself to one bottle of Madeira a day, which rendered him notable among his intimates, though one bottle was considered better than none.

John Rutledge was a two-bottle man, and proud of it. He agreed with his friend, Mr. Laurens, that one bottle a day might be sufficient when a man dined *en famille,* but if there were guests he claimed a man should drink two bottles at least.

This Madeira habit, to which Rutledge and the others were devoted, was of English origin, dating back to the British treaty of 1703 with Portugal when Madeira supplanted French wines. Before that claret had been the favorite English wine, but to continue drinking claret was considered unpatriotic.

John Rutledge installed in his cellar as many pipes of claret as of Madeira, to please his Huguenot friends and relatives, but for himself he stuck to the drinking habit he had formed in England.

Late in 1763, in good time for Christmas, John and Elizabeth moved into the new Broad Street home. It was a social event of the first consequence in Charles Town. They had twenty slaves, chosen by John from those belonging to his mother, taken in partial payment for the money he had advanced her. The butler was their ostensible chief, but the game cook ruled them.

In May of 1764 John Rutledge was appointed Attorney General of His Majesty's Province of South Carolina. He was in his twenty-fifth year, eleven years younger than the youngest man ever to hold the office previously.

7.

The appointment of John Rutledge as Attorney General was an attempt by the Governor, Thomas Boone, acting for the Crown, to break up the sovereign hold of the triumvirate over the affairs of South Carolina and it was part of his subtle contest with it.

Rutledge was young; he was amiable; he was of the aristocratic tradition. The Governor had reported that he readily could be absorbed into the imperial structure, if given a share of the regal bounty. It was a small share, to be sure, but a little was all that a colonial could expect. The Governor thought that he would make Rutledge an authentic King's man.

Similar reasons had influenced Parsons and Pinckney, and the chief clients of the port, when they turned to Rutledge. They, too, counted on the apparent pliability of his youth; they felt that his potential ability could be fostered to their advantage and manipulated as they desired.

The new Attorney General was a like a Chinese in outward reverence for age and authority. He deferred to his elders with a charming youthfulness which disarmed all opposition. But from Uncle Andrew he had acquired the instinct never to tell all he knew.

Neither Parsons, nor Pinckney nor the Governor could know for some time what steel lay under the Rutledge velvet. John was almost like a son to Parsons; yet, when they appeared in court against each other in a trover case, Rutledge whipped his mentor and then invited him to dinner.

Charles Pinckney favored John because, in addition to his obvious talent, he came of such good old Charles Town stock (the Hexts antedated the Pinckneys by eight years); and when they appeared in court with the counsel table between them and Rutledge came away with the verdict, John sent Pompey to Pinckney's office with a case of cognac.

Those he defeated seldom held anything against him for winning. He did not swagger in victory. He had a way—a smile, a little modest self-depreciation; almost an apology. His victories seemed not to be personal, but something apart from him—like his eloquence.

It was almost as if he had a dual personality. He was a pleasant and courteous fellow, not disputatious, and always with an engaging question to ask about the other person's opinions. He seemed, in fact, to have no opinions on general subjects; one might think that these important matters were beyond him. He was always willing to listen. Of this subtlest of all flatteries he was an adroit master.

The loquacity of his superficial father had given him deep distrust of promiscuous talkers and of ready retailers of ideas picked up at random. The tuition of his worldly mother had been more effective than she realized, for while he absorbed her social reticences and distinctions, their expression was his own. In addition, he developed a passion for people and affairs which led him into ever widening contacts. During his three years in England and Ireland he had given a minimum of time to book study; but he had pursued public men, pushing his way into inner sanctums, absorbing the gist of the personalities that came his way. These habits grew on him. When he spoke it was only of those things he knew: facts, personalities which he had seen and understood. Often his remarks about purely local affairs were startling in depth and clarity; they came oddly from one so young and were uttered without conceit.

These qualities captivated his elders, for he took no issue with them in the field of political speculation or in the realm of ideologies where he might touch their vanities. He disarmed them by leaving their prejudices to them, and so they were content to be led, though they did not realize it, by one who, to them, was little more than a child. Each elderly person of consequence felt he had John's support because John listened and absorbed and reserved his energy for expression in some homely field where it could be recognized instantly that he had gone to the heart of the matter.

This was the man who was already the uncrowned king of South Carolina, though no one yet recognized the fact, least of all himself.

Then there was the other John Rutledge, the lawyer, who never lost a lawsuit, who managed somehow always to be on the winning side in the Assembly. Or was it that the Assembly always agreed with him? No one could say which.

A myth began to grow up around the name of John Rutledge. Some in Charles Town asserted he was invincible because during his years abroad he had come in personal contact with the throne; he was, they whispered, the chosen favorite of the House of Hanover.

There was grumbling about him and against him, but it never came to anything. Whenever anyone came into his presence antagonism melted away. Light emanated from him. The general feeling was expressed in a throw-away handbill which was tacked to the bottom of a political poster:

"Pierre, the Court went against you."

"Aye, but 'twould a bin different an' I afforded to retain John Rutledge."

It was the custom for each member of the bar, at least once a year, to appear, fee gratis, for some poor client unable to hire a lawyer. The court made the assignments. Just before he was appointed Attorney General, Rutledge was assigned by the court to defend one Colton Sparkins. The charge was "assault by diverse and sundry beatings of a negro slave named Jeremiah."

Colton Sparkins appeared before the Court "by John Rutledge, his attorney, and maketh herewith his plea unto the charge aforesaid, namely that he is guilty as charged, and he begs leave to submit also to His Majesty's court, most respectfully, by his attorney the John Rutledge aforesaid, that in mitigation of his offense he declares that he had so partaken of spirituous liquors on each of the sundry occasions mentioned and at each of the places enumerated aforesaid, that he had no clear knowledge of his offense, and, MOREOVER, that he never at any of the times or places specified had of his own knowledge a clear perception of what he now knows to be the upright and meritorious character of the aforesaid negro slave Jeremiah."

Colton Sparkins was fined five pounds. He might have been sent to jail for two years. He was fortunate indeed to secure such charity counsel!

This was as near as Rutledge came to criminal practice, until he became Attorney General. Then, in his ten months' term as King's Counsel he had plenty of such experience, all of a minor nature except one: the Jared Mangin case.

Mangin was a sub-overseer, in charge of slaves on an indigo plantation. It was charged that he "feloniously and with malice aforethought did unto death a female slave of the name Deborah, the property of his employer."

To bring this indictment was probably the hardest decision Rutledge had to make while Crown Prosecutor. There was precedent for his doing so. Twice before since 1670 in South Carolina white men had been tried, convicted, and executed for killing Negroes. There was "law" for the prosecutor to lean on, either way. The white man could be let off with a slight imprisonment, and most frequently was, on the plea that a Negro was a chattel and that his destruction could not be a capital offense, but only "conversion of property." Or it was possible, and twice had so happened, that the Court could be asked to invoke the ecclesiastical law, which held that a Negro possessed a soul capable either of damnation or salvation, like any other. If the Court "went church" it was hard on the accused. He could appeal, of course, but the High Bench in London was nearly always "high church."

Before bringing the indictment, Rutledge consulted his colleagues,

Parsons and Pinckney. He laid the facts before them: this Jared Mangin was brutal and shiftless, often drunk. He had drifted from plantation to plantation, never in one employment more than two years. Twice he had been discharged because his employers disliked his relations with female slaves. The dead woman, Deborah, had resisted him openly in the presence of both blacks and whites (an episode extremely rare and in itself proof of great provocation) and he had brazenly clubbed her. Moreover, he was defiant about it, claimed that her value was no more than two hundred pounds, and that so much was coming to him.

The affair was already notorious. Something had to be done. To let the accused off, or to prefer a lesser charge, and thus void the possible uprising of the Negroes in case of conviction, would, at the same time, let down discipline among all the lesser whites, the overseers, the factors, and the white workmen, who, always in physical contact with the slaves, were constantly tempted to assert "white supremacy."

The moral aspects of the Negro question were not in the words or minds of the three attorneys as they discussed the Mangin case. Equality of the races in the moral law was taken for granted. There was enough variety in statute law to achieve any effect they desired. The problem, therefore, was solely one of discipline; the decision, in the highest sense, administrative.

Parsons, Pinckney, and Rutledge and all their clients owned plantations and slaves. All of them constantly wrestled with the problem of finding agents to rule and work the slaves effectively. It was a problem never quite solved. The triumvirate realized there must be some way of dramatizing the obligations of authority; the "law" must post a stern warning to bullies. Parsons and Pinckney advised Rutledge to proceed.

The trial was held in the Court of Common Pleas before Chief Justice Shinner. When the jury was chosen and in the box the Justice removed his wig, revealing a half bald, carroty pate, sloughed down in his chair, mopped the sweat from his forehead, poured out a tumbler of rum, downed it, winked broadly at the Attorney General, and, with a loose gesture, turned the Court over to him.

Rutledge, the essence of legal decorum, in high wig, lace ruffles and silk gown, was embarrassed and disgusted, though he could not show it. There sat the Chief Justice of His Majesty's Province of South Carolina, rapidly getting drunk in open court, at the beginning of a sensational murder trial.

The facts of Shinner's history had not been locally printed, but letters from London containing the pertinent information had brought the sinister revelations. The Corner knew that Shinner, never a member of the bar, had been born in Cork of a Liverpool father and an Irish mother; that he had been a pot-house hanger-on; that one day an English tourist in Cork sent him with a note to the woman with whom he was traveling; that Shinner surprised this woman in the arms of another man. Quick to see his advantage, Shinner had prevailed on her to induce her traveling companion to give him a job. What could he do, she asked. "Carry messages," replied Shinner.

The Englishman was Lord Halifax, chief of the Board of Trade and Plantations, in effect, the King's Minister for Colonies. He appointed, as runner for the Board, Charles Shinner, whose duty it became to carry bills and answers in equity between the courts of England and Ireland.

Before long the runner, who had learned one effective means of advancement then in vogue in England, attached himself to an English lady who was interested in a lawsuit in Ireland. What secret of this lady's he possessed is not known, but it was enough. She induced her brother, close to the throne, to secure the appointment of Charles Shinner as Chief Justice of South Carolina. She wanted him far away. Thus, "an illiterate ignoramus unfit for any place of credit in England or Ireland was sent to one of the principal colonies of America to sit in judgment on the fortunes, lives and liberties of His Majesty's subjects there." Nor was there any known way to replace him or to impeach him—short of gaining the King's ear—and no South Carolinian had that.

The greeting of the Chief Justice to Rutledge in his chambers after the latter's appointment was said to have been, "Now, me bye, as one mick to anither, th' Court's yours." The gesture in open court at the beginning of the Mangin trial was of the same sort.

So, before a shiftless, illiterate judge, becoming more intoxicated by the minute, Rutledge tried the discredited overseer as hastily as possible, and got a verdict; whereupon, rising unsteadily to his feet, without permitting the convicted man a moment of adjustment, and winking at the Attorney General, like a low-comedy roustabout, Chief Justice Shinner pronounced sentence: "To hang by yer neck until dead, an' may God ha' mercy on yer soul—fer I won't—hic!"

The night of the Mangin verdict Parsons, Pinckney, and Rutledge met tensely on the second floor of 116 Broad Street. The unspeakable Shinner had so bungled the trial that its salutary effect was probably lost—and might be worse than lost.

There was about it a feature even worse than the judicial debauchery visible in court. The complicating factor was that Shinner had acquired an octoroon female slave, whom it was known he favored. This would lend support to the view that he had used his power as a judge to send to the gibbet a white man less considerate of the Negroes than himself.

That Shinner had only subordinated himself in the usual way to the wishes of the Attorney General, whom he would have followed as readily if the direction had been opposite, meant nothing. The slaves would make their own interpretation.

Rutledge and his colleagues did not attempt to deceive themselves. They were well aware of the astounding efficiency of the grapevine communication among the slaves. By now the word had spread to the uttermost plantation that the blacks had a friend on the High Bench placed there by the distant English King, benevolent patron of all his subjects alike, both white and black, and that he was going to hang a white man for killing one of them. In unison, everywhere in the province, the Gullah eyeballs would be turning piously upward, the dark lips would be framing hallelujahs.

Parsons and Pinckney considered having Rutledge acquiesce in an appeal, which of course Shinner would grant or not, exactly as

Rutledge requested, and so put off for perhaps a year the fatal day, while the prisoner Mangin would be kept in jail. However, firmness won. The three decided that though the pill was bitter they would swallow it at once. Rutledge sent Pompey to the house of Lieutenant Governor Bull that night, Governor Boone being in England, with an order to which he first secured the signature of Shinner. The whole episode showed how practically vital affairs were settled on the second floor of 116 Broad Street.

At noon next day the drums began a muffled beat; the trumpeters lifted up their instruments and blew three long blasts which could be heard throughout the Town. Through a door in the wall of the prison a group appeared bearing in its midst the inert form of Jared Mangin, whose legs had failed him and who was muttering to himself.

At that moment a wild shout shattered the ominous silence. A light carriage drawn by prancing horses careened up the Broad Path, casting a cloud of dirt, and dashed through the scattering spectators, halting just in front of the guard. Out lurched Shinner, his wig awry, his clothes disheveled; he forced a way through the line of soldiers just as the condemned man was being carried up the steps to the gibbet. As the Chief Justice advanced he jeered and execrated the miserable creature.

Colonel Pinckney, military commandant in charge, was horror stricken. His impulse was to order the gross offender to be expelled from the scene, but he hesitated. Before him was Shinner; and, though he was muttering fantastic gibberish, still, he was Chief Justice, and Colonel Pinckney was merely an officer of the Court. The Colonel ordered the jailor to hasten. In a moment the debased Mangin kicked off into eternity—with Shinner leering before the gibbet.

This travesty of justice was an insult to all the cultivated instincts of the rulers of South Carolina.

Yet they felt morally responsible. The public demoralization which ensued stemmed from the government. The whole despicable account was chalked up to Chief Justice Shinner and, beyond that, to the system which produced him.

8.

For the rulers of Charles Town the problem of the Chief Justice, baffling as it was, and professionally humiliating, was not so difficult as the problem of the Governor.

Thomas Boone had come among them, only a few years before, with every engaging prospect. Though a "foreigner," born in England, he had lived a few of his early years in South Carolina and owned a fine plantation there. Before returning to the scenes of his early life, he had been Governor of New Jersey where he had been greatly liked and respected. Word of his popularity in the North preceded him to the South.

When Governor Boone and his lady arrived in Charles Town in December, 1761, there had been the customary ceremony. A militia regiment was drawn up in Broad Street, with a company of artillery before Granville's Bastion. Then there was a parade to the Council Chamber for the reading of the Commission before the Council; next, an equally formal parade to the State House with a second reading of the Commission before the Commons; followed by an "elegant entertainment" at Poinsett's Tavern.

Both the Council and the Commons, in addresses, declared that if South Carolina had been asked to choose its own Governor it knew of no gentleman whom it would have preferred to Thomas Boone. Equally important, with all the first ladies of the colony grouped around Mrs. Parsons, Mrs. Pinckney, and Mrs. Leigh in the front row, it was also asserted, officially, that no woman was more desirable, as First Lady, than the gracious Madame Boone.

If this sounded like the usual genuflection, still there it was, the official record and a social fact. The Governor and the people had a joyous "honeymoon" through the holidays.

As senior member of the triumvirate, Mr. Parsons, with his lady, first entertained the Governor and his lady at dinner; then Colonel and Mrs. Pinckney; then Mr. and Mrs. Leigh. (This was a year before Rutledge replaced Leigh as a member of the triumvirate and a little more than a year before Rutledge's marriage.) Then other leaders

entertained the Governor and his lady, and were, in turn, invited to
the Governor's Mansion.

Priorities in this miniature social hierarchy were well established,
based on the procedure at St. James's, as reported in the Court Circular. In Charles Town the members of the triumvirate corresponded
to royalty in London, the members of the Council to the leaders of
the House of Lords, the Speaker to the prime minister, and so on.
No outsiders were desired or permitted. It is difficult to conceive what
earthly power would have attempted to alter the established procedure. Apparently Governor Boone would not, when all seemed
well in the best of all possible worlds. Through the height of that
first winter season social life was gay and attractive in Charles Town.

Then, without any formal announcement, it was learned that
Mrs. Boone, and her two children, had sailed for London. The ship
had gone before the *Gazette* said anything about it. It was assumed
she had gone to take the children to English schools. That was the
customary reason for which matrons of the colony took their children
to the mother country—and one readily understood. Usually, however,
the event required a season for preparation, with all the necessary
farewells.

The Governor treated the event casually and without explanation.
His manner was such that no one questioned him closely. Then he
invited the members of the triumvirate and their wives to dinner;
the members of the Council and their wives and the Speaker of the
Commons with his wife were also asked. It seemed as if he were
beginning over again, for this was the fifth banquet of the season,
not the first; yet it was no obvious violation of any known precedent
and the accepted leaders of the Town went happily, totally unprepared
for what they met.

They found a new hostess. Receiving with the Governor was a
"lady" not his wife and not a relative. Governor Boone offered no
explanation. This was his friend, Mrs. Wortnington—that was all he
said. Where she came from, why she was there, he did not deign
to explain. No one dared to ask. The Governor was the personal
representative of their sovereign, answerable solely to the King. Were

they parochial enough to expect that he would consult them, or inform them about his personal affairs?

The next day the triumvirate met—*en camera*. Here was a problem of state, profound and far-reaching—how far-reaching no one present had the imagination to foresee. However, the consideration given was only formal. There could be little doubt of the decision. There was a simple way to answer the Governor. It was negative, yet most decisive. Not one of the ladies paid a dinner call. Not one of the group invited the "friend" of the Governor to dinner, or to tea, or to lunch, and when by chance they passed on the street the ladies did not "see" her.

There was no slightest deviation from what the rulers of Charles Town considered to be the correct social position. Their Governor could have but one lady and that lady must be his wife. If this was lese majesty, let him make the most of it. If divorce was in the air no one ever mentioned it. Divorce was not only unheard of; it was unthinkable. The South Carolinians were like the Mongolian tribe which had no knowledge of marital infidelity and consequently no word with which to express adultery.

Boone tried to laugh it off, at first. He said they were provincial, narrow-minded, bigoted, with no knowledge of the great world; they were strangely and unexpectedly puritanical in what he had believed was a liberal social atmosphere; they were unsophisticated peasants! All this the Governor uttered at first in hurt surprise, then in derision.

The rulers of Charles Town, nevertheless, knew the customs of London. They knew the King did not invite his royal advisers and his ministers to the palace to meet a woman who was not the Queen. Then Boone shifted the war to the field of politics. Here it appeared the advantage must be with the Governor.

The first intimation that Boone intended to make a real fight of it was soft and courteous. He announced that he reluctantly had come to the conclusion, after a careful study of the election laws, that the Assembly as constituted had been improperly chosen. He dissolved the Assembly with an apology and issued writs for a new election.

Here was something so startling that at first no one would admit its implications. For more than a generation, or since 1719, no governor had dared to question either the legality of the election or the power of the Commons House of Assembly, though every governor possessed technically, as did Thomas Boone, the King's authority to prorogue.

The situation resembled, in principle, that in which Charles I had prorogued his Parliament. Governor Boone might easily have read what happened to Charles for his rash attempt to obstruct free-born Englishmen. So also he might have known more about the social customs at St. James's. It was his opinion, however, that he was dealing with "provincial peasants." How far he was goaded into this view by the "lady" in his residence is not on the record.

The Commons heard the Governor, but did not go home as he ordered them to do. Instead, they referred the matter to the triumvirate and adjourned for twenty-four hours. After hearing from the triumvirate the Assembly, on reconvening, went about its business as if nothing had happened; yet it punctiliously appointed a committee to investigate the assertions made by the Governor and to report on the prorogation. In due time—a full week—the Commons received the report of its committee, adopted it favorably, and transmitted it by messenger to the Governor, who thus was properly informed that his "Parliament" had carefully inspected the election laws, had found them to be correct, and that it was not necessary for him to dismiss it. This was explicit and final, like the preliminaries of a street duel. The issue was now drawn even more clearly. Who was the ruling power in South Carolina—Governor or Commons? King or People?

Boone did not pick up the challenge at once. He realized he had bitten off something it would be hard to chew. Neither would he admit defeat. He reported the affair to London and was advised to go easy. The head of the Board of Trade and Plantations, his immediate superior, had heard something about the lady in the case. Boone bided his time until fall.

In September, 1762, when the new Commons, elected in the normal course, came before the Governor, Rutledge had displaced Leigh and was the new third member of the triumvirate. He went with his fellow members to the Governor's Mansion to take the oath of allegiance. The oath could not be administered, the Governor said, because one of the new members, Christopher Gadsden, was not properly qualified, as the church wardens who returned him had not been sworn before they made their declarations. The others might swear allegiance, if they desired to do so. Instead they refrained and withdrew to confer.

The Commons waited a day for the triumvirate to thrash it out privately. Parsons, Pinckney, and Rutledge saw in this new challenge something more serious, to them, than proroguing the Commons, especially since the Commons had gone on meeting just the same. As lawyers they saw that here was something basic—an attack on that which it had taken parliamentary government four centuries of conflict to establish; namely, the right of the Commons to judge the qualifications of its own members. Once that right was waived there might be nothing important left.

However, did the Commons want to qualify Mr. Gadsden? Here was a neat problem for the triumvirate to resolve. It would require all the statesmanship at their command to give the correct answer. The issue had been raised, by a curious legerdemain, from the drawing room to the inner sanctum of the state house. Mr. Gadsden was, in their own private opinions, a bit of a blatherskite. He was a reformer of a noxious type. He could orate for two solid hours—and habitually did so—on the subject of Liberty. He interspersed his remarks plentifully with quotations from Greek and Latin authors, and recently he had taken to a study of Hebrew, thus augmenting and lengthening his repertoire, which was the special and enormous delight of the mechanics and artisans of the Town whom he later organized into a group known as the Liberty Boys. He was wont to address them six nights a week—never on Sunday, for he was a deeply pious man—under a great oak on the common which in due time was known as the Liberty Tree.

It was the mechanics and artisans who had elected Mr. Gadsden, almost unanimously, to the Commons, from St. Paul's Parish. The church wardens might take an oath or not; there could be another election or a dozen or none; everyone knew that Mr. Gadsden would still be the overwhelming choice of St. Paul's.

Unfortunately—and this is what made it especially hard for the triumvirate—Mr. Gadsden recently had let slip a disrespectful reference to George III. It was said he was in correspondence with another agitator of his type in Boston, named Sam Adams. It was this fact, no doubt, which justly had alarmed the Governor. The Ministry in London had given Boone no encouragement when he prorogued the Commons, but what would be the London attitude when it was known the King's *alter ego* in South Carolina was determined to keep from the Commons one who in public assaulted the King? It appeared that Governor Boone and his "lady" had improved their position.

The triumvirs had more than political disagreement with Gadsden to deter them. (It went without saying they did not approve attacks on the King.) So far as they were concerned Christopher Gadsden did not "belong." Though his father had been an officer in the royal navy he himself never had been commissioned and had been only a purser in the merchant marine. That was a severe social handicap in an essentially British hierarchy.

In his early twenties Gadsden was an intimate of Henry Laurens, and the two swore vows of chastity, temperance, and frugality—a monastic regimen. Keeping his vows, to which he added that of taciturnity, Laurens scaled the heights, while Gadsden, who copiously explained everything to everybody, lost much of the money with which he started and soon retired and invested what he had left in a wharf, which ran itself.

Gadsden was a great denouncer of alcohol. He parted company with Laurens when he found that Henry had temporized with at least one of his vows, and was drinking up to a bottle of Madeira a day and doubling his money every three years. Gadsden also denounced lewd women. He denounced European fashions for "good" women. He denounced horse-racing. He denounced popery. All of these, however, were only warming-up exercises for what later became the chief object of his denunciation—George III. As a denouncer, Christopher Gadsden had no rival in Charles Town. Gadsden never denounced slavery, however. He owned slaves. His friend, Sam Adams, likewise a purist and an honest, pious, frugal man who personally owned a bond-woman, did not discuss slavery, either.

This was the man the triumvirs were asked to champion. A man of no background, of little property, and an awkward fellow in the drawing room. However, Christopher Gadsden was a duly elected representative of the people. The *demos* had put its finger on him. Should Runnymede and the Rump Parliament be forgotten?

The triumvirate conferred solemnly; the youthful Rutledge silent, but listening respectfully to his elder associates. The triumvirs advised their associates in the Commons—which included a much more than two-thirds majority of the thirty-six members—that "nothing should deprive the House of its just claim solely to examine and determine the validity of the elections of its own members." Whereupon, the Commons so notified the Governor, with seven dissenting votes. The Governor at once dissolved the House for "contumacy"—a word then well understood.

This was the second slap from Governor Boone. When he prorogued them, they had overlooked it, as a sort of error in etiquette; but that word "contumacy" had more bite in it. They promptly met and voted, with seven stiff Tory dissenters (the only members not under tuition to the triumvirs) that henceforth they would have no "intercourse" with the Governor. They laid the Governor's messages on the table. They refused to pass the tax bills he recommended. And they failed to appropriate salaries for the Governor or the Chief Justice.

This was serious. The Governor possessed a simple remedy, one that would have settled the affair promptly. He was sovereign; his commission charged him with authority to command the military. He had only to order out the militia and direct it to station guards at the doors of the House, while the Commons was ordered dispersed *"vi et armis."* That would be decisive.

However, to take this obvious step he would have had to deliver his orders to Colonel Charles Pickney, commandant of the militia, and one of the triumvirs who directed each move of the Commons. If Governor Boone ordered Colonel Pickney to close up the Commons, would Triumvir Pinckney obey? And if he refused to obey, what then? Evidently the Governor did not want to learn the answers to these queries, for he never issued such an order.

Boone might have precipitated an armed conflict between South Carolina and Great Britain in 1763 or 1764, if regular soldiers of the mother country had been available, but those who had been there had finished up their job of subduing the Indians and had left the colony. So he applied to the Ministry in London, for the third time; and for the third time Lord Halifax advised him to be "more tactful." So Boone "tactfully" went on about his business of signing unimportant documents (without salary) while the Commons went about its customary ways.

Meanwhile, *pourparlers* were exchanged. The next election found Sir John Colleton among the members of the Commons. He was one of the two knights in the colony, presumably, in the mind of the Governor, a Tory, though as events proved a stout Whig. Sir John was a stickler for proper form and refused to sit in the House until he had been legally sworn in by the Governor. This put the House in a hole. It had a knight and wanted the glamour of his presence during sessions, but it could have him only on his own terms. He had to be sworn by a Governor who, to the Assembly, did not practically exist.

Again the aid of the triumvirs was enlisted. Parsons, Pinckney, and Rutledge went into session and then suggested to the House that it proceed just as if nothing had happened. So the House voted that two members should accompany Sir John Colleton to the Executive Mansion to receive the oath, which the rest of them had been obliged to go without. The Speaker appointed Mr. Moultrie and Mr. Gadsden, the person who was politically non-existent in the eyes of the non-existent Governor. Arrived at the Mansion, and ushered into the presence of the executive, the three—Sir John, Mr. Moultrie, and Mr. Gadsden—informed His Excellency that Sir John had been sworn in properly by the Commons and now desired the state oath from the Governor.

His Excellency smiled upon Sir John but coldly informed Messrs. Moultrie and Gadsden that the House had no right to order any person into his dwelling place, whereupon he called his servant to open the door. Moultrie and Gadsden bowed themselves out and as Sir John followed them he was plucked by the sleeve by His Excellency who said, quietly, that if the honored knight had any business to transact with the Governor His Excellency would be only too pleased to transact it.

Later—in the Commons—Sir John Colleton appeared and announced that the Governor had given him the state oath. Though the law required that there must be two witnesses to this momentous official act, the Commons by resolution declared that in this instance the personal statement of the new incumbent would be accepted as sufficient.

So the great quarrel was patched up and revolution averted, for a time. The Commons functioned on its own terms. Salaries were unpaid, while the "lady" remained in conspicuous residence at the Governor's Mansion. Official social intercourse with other members of the government remained suspended. This sort of nonsense went on for three years.

It became very involved. The colony employed an agent in London, named Garth. He, in turn, employed an important lawyer named Dunning (afterward Lord Ashburton) to put before the Board of Trade and Plantations the colony's case whenever Governor Boone made complaint. So there were two main lines of appeal going up constantly to the Ministry; one from the sovereign's *alter ego,* one from the people as sovereign in the Commons.

When Boone wrote in, reporting his "indignities" and how vigilantly he had upheld the honor of the throne, Ashburton appeared and delivered a legal argument based on the British constitution, and meanwhile in the coffee houses gave currency to the facts about the lady in the case. The Ministry took no action, except to give Boone leave to come to London in person and plead his cause. The Governor considered this humiliating and for a long time did not accept the invitation.

Thus, South Carolina was, in effect, free and independent. The Governor was only a figurehead. The Chief Justice was an easy tool of the ruling authority. Actual power resided, through the Commons House of Assembly, in the triumvirate.

The mother country permitted no such license in any other American colony. South Carolina was the favorite because the relationship was so prosperous for both sides that neither wished to disturb it. Those were the years that would ever after be referred to in Charles Town as "the good old days." South Carolina was the plum of the world.

Already the colonists of New England had touched the rock bottom that lay so near the surface of their farms and were turning to manufacturing for a living. The northern coasts were sprouting shipyards, and every year saw an increase in Yankee merchantmen. New England was setting herself up as a potential rival, and in some degree as an actual rival, of England.

England established colonies to create markets for her manufactured goods and to get the agricultural products she needed at her own price. New England perverted the British colonial system when she became a competitor by manufacturing her own goods. To make it worse she diminished exports from her soil; and still worse, the Yankee merchantman increased his hold on the seven seas. All this was putting the northern colonies in the black books of the mother country. And the reprisals put the mother country equally in disfavor in the North.

In South Carolina the situation was reversed, and to such an extent that when a shipyard for the construction of ocean-going vessels was proposed for Georgetown, neither Parsons, Pinckney, nor Rutledge could be persuaded to draw the papers, so considerate were they of the larger issues which might be adversely affected. No other attorney was considered. South Carolina's value in the eyes of the London Ministry—and this doubtless influenced every official act—lay in her lack of manufactures and of shipyards. Moreover, there was no apparent prospect that she would ever have any. Rice and indigo were South Carolina's chief staples. Neither could be grown in England where the population had constant need for both. Also, both products were in world-wide demand. Out of the regulation of the commerce in these two chief staples came the advantage which South Carolina had over New England, Virginia, and Maryland. A bounty of sixpence a pound was provided for indigo in 1748, when it had just been discovered and was an infant industry; England wanted South Carolina to produce a rival to the then superior French brand. By 1760 the Carolina indigo was better than the French but England did not rescind the bounty. The South Carolina planter still got his sixpence a pound bonus though he had learned to produce better indigo than the French and at less cost. In the decade of the 1760's, South Carolina indigo was more valuable to England than the mines of Peru and Mexico were to Spain.

With rice the situation was similar, but the volume of business was greater. England wanted nothing to disturb the rice culture, so she altered the Navigation Act, which so oppressed New England and Virginia, to permit South Carolina to ship rice to ports south of Cape Finisterre, including Portugal and the Mediterranean, without first sending it to England, provided the English market had been satisfied first.

This was a voluntary exception in the arbitrary control established over colonial commerce, for none of the other colonies was permitted to trade except through England. Thus South Carolina rice merchants had the chance to sell about a fifth of their product without paying direct toll to England. That fifth spelled the margin of excess profit and that was why sellers like Laurens, Brewton, and Legare doubled their capital about every three years. The chief planters were nabobs. To the Crown of England the rice of South Carolina was on a par with the rubies which Clive had just seized in India.

The trade was open, free, and legal, and a monopoly. It made real a shopkeeper's dream of paradise—great profit without violation of the law. It was the chief business of Parsons, Pinckney, and Rutledge to preserve this situation; and they were enriched by doing so. George III and Thomas Boone reigned; the triumvirate ruled.

9.

The first child of John and Elizabeth Rutledge was born in the spring of 1764 in the new Broad Street house and died there before it could be christened. Their second child, a girl named for her grandmother, Sarah, was born in June, 1765.

Rutledge had resigned as Attorney General three months earlier, after only ten months in the King's service. The reason given was that he must provide for his growing family. The Attorney General received as salary a hundred and fifty pounds per annum. His professional income the year following his resignation was above three thousand pounds.

However, the real reason for Rutledge's resignation was political. The triumvirs were facing the most disturbing question that ever had been brought before them: What answer should be made to an invitation from the General Assembly of the Colony of Massachusetts Bay to attend a "congress" of all American colonies "to take deliberations concerning the Stamp Tax proposed to be levied—"

Never before had the colonies in all sections of the country met together officially. If it convened, this would be the first American Congress. The mere mention of the possibility raised profound issues. Here was a crossroads of history. Which way was South Carolina to go?

If the triumvirs were to consider this with a free hand it would not do to have one of them in the King's pay. They realized well that the issues involved went far beyond the proposed Stamp Tax, which had been devised as a means of getting the colonies to pay part of the expense of the late French and Indian War. Prime Minister Grenville, the Tory who succeeded the Whig, Pitt, was the first responsible minister personally to study colonial reports—a minor detail in the affairs of empire—and he noted the comparatively large number of legal documents filed in America. This gave him the idea of taxing them. He thought such a tax would be hidden and painless. As an afterthought he added a tax on newspapers. The aroused hornets' nest astounded everyone in England.

The triumvirs of Charles Town had this to consider: a fierce and protracted protest was being raised by Gadsden and Timothy and was fast getting complete hold of the populace, but not a word was ever uttered against the real rulers of Charles Town, Parson, Pinckney, and Rutledge, or the rich clients they represented. The author of all their woes, the agitators said, was that shadowy distant Ministry, and the King whose power was becoming increasingly oppressive. The King was denounced; the triumvirs were immune to criticism. At first glance it seemed to be an ideal situation for them.

However, it was more complex than that.

The complexity began with their relationship to the Indians. South Carolina had just ratified a treaty to end all Indian treaties. The red men had agreed to withdraw as far inland as three hundred to five hundred miles. The whites thought they would never have any more trouble. This had been true for eighteen months, and as a result there was an expansion of settlement and a freedom of life never before known. The blessings resulting from this marvelous fact could hardly be overestimated.

Who had done this? The soldiers of the King, assisted, of course, by colonials; yet on the King had been not only the chief financial responsibility, but the moral burden as well. Many sensitive souls were questioning the manifest and numerous injustices to the original owners of what was now realized to be a paradise on earth. The Indians' lands had been taken, their homes looted and dispersed, often their lives forfeited, and now they were enduring the final process of expropriation—their reputation was being destroyed. In the beginning they had been noble red men; now they were treacherous savages, because they fought desperately for their lands and homes.

The white men had broken each of the first six treaties with the Indians; and this legal and moral fault was laid on the broad shoulders of the King, because his generals had violated the treaties. His commanders had persuaded Indians to give themselves up as hostages and then had ruthlessly executed them. Yet when these events were discussed in church or home or in letters to the *Gazette,* and the inference made that the appointees of the triumvirs (colonial commanders) were responsible, the blame was always sternly laid to some "ignorant" or "brutal" agent of the King. The South Carolinians readily accepted this exoneration of their local rulers (for whom they were responsible); they were not unlike other citizens in other colonies who desired to enjoy moral immunity along with physical possession of the new conquest. This made the King a great moral convenience, a sort of scapegoat. To the South Carolinians it was pleasant to believe that it was the King who despoiled the Indians. It was only incidental that they themselves kept the spoils.

If the King was a moral convenience in the conquest of the Indians, who had little if any effective power to strike back, he was even more important as a scapegoat to the triumvirs in their relations with the steadily increasing numbers of settlers, laborers, and common people whose only possessions lay in their capacity to toil, but who yet were white and legally free.

Inured to the idea of slavery which existed all about them, much more than half the white population lived in a condition only theoretically better than that of the blacks, who at least had social and old-age security.

Every vessel that had arrived for a hundred years brought indentured immigrants: that is, white persons who had agreed, in writing, to give a term of years of labor to pay for their passage. To this they often added bonds to cover their remaining years, in return for unimproved land, for which the "owners" had paid neither the Indians nor the King. If they rebelled there were the courts and the law of contracts.

These conditions—and the many others growing out of them—were, in reality, the undertow of the rising revolution; a slowly gathering force which was to become a tidal wave. They were never brought forward directly in the eighteenth century as political capital by anyone in America. Instead, in Charles Town, as elsewhere, the crowds were fanned into a white heat of indignation against the Stamp Tax, whose chief revenue would come from public documents. To a man like Henry Laurens, for instance, from whom the tax probably would take more than from anyone else in the community, it might not mean more than a hundred pounds a year. He did not object to it seriously. Benjamin Franklin, who was consulted unofficially by Grenville before the act was passed, had approved it. So did John Rutledge, and his colleagues of the triumvirate, at first.

The item in the Stamp Tax that chiefly accounted for the opposition was the tax on newspapers. Every separate issue of every separate newspaper would be obliged to carry a twopenny stamp which could be purchased only with cash. The colonies had twenty-two newspapers; practically every one would be obliged to suspend if the Stamp Act held.

The South Carolina *Gazette,* like each of its twenty-one colleagues to the north, was giving up large portions of each issue to the "horrors" of the Stamp Tax. It had no room for any accounts of what to it were comparatively trifling events, such as the Cooke-Lennox and the Jared Mangin cases, but it published interminable columns about the "unspeakable atrocity" of the proposed tax. Mr. Timothy was so breathless he ran out of English and imported a font of type in the Greek alphabet and used it liberally, with thoughtful translations, so that anyone could know what had hapepned to the tyrants of Syracuse and Sparta. Mr. Gadsden was also breathless about it, in Latin and Hebrew as well as in English.

There was a legal point involved—taxation without representation. The lawyers winked at that. It was Peter Timothy, the editor, and Christopher Gadsden, the wharf-owner, who informed the crowds about the coming violation of the constitutional law.

Knowing all this only too well, why should the triumvirs commit South Carolina to an inter-colonial Congress on a matter which, in their minds, concerned only them and the mother country? They had very little, if any, sense of being "American." Their feeling of antagonism against their northern neighbors far outrode any resentment they held toward Great Britain. And every other southern colony felt the same way.

In fact, North Carolina had already refused to send delegates to the New York Congress; so had Georgia; and the Virginia House of Burgesses had been prorogued so as to avoid taking action on the matter. If the triumvirs should decide to send delegates to New York, South Carolina would be the only southern colony represented.

The crowds in the streets were demanding just that, however, and shouting for it as they had never shouted for anything before. Gadsden was aggressive and obstinate, but he commanded only three to seven votes in the Commons, and Rutledge shrewdly realized that Gadsden was only an echo.

The original protest came from the North; from Sam Adams, who was beginning to stir up the town meetings to register his will. It was a prodigious triumph of organized propaganda, the first in the history of America, and its repercussions were being felt in South Carolina.

With all his political skill, however, Sam Adams was as yet only a rebel. The Governor and courts of Massachusetts defied him and functioned loyally for the King. No member of the General Assembly in Boston had even thought of setting them aside, as the South Carolina Governor had been set aside by the Commons. Parsons, Pinckney, and Rutledge already had accomplished noiselessly in Charles Town what Adams and Otis were talking about so violently in Boston.

Thomas Boone cast the die. The Governor accepted the three-year-old invitation of the Board of Trade and Plantations to make a personal call upon its members and state his grievances and, with his "lady," he sailed for London. Between him and his real masters, the triumvirs, was dropped the obligatory three-months' wall of silence. No sooner was the ship that bore the Governor and his feminine companion beyond the outer islands than Parsons and Pinckney met with Rutledge in the drawing room that looked down on St. Andrew's Hall. With apparent readiness they arrived at a unanimous decision.

That night word spread about the Town that Mr. Rutledge would speak the next day in the Assembly. Before eight o'clock the next morning the state house was jammed. The tiny spectators' gallery could hold only a small fraction of those who came. Business was almost suspended and the throngs spread along Broad Street and overflowed The Corner.

When the Speaker took the rostrum all but one of the thirty-six members were in their places. Two, summoned by the triumvirate, had ridden all night from their plantations to be on hand. As soon as routine business was disposed of, Mr. Rutledge rose and asked for personal privilege, which the Speaker granted.

The youthful triumvir stepped down into the well and faced the Assembly and the gallery. He was pale. For hours the night before he had listened silently to the adjurations of his elder colleagues who were entrusting to his single voice the aegis of the state. He could see them as they sat in front of him—Mr. Parsons, with ruddy face and bald pate, on the aisle a few rows back; and, in the far corner, with iron-gray hair and severe expression, Mr. Pinckney, in his red uniform as Colonel Commanding.

The crowds in the street were hushed. The Governor was on the ocean. The Lieutenant Governor was a factotum in their hands. The actual executive power of the province was about to speak.

Rutledge began quietly, as if in casual conversation. The doors and windows were open, but the people in the street and on the stairs could not hear distinctly. They asked each other: what was he saying? Whispers carried the news from the doors into the halls, down the stairs, into the street. He was talking about the King; he was praising the King. They became deathly still. Now his voice became a little louder and even on the street they could hear him. Yes. He was recalling what they owed the King. Was it not to the bounty of the King they were indebted for all the blessings of this new land?

For many, many months they had heard nothing like this. Most of them felt quite the opposite. But no open protest was made. So that was the decision! The triumvirs were King's men. Sullenly and silently they listened.

The voice of the orator rose. It lashed like a whip out of the open doors. What was that he was saying? They were Englishmen, and the sons of Englishmen, and free-born. The rights due an Englishman were theirs by birth. Even down at The Corner they heard the peroration: "And if we are wronged our King shall know it, and he shall right the wrong—for His Gracious Majesty will not willingly let into serfdom his loyal and dutiful subjects."

Was Rutledge carrying water on both shoulders? What had been the decision? In a little while they heard; Rutledge had moved that the Speaker appoint three delegates to the New York Congress. The motion had carried, with only five dissenting votes. His loyalty had been so eloquent he had convinced two of the seven Tories. And the Speaker had at once appointed Christopher Gadsden.

The people's champion—Captain Gadsden—was to go to New York and join with the great patriots of Boston in defying the King! Now they could shake their fists right in His Majesty's face! John Rutledge was all right, after all—perhaps a bit cautious, as a responsible man should be—but just the man for them.

The other delegates were Thomas Lynch and John Rutledge. The three names had been chosen the night before by the triumvirs and placed on the Speaker's desk just before Rutledge spoke.

Lynch ranked as the wealthiest planter, after Middleton, in the province. He had just built in the Town an imposing mansion with cypress timber cut in his own mill on the Santee. Though a Whig, he was conservative. The triumvirs selected him as a foil to Gadsden.

The secret instructions of the triumvirate to Rutledge were to avoid taking any action that would bring about a breach of relations with the mother country. The delegates were to look, listen, to talk if necessary, and to report. Frontier spirit ruled; they were scouts entering enemy territory.

At the last moment it was understood, with the triumvirs, that if Lynch and Rutledge should agree on any action it should become the official decision of the delegation. Gadsden was not informed of this, though he had agreed the three should act as a unit and be bound by a majority. This tied Rutledge to Lynch but prevented his combining with Gadsden, as against Lynch—a device of Pinckney's, who felt that his young associate might need the steadying influence of an older man like Lynch. Apparently none of them, from Pinckney to Gadsden, realized either the subtlety, the certainty, or the swiftness of Rutledge's leadership. They doubtless felt he was not experienced enough to be in their class—but that he was coming along—a most promising young fellow, whom they liked very much. Each might have said to himself secretly that that was the kind of son he would like to have.

As they boarded the vessel that took them north, just after the middle of September, 1765, one Charles Towner complained, "There go two old men and a boy to represent us." Lynch was in his fifties; Gadsden forty-three; Rutledge just turning twenty-six.

To the "boy" it was just another triumvirate. By this time he understood how a triumvirate works.

I.

THE South Carolina delegation, enjoying good winds, arrived in New York five days ahead of the opening of Congress, and three days ahead of the men from Boston. Gadsden went to a boarding house. Rutledge and Lynch went to the most fashionable tavern, the Kings Arms Inn, built on the first hill on Broadway, between Cedar and Liberty Streets. They all considered London their capital and felt as Rutledge did when he wrote to his mother, "This is my first trip to a foreign country."

From the Kings Arms balcony, where the inn kept a spyglass mounted, Rutledge could see far beyond the lower tip of Manhattan Island. It was like his own city. There was the Hudson; just like the Ashley, it seemed; the East River was like the Cooper; each city had a similar bay, with Staten Island and Governor's Island in place of James's and Sullivan's. Charles Town and New York! Two matchless natural ports for man's convenience—two apparently equal gates to empire!

Yet—were they equal? Rutledge took their measure calmly. The Hudson seemed twice as wide as the Ashley and twice as deep; into the East River could be poured several Coopers; the harbor beyond seemed much deeper than his.

For the first time, during the past year, more tonnage had cleared New York than had gone out of Charles Town. When Rutledge's ship lifted anchor sixty-three vessels were visible from Granville's Bastion; when the same anchor dropped off the Battery eighty-seven sails were visible; reports indicated this to be near an average. Was the sceptre of commercial empire in the colonies moving north?

In population the towns were about the same: approximately fourteen thousand persons in each. In Charles Town, however, eight thousand were Negro slaves; in New York only two thousand were slaves. These facts altered the situation and produced two different civilizations.

Rutledge found that a prime Negro could be bought on the Battery for seventy pounds. The same man would bring three times as much in Charles Town. The Dutch in New York, rather than the English, valued slaves, who were being discarded as field hands. Because of the high license required in New York for transfer of title to a slave it was the custom to buy them in Newark, where there was no license, and then bootleg them across the river at night. This was a curious evasion of statute law which the South Carolinians confronted for the first time.

Negro beggars accosted Rutledge in front of his inn, and this was a novel experience. He learned that in New York slaves were "freed" when they were too old to work profitably. Though Charles Town had four times as many slaves, none were ever seen begging.

Other customs were also reversed. In New York most men chewed tobacco and spat anywhere; in the South the only tobacco chewers were Negro field hands. After dark, lower Broadway and the Battery swarmed with street-walkers; one never saw a prostitute on the streets of Charles Town. A man who ventured on Corlear's Hook, or along South Street, after sundown, took his life in his hands; the waterfront in Charles Town was as safe as church. Chalked on the new stone abutments for the graveyard of Trinity Church Rutledge could read, "Rag of the whore of Babylon." If anyone in Charles Town ever felt like that about the Church of England it had not been publicly expressed, even in secret night writing.

In Chapel Street, where Rutledge went to the theatre, he was warmly greeted by his friend, David Douglass, manager of the Hallam Company, who confided that they were living perilously. Rotten eggs were thrown at the actors nightly, not as dramatic criticism, but as a note tied to a bunch of decayed vegetables put it: "It is highly improper that play actors should appear when great numbers of poor people are starving." The *New York Weekly Post Boy* had underlined this by saying, "It is hardly deemed seemly that a play house should continue in our midst where many might be tempted to forget their business and squander their money."

Nothing like that ever had occurred in Charles Town. Douglass was counting the days to the end of November when the Hallam Company would sail for South Carolina—and civilization.

As Rutledge went about the gangling, active port, superficially, at least, more alive than his own, he found that no one had yet thought to establish a department store like that of the Lennox Brothers. New York had four or five markets where food and commodities were sold from open stalls, but neither an emporium nor separate specialized stores. Hucksters strolled about the sterets, offering goods. Marketing, on the whole, was done in the mode of medieval England.

All day, before the Kings Arms, as elsewhere, pigs and chickens roamed at will. Rutledge was waked by lowing cows being driven past the inn to pasture. In Charles Town domestic stock was largely confined to the plantations, and the walled gardens were given over to flowers. In New York the backyards were pig pens and cow stables. To keep their backyards clean and thus protect their livestock, house-wives emptied slops from the front doorways into all streets, even on Wall Street and Bowling Green.

Two towns could hardly be more different. South of Queen Street, in Charles Town, there was order and strict discipline; slaves were in their places at all times; all persons retired to their private affairs behind high walls; the streets were swept daily; everywhere there was an atmosphere of aristocratic seclusion. New York was a frontier Babylon.

Despite the rising tide of ships' registry Rutledge found that New York was much more discontented than his own country. The North was given over to the despair of post-war adjustments. The *Weekly Post Boy* dared speak of "the severe depression of the times" which its readers believed to be a terrible and unaccountable affliction.

The Kings Arms' manager told Rutledge that local merchants, warehousemen, factors, and others were frankly saying good times would never return until they could get back the Dutch. Everyone was talking about "the good old days under the Dutch." No one would extend credit, and money was even scarcer than in Charles Town. The gold pieces of eight with which Lynch and Rutledge paid their way lent them the glamour of nabobs, for everyone feared each piece of gold he saw would be the last and seldom was one spent. Since the King's soldiers had gone away, eighteen months before, trade had sunk to unbelievably low levels. Men were muttering, "War is a good thing; see what it does for business."

Lynch and Rutledge were invited to the homes of the patroons De Puyster, Van Rensselear, and Lorillard, and met the wealthiest men of the province. In the town houses they found mostly white servants. Madeira was a rarity; claret and beer were served largely, and much pastry, a novelty for the southerners.

The New York patricians looked upon the assembling of an American Congress—the first, and the last, they thought—as a stupidity whose only importance was the opportunity it afforded for entertaining these attractive visitors from the South, interesting solely because of their reputed wealth. (Lynch and Rutledge only were invited; the patroons had heard that Gadsden was a demagogue and they had no use for such.)

The worldly tolerance of the New York hosts was evidenced in their overlooking the fact that their guests were also politicians, an oddity, to them, difficult to explain. The New York delegates to the Congress were men whom none of the patroons would invite to his home. They were sure nothing good could come from politics, an occupation they believed to be only for barroom loafers, not for gentlemen.

Rutledge found that, in the legal profession, also, New Yorkers had no time for politics. The only interest New York lawyers expressed in the laws of England was how to take advantage of them. It seemed never to have occurred to them that they could command, control, or rewrite those laws.

Nevertheless, the New York bar claimed leadership of the professions, and, to make it exclusive, declared their calling overcrowded —there were thirty-two practitioners; they had just adopted a rule "greatly to impede the lower class of people from crowding in." The rule set up an impediment, consisting of a fee of two hundred pounds required of any man aspiring to a clerkship. Times being as they were, this worked; in the past year only one aspirant had produced the necessary fee, a young Huguenot whose accent caused him to be called a Frenchman, named John Jay, who had paid Benjamin Kissam two hundred pounds for the privilege of "reading" law in his office. Jay, twenty years old, clerking in a Cherry Street office in the fall of 1765, heard of John Rutledge, who promptly became a figure in the city, but the South Carolinian had no knowledge then of the Huguenot law student.

The most impressive thing in New York, Rutledge wrote to Parsons, was King's College. Why, he thought, could not Charles Town have a college of its own? He promised himself to do something about that on his return.

The day after Rutledge put up at the Kings Arms Inn, New York was startled by the arrival of two hundred Indians, heavily armed, but without war paint and in holiday attire. They came down the Albany Post Road as the retinue of Sir William Johnson, High Commissioner of His Majesty to the Six Nations, who was arriving from his castle a hundred miles beyond Albany for his annual visit.

Sir William owned more than thirty trading posts between Detroit and Albany, and as such he was America's first chain-store proprietor. Since he bought more goods than any other six persons in America combined, he was the original fall buyer. Every avenue of trade was stimulated simultaneously on his arrival. He would buy enough goods to affect all the trade balances for a year and his advent was naturally of far greater importance than the convening of the first American Congress, which brought only twenty-three strangers to the inns and boarding houses for a few weeks.

Sir William was met with a fife and drum corps at the Harlem River and he encamped just below the new canal, a mile above the Common. Here, far from the outermost houses, and a little southeast of budding Greenwich Village, he pitched camp in a meadow by the side of a stream. He disdained the comforts of civilization. He was an adopted Mohawk and with him were three of his many Indian wives and five of his papooses.

If America had a potentate it was Sir William Johnson, for he had tipped the scales in the late war. Due to him and his Iroquois, North America would be English, not French. Moreover, he was the only man on the continent, if the triumvirs of South Carolina were excepted, who had stood up successfully to the English King and he was willing to do it again, any time, if the English should attempt to outrage his Indians. Pontiac and Red Jacket were his brothers by every equation, including marriage. When the great chiefs came to him they slept under his roofs in his beds, and when he visited them he slept under their blankets by their fires. He spoke their languages; their sisters were his wives; his children had their blood.

John Rutledge hired a coach and rode out to the Mohawk camp to call on Sir William. As Rutledge entered the tent of the High Commissioner, nude red braves, Seneca warriors, lifted the flap. The visitor had never seen such native males, sleek, alert, silent.

"I see you've come to comb the King's hair!" Sir William shouted as he greeted the young southerner. "Good! Only don't take his wig off!" He laughed uproariously.

After they had talked a while, Rutledge wanted to know about the operation of the Hodenosenee, the parliament of the Six Nations. Sir William explained: each nation was sovereign internally, but externally, especially in war, the council of sachems was supreme; this gave individuality to six nations, yet they had the united strength of one; the autocratic power granted the chiefs in war was for limited periods and was not hereditary.

"If England is ever to become a great nation," the High Commissioner summed up, "she must go to school to the Iroquois. The Six Nations control this continent, not by accident, but through the triumph of their science of government. If it had a chance their system could master Europe—or the world."

Here was the most startling contrast of all for Rutledge to note between New York and South Carolina. At home the Indian Commissioner, John Stuart, after spending time with the Indians, as he must and did, and before associating with persons like the members of the Rutledge family, would spend at least twenty-four hours alone, being fumigated. Nor was the fumigation only physical; he wanted to destroy the intellectual odor, for he believed concretely and absolutely in the dogma of race supremacy. Indians, he asserted, were wholly incapable of grasping the meaning of English law, particularly when it penalized whole tribes for the acts of a few members, and especially when those acts were instigated for the purpose of supplying a pretext for expropriation. Often he had failed even to argue the point with the Chickasaws and the Cherokees; he had saved his scalp only by running. If he had wives among them, or papooses, no one in Charles Town knew it.

The contact with Sir William extended over several weeks, for Rutledge had Johnson down to dine with him at the Kings Arms and he traveled out to the Mohawk camp again and again. Rutledge knew as well as Stuart the white man's formula for consolidating Indian conquest. Heretofore he had accepted it without examining its bases. Pragmatist at heart as he was, here was something at hand for which his instincts were searching. And, fortunately, he had been trained by Uncle Andrew never to reject any idea without investigation. That he was the first man to see a revolutionary application of a profound principle of statecraft did not deter him.

Rutledge never had been in the least convinced by any of the rebellious agitation of Christopher Gadsden. Neither Gadsden nor Sam Adams had disturbed his settled conviction of the fundamental correctness of the British governmental system. They proposed to tear down, but they were not constructive; they offered no replacements.

Now, as in a lightning flash, he saw what might prove to be an answer to that dual problem of Shinner and Boone, the debauched judiciary and the debased governor.

It was not in Sir William's nature to argue. For a long time now he had ordered people and they obeyed; he had ordered even the King. John Rutledge was another of the same kind, only this was his period of gestation; he was at the ripe moment of his youth. He was still listening.

Thus, when Sir William Johnson, owner of more land and commander of more trade than any other person in America, described the workings of the Hodinosinee for the thin South Carolinian, he had an attentive audience.

Rutledge learned at first hand of the governmental wisdom of the Iroquois in their use of two ingenious devices to distribute power evenly, while centralizing its sovereign effect and giving final authority to a judiciary of chosen elders.

From the moment of his meeting with Sir William Johnson, Rutledge ceased being merely a transplanted European and began an intellectual rebirth as an American.

2.

The delegates from Massachusetts Bay arrived on October 7, in the fast time of six days over the Boston Post Road, but New York generally gave little attention. It was absorbed in the Mohawks and the plentiful money bags of Sir William Johnson.

The next day twenty-six congressmen came together in City Hall for the the first American Congress and elected Timothy Ruggles of Boston President. That Massachusetts Bay should have the presidency and direct the gathering seemed logical, for it was Puritan New England which had taken the initiative in this attempt to get together with Dutch New York, Quaker Pennsylvania, Catholic Maryland, and High Church South Carolina.

It was a calamity that Virginia—the most populous of all the states—had not responded, a misfortune that North Carolina sulked in her tent, unfortunate that Georgia did not come. But South Carolina was present. So the Boston men could not too highly praise and honor Lynch, Gadsden, and Rutledge.

Ruggles dominated the Congress, but he gave two-thirds of the committee chairmanships to South Carolina. Gadsden had only to waggle his finger to be recognized; he talked so much that at one time he collapsed with exhaustion; he never before had had such a chance; he took up a quarter of the time of the whole Congress.

Ruggles thought it best to offer the chairmanship of the Committee on Resolutions, which might be the spearhead of the body, to Lynch, the senior member from South Carolina, but the Santee planter said, "No. Rutledge is your man." Ruggles agreed, and thus the official utterance of the voice of America to the mother country and to the whole world was entrusted by the Congress to its youngest member.

Rutledge quickly saw that the Congress would be controlled by four men, Ruggles, James Otis of Massachusetts, John Dickinson of Pennsylvania, and himself. Ruggles had the chair. This put the floor into the hands of Otis, Dickinson, and Rutledge. It was another triumvirate.

The nephew of Uncle Andrew, whose adroit progress always had been based on accurate estimates of key personalities, realized that secure possession of this political knowledge must precede any possible grasp of the principles of statecraft involved. His first task was correctly to gauge the other three leaders.

Ruggles had the room adjoining that of Rutledge at the Kings Arms and this greatly facilitated their mutual cultivation. In the late war the President of the Congress had been a general, and a good one. He was chief of the Boston bar; he was six feet six inches in height, lean and hard. As he talked to Rutledge he had to bend over, for the South Carolinian was nearly a foot shorter.

Yet—and this weighed more than anything else with the Bostonian—Ruggle's fee as a lawyer was "fifty pounds to look into a case," while it was established professionally that John Rutledge required double that. As they compared notes it was revealed that the two might have belonged to different eras, as well as to different colonies, for while they used the same legal codes, it was with opposite techniques.

Rutledge had just represented Henry Laurens by brief before the High Court of Admiralty in Bristol, England, and the British judge had taken occasion to remark in his decree giving judgment against an English debtor, "The word of Henry Laurens, or of his attorney,

John Rutledge, require no confirmation in this court." Such an appraisal of character had never been uttered by any English court of any Boston merchant or attorney. The New England, like the New York, attorneys were obliged to be conversant with at least seventeen ways of circumventing the Trade and Navigation Acts. Their clients, the leading merchants of the northern ports, were practically all smugglers under the law, while southern merchants dealt in the clear. Timothy Ruggles, in a letter to Sam Adams, written from New York, said, "John Rutledge is aristocratic and upright."

What cemented the friendship between Ruggles and Rutledge was the discovery by the former of the secret instructions from the triumvirate which bound the South Carolinian, for the Bostonian was at heart an uncompromising Loyalist, and his tolerance of the rebellious utterances of Gadsden and Otis, as well as of Sam Adams, was merely on the surface.

From Ruggles, Rutledge got his first intimate estimate of that potent personality with whom he and Parsons and Pinckney had been coping at great distance for two years, the man who had produced this assemblage, practically single-handed. Rutledge asked about Sam Adams.

Ruggles said Adams was a most pious man. To that fact he said he owed his own choice as a delegate, for Adams had had sole choice as to who should represent Massachusetts Bay and he would have only devout Christians. He preferred Presbyterians, would accept Congregationalists, but not Episcopalians, whom he considered to be practically papists. Just a few months earlier he had blocked selection of Benjamin Franklin as agent in London for the Bay Colony because it had been verified that Franklin as a boy in Boston had pleaded with his father to bless a whole barrel of beef in the cellar so as to avoid the many piecemeal blessings at table, and this attempt to make a single job of the fractional appeals for Grace had rendered Franklin unfit for public duty—in the opinion of Sam Adams. Ruggles, fortunately, was the son of a Congregational minister, and so Adams had accepted him readily as head of the delegation going to New York, without too careful an inquiry into his Loyalist leanings.

Rutledge wanted to know why Adams was not there himself, for Gadsden had come and so had Otis. "Because," said Ruggles, "he has but one suit of clothes and there are so many holes in the trousers he is not presentable."

Ruggles then confirmed what Rutledge had heard before: that though Adams had been a law student he never practiced; that though he was the most prolific journalist in the colonies he never was paid for writing; that though an excellent speaker he rarely mounted a rostrum; that though an ardent advocate of the democratic principle of the town meeting he usually avoided calling one until he felt sure the men he could rely on were in control; that though he inherited quite an estate from his father he had lost it through bad management of the brewery which was its principal asset. "He made bad beer," said Ruggles.

Adams lived through the charity of friends, the labors of his wife and children, and an occasional small stipend for clerical work. For years he had been a tax collector, but an audit of his books showed he was unable to account for several thousand pounds, which friends made up, and the rest was forgiven. The authorities did not prosecute for fear his political adroitness might enable him to persecute them. Moreover, no one believed him to be venal. For years he had been an assemblyman, without salary.

Then what was this Sam Adams, if neither lawyer, journalist, business man, public official, nor man of means?

"The greatest *agent provocateur* who ever lived," said Ruggles. "John Wilkes is a baby beside him. Hardly an issue of any paper in Boston, New York, Charles Town, Philadelphia, Norfolk or Baltimore appears without a letter from him, but never over his own name. He uses twenty-five different names. He writes from morning to night and half through the night. All post boys are burdened with mail from and to Sam Adams. The Committee of Correspondence, which he has organized, pays the postage, else he would be dumb. All to one purpose only—to pull down the King in these colonies and drive the British government from these shores."

Ruggles and Rutledge faced their problem frankly. How should they outwit Sam Adams? This firmly united them, for neither believed it desirable or possible for the colonies to be independent.

Rutledge became the floor leader for the President and it was essential to their strategy that neither should too openly display Loyalist leanings. On the Resolutions Committee with Rutledge, Ruggles placed Dickinson of Pennsylvania and James Otis of Boston.

With Dickinson, Rutledge established what was to be a lifelong friendship, though at this time they were far apart politically. The Pennsylvanian was a responsible man of property, a farmer, whose mind leapt all the barriers. He foresaw the necessity for independence and stoutly declared for it and with a frankness which seemed impersonal. He could write and he could talk; he felt that was all that was necessary; he scorned political intrigue, as something unworthy.

Rutledge never openly opposed Dickinson, any more than he openly opposed Otis or Gadsden. Neither did he agree, either publicly or privately. His position was always one of considerate reserve and he utilized the fact of his youth as a plausible reason why he should not be forward in his opinions on the revolutionary doctrine.

The other floor leader was Sam Adams's choice, James Otis, chief orator of Massachusetts and only a few years older than Rutledge. He had been Attorney General of the Bay Colony and had resigned, but in a different spirit from that which had occasioned the resignation of Rutledge in the South. Otis had resigned from office with a gesture of defiance and was more of an avowed rebel even than Sam Adams.

Otis was vehement, uncompromising, the idol of Boston crowds, and like Gadsden in that if he could make a speech he was well satisfied. He hated opposition, but was responsive to sympathy. Rutledge appealed to him as one former attorney general to another and won a confidence he never lost.

Before the Congress was over Otis turned from extreme radicalism —he had wanted not only repeal of the Stamp Tax Act, but of the Trade and Navigation Acts as well, and he had also wanted the colonies to be represented in Parliament, a plea that usually struck fire in the crowds—and agreed, at least as to procedure, with his

southern brother. Apparently Otis did not realize—not until he returned to Boston and talked with Sam Adams—that he had changed.

How warily Rutledge carried himself is measured not only in
the personal friendship of Dickinson and Otis, but in the fact that
both Lynch and Gadsden, his colleagues, though politically and tem-
peramentally at opposite poles, readily followed his lead—after they
found he had the complete confidence of President Ruggles.

A week of public sessions went by and Rutledge had been faithful
to the triumvirate's instructions not to commit South Carolina to any
expression of disloyalty. However, it then became apparent there
must be something tangible to show for the coming together of so
imposing a body. There had to be at least some resolutions. All
agreed on that. Rutledge was now in the most difficult position he
had ever been in, and he must follow his ruling instinct—to serve
as an attorney.

As an attorney for whom—or what? For the Charles Town
triumvirate and the propertied interests they privately represented?
Or for the Province of South Carolina? Or for the nine colonies,
now bound together, though only tenuously, for the first time? Or
should he rise above the interests of the colonies and be an attorney
for the empire, a true servant of the King to whom he had sworn
obedience?

Could he include all these loyalties in a single act? If so he might
emerge a statesman.

On the ninth day Rutledge spoke publicly for the first time. The
Congress was half over. Lynch had been heard twice, Gadsden eleven
times, and every other leader at least once. Rutledge's agreeable personality was such, combined with a reputation as an orator, that he
was given close attention. What others *said* was noted; only *how*
Rutledge spoke received comment. "He was eloquent and pleased
all," was the full report.

The Loyalists liked his devotion to the King, but he also pleased
the radicals in disapproving the Stamp Tax Act, though he did this
with measured legal technicality gleaned from Parsons. His new
friend Otis became his champion to the radicals who felt he should

be more outspoken, by explaining his semi-official position at home, and assuring them they had a friend within the royal ramparts. Neither side felt he was wholly one of them, and yet each felt that he was impartial and that it was important to win his favor.

Dickinson wrote to the Committee of Correspondence, "As he matures he doubtless will be one of our chief supporters." Ruggles, to Lieutenant Governor Hutchinson of Massachusetts Bay, wrote, "Rutledge has the fire of youth, but as he matures his natural conservatism will hold him steady."

So, as the last half of the Congress began its sessions, and reached its vital moment, Rutledge was in a controlling position, with the confidence of each leader and of the whole body, also, while he held the key chairmanship. And now the question was how to use this power?

The congressmen had no illusions about their ability to influence London. How could this scant handful of colonials, without recognized powers or defined instructions and with the most important colony, Virginia, not represented, hope to cause the autocratic House of Commons to undo what it had done? It was almost as absurd as hoping the King could be induced to unsign what he had signed. Neither was suggested as a serious possibility. They felt that the only true aim was to try to rouse the hinterland.

Rutledge proposed that they have two memorials, one each to the House of Commons and the House of Lords. There was no opposition, especially when he asked his friend, Dickinson, to prepare the memorial to the Commons, and then asked Otis to help him on the memorial to the Lords. As the Commons alone had the power to levy taxes, a memorial to that body was looked upon as the only one that could be important.

Dickinson prepared a stout and ringing essay of protest, accusatory and uncompromising, in plain words. After it was adopted everyone of the twenty-two journals in America, threatened with extinction by the Stamp Tax, hastened to publish it with approval.

The memorial to the Lords was quite different. It began in praise of the King; rehearsed his undisputed rights together with an assertion of the loyalty of his American subjects. Then, tactfully, almost incidentally, it mentioned the duty of the King to his subjects, and then spoke simply of only one right of the subjects, the right to be *heard* by the King. By the easiest stages the indisputable point was reached that the colonies had not been heard officially before the Stamp Tax was levied. Nothing else was noted.

It was dry reading, this memorial to the Lords, especially the latter part which was merely a legal brief, and with only one authority quoted, Blackstone. Otis, who helped in the preparation, brought to Rutledge quotations from Coke, a Whig, but Rutledge discarded them and used only the Tory Blackstone.

Mr. Garth, South Carolina's London agent, had told Rutledge of a curious failing of George III, who believed himself to be a lawyer because he had read Blackstone in manuscript before publication. This was the only law book he had ever read and his memory was not good, for he trusted notebooks altogether, but the name Blackstone was a power with him.

Nowhere did the memorial to the Lords question the *right* of Parliament to tax the colonies and only in conclusion did it explicitly *request* (it did not *demand*) repeal of the Stamp Tax Act.

Congress passed the Dickinson Memorial with cheers, and the Rutledge Memorial without enthusiasm. The feeling about the Rutledge document was that it would do no harm. The Commons alone counted and they had been properly told!

Congress adjourned and the Athenians departed from Babylon. While Lynch, Gadsden, and Rutledge were sailing for Charles Town, the political storm that had been brewing for five years broke over America, for the King's ships arrived with the green stamps.

In Boston Lieutenant Governor Hutchinson's house was torn down and his library scattered in the street; in Philadelphia the stamp distributor was mobbed, and resigned; in North Carolina the King's officers who tried to sell the stamps were tarred and feathered; in New York the distributor boasted he "would force the stamps down the throats of the people," so the people took his house to pieces and chased him into the Flushing meadow where he found refuge in an abandoned outhouse, with only his stamps and his sword. In Georgia a few stamps were sold and when they heard about it in South Carolina a boycott was declared on "that infamous colony in Georgia."

Rutledge, Gadsden, and Lynch arrived in Charles Town to find in front of Dillon's Tavern a gallows twenty feet high; on it hung an effigy with a label, "Liberty and No Stamp Act." Some stamps were believed to be in the province. Lieutenant Governor Bull denied knowledge of them. Searching for them, a mob invaded Henry Laurens's garden and wrecked it, and took wine from his cellar because it was said that Laurens favored the tax. Finding no stamps, they went to the house of the Chief Justice. Shinner, a practical diplomat, asked them in and made a punch for them, drank the toast, "Damnation to the Stamp Act," and so was spared.

Sam Adams had done his work well from Boston to Charles Town. The authorities were not prepared and none of them knew what to do. It was a political earthquake. But the play was not finished. The curtain had not risen.

Rutledge came back to 116 Broad Street early in November. The colony was paralyzed; business at a standstill. Fortunately for him the memorial to the Lords was not published, and his respectful wig-doffing to the throne did not have to meet the test of mob psychology. The *Gazette* was suspended, and so the citizens of Charles Town who had come to believe in the youthful attorney did not know of the tone their trusted "voice" had used in addressing the Lords.

In London, in a room looking on St. James's Square, there was a man only fifteen months older than John Rutledge. He had no wise uncle to tell him how to be a King, but only a German mother whose pride was at stake. What did these English think—that they had imported a royal rubber stamp? She insisted it was up to George to show them that a King should be a King indeed.

George arose every morning at six and was at his desk until after eight every evening. Watching everything he made careful notes—of what he could see—in orderly, ruled notebooks: the hour and minute the guard was changed, the names of assistant rectors, the cost of new buttons, etc. He would have made an excellent accountant's clerk. Twice each day he prayed publicly; he subscribed liberally to the church and everything he did was endorsed by the archbishops.

The political object of George III was extremely simple. He wanted to rule; that was all. When his grandfather died, bringing him to the throne, the Whigs, in power, indicated they expected him to be only an ornament, while Parliament and the Prime Minister ruled. This was coming to be the English custom, but George's mother did not like it, so George proposed to put the Tories in power.

The Whigs, headed by the first statesman of the age, William Pitt, had given the country victory on the battlefields of five continents. That looked like a hard combination to combat, but George was a competent politician; he estimated his resources, studied his adversary, and waited for the opportunities.

He never considered dismissing Parliament; he found safer ways. He began by bullying, but this worked with only a few members. Some were amenable to the lure of having wives and daughters welcomed at the Levee. Then there was the annual King's list; George made this a semi-annual affair and increased the distribution of knighthoods and marquisates. Still the scales did not tip; the Whigs and William Pitt still ruled.

George had been on his job less than three years when he decided to wait no longer; to give power to his arm he began using "gold pills." These were administered in the form of neatly sealed plain envelopes delivered on quarter-day to stubborn members of Parliament; usually fifty pounds in a container, but, in rare cases, as much as a thousand pounds.

At last the King had found the secret; he could not bully nor lure nor seduce Parliament sufficiently to control, but the balance of power was purchasable, so he bought it. The process took more than a year and was not unduly expensive. The average amount paid by the King to capture a member of Parliament was fifty pounds; a

Corromantee houseboy on the Battery in New York cost little more. George III bought control of Parliament, which meant the empire of Britain, and thus practically the rule of the contemporary world, for a sum about equal to what a South Carolina gentleman would be obliged to pay for the necessary outfit of slaves properly to man a thousand-acre plantation in the low country.

This was the Parliament in which American crowds were furiously battling to be represented, and on it every colony modeled its Assembly. It consisted of about four hunderd "statesmen" (mutton and beef eaters), many of whom had bought their seats at auction, and then had sold their use to the King for less than they had paid for them.

Thus—while the first American Congress was in session, an episode unknown officially to the British Parliament until after it had adjourned—George III came to rule single-handed the most far-reaching nation then in existence. It kept him fully occupied; he was the busiest man in Europe. He personally sealed his "gold pills" in their paper containers and obtained receipts for their delivery. He noted also the registered opinions of each member of Parliament, in both houses. In addition, he acted as party whip, told the Prime Minister what to say, and, when the appointee argued unduly, he changed ministers.

Nothing is better proof of the adroitness of George as a politician than his method of dealing with Pitt. At this very moment in 1766 the King "owned" Parliament, yet the opposition under Pitt was such that he avoided disclosing the fact. He was determined to win Pitt by some method other than the use of force and was searching for the statesman's weakness—desire for a title—which he had not yet discovered. This duel between George and Pitt had begun when the Stamp Act question arose.

The King knew nothing of the Stamp Act when it was passed, and Pitt paid little attention to it for a long time, as it was a very minor matter in the affairs of empire. Suddenly the King heard that colonials were pulling down governors' houses because of it.

The "Patriot King"—for so he styled himself—was startled, for after going to so much expense and trouble to control Parliament, he could scarcely evade responsibility for one of his policies after it was established.

George often referred to the American colonies as "British farms." He looked upon himself as a farmer; he owned several farms in Hanover, Germany, and had just bought one in Sussex, which was run by a tenant. In the summer the King would go down, look things over, and issue orders. Imagine a tenant telling the King how to run his farm! George was not imaginative enough for that. When the American "farmers" began destroying property there seemed only one thing to do—use force. At this point, however, the affair became complicated for George because Pitt championed the "farmers."

The Great Commoner, as his followers called Pitt to distinguish him from the Patriot King, thought he had found a good issue with which to control the Commons. He was told that George had bought the control, but the evidence was not all available and he was not sure, for George locked up his receipts for the "gold pills." Pitt rallied his forces and the leaders made some ringing speeches for the Americans, but a poll of the house showed that a motion to repeal the Stamp Act would be lost. It looked to Pitt as if the gossip about "gold pills" was justified.

At this point the memorials from the New York Congress arrived. The one to the Commons was sent to committee, was read by the chairman, and was dropped like a hot potato. The ruling Tories read it derisively and said it was almost treasonable; it challenged the *right* of Parliament to tax; it *demanded* repeal of the Stamp Tax. The chief argument was that it was unjust to tax the colonies as they were not represented in Parliament, but did they not know that nine-tenths of the people of England were not represented? The whole paper was—to them—so specious and annoying that they refused to report it to the King lest he become angry. Pitt moved to bring the matter to a vote; the Tories buried it in committee.

In the Lords, meanwhile, the memorial from America was kicking around, hardly read. It seemed inoffensive enough and no one took the trouble to denounce it. Then news arrived of the chasing of the stamp distributor in New York. Some members laughed about that; others became choleric and declared they would move to investigate the War Office.

In this dilemma Pitt met Lord Rockingham one day in the lounge and had a casual chat, one of those off-stage confidences frequent between opposition leaders in England, and especially requisite when colonial policy was at stake.

Rockingham, for the moment was Prime Minister, and was rather bewildered in his important office. He, like Pitt, suspected the King's use of "gold pills" and was the temporary beneficiary of their potency, but he also shared the confidence of the King to the extent that he knew the royal desire to propitiate the Great Commoner.

Now that the issue in America threatened to rise from the field of debate to one of armed conflict there was a different face on the matter. Rockingham felt drawn to Pitt. As they discussed the situation and Rockingham revealed that the King was ignorant of the written appeals from the colonies, Pitt asked if the Minister had read the memorial to the House of Lords. "No," said Rockingham.

"Read it," said Pitt. "The Americans have found a barrister. The reasoning is close and sound, but it is most respectful. I suggest His Majesty see it."

So John Rutledge stood before his King, in parchment: the attorney for the distant people to their chief magistrate. The King read. The opening phrases made him tingle with particular pleasure. This verified what he really believed: those newspaper reports of the tearing down of governors' houses must have been exaggerated. Here was an official document saying the Americans respected their King; they loved him; they were loyal; they had not been heard before the Stamp Act was passed; well, neither had he; and what was this? Blackstone? Yes—that legal writer—the one he had read in manuscript when he was twenty-two; a stout Tory, too. George remembered. And was he not a constitutional monarch? And had he yet found the crack in Pitt's armor? Was this a time for a real test of strength, on such an issue? He sent for Rockingham.

Three days later the Commons repealed the Stamp Tax Act.

The King signed the repeal at once and that night a ship cleared to carry the glad news to America.

It was May 6, 1766, when the ship came to Charles Town. A distracted populace received the astounding "intelligence." Bonfires were lit on every block; the church bells rang until midnight. The South Carolina Assembly, only a week later, passed unanimously a resolution asking John Rutledge, Thomas Lynch, and Christopher Gadsden to sit for their portraits "to be drawn at full length and to be placed in the assembly room that the memory of the signal service they have done to their country . . . may be transmitted to and remembered by posterity."

Shortly afterwards the King found the crack in Pitt's armor, but not before the future Earl of Chatham declared, "These Americans are not bastards but the sons of Englishmen." And this was no tavern expletive but a solemn adjuration on the floor of Parliament made by the most eminent living Englishman for all men, Thomas Boone included, to hear and ponder.

The wonders seemed unceasing, for next Charles Town heard that Boone would never annoy them again. South Carolina had a new Governor, His Excellency Lord Charles Greville Montagu, only twenty-four years old and with an indisputable title; he was the second son of Robert, third Duke of Manchester. His bride of three months, Lady Montagu, came with him. The cup of joy ran over.

Throughout the colonies men breathed freely again. The dreadful Stamp Act was no more. The tyrant had retired. In Boston, however, Sam Adams quarreled with James Otis for signing the memorial to the Lords—Sam had correspondents in London who told him what had happened—and Otis and Adams parted company politically. Otis said he could not understand exactly why Adams was so upset, but added, "The old bear vowed he never again would get to his hand another stick like the Stamp Act."

Nor did Adams approve the method Ruggles had employed to woo the South by giving so much authority in the Congress to South Carolina. "The tail," he growled in a letter to Partridge, "wagged the dog."

It looked, indeed, as if Sam Adams's five years' labor had come to nothing. He would have to quit or start all over again.

Many of the people of Charles Town believed the King—the Patriot King—was responsible for their good fortune. The mechanics and artisans credited Gadsden; many shrewd voters said it was due to the new Earl of Chatham; the actual rulers of the port looked to the true source, the triumvirate. Parsons and Pinckney, fully informed, realized that the young man who spoke for them also led them.

I.

THE triumvirate's major problem, an obnoxious Governor, was solved. There remained the problem of Chief Justice Shinner. They could and did use him exactly as they pleased, in so far as official procedure went, but they could not keep him sober in Court, nor educate him so he could write his own opinions, nor regulate his personal conduct off the bench. They might have been cynically content to retain the substance of the courts, as they did, and let the appearance go, but it was not written of them unknowingly that "the Charles Town men of that era were so sensitive that the slightest stain upon their honor was like a wound."

The attitude of the triumvirs was professional. The sovereignty which they had assumed lay in the practice of the law. They held themselves accountable for the responsibility which went with the authority.

The problem of Shinner was the first to face Rutledge after his return from New York. He began it in a truly Rutledgian manner, by a move far on the left flank. Never did he make any open criticism of the chief of the South Carolina bench. Rather, he introduced into the Assembly a motion "to enquire into the state of the courts of justice."

Then he turned the spotlight of debate on the up-country as if, only in that region, there existed a "state of the courts of justice." The only courts in the colony were in Charles Town, and this fact created a somewhat lawless situation elsewhere.

From Orangeburg to the Waxhaws lived a population as foreign to the low-countrymen as the Dutch of New York or the Yankees of Boston. For a hundred years these people had been coming in overland through Pennsylvania and Virginia, and occasionally up the rivers from the seacoast. They were English only indirectly. The Lutherans among them held passively to their religion, but the Scotch and Irish were fixed in Presbyterianism. When an up-country man "went to law," he had to travel to the seaport, and when a Presbyterian had his cause tried before a jury of Episcopalians he declared that his fundamental English right of trial by a jury of his peers had been violated. Episcopalians were not his peers.

Up-country political leaders had capitalized on this situation. They had organized groups of armed men called Regulators, who went about the country dispensing summary justice, without legal form. The South Carolina Regulators were the remote ancestors—in spirit—of the western Vigilantes. They mingled the vices and the virtues of the frontier.

In the debate on the subject of a Committee on Justice, as Mr. Timothy christened it, Rutledge directed the talk solely to the problem of the Regulators, though the powers of the committee, as defined by the Assembly, were so inclusive that they touched the matter nearest his heart. The next important matter was the choice of a chairman.

The Speaker of the Assembly was Peter Manigault, a client of James Parsons. He turned to the customary source for guidance in the appointment. So the matter was settled at 116 Broad Street over the dinner table, where Pinckney and Parsons joined Rutledge. The next day Speaker Manigault appointed—not a lawyer—but the most conspicuous reformer of the colony, Christopher Gadsden.

The entire maneuver—of which this was the second step—was aimed at the personnel of the governmental structure. They had no direct access to the King's ear, but Rutledge's study of the colonial statutes convinced him that it was possible to get rid of the Chief Justice through a complaint by petition. If the Assembly, direct representative of the people, asked for something, the Crown must consider the request seriously, even though it involved removing a Chief Justice appointed by the Crown. In a way, it was repetition of the maneuver whereby the Stamp Act was repealed.

However, Rutledge felt that such a complaint would have to be unanimous to be effective. The former Attorney General could have moved without delay and with an easy majority, for the bar was with him to a man, as were most of the assemblymen. But there was a noisy minority of mechanics and artisans, and Rutledge felt he must have them behind him also if he was to succeed.

In this commotion the red-headed Shinner, himself a first-class politician of the pot-house variety, was a complication. The Chief Justice liked to pull off his wig and half remove his gown in court. Whenever he felt warranted—that is, if the litigant was indiscreet or unlucky enough not to have one of the triumvirs appear for him— he would decide against some highly placed person and indulge in ribald jests in delivering the verdict. This conduct was offensive to members of the bar; but to the town laborers it was meat and drink. If the question of Mr. Justice Shinner's removal from office had been left to popular vote he might have won.

That, of course, was the reason Christopher Gadsden was chosen to head the Committee on justice. Only Mr. Gadsden was never informed of it. His followers believed he was selected because of his success with the Stamp Act. They told him and each other that their "Lion of Liberty" would clean up the situation quickly.

All the talk, however, continued to be about the Regulators, those fierce posses of half-wild men who were overrunning the up-country, and who might, the agitators said, sally down on the port at any moment. Gadsden himself was eloquent on the subject of this menace, and nightly under the Liberty Tree he denounced the situation which could produce the Regulators. Thus he aspired to become the champion of the up-country, while protecting the low-country.

Between Rutledge and Gadsden there was constant political conflict, for they were exact opposites. Gadsden blurted out all his feelings whenever he spoke; Rutledge spoke only to achieve a premeditated political effect. Gadsden was socially an outsider; Rutledge an insider. Gadsden's mind was untrained; Rutledge's disciplined.

Often the two clashed and the spectators would be treated to what seemed the doughty spectacle of two oratorical champions about to fight to a finish. Yet the finish never came, and, oddly, in each important crisis, the two men stood together.

Rutledge observed the amenities touchingly, for he always treated his elders with deference. Gadsden was nearly twenty years his senior. So, in debate, he always permitted the Lion of Liberty to have the last word. If he had failed to anticipate his opponent's arguments, he let them go unanswered.

This rule, however, did not influence votes in the Assembly. There Gadsden often lost, but Rutledge never.

After Gadsden was appointed Chairman of the Committee on Justice Rutledge, though having secured his appointment, actually wooed him, even if the marriage was by proxy. Andrew, John's oldest brother, was courting Gadsden's daughter Elizabeth. This alliance between the Rutledges and the Gadsdens turned out to be not merely a romance. It influenced the history of South Carolina. For Gadsden went on "blowing great gales," as a local writer described it, about the disgraceful situation concerning the Regulators; while what the triumvirs really wanted was to eliminate Charles Shinner. Parsons and Pinckney could not decide how to show Gadsden the real point, and it was therefore up to Rutledge.

Though in the Assembly he sat next to the only knight there, and had traveled to New York in company with the exclusive Thomas Lynch, Gadsden was still outside the social pale in Charles Town. Who could tell what afflatus this supplied to his perennial sense of protest? John Rutledge shrewdly estimated this situation and found in it the advantage he required.

Planters were at the top of the Charles Town social hierarchy. Merchants, no matter what their wealth, were on a distinctly lesser plane. Christopher Gadsden was not even a merchant; he was the servant of merchants. All he had achieved politically helped him not a whit socially. Thus, when the oldest brother of John Rutledge came to court his daughter it was an important event.

The Rutledges were secure in the inner circles of planter aristocracy. It was almost forgotten how close they had come to financial disaster. John's political ascendency might have been socially negligible in itself, but, allied to the Hext-Rutledge background, it placed him on a provincial throne.

John was brother Andrew's financial backer. He advanced the money with which Andrew purchased a piece of land and built a Rutledge warehouse near the Gadsden wharf. Andrew Rutledge, merchant, was installed here when he met and won the heart of Elizabeth Gadsden. Christopher consented to the marriage and gave as dowry a thousand pounds, half in cash, half in real estate. Andrew and Elizabeth were married September 29, 1767.

This marriage was a bigger feather in the cap of Christopher Gadsden than the repeal of the Stamp Act, and it crowned his appointment as Chairman of the Committee on Justice. Evidently he believed it would realize his fondest ambition by placing him definitely in the charmed circle of Charles Town society, but he soon learned that social preferment is elusive.

As the father-in-law of Andrew Rutledge, Christopher Gadsden was now a connection of that leader of the *ancien régime,* Mrs. Sarah Hext Rutledge. Andrew and his wife Elizabeth were always welcome at the manor and the town houses of the Rutledges. Mr. and Mrs. Christopher Gadsden were invited formally once, to a family gathering, but not to a social event with the first families.

This could not be accepted as an affront by the Gadsdens, yet it was chilling. Meanwhile the Chairman of the Committee on Justice was declaiming against the Regulators. About the Town they said, "St. John's palace looks down on St. Andrew's and St. Patrick's." They referred to the fact that the St. Andrew's Society was next to 116 Broad Street on the west, while the St. Patrick's Society had a home around the corner to the east. When John Rutledge saw that the senior Gadsdens were affected by his mother's failure to invite them to the exclusive social events—and it is likely that her social moves were taken only after conference with her eldest son—he asked them to dinner at "St. John's Palace."

The morning after that first dinner at "St. John's" Chairman Gadsden was more eloquent than any member of the bar concerning the disgraceful and unprofessional conduct of the Chief Justice, and when he submitted his report to the Assembly the following week it dealt solely with these alleged deficiencies. The speech with which he presented it to the Assembly—a second dinner at the "palace" had been given to the Gadsdens the night before—was so devastating that it won the vote of every Gadsden supporter. As the triumvirate's following was already assured, that made it unanimous, thirty-six to nothing. Here was absolute provincial unity!

Curiously, this report contained none of Gadsden's customary windy invective, but was a convincing, lawyer-like indictment of Mr. Justice Shinner, naming dates, places, and events, with witnesses and citations. The Justice did make a reply, which was written by a clerk. The Governor, the youthful Lord Charles, who knew what had happened to his predecessor when he opposed the triumvirs, and who also had dined at the "palace," did what no other governor ever had done. He exercised a prerogative which Mr. Rutledge pointed out to him was his under a statute of the proprietary government. He suspended Mr. Chief Justice Shinner, "until His Majesty's pleasure shall be further known."

The discomfited Shinner was helpless. He was caught unaware and had no chance to rally popular support. His only visible enemy was the popular Gadsden, who was not even a lawyer, and who yet had brought about the downfall of the Chief Justice with a public document so ably presented that the Governor was willing to send it up to the House of Lords, where it was sustained.

First the triumvirs had set aside a governor whose social ways did not please them. Now they triumphed again, and put out of office a chief justice whose professional conduct they considered offensive. No violence attended either act. Both had been accomplished deftly without disturbing the machinery of government.

Chairman Gadsden took a year for further deliberation and then presented a court bill which the Assembly passed. This extended the courts to the up-country, liberated procedure, and took from the Regulators their justified source of complaint. Credit for both these reforms went to Gadsden. He had the voice and the name which championed them, while Rutledge was looked upon, then and later, as a reactionary. Actually, nothing ever passed the Assembly without Rutledge's approval.

John was also caring for his family. He had bought the warehouse for Andrew; he still supported Thomas in his losing management of the Stono plantation; and when Hugh went to London, John supplied half his expense money, which their mother could not meet in full. John told Hugh what he should do in London, but Hugh did not like the instructions. He took the money and went his own way.

It was different with Edward. He apparently adored John, listened to him and imitated him in all ways he could. John felt toward Edward as if he were a son. For three years Edward was a student clerk in John's office and when he was eighteen he too wanted to go to London. Hugh was still abroad and Sarah was unable to do what she wished for Edward, so John equipped his youngest brother for the great experience, paid his way entirely, and sent him to study for four years at the Middle Temple.

On the very next ship after Edward sailed John, now thirty, wrote to his eighteen-year-old brother: "I hope that whatever you attempt you will make yourself completely master of; for nothing makes a person so ridiculous as to pretend to things which he does not understand; and it will not be sufficient for a man, in such a case, to rest satisfied, because he may pass as a complete scholar among those with whom he may have to do in general, who, perhaps, may know little about the matter; such a one may meet sometime with his superiors, and in what situation will he then be?"

After giving specific advice as to where and how Edward could be instructed in the branches of the law he most desired to learn—the common, the probate, and the admiralty—John continued, "The very first thing you should be thoroughly acquainted with is the writing of shorthand, which you will find an infinite advantage, and by no means fall into the too common practice of not attending a place of worship. . . . If you stick to French and converse generally in that language you may soon be master of it. . . . I know nothing more entertaining and more likely to give you a graceful manner of speaking than seeing a good play well acted. Garrick is inimitable. Watch him well and you will profit by him."

The paternal elder brother added, "You should not confine your-self to the securing men's properties, without regard to their liberties and lives, which are the more preferable."

2.

When Hugh returned from London, John stood sponsor for him, secured his admission to the bar, and handed him his first case. Hugh was tight-lipped and secretive. Before John knew what he planned he had purchased the lot next door to 116 Broad Street, had torn down the dwelling there, and was building a residence more ornate than the "palace."

Hugh got the necessary money from a prosperous marriage. He did better than Andrew for, with Ann, his bride, he had a dower of ten thousand pounds from his planter father-in-law, Thomas Smith. He spent much of it on this house. He raised the new roof a floor above John's, set the house back of John's ten feet, and gave it more space on the sides than John's had. Indeed, he had twenty feet more frontage on Broad Street. Then he added thick columns of cream colored granite to the front porch.

People might talk about John's residence being the "palace." Hugh's looked more like one. Many a client—minor, of course—from distant parts of the Town, or from out of town, being directed to the residence of "Mr. Rutledge" would pass by the now seemingly second-ary structure at No. 116 and ascend the steps between the massive granite pillars, next door.

When Edward returned from Middle Temple, John stood sponsor for him, secured his admission to the bar, and then handed him his first case.

His mother could not set her youngest up in a style comparable with that of either of his brothers and Edward was determined to go into politics at once, despite John's advice to wait. A political career in South Carolina was impossible without a background of wealth.

Sarah Rutledge now found her opportunity to rule her family. Edward had a childhood playmate, Mary Everleigh, whom he wanted to wed. Sarah favored Miss Middleton, the most desirable heiress in the province, the girl whose dot she had desired to put behind John's career. Miss Middleton was eleven years younger than John and only one year older than Edward.

So Edward married Henrietta Middleton. The dot was seventy thousand pounds. This made the youngest Rutledge brother the wealthiest of all. Edward purchased the lots directly across the street from John's house and Hugh's, a space larger than that of the other two houses combined, and soon he built on it the largest house on Broad Street, more than a full foot higher than Hugh's, a story above John's, thirty feet wider, much deeper, and with enormous grounds.

Clients and others searching for "Mr. Rutledge" now had a choice of three houses, and the "palace" of the triumvir was the least of them. Both Hugh and Edward found a comfortable legal practice— from clients John was too busy to serve. Both proved to be able lawyers and competent politicians.

The new Circuit Court system stepped up the "law business." "Shire" towns were appointed at Beaufort, Georgetown, Cheraw, Camden, Orangeburg, and Ninety-Six. At first none of these had lawyers and the bar of Charles Town "rode circuit."

From the winter of 1769-1770 on, John Rutledge spent at least four months of each year in the saddle, stopping at local taverns. The first year he helped establish the courts, and afterward he attended them. His office was in his tricorn hat with violet facings. He was an early riser and after Court adjourned, about two in the afternoon, he made it a rule never to discuss business. Those who sought his advice had to get it before ten in the morning.

In each of the six towns—the largest had only fifteen hundred inhabitants—there was usually a line waiting for Mr. Rutledge each morning of his stay. He would stand in the path at the edge of the street either before the tavern or the court house, talk to each comer in turn, and give a verbal opinion. Following this he would take a pad from his pocket and sketch his conclusion in a few words. Often he wrote only a dozen words, seldom more than fifty. He signed his initials, wrote the phrase "Given on circuit," to indicate he was without lawbooks, and added a receipt for the cash paid.

When the slip was given he would receive his fee, or a retainer. He kept no account books on circuit and relied on his clients' records of their transactions. His rich clients in Charles Town were usually under annual contract. These takings from the circuit riding, however, were enormous. On a single morning in Orangeburg he took in, before breakfast, cash fees totaling more than a hundred guineas. His income, after the circuit was established, doubled at once, and eventually tripled.

In the fall of 1771 John Rutledge was trying a case in Beaufort when a rider from Charles Town galloped in with a message asking him to return at once and defend a man accused of murder. Except as Attorney General he had never appeared in court with a human life at stake. This case, however, was political. Its repercussions would reach to New York, Boston, and perhaps to London.

The accused man was Dr. John Haley, a physician three years younger than Rutledge, and son of a doctor who had been a colleague of his father's. The younger Haley, however, was unknown to Rutledge. Dr. Haley was a man of modest means and of no particular social position. He had allied himself with Gadsden's Liberty Boys and had made a speech or two under the Liberty Tree.

The dead man, Delancey, had been the brother of Mrs. Ralph Izard, who had important family connections. Also, he had been the son of the Chief Justice of the Province of New York. His body had been found on the second floor of a public house in St. Michael's Alley, and Dr. Haley was found alone beside it, and with a smoking pistol.

Rutledge rode all night to reach Charles Town for the preliminary hearing and arrived only an hour before Court convened to find that Dr. Haley already had four attorneys, among them Hugh Rutledge.

The Town was seething with political passion. The deceased man had been a Royalist; his father in New York was a prominent northern Royalist. Shortly the colonies, from Savannah to Boston, would be aflame with the report that a South Carolina rebel had killed a New York King's man.

The fires of the rising Revolution had been smouldering. Here seemed to be a vital spark to rekindle them. Indeed, as it turned out, for more than two years, or up to the time of the Boston "massacre," the Haley-Delancey case in Charles Town was the high talking point in colonial politics.

For John Rutledge the case involved his family, professional, and political relations. Until this moment he cautiously had maintained the *integrity* of his loyalty to the King, and equally his *reputation* for loyalty, while, as a triumvir in control and a virtual ruler of South Carolina, he had accorded full parliamentary opportunity for all outspoken critics. He believed that every desirable reform could be accomplished as readily as he and his associates had accomplished the removal of Boone and Shinner, repealed the Stamp Act, and extended the courts. The Loyalists of the port were his friends, almost to a man, and politically they were his supporters. He made them feel that his conduct of affairs was the best insurance against disorder. Some of them were his best-paying clients.

The Haley-Delancey trial, however, would force his hand. If he appeared for Dr. Haley, how could he escape being classed at once, and perhaps permanently, as an enemy of the Royalists? For nothing was talked about in connection with the case except politics. It was asserted that Haley had killed Delancey with the boast that thus rebels would treat their King. Royalists were demanding summary punishment as a political warning.

In John's absence on circuit, Hugh Rutledge had seen his chance to make both political and professional capital. He hoped John would not want to appear, and, if he did, that it would be too late when he returned. Thus, if Hugh could help in acquittal and be identified with so prominent a Whig cause he would be established as a leader of the rising Whigs, and this would probably place John securely in public estimation as a Royalist. Hugh wanted to be the leading Whig Rutledge.

If John was tempted to let Hugh have his way no one knew it. He had less than an hour in which to grasp the inter-family, as well as the political, problem, to say nothing of the legal aspects of the case. He did not confer with Parsons or Pinckney. When the Chief

Justice ascended the bench and the clerk called, "His Gracious Majesty, George III, King of England and of Ireland, and of the British possessions in all lands, versus John Haley; defendant to the bar," five attorneys, each in full wig and gown, stepped forward. John Rutledge was at their head. He had just turned thirty-two, but in experience and authority he might have been at least fifteen years older.

The Chief Justice, Thomas Knox Gordon, a Dublin lawyer, had been over from London only a few months. He was a sturdy Royalist, like his colleagues in the Province of New York, but, unlike Shinner, he was a properly educated barrister. He had dined at the "palace" and his relations with the triumvirs were cordial. No doubt he was surprised at the appearance of John Rutledge for the defense. Before a word could be uttered he demanded the presence of the accused.

Then it appeared there was no prisoner. Dr. Haley had not been apprehended. The fact was news to John Rutledge, but he conferred with his associates and then announced to the Court that if the trial could proceed he would guarantee the appearance of his client in due time. The Court accepted this guarantee and then granted three days' recess so that Mr. Rutledge might become acquainted with his case.

The battery of distinguished counsel, and their client, dined at 116 Broad Street that afternoon. If Hugh Rutledge and the other three associates were a little discomfited at the appearance of their triumvir as chief counsel, they nevertheless dutifully submitted to him what they believed to be the best defense. It was political. They felt sure that a judicious choice of a jury would ensure that an aggressive Whig would not hang—provided the political angle was stressed.

John Rutledge listened to it all carefully and then turned to his client, saying that if the accused man should persist along the lines indicated he would withdraw. He added the only terms on which he would remain. The conduct of the defense must be entirely in his hands and he wanted it understood that he did not propose to permit politics to enter it.

Until this moment Dr. Haley had believed that his only chance to escape the noose would be an appeal to Whig political sympathy.

He had challenged Delancey to a duel and then he had violated the code by proposing the weapons and the terms. To this there were witnesses; nor could he deny that he had killed the man. Naturally he wanted at his side the best attorney in the province, one who never, in his maturity, had lost a case. But the terms were drastic. Hugh and the others were shocked. Hugh even went so far as to ask John what he proposed. This was fruitless. John would not show his hand, even to an associate counsel who happened to be his own brother.

Dr. Haley, who was neither the first nor the last to do so, gave in, to that will and accepted the terms. He placed his life in Rutledge's hands, without knowing how he would be defended.

Three days later the defendant entered the court room with John Rutledge and, when his name was called, stepped into the dock.

3.

The prosecutor was Egerton Leigh, the new Attorney General. His former lucrative practice being now in the hands of his opponent, it was necessary for him to accept the meagre official stipend attached to his position.

The Attorney General charged that "Dr. Haley, an extreme member of the rebellious and obnoxious Liberty Boys" had deliberately provoked a quarrel with the visiting "inoffensive and modest Loyalist from New York" and then had "willfully done him to death."

A more solemn charge was added—"treason." Dr. Haley was examining physician of the port and annually received fifty pounds in consular fees. In accepting the job he had taken an oath of allegiance. This, Mr. Leigh declared, had been violated.

John Rutledge pointed out that the written charge did not mention treason. The Chief Justice ran through the papers, nodded his head to Mr. Rutledge, and admonished the Attorney General to make no further reference to treason, adding, "The penalty for the lesser crime is equally death by hanging."

The judge beamed on the triumvir. Those who knew the undercurrents of court procedure were chilled at the prospects for the defense; they felt the judge would favor Mr. Rutledge wherever possible as he already considered him to be on the losing side.

The character of the jury was the point on which Hugh Rutledge and his associates had been most insistent. They felt firmly that one or two good stout Liberty Boys there would prevent conviction. This was also obvious to the Attorney General who had seen to it that a double jury list be impaneled. He was prepared, he said, to exhaust his challenges if need be, or even move for a mistrial if compelled to accept anyone who would admit being a Liberty partisan.

To the amazement of all, including Mr. Leigh, the Attorney General was allowed largely to have his way in choosing a jury. This became apparent when John Rutledge accepted William Wragg, an outspoken Royalist, one of the most conspicuous in the Town. Leigh, especially, wanted him as foreman and Rutledge agreed. Nine others of the same class were accepted.

John Rutledge objected only to Jonas Simpson, a butcher, and Hezekiah Appleby, a contractor. This seemed curious because both were outspoken Tories, as much so even as Wragg himself. Both, however, were of the small tradesman class; they depended for a livelihood largely on Royalists. Rutledge did not ask either of them any questions, but challenged each peremptorily.

Leigh then accepted Joshua Fewtrell, of an old but not rich family, believed to be Loyalist, and Ponsonby Williams, of similar background. Each was of independent if slender means. Rutledge accepted both readily.

A gasp went through the court room. This was most amazing; an alleged traitorous killer was to be tried for his life by twelve of the most conspicuous and unblemished Royalists available in Charles Town. There was not a Liberty Boy on the jury, not a Whig! What could be John Rutledge's purpose in neglecting what his associates and all their friends considered to be a first essential in the conduct of the case?

The trial began. In his direct evidence Leigh proved that after two hours of drinking with Delancey on the fatal night, Dr. Haley had challenged him; that Delancey accepted instantly, saying he would meet the doctor any place any time, and the sooner the better; that Haley had proposed that they go, alone, to an upper room of the tavern they were in and shoot it out with pistols, immediately; that Delancey had agreed at once; that Haley sent a servant to his home in the next block for duelling pistols; that when the pistols arrived they were found to be double-barrelled; that Haley offered the choice which Delancey made without a glance; that the tavern keeper had supplied a vacant room on the second floor; that the room was no more than fourteen by sixteen feet in size and had contained only a small bed, a table, and two chairs; that the two went up, unaccompanied; that shots were heard shortly; that spectators had rushed up and found Delancey dying from a wound through the heart, and Haley untouched. The prosecution rested.

John Rutledge caused a great stir by placing the defendant on the stand as his own first witness. Rutledge asked what had happened in the upper room.

"I lighted two candles," said Haley, "set them on the table in the center of the room and closed the door. Then we placed ourselves across the table, each against a wall, about four paces apart. I gave the signal."

"Who suggested these rules?" asked Rutledge.

"I did."

"Did Mr. Delancey object?"

"He accepted them with one word—'Yes.' "

"Was that in the taproom?"

"Yes, sir."

"Now, then," asked Rutledge, "how many drinks had you taken?"

"Seven or eight rumbullions, sir."

"Were they all rumbullions?"

"Yes, sir. I make it a rule not to mix my drinks."

"What had Mr. Delancey taken?"

"I do not know what he had before we met, sir, but with me he drank tumbler for tumbler."

"As a medical man do you consider that either of you was drunk?"

"No, sir. On the way up the stairs I noticed that once he lurched against the wall, but only slightly. I walked steadily."

"In the room, what remarks were made?"

"When Mr. Delancey placed his back against the wall he said, 'Maybe you think I can't shoot straight enough to hit you, but you'll see.' I replied, 'It is my professional experience that a man who can't think straight can't shoot straight.'"

"Then what happened?" Rutledge asked.

"He raised his pistol and so did I. Then I said, 'Ready!' I saw he was set. Then I said, 'Fire!' I waited to give him the first shot, and it went wild. I could see clearly in the candle light and saw him shift his finger to the other trigger. I waited until he was about to pull and then I pulled my first trigger. His second shot was as wild as his first, but mine went true."

Rutledge continued, "Now, then, will you tell us exactly what was said, on the lower floor of the tavern, to cause your challenge?"

"It came about, sir, through my remark that the Tories in Boston and New York are influenced in their political opinions solely by money reasons, which I said is proven by the fact that the northern Whigs are all poor men. Then I said that in South Carolina neither Whigs nor Tories are influenced by a property interest, and, to prove that, I told him that some of our wealthiest citizens are Whigs. He shouted out that this was a lie. I asked if he meant to say I was a liar. He replied—'Yes.' So I challenged him."

At this point John Rutledge rested.

The Attorney General strove, by cross-examination, to establish that Haley was partially drunk, and so was mistaken as to the number of shots fired. After the defendant left the stand several witnesses testified they heard only two shots.

In rebuttal Rutledge put on the stand his old friend, the carpenter, Walter Greenland, who placed in evidence as an exhibit a portion of the wainscoting which he testified he had cut from the wall in the duelling room, at a point directly behind which Dr. Haley had stood. In it was embedded one bullet. Six feet away, Walter testified, was the mark of another. He also produced a bullet which he swore he picked from the floor. A third bullet had been found in the body of the deceased.

Then Rutledge placed the duelling pistols in evidence. In one a single charge remained; from the other both bullets were gone. Finally, he called four witnesses, each of whom testified he had heard Delancey call Haley a liar.

In his address to the jury, Attorney General Leigh occupied about three hours. Half of it was a diatribe against the Liberty Boys, "that element of unprincipled rabble which defies law and order and the decency of our Beloved Majesty, in our very midst." Then he dwelt on what he declared to be the defendant's violation of the law of hospitality.

"Was it not," cried Mr. Leigh, "a despicable advantage for a southern gentleman to take of a distinguished guest like the visiting son of a neighboring chief justice to impose on him his own code of honor, and then flagrantly to violate it by naming his own weapons, and then further to depart from its accepted standards by suggesting that he, himself, the challenging party, give the fatal signal? Such a man is so lost to finer sensibilities that he has lost that sense of honor for which he pretended he would stake his life."

Mr. Leigh dwelt on the effect of eight rumbullions, and added, "Dr. Haley was, in effect, drunk, yet as a physician he was morally and legally responsible."

The peroration was in the nature of a funeral oration over the body of a fellow Mason—Leigh held the chief office in the Masonic order in Charles Town—and in part used the language of the accepted Masonic ritual, though without actually referring to Masonry. Judge Gordon was a Mason, as were seven members of the jury. The dead man also had been a Mason.

John Rutledge spoke for twelve minutes in defense of Dr. Haley. Not a Mason himself, he did not mention Masonry. He did not mention the Liberty Boys, or the King, either.

He rehearsed the evidence briefly, speaking with respect of both Delancey and Haley, neither damning one nor praising the other. Then he picked up the *Actes of the Assembly* and read the section on homicide; he re-read the section on self-defense. Then he read, from Coke, a comment on the common law of England, which declared that from the most ancient times self-defense had been considered by the English people an adequate reason, under the law, for the taking of a human life.

It was all pure reason, compact, spoken as if in the quiet of his own drawing room to a group whom he knew socially, and from each of whom he asked the understanding of a friend.

The method, of course, was subtle and telling. Ramsay wrote of it, "When Rutledge spoke it was as if he transported us, by some magic, to an ancient place, far removed from all feeling of the day. We were all like little boys listening to a revered headmaster, whose words were eagerly absorbed, so they might be forever treasured. If one recalled those words and quoted them they seemed cold with logic, and dry with facts, but as they were uttered the voice of the speaker was so charged with feeling, and his mouth so trembled as if he were on the verge of breaking down with the excess of emotion, that everyone was filled with indescribable pathos."

Rutledge concluded, each word weighted with a pause and saturated with unexpressed emotion, "The facts, gentlemen, are clear, I believe. The deceased, whose untimely end we must all sincerely mourn, had the misfortune to speak falsely of this defendant as an alleged liar, and this was in a public place, before witnesses. He then, most unfortunately, repeated his offense. For this he was asked to answer under conditions to which he voluntarily agreed. With cautious self-discipline the defendant permitted to his opponent the first shot. Only at the last fatal second, with his life again in peril, having once risked it in chivalrous abnegation, and finally only in self-defense, he fired at the moment when the deceased was taking his second shot. I submit to you that his conduct was exemplary. And I feel confident that your verdict will render the indicated justice."

Egerton Leigh began to realize why John Rutledge let him pick the jury, objecting only to tradesmen, assured that to those of "the tradition" personal honor outweighed politics and fraternal oaths.

The jury acquitted Dr. Haley.

All northern papers hailed the Haley verdict as a great victory for "Liberty." It changed Sam Adams's mind about John Rutledge. Yet the Charles Town Loyalists believed in the young triumvir more than ever. Demands on his professional time increased. From New Jersey came an offer of a thousand pounds if he would go there to defend a young merchant accused of murder. Rutledge refused; never again did he appear for a homicide.

The Liberty Boys were overjoyed; they lit bonfires, held a public dinner, Dr. Haley became a hero. But none of them claimed John Rutledge as one of them. He was not asked to address them; he held aloof as he always had. They regarded him as a supreme pontiff who, in a bitter crisis, refused to be prejudiced against one of their number because their political opinions threatened an order which he basically upheld.

Parsons and Pinckney leaned more heavily than ever on their young associate. Here they had found an astute moderating influence which never failed them. Who else could have so handled the Haley trial that both sides in Charles Town were satisfied?

The emergence of John Rutledge into his unique place in the history of his state and nation almost may be dated from the Haley trial.

4.

One day late in 1772 Rutledge rode into Ninety-Six, so named because it was ninety-six miles from Keowee, the chief Cherokee settlement. Two hundred miles northwest of Charles Town, it was the frontier and the Indians were just a day's journey beyond.

Two days before the opening of Court the circuit-riding barrister put up at the only tavern in Ninety-Six. He knew he was in enemy country, for he had been warned that the religious feeling would prevent his winning a case in Court. He found no Liberty Boys. The coonskin caps apparently covered loyal heads.

The man who, in one afternoon at The Corner in Charles Town, could learn the prevailing responses in the first community of the province, learned much at the Ninety-Six tavern in one evening. The backwoods Huguenots, it seemed, remembered the Edict of Nantes and wanted no trouble with any ruler. The Germans thought of George III as one of themselves and believed that as long as he was on the throne they were better off than the English. The Scotch and Irish believed that, as dissenters, their only protection from brutal assault by High Church dignitaries on the coast was in the Crown. Everyone secretly upheld the Regulators because the Regulators told them that the Liberty Boy agitation in the port had been started by greedy merchants who wanted to escape taxes.

In addition to all this, Rutledge had to meet the suspicion which countrymen held for the city man. One of his timid interlocutors became bold enough to ask him if it was true that men named Heyward, Middleton, Drayton, and Thomas Lynch, Junior, were "speechifying" with the Liberty Boys. Rutledge admitted it and then a bolder heckler demanded to know if it was not true that Hugh Rutledge was speaking publicly against his King. John nodded silently.

The tavern became so crowded that the proprietor had difficulty selling drinks and so made a thrifty suggestion: Would the visitor address them publicly the next night? Instantly Rutledge accepted. A bold wag cried, "Will 'e talk in th' kirk?" Smilingly the visitor accepted this also.

It was the general belief in Ninety-Six that no Episcopalian would enter a "kirk." There were bets that Rutledge would not be there as agreed the next night. Among those who came many boasted that they would make a row if Rutledge "rode Liberty," and, "Hadn't he admitted his brother was one of them?" Word spread to the farms. The kirk was packed with those who wanted to see in person this "chief nabob of them all." Did he not "hold the Commons in his pocket?"

Rutledge appeared without a wig, without even powder in his hair. He talked half an hour and told them what a beautiful country they lived in. Also he made several dutiful references to George III. It was incredible; he seemed one of them; his mind was just like theirs, only more articulate.

As he seemed so "folksy," a heckler was emboldened to demand to know if John Rutledge was not an Episcopalian. He told them, smilingly, from the Presbyterian pulpit, that he was born and baptized in the High Church faith, that he attended service regularly, always paid church dues, but never held any church office, not even that of vestryman.

"Why?" demanded the heckler.

Rutledge replied patiently that he did not believe that religion should enter politics, that every man had a right to worship as he pleased.

A religious hothead seized the floor and attacked the High Church "to the very face of the best of them." Though Rutledge seemed to have won his audience so far this was what most of them had come for—a religious argument. That was their chief excitement, next to a cock fight. This looked as if it might be a good one when the Ninety-Sixer cried out that it was a "bloody shame" the High Church law in South Carolina should be above the common law.

Rutledge did not reply as he might have with a legal quibble on the practical point. Instead he said calmly that he agreed with them, that he did not like to have a church law, in civil affairs, superior to the civil statute. A gasp went over the kirk. Was the chief triumvir not willing to fight? The heckler was not through. He demanded to know why Rutledge did not change the situation, crying, "Ain't you the boss?"

Silence fell on the crowded kirk. They thought they had him cornered. Rutledge waited for complete silence. Then he spoke to them as if they were members of his own inner circle at Charles Town. He asked them, as friends, and as loyal South Carolinians, if they did not think there was enough bad blood already aroused. "Do you not realize," he concluded, "that to change the church law would require a contest with His Majesty's government? Do you think that at this time we should further embarrass our gracious King?"

He had appealed to them as Royalists, had advised them gently, had placed himself with them. The heckling stopped. The next day he tried a petit-jury case before a mixed panel of Huguenots and

Presbyterians and got a verdict without the jury leaving the box. After that no litigant in Ninety-Six who could afford his services would have any other attorney.

In Charles Town, a few months later, Rutledge entered an action which had a curiously far-reaching effect on his up-country political fortunes. For a client he had secured a judgment of two thousand pounds against a prominent communicant of St. Phillip's Church. By placing his property in the names of other members of his family the debtor evaded the usual legal consequences. Whereupon Rutledge sued him in the ecclesiastical court, asking for his excommunication from the church on the ground that he was guilty of immorality in evading his just debts when he was able to pay them.

This set the Town, and the province, by the ears. The situation was extremely startling, something no one had ever contemplated before. It was even more sensational than the Cooke breach of promise case. Excommunicate a man for putting his property in his wife's and his children's names? It was possible to try a man in the ecclesiastical court for immorality. That had been done before; but not that *kind* of immorality, and, besides, *was* it immoral?

John Rutledge seemed to think that was the only question and that propounding it to the church was not remarkable. Surely, he said, the church has a civil power, and standards of morality are its special province. To whom else could one appeal for such a ruling? Rutledge insisted that the only point open for decision was a definition of morality, a specialty of the church, and that if his contention was upheld naturally the church would be obliged to excommunicate. He refused to discuss the matter privately and calmly awaited the sitting of the ecclesiastical court so he might present his evidence and arguments on that point.

If anyone but John Rutledge, undisputed leader of the bar, and at the same time a devout and churchly man, had filed this action it might have been frowned out of hearing, or the court itself might have pettifogged the issue so that it never could reach a hearing.

However, the ecclesiastics had this to consider: the coming session of the Assembly would be asked to vote a sum to pay annual salaries of the churchmen. This was routine, of course, and nothing heretofore had disturbed it. It could not be forgotten, however, that the Assembly had held up salaries for the Governor and the Chief Justice. Would John Rutledge dare such a thing with ordained officials of the Church? No one could say. No one asked him. It was known, however, that he never threatened; he acted. After he acted it was usually too late for anyone he opposed to make effective argument.

There was deep grumbling in important church circles. Many pious, dues-paying members were scandalized. Nevertheless, the presiding churchman set a date for the trial, and appointed two ministers to sit with him in forming an ecclesiastical court.

Now it was necessary for the defendant to prepare his case. He would have to defend his morality in a legal document; a man whom everyone knew attended church twice each Sunday and at midweek vespers. It was preposterous. Yet he dare not continue without an attorney highly placed in the Church. What attorney could defeat John Rutledge?

The harassed debtor certainly needed a brilliant attorney, for excommunication was a terrible punishment. Its rarity, with its accompanying penalty, social obloquy, made it more ominous than incarceration behind the walls of the jail.

The prospect proved to be sufficient. Two days before the date set for trial the debtor paid, in full.

Meanwhile, the up-country was agitating for representation in the Assembly, even as the colonies agitated for representation in Parliament. At Ninety-Six it was decided to select a delegate to go to Charles Town and plead personally for representation.

When the votes were counted in the kirk it was found that Ninety-Six had elected John Rutledge as its delegate to appear in Charles Town and plead its case in application for a legislative seat in the Assembly. Not a speech had been made in his behalf; no one had nominated him. The election was totally without his knowledge.

The voters of Ninety-Six were taking a short cut to power. It was frontier political mathematics; they knew the shortest distance between two points. Instead of electing one of themselves to go to Charles Town they jumped in the driver's seat.

When elected a delegate from Ninety-Six, Rutledge was holding three seats in the Assembly: his perennial membership from Christ Church and two others. Within two years the Assembly passed a bill providing the up-country with four new districts, each to have ten delegates. Ninety-Six was one of them.

Early in 1774 the up-country was represented in the Assembly for the first time. John Rutledge sent word to his friends there that he would like to have the name of his brother, Edward, substituted for his, and this was done. Evidently Ninety-Six accepted the endorsement without examination of the political views of its new member, for when they learned that Edward was a Liberty Boy he was not re-elected and was obliged to find another district for which he could stand.

Edward was going rapidly ahead of Hugh as a conspicuous revolutionary, and was competing with other rich young men—sons of the Middleton, Heyward, and Lynch families—for the suffrages of the followers of Liberty.

In the *Gazette* Mr. Timothy celebrated Edward, and ignored John, who would not contribute either cash for paid cards or written contributions. Edward, however, kept his professional card always alongside the contributions of Gadsden and of that mysterious "Obiter Dicta" and "Pro Bono Publico" of Boston. Whatever the signature they were alike in thinly veiled references to "tyranny." Each contained similar involved arguments against the distant government. John was silent. On the major political issue he said positively nothing.

The Crisis had come. The forces on both sides were set. The drama was written now and was ready for production.

Where did John Rutledge stand? In 1775 no one could say.

5.

The real American Revolution occurred between 1760 and 1775. It was then that the minds of the men of the colonies were being prepared for one of the great adventures of history. The war of 1775-1781 only proved and established an event that already had taken place.

During the earlier period John Rutledge came to mental maturity. No other leader in the colonies during those critical years, except Sir William Johnson who died in 1774, held a place of such power and responsibility as he did. He carved from shifting, obscure conditions a secure, well-defined sphere of influence in which he ruled positively, though anonymously. This unique power depended largely on his sensitive perception of change and his ability to reconcile it with what he believed in.

Rutledge was not a crusader whose revolutionary temperament was apparent. His logic was so potent that he abhorred ignorance, waste, and futility, especially of his own powers. He never discouraged reform and he always was ready to use new techniques. At heart he was a pragmatist, an empiricist, like all men of action. Ideas, as such, had little appeal to him. When they entered practically into affairs he studied them as forces, but none to him was ever sacrosanct.

For Rutledge the word liberty was not a slogan; the duelling code was not a religion; the organization of the church was not sacred; and allegiance to the Crown, which from birth had been the essence of a life fundamentally loyal in nature, was, nevertheless, no more than a political symbol. If he was Oriental in his obeisance to the King, it was not personal servility but his recognition of sovereignty. Mentally he was a free man.

As the Revolution rose to its crisis where, at last, all men had to come forth and declare themselves, John Rutledge might well have paused. In 1775 his cash income from earned fees was above nine thousand pounds, perhaps a quarter more than that of any other professional income in the colonies; it came largely from exporters and importers, whose economic interests were most closely identified with Great Britain.

The components of his fortune—practically all earned by himself in fifteen years—were: about sixty slaves taken from his mother in payment of money advanced; fourteen parcels of real estate, nine in

city property and five in small plantations. The assessed value of his
estate was around seventy thousand pounds.

In public estimation, especially in the North, Rutledge was a
"rich planter." Such associates as Henry Middleton, the Draytons, and
Thomas Lynch had much greater estates and many more slaves.
However, Rutledge had a demonstrated and unique earning power,
which, if sustained for another fifteen years, might make him one
of the richest men in America.

As the war clouds rose so did his perturbations. If it came to
armed conflict he would have to risk not only his "life, fortune and
honor," but also that place and power which was his alone and
which was delicately adjusted to all the complications of colonial
life within the imperial sphere.

Who but a bold and fearless man could venture so much? And
for what? Not for material gain, certainly, for property losses would
be certain. Was it ambition that decided him or the disinterested
vision of the statesman who had taken communal authority on himself
and who felt the moral obligation to express it for the best interests
of the community? Or both?

Rutledge had no chance to make a dramatic decision at any
one point. The history of the whole fifteen-year period is of a piece.
Again and again he could have taken the stand, which was indicated
by his property and professional interests, with the Tories, in support
of the Crown. Yet, in each crisis, his influence was thrown to the
other side, not openly, but with a certainty which seems uncanny
in ultimate purpose.

The Revolution in South Carolina was almost orderly in comparison with its turbulence in Massachusetts. In written history, Massachusetts usually has been accepted as the center of events, but it was,
in fact, no more the center than South Carolina. Great Britain's
acts affected both at the same time, and with similar results, but with
clearer definition in South Carolina. The chief reason for this greater
clarity lay in the character of the South Carolina leadership.

At base there were two revolutions, proceeding at once and on parallel lines, each with a period of gestation running from 1760 to 1775. There was the revolt of the people and the imperial civil war.

These two revolutions were not cleanly separated. They over-lapped at all points and times, but, broadly speaking, the revolt of the people dominated in Massachusetts, while in South Carolina the story was chiefly that of the imperial civil war. This was solely an economic conflict for trade and profit. South Carolina was no longer the Crown's favorite; the bounty on indigo was gone and so was the rice differential.

The Liberty Boys were never a serious menace to Rutledge and his associates, but they were always a problem. They were kept under control, and, when action finally came, they were not in the saddle.

A curious affinity between the Liberty Boys and the Regulators—one Whig, the other Tory; one low-country, the other up-country—eventually brought them both under the same banner as rebels. Each, if a reckless, was also a dynamic force. Rutledge mastered them both, harnessing each as an integral part of the political machine he developed. Thus he diverted a destructive tendency to a constructive end. This was the subtlest and most difficult test of his statesmanship.

The real basis for his power, of course, was the support of his immediate associates. These leaders, the planter aristocracy, cast the die in taking sides in the imperial civil war and when the time came it was Attorney Rutledge who showed them how to get what they wanted.

Before the die was finally cast none of them believed in inde-pendence. Rutledge believed, as did all the others close to him, that he was merely working with Pitt, Barré, Burke and others in London in a contest within the mother country, not against it. If Rutledge had any realization of how far he was traveling on the road to practical independence there is nothing to indicate it. He was a subtly decisive factor in achieving independence, yet it evidently was not by crafty design, but by instinct. He hewed to the line of daily necessity and let the chips fall as they would.

Bit by bit, brick by brick, fact by fact, the planter aristocracy, guided by Rutledge, built this independence. Before anyone realized what had happened they controlled the courts and the churchmen and set aside the Governor. The proroguing of the Assembly meant no more than changing the meeting place from indoors to outdoors. Rutledge always found a legal way around any difficulty. Troops did not appear. There was no "massacre," as in Boston, nor any threat of violence, for a long time.

In Massachusetts, when Governor Hutchinson dismissed the Legislature, Sam Adams locked the door and kept the members in, and so defied royal authority. The only answer to that was armed force. When the tea was sent, at a price cheaper than before, but with the obnoxious duty added, Sam Adams persuaded the Liberty Boys to dress up like Indians, and, at night, to throw the tea in the harbor. The royal answer to that was a blockade of the port of Boston.

In Charles Town the same events happened and at the same time. When the tea came the Liberty Boys were advised by John Rutledge to seize it openly. So they rowed out on a bright day without masks, with the whole town looking on from wharves and windows, and, in a holiday spirit, took the tea to an obscure warehouse where it finally molded and was forgotten.

Then the Governor at Charles Town dismissed the Assembly, locked the state house door and put the key in his pocket. The members calmly adjourned to The Corner, and sent a messenger for John Rutledge. He came promptly, took his place on the bench below the magnolia, and advised them to organize themselves into a Committee on Public Safety. There were sixty-four present, including up-countrymen, but they had not been counted, and someone asked Rutledge how many he thought should be on the committee. From the bench he answered, off hand, "Ninety-nine."

So, within an hour, the Committee on Public Safety in South Carolina—the responsible public body which organized and carried out the Revolutionary War in the South—was created. Later it included more than ninety-nine members. It proceeded to consider all the questions the prorogued Assembly would have considered and acted on them promptly. After they were acted upon they had the effect of law. Except for the impotent Governor no one in the province disputed them.

It was revolution by advice of counsel. The South Carolinians were not looking for any trouble. They intended to avoid trouble, if possible. It seemed to them they were normally going about their business as a group of gentlemen who always had had their way and saw no reason to change their habit. They did not anticipate that the result of this temperamental peculiarity would be war.

The Liberty Boys indulged in the protests customary in the North against "search and seizure," against "impressment into virtual slavery," against the quartering of troops in private houses—though there was little enough of that—against the "despoiling of women"— which happened only at a distance—and against "the brutal violation of human rights." Very little of this actually had happened to them; it was chiefly in prospect.

The Committee on Public Safety did not endorse these protests. All governments and all armies of the time were "practising brutal violation of Human rights," just as the newly formed American army in the North presently would be doing.

Their problem had many facets and brought about much debate, but at heart it was quite simple: who would get the profit from the carrying trade between the colony and elsewhere, South Carolina or Great Britain? It was no more complex than that and Attorney Rutledge kept the core of the problem steadily in view.

Great Britain always had had the lion's share of the profit from this trade, and this was accepted by tacit agreement. Lately, however, with changes in the Ministry, she wanted it all. South Carolinians wanted that to which they were accustomed. Much oratory and much ink were spilled over this issue, but if it had been eliminated there would have been no imperial civil war. The Attorney for South Carolina would not have advised it.

The colonists thought they knew a way to bring Great Britain to her senses. They called it "non-importation and non-exportation agreements." It was the original isolationist policy. By bottling themselves up they believed they could defeat the mother country. South

Carolina had tried it, but without inter-colonial unity, and it had failed. Now the northern colonies proposed that they all make common cause of isolationism as a general American policy. In each colony there were objectors, but it appeared that a majority in each believed that isolationism would settle everything.

Again—after nine years—the call came from Massachusetts Bay Colony to South Carolina to attend an American Congress. It was to be in Philadelphia, and, ignoring the assemblage in New York in 1765, this was to be called the First Continental Congress.

The Governor said that the Assembly was not in session. So he refused to issue the call. Nor would he open the state house; he held the keys. The Committee on Public Safety, however, met at The Corner.

In Boston Sam Adams kept the state house key and locked out the Governor; in Charles Town John Rutledge left the state house to the Governor, and assembled his legislators under the trees. Otherwise the procedure was quite similar.

The Committee decided to send five delegates to Philadelphia. Two tickets were nominated, one by the planters and merchants, and one by the mechanics and artisans. John Rutledge headed both tickets so he was the unanimous choice for chairman. The mechanics and artisans won, and the other delegates were Henry Middleton, Christopher Gadsden, Thomas Lynch, and Edward Rutledge. Not one was a mechanic or artisan.

In open meeting the committee instructed its delegates. The chief question was: Should South Carolina join in the non-importation and non-exportation agreement? John Rutledge spoke against it and the committee sustained him.

Then a motion was made to bind the committee to this. Rutledge leaped to his feet on the bench under the magnolia. "Give us no instruction whatever," he cried. "Invest the men of your choice with full authority to pledge the people of South Carolina to abide by whatever they agree to. Less than plenary discretion to this extent is unequal to the crisis."

From the depths of the committee came a voice, "And what shall we do if our delegates make a bad use of this authority?"

Rutledge wheeled on the speaker and cried, "Hang them!" The motion was lost, and a substitute, suggested by Rutledge, giving the delegates full authority, was carried.

Fifteen hundred pounds was appropriated for expenses of the delegation, and was promptly tossed in a hat. The artisans and mechanics had triumphed, but the planters and merchants chiefly paid the bill for the journey north. Under Rutledge's leadership were two Liberty Boys—one his personally loyal young brother, the other the father-in-law of another brother—and two conservatives who never had opposed him.

All effective connection with the distant Crown had been severed. John Rutledge faced Philadelphia with powers that were practically autocratic.

6.

While the Charles Town boat was sailing north to the Delaware a stage coach was bumping south along the post road from Boston with the four delegates from Massachusetts Bay Colony. They were poor men. Two of them depended wholly on the forty pounds a year each earned as assemblyman in Massachusetts, where it was possible for a native politician to exist professionally. The other two were small-town attorneys, not considered capable of practicing in the metropolis of Boston, and for whom a hundred pounds was an average yearly income. The traveling expenses allowed for all four was five hundred pounds.

They were in joyous holiday mood, for this was the first time any of them ever had been outside of the Bay Colony. Now they were on a junket at public expense, living in a style much better than that to which any of them was accustomed.

Their chief was a paunchy, dour man of fifty-three years, "the wizard of the folk motes," Samuel Adams. When he had been selected as first delegate his neighbors had quickly faced what they accepted as a communal problem, how to avoid collective disgrace which would

come to them in Philadelphia if Pro Bono Publico appeared there
dressed as they knew him. This calamity was avoided by sartorial
gifts. So he rode in a new buff waistcoat, fresh lace and linen, whole
breeches, a new pair of shoes, and a "surtout" newly fitted by Boston's
leading tailor, the gift of two fellow deacons. In a hamper by his
side was an extra pair of breeches, and a spare waistcoat. For the
first time in his life Sam Adams was well dressed.

Nine years before, Adams had remained at home and let Ruggles
and Otis go to New York. Now Otis was in a madhouse confined
to a strait-jacket, and Ruggles, still a stubborn Royalist, was tearing
his life up by the roots. He was about to depart for Nova Scotia and
oblivion. Adams was in personal command. He was the Father of
this Revolution and he was prepared to be on hand at its parturition.
This was not the first, but it was *his* first Congress.

The "wizard" had written fifty thousand letters and had manipulated twenty or more newspapers and hundreds of speakers. He had
nurtured the town meetings with unerring skill, pinching them off
when they did not please him, fanning them when they were too
hot, flattering their vanities and obscuring the realities from them,
until they piped in concert the tune he set for them. The blockading
of the port of Boston by the British fleet was his masterpiece. He felt
that his lifework was practically achieved and that this free ride was
his reward. He had no further plan, but he was grateful that he
could be on hand in Philadelphia and be sure that nothing was done
to mend the open break between the colonies and England.

All the Massachusetts delegates were of his choice and the youngest was a lawyer, "of no great reputation, talent or weight," John
Adams, of Braintree, his cousin. Sam had picked Cousin John because
he felt sure of him as a relative and thought of him only as an echo.

However, John was already beginning to act like the founder of
a dynasty. He might not have asserted himself as he did if it were
not for the smug security he felt in knowing that he could earn a
hundred pounds a year at his profession while away from the public
till. It pleased him to think that Sam Adams never had earned a

shilling otherwise. John was quite ready to skim the cream off the pot of revolutionary fervor.

John did not take a back seat. He kept a diary. "At New Haven," John noted naïvely, "as we came into town people were crowding at doors and windows as if to see a coronation."

All went merrily until they reached the suburbs of Philadelphia and there they had a shock when they met several local Sons of Liberty. "We invited them to tea," the Adams diary records, "and they represented to us that we were being pictured as four desperate adventurers—as artful, designing men—that we were all suspected of desiring independence, of having nothing of our own to risk yet being resolved to entice men of substance into our net, and so lead them to their destruction, and for our benefit."

The Philadelphians counseled, "If you use that word 'independence' or give a hint or insinuation of it you are done."

The holiday mood of the traveling Bostonians was shattered. They entered Philadelphia downcast. The South Carolinians had been there for three days; the Virginians for a day. The Bostonians prepared to forget about "the coronation."

Philadelphians did not regard the Congress very seriously. Their attitude was not unlike that of New York nine years before. This assemblage meant that fifty-three strangers were in town and that would help business in the taverns, rooming houses, livery stables, and night resorts; that was all. The town had a few Liberty Boys, but they were not of the best families nor very conspicuous. They complained bitterly that they did not have the support given "Liberty" either in Charles Town or in Boston.

Philadelphia was, in fact, quite blasé about the whole affair. It was the metropolis of the colonies, and considered itself far above other cities. The trouble in Boston was looked upon as a distant local disturbance that soon would be adjusted. What Charles Town did was only a "foreign" curiosity.

The principal tavern was Frye's, and there the South Carolinians stayed, taking all the second floor, directed by John Rutledge, who was manager of the delegation. Mrs. Rutledge was with him. Edward had brought his wife, too, and so had Henry Middleton. This made it almost a family party, as Edward's wife was Mr. and Mrs. Middleton's daughter. They brought their own body servants and it was commented, a little ruefully, if not resentfully, that South Carolina had monopolized the principal hostelry.

The South Carolina servants brought with them the ingredients for the rumbullion, the bombo, and the sangaree. An Irish barman at Frye's served a French drink called a julep. John Rutledge told Pompey to learn how it was made, so he could carry this important secret back to the South with him. The barman confided that originally the base had been cognac, but that he used Irish whiskey with crushed mint leaves, crushed sugar, and crushed ice. The ice made it expensive, but the mint julep, as served by John Rutledge's Pompey, became the king of drinks at the Congress.

The delegates, with their ladies, drove about the great metropolis and enjoyed its sights. Here was a city with nearly twenty thousand people, mostly white. The principal thoroughfare, Market Street, was a hundred feet wide and paved in part with brick, an astounding municipal luxury. Broad Street, in their city, was only forty feet wide, while Tradd and Elliott were only twenty-four. Here in comparison was a truly magnificent thoroughfare.

Two days after Rutledge and his party were settled the delegates from Virginia drove in and applied for accommodations at Frye's, but unsuccessfully. They put up at the house of a tradesman around the corner. At first there were only three Virginians: Peyton Randolph, a leading figure in the House of Burgesses; Patrick Henry, the golden orator whose name was already a household word with all potential rebels; and a country gentleman who had no known political views of any kind, who had neither written nor spoken anything in public concerning public events. Fourteen years before he had been a colonial officer attached to the British army, and despite his apparent lack of military skill he enjoyed an excellent reputation which was enhanced when he became the heir to his wealthy half-brother and married the richest widow in Virginia. This was George

Washington. He was alone; Mrs. Washington had remained on the plantation.

Just before the opening of Congress twenty-five of the delegates dined together at Frye's. Here John Rutledge first shook hands with Sam Adams. The man born to the purple met the ragged adventurer arrayed in the fine linen and velvet given him by his admiring neighbors. Rutledge presented Adams to Mrs. Rutledge. Then he presented the other men from Massachusetts: John Adams, Cushing, and Paine.

South Carolina and Massachusetts were reaching out for each other, though perhaps neither fully realized what it meant. "We need South Carolina," John Adams noted in his diary. "That must be our first objective." That was from the pen of John, but the tone is Sam's.

In hospitality, at least, the "objective" seemed quite possible, for John Rutledge asked the men from Massachusetts to join him in his rooms where Pompey mixed and served a bombo. Its base of Jamaica rum proved to be too stiff, so Pompey served a negus made of wine, sugar, and water. John Adams, Paine, and Cushing enjoyed a negus with their host, but Sam Adams preferred tea.

In spite of this hospitality, John Adams was not encouraged, for when he returned to his room he wrote in his diary, "John Rutledge still maintains that air of reserve, design and cunning."

After John Rutledge's negus-tea party, Sam Adams rose to what was often said to be the greatest sacrifice of his career. He sent Cousin John to the South Carolina delegation to propose that the Congress be opened by an Episcopal clergyman. Edward Rutledge, after conference with John, returned to the rooming house with a formal reply: so far as South Carolina was concerned, the Congress could be opened without prayer. Sam Adams at once went out and called on an Episcopal clergyman and requested him, in the name of Massachusetts, to open the Congress, and "if desired, with a prayer from the psalter of the High Church."

The religious issue was a smoke screen, of course, behind which the gathering clans were taking each other's measure. As yet they were not friendly. Each was wary and distrustful of the other. Suspicion clouded every move toward union.

If Rutledge appeared to John Adams "reserved" and "cunning" it was because he was following his custom, established in the Charles Town Assembly, and observed before in New York, of waiting for all others to declare themselves before he showed his hand. He had plenary powers but he held them in reserve. And this almost undid him, for he now faced, for the first time in his life, an opponent fit to compete with him in the field of parliamentary action.

There were only a very few men in that Congress who had demonstrated their ability to lead. Gouverneur Morris's comment on them—"what a lot of rascals"—was not unfair. The Virginians, the South Carolinians, one or two of the North Carolinians, a few of the Pennsylvanians, and the men from Massachusetts were the only ones fit for so momentous an assembly. Most of the others, seventy per cent of the whole, did not amount to much.

Among the fifty-three delegates only two were politicians of first-rate skill and experience: John Rutledge and Sam Adams. Each, in his way, was a master. They were about equal in will and courage, and also in possessing the gift known only to great leaders, of accurately sensing public feeling before it has been expressed. Each also possessed that mental and psychic power by means of which public feeling could be turned into channels of his own design. Otherwise, they were as far apart as the poles.

Sam Adams was at all times ruled by one idea, even when he shrewdly masked his purpose, as he did cannily for years, and still persisted in doing at the opening of this Congress. That idea was that the colonies should be independent of Great Britain. Beyond that he saw nothing.

John Rutledge realized this fully. He had "cracked many a hard nut," as a supporter from Ninety-Six said of him, but here was the hardest nut he had yet encountered. He wanted the support of the northern colonies to help South Carolina get a better trade advantage with Great Britain but he did not expect to proclaim political independence to get it. He was, at that moment, a colonial first, an Englishman second, and an American third. He felt strong and confident because he knew that a majority of the members of the Congress, as then constituted, were of the same kind. Incidentally, that was also the opinion of Washington, the country gentleman from Virginia.

Sam Adams moved swiftly and surely to get control. He not only let the sessions be opened with an Episcopal prayer, he seconded the nomination of Peyton Randolph of Virginia (proposed by Thomas Lynch) for President. So the South had the chair. He seemed to offer two ólive branches and it appeared that Massachusetts had "no desire to lead the south into her net and tyrannize over them for her own selfish purposes."

Then came the real coup. With the initial business went a motion that the votes should be counted by colonies, not by individuals. Virginia had seven votes (four more delegates had just arrived), South Carolina five, and Massachusetts only four. There were more northern colonies than southern, but if Pennsylvania were counted with the South, and she leaned that way, the southern interests could command more individual votes. Also, individually there were more moderates than radicals. It was to the advantage of the South as well as to that of the moderates to vote by delegates.

Apparently, only Sam Adams saw this from the start. He consorted day and night before the opening with his adoring pupil, Christopher Gadsden. Then, in the first debate, Gadsden, the Lion of Liberty, was on his feet with a blunt call for a vote by colonies. Sam Adams was rushing John Rutledge off his feet at the first impact by the simple expedient of leading off with Rutledge's associate.

Congress now enjoyed the spectacle of an open South Carolina wrangle. Lynch, Middleton, and Edward Rutledge spoke against voting by colonies. John Rutledge spoke last and was clearly puzzled; he sensed what he was up against and how he had been handicapped from the start; Gadsden was his Achilles' heel.

However, the conservatives in Congress were whipped by that first bold move which came before the issue was defined. The decision to vote by colonies was carried by the narrow margin of two votes.

Thus it was clear that Rutledge was not to have a repetition of his easy victory in New York in 1765 when he dealt with Ruggles and Otis. Sam Adams was not of the same caliber of opposition: he knew exactly what he wanted; he was accustomed to dealing with assemblies partly apathetic, partly hostile; he knew better than to show his hand; and he was fully aware of Rutledge's powers.

The value of the victory to Adams appeared in the first major business, a resolution prepared by Joseph Galloway, of Pennsylvania, providing for an administrative separation of England and America, the colonies remaining under the Crown, yet having full authority to levy taxes, while all equities of the carrying trade would be administered by a joint commission. It was an enlightened proposal, and, if it had been adopted in Philadelphia and ratified in London, would have prevented the war.

Rutledge favored the Galloway plan and was its floor leader, but the radicals under Sam Adams marshalled their forces, denounced it as a Royalist plot, and defeated it by seven colonies against six. Except for Christopher Gadsden's, every southern vote, including that of George Washington, as well as a comfortable minority in the North, was for the Galloway plan. If the votes had been by individual delegates, the plan would have succeeded.

There were no reporters present, and so nothing was known publicly at the time about the Galloway plan. Sam Adams moved to have the minutes expunged from the record, and they were, seven votes to six. Sam did not want the people even to know of the existence of such a proposition.

The First Continental Congress then plunged into the trough of the sea, and followed the historic inclination of parliaments: towards internal strife, indecision, and inaction. For weeks it debated aimlessly, met in committee, considered reports, and agreed on nothing. After a month of this it seemed it would have to adjourn.

This placed upon John Rutledge the onus of following his natural bent, that of the constructive builder. He found himself at a parlia-

mentary disadvantage and yet the moderates, whose desires he articulated, appeared to be in the majority.

7.

Many of the provincial congressmen felt that their trip to Philadelphia was a success, however, for they were learning gambling
games of which they never had heard; pharo, vingt-et-un, macao, and
loo. The barman at Frye's had received from Pompey in exchange
for the secret of a mint julep the recipes for the bombo and the
sangaree. Thus cultures were being extended and exchanged.

President Randolph appointed a general committee to take over
the important business, leaving other delegates to their diversions.
On it were the two Adamses, Thomas Lynch, and John Rutledge.
This general committee of twenty-six—two from each colony—was no
more effective than the whole Congress. Then it was suggested,
indirectly by John Rutledge who did not want his hand to appear,
that for the sake of facility a sub-committee of the junior members
be appointed. This dropped Lynch and Sam Adams, leaving Massachusetts represented by John Adams and South Carolina by John
Rutledge. Rutledge, accustomed to leisure in his own Assembly, had
had time to think out the parliamentary procedure and to evolve
his characteristic adroit approach.

What happened then—in this sub-committee, which lacked power
—was the crux of the Congress and a momentous crisis in the history
of America. "After several days' debate," wrote John Adams in his
diary, "it seemed as if we never should agree on anything. Then Mr.
John Rutledge of South Carolina, addressing himself to me, was
pleased to say, 'Adams, we must agree upon something; you appear
to be as familiar with the subject as any of us, and I like your ex-
pressions—'the necessity of the case,' and 'excluding all ideas of taxation, external and internal,'—I have a great opinion of that same
idea of the necessity of the case, and I am determined against all
taxation for revenue. Come, take the pen and see if you cannot
produce something that will unite us."

"Some others of the committee seconding Mr. Rutledge I took

a sheet of paper and drew up an article. When it was read I believe not one member of the committe was fully satisfied with it; but they all soon acknowledged there was no hope of hitting on anything in which we could all agree with more satisfaction. All therefore agreed to this, and *upon this depended the union of the colonies."*

This saved the sub-committee from disunion by a narrow margin, and it reported unanimously to the Committee of the Whole. The resolution was not very strong. It had a reservation whereby the timorous could still cling to the British Parliament, and asserted by only the narrowest of margins the right of the colonies to assess their own taxation. It implied, without admitting, that the mother country might control trade. In reality it was a dilution of the Galloway plan, so thin that Joseph Galloway himself never recognized it, yet its conception at the pen of John Adams, and its endorsement by the whole Congress, was a demonstration of the statesmanship of John Rutledge.

Sam Adams, who liked devious paths to a simple goal, who was a master of indirection and enjoyed nothing better than being a drama-tist behind the scenes writing the parts for the actors out front to speak, was now involved unexpectedly in the script of a super-dramatist. He did not like the Resolution; it was too conciliatory; *and* it contained an open door to negotiation with the Crown. But Cousin John had written it under his very nose.

What Sam had done to Rutledge by reaching into South Caro-lina and inducing Gadsden to make the move which gave his radicals control of Congress, Rutledge had now done to him by reaching into Massachusetts and inducing Cousin John to write the covenant. It was a deft and telling riposte in the undercover parliamentary duel.

Sam Adams wanted the union, but only on his own radical terms. John Rutledge also wanted the union, but on moderate terms. Rut-ledge had his way, and Congress found itself. There was to be neither northern tyrant nor southern dissenter.

The Committee of the Whole agreed to recommend the report to Congress. Finally, Congress passed the resolution with *all thirteen colonies in agreement.* That Act of Congress, never given a name, might be called "The Original Act of Union." In a basic sense it was the most important act ever passed by any American Congress. Until it was voted upon and passed, unanimously, there was no American union of states. After it was passed, and continuously, from that moment to this, there never has ceased to be an American Union.

Sam Adams did not nurse a grievance; he was just as ready as John Rutledge to seize any shred of success that he might build into his eventual purpose. So now he appealed to the sense of unity recorded in the Resolution of Union and moved to his major objective, a non-importation and non-exportation agreement. He wanted violence and nothing short of war could be more violent than a boycott.

However, he did not ask for a complete boycott. The northern states had long thriven by evading the English trading laws, while South Carolina always had observed them. It would have been simple enough for the North to carry on this habit of law evasion, in which her merchants and mariners were expert, but Adams balked at the idea of facing his own constituents with the necessity of violating a law to which they had agreed. What he asked for was a boycott on only a few articles and with England only. As only a small part of the New England products went to the mother country and nearly all of South Carolina's went there, this was a disproportionate sacrifice. There were other differences to make it more complex. As a result Congress became hopelessly deadlocked.

Then John Rutledge made a sudden proposal which startled everyone, including his own associates. He moved that the thirteen colonies bind themselves, in the most solemn manner, to cut off every trade relationship with Great Britain, and at once. If adopted, it would have been a completely isolationist policy, and was directly contrary to what he had advocated before he left home. But he had been given plenary powers; he was within his rights. Middleton, Lynch, and Edward stuck with him, though surprised; Gadsden was against it, but under the unit rule, he was helpless.

The whole Congress was stunned. This would be, if adopted,

an heroic cutting of the Gordian knot. It was taking Sam Adams at his utmost word and binding him to it. While all colonies would suffer they would suffer equally. If the agreement was kept in good faith no Yankee ship could go into illicit carrying trade. The colonies would be half paralyzed, but England would feel the blow seriously.

Rutledge made a quiet argument in support of his resolution and in conclusion, for the first time in that Congress, "spellbound" them. "Why trifle with the idea of an embargo," he cried, "unless we are willing actually to have an embargo? Let us be done with compromises. This is the only way to test what can be done by an arbitrary control of trade. If we are to fight let us fight completely and with all our weapons. And let us go in equally, and mean it!"

A Maryland delegate leaped to his feet and cried, excitedly, "This is the only decisive proposal I have ever heard. It is the only sure way to bring England to her knees."

It would be total war, at once. It would allow no ship to depart, let no ship land. It was too much for Sam Adams. He got slowly to his feet and hesitantly said, "Personally I am in favor of this, but I dare not vote it and be obliged to return and face my constituents who have not authorized so drastic a step." Rutledge also would have been obliged to face constituents whom he himself had told in advance what to do with delegates who abused their powers, viz.: "Hang them."

This was not necessary, for the vote was twelve to one against Rutledge's resolution. Perhaps the denouement indicates an ulterior motive. Now Sam Adams thought he saw his chance; he would cut away the middle South from the deep South and so have his way. He proposed the limited non-exportation and non-importation agreements, favoring New England, but not to go into effect for a year, which would give Virginia and Maryland a chance to market their current tobacco crops. It appeared that this would carry.

Rutledge, however, was ready for his final stand. He took the floor, and, in contrast to his previous, emotional appeal, read a few statistics, which he had gleaned from his Philadelphia colleague, James Wilson. These showed that only about five per cent of the

New England items Sam Adams had included were traded with the mother country, while sixty-five per cent of South Carolina's rice and a hundred per cent of her indigo went to England.

Then Rutledge brought out his drawing-room manner, and those who knew him would have been especially warned. "These figures, gentlemen," he said, "will reveal to you that if this association is perfected the northern colonies will suffer very little, for they can still carry on their trade with Europe and pay indirectly their debts in England while if South Carolina enters into it her chief businesses are ruined. I think it is not unreasonable for me to say that if we are to bear burdens in the cause of America they should be as equal as possible. This proposed association looks like a commercial scheme, among the flour colonies, to find a better vent for their flour indirectly into the English market, by preventing, if possible, any rice from going into that market. In this, of course, I have not consulted my constituents, and am speaking only for myself, but I can never consent to the people of South Carolina becoming the dupes of the people of the North, or, in the least, to yield to their unreasonable expectations."

It was said "apologetically" and "with a tremble in his voice." The proposal for a united embargo had been uttered with a ringing defiance that stirred even Patrick Henry, but this came out, with that "unutterable sob," as if he were infinitely reluctant.

However, it was an open declaration of sectional hostility, on the floor of the Congress. Until that moment such a thing had been avoided.

There was a hurried consultation among the Massachusetts delegates. Then Mr. Paine politely inquired what Mr. Rutledge could propose as a compromise. Mr. Rutledge replied, promptly, as if all his previous moves had been only calculated preparation for the question, that South Carolina would come into the association if rice and indigo were excepted.

Congress went into an uproar. So that was South Carolina's ultimate object—to be the colony favored over all; to continue, by consent, of the American union, the place she previously had held under the British Crown!

She had no support. When Rutledge brought the real issue into the open frankly, and met it boldly, with irrefutable figures, he found himself, except for three of his own colleagues, utterly alone.

Sam Adams quickly saw he could force a vote and win, but did he want to do that and run the risk of South Carolina withdrawing entirely? He wanted complete union as much as Rutledge had seemed to want it earlier. He proposed adjournment.

The Congress waited a week to give South Carolina, "that colony of hot-heads," a chance to cool off. However, the demands of Mr. Rutledge were not changed. Then Sam Adams proposed a compromise. If South Carolina would be content with the exception of *one* commodity the others might agree. Rutledge said, abruptly, "All right. We take rice."

Thereupon Congress unanimously agreed to the non-importation and non-exportation association, excepting rice, and adjourned. The boycott never went into effect; events nullified it.

No concrete purpose was achieved by that first Congress. There was only a moral victory—union had been established.

When Patrick Henry came to the first Saturday night meeting in the country store and his neighbors gathered around for a report on what had happened in Philadelphia, William Wirt asked, "And who do you think was the greatest man in the First Continental Congress?"

"If you speak of eloquence," replied Henry, "Mr. John Rutledge of South Carolina is by far the greatest orator."

8.

The day after he returned to Charles Town John Rutledge appeared before the Committee on Public Safety, meeting at The Corner, and, from his bench, made a full report of what had happened in Philadelphia, repeating his arguments, but with no plea for endorsement. It was one of the longest public speeches of his life and lasted "more than an hour." Then he mounted his horse and rode to Beaufort, the first "shire" town on the circuit. Behind him Rutledge left a fierce discussion. For the first time in his career he was bitterly assailed by a large part of his own people.

The indigo growers, nearly half the low-countrymen, were furious because they declared the embargo would ruin them while the rice growers would be enriched. The cattle men, the hemp growers, the corn planters, the salt men were similarly outraged. The lumbermen appointed a committee to plan a reprisal. All lesser industries were up in arms.

With his political career at stake Rutledge turned his back on the debate and left his interests in the hands of his friends. Parsons rose from his bed and was carried to The Corner. Colonel Pinckney, the chairman of the Committee, defended his young associate zealously. The second day of the debate a lumberman from the Santee ventured to put in public words what many were saying privately.

"When we voted full powers to our delegation," he cried, "and someone asked what should be done if the delegates abused their powers John Rutledge replied, 'Hang them.' I say they have abused us! We should call in the Regulators!"

Thomas Lynch rose. In Philadelphia he had been described by John Adams as "a calm, judicious man."

"Certain facts," said Lynch, while all listened, "we should keep in mind. Mr. Rutledge owns about eighty acres of rice land. All else that he plants is in indigo, though he also owns a little lumber. Mrs. Sarah Hext Rutledge, his mother, mills no rice; she has only indigo. One of his brothers has a hundred and fifty acres in rice, and over eight hundred in indigo. That, I believe, is a fair estimate of the Rutledge holdings; only a small fraction is in rice.

"Now, it happens that I was with Mr. Rutledge in Philadelphia the day we received from Massachusetts the proposal that we secure agreement on only *one* commodity for exemption. Without asking my opinion, or that of anyone else, and without any hesitation, like that [snapping his fingers] Mr. Rutledge said, 'Rice!' The others agreed, except Mr. Gadsden who believed we should have no exemption.

"Therefore, gentlemen, I submit, was Mr. Rutledge making a selfish abuse of his powers, or, as best he could under the circumstances, without the slightest apparent consideration of his own interests, for his personal profit would be much greater if he excepted indigo, was he making an important decision for the greatest good of the greatest number?"

This received wild cheers, but the debate grew more bitter and protracted. No one wanted to hang any of the delegates, but apparently many of them would have hanged Sam Adams. Pinckney saw how the wind was blowing and held off the vote, for if the Committee did not ratify the work of the delegates at Philadelphia it might mark the end of the rule of the triumvirate. Never before had that rule been so seriously challenged.

Either horn of the non-importation dilemma was a cruel point for the impalement of South Carolina. If rice was not exempted a great blow would be dealt the chief business of the colony. If it was exempted a new and just ground of offense would be offered the up-country, for rice, which could be grown only near tide water, would be helped at the expense of the products of the inland sections.

That was why Rutledge rode so rapidly "on circuit." He knew the real peril of schism among them was in the up-country. So he faced quickly the prejudices and localized indignation of the shire towns where, on the tavern steps of an evening, or before the court house in the morning, he could talk it out man to man. He realized that unity was necessary in South Carolina as in Philadelphia. Thus he bared his breast to his rural critics and assured them that the non-importation association was only a temporary measure.

Meanwhile, in Charles Town, the Committee seemed on the verge of refusing to ratify the work of its delegates. Colonel Pinckney held off the vote for many weeks. Finally, in uproar and confusion, it was taken, and resulted in eighty-seven to seventy-five favoring ratification.

This was the nearest to defeat John Rutledge ever came on a major issue among his own people, and it was on a measure in which he had gained a signal victory for them.

Two days later the Committee unanimously re-elected John Rutledge and his four associates as delegates to the new Congress "to further measures . . . which shall appear to be necessary for the recovery and establishment of American rights and liberties, and *for restoring harmony between Great Britain and her colonies.*"

This was the "instruction" of the so-called First Congress of South Carolina to its delegates to the Second Continental Congress. Official resolution was one thing, the temper of the people another. While the delegates were getting ready to leave for what looked like a long absence from home an episode occurred which emphasized the quick and perilous sands which underlay the whole situation. For against Rutledge had appeared a new rival, the most menacing he ever faced locally.

This was William Henry Drayton, who had joined forces with the Liberty Boys and was now out-roaring Lion Gadsden. He was from one of the oldest, wealthiest, and best-established families in the South Carolina hierarchy, for the Draytons ranked, in all ways, with the Pinckneys, Rutledges, Middletons, and Lynches.

William Henry was thirty-three years old, of boundless ambition, well endowed with every apparent requisite for success; and he knew what was at stake—sovereign control of the colony. Educated as a barrister in London he had not practiced law except sporadically, for his private fortune was ample. He had a charming personality and was very effective as a writer and speaker. He was always ready with references to Cato of Utica and to Cicero's letters to Atticus, and on the slightest prompting, or to any audience, he was ready to tell what had happened in the Long Parliament and how the Roman Senate had acted. In London, where he lived for years, he had been a stiff Royalist, and had made every possible approach to court circles, though unsuccessfully. Rebuffed at the capital of empire he had returned, only two years before, to Charles Town, and had thrown himself into the cause of "Liberty." Under the Liberty Tree his elegance and distinction were rapidly stealing the thunder of the cruder Gadsden. Drayton was the new political darling of the "mechanics and artisans," and this was rendered all the more piquant by the fact that he was a member of the King's Council.

The trifle which first threw William Henry Drayton across the path of John Rutledge was the arrival in port of a South Carolina family which had been living in England and was returning home to share with old neighbors their fate in upset times. This family brought furniture and horses used in England and asked permission of the Committee to land. Permission was granted.

Before the horses could be taken from the ship, however, some Liberty Boys raised the cry, "The Association is broken." Along East Bay hundreds assembled and all could see above the deck-rail of the vessel lying only a cable's length off shore the heads of the English horses. Furious demands were made that the Committee should rescind its action.

Edward Rutledge appeared and strove to be heard. He tried to censure the people for questioning the acts of the Committee. He was howled down. Meanwhile, a voluntary posse was formed and swore it would prevent the "outrageous" landing of the "illicit beasts." In the face of this hysteria the owners made no such effort, but agreed to wait for a re-hearing.

A day was set, but not all the members took it seriously; only sixty-nine, most of whom lived near-by, were present. This was less than half the Committee. Nevertheless, these, on a pleasant summer afternoon at The Corner, proceeded to reconsider this problem of foreign and domestic policy: should the driving horses be embargoed or non-embargoed? The Liberty Boys declared that if they were allowed to land on the holy soil of South Carolina it would be another bloody outrage committed by the King.

Gadsden got in the first blow. It would be monstrous, he declared, to let these horses land, for it was not even claimed they were born in South Carolina. They were undoubtedly wholly English, and if they came in and word of it reached the North, the colonies up there would justly declare that South Carolina had broken the Association.

A popular clergyman followed, and then leaders of the butchers,

the cobblers, and the carpenters. Each put thumbs down on the foreign beasts: let them either go back to England or be dumped over-
board and drowned. South Carolina was not to be contaminated
by English horses.

Then Thomas Lynch, Edward Rutledge, Rawlins Lowndes and
Thomas Bee, men who ordinarily carried great weight, appeared
in favor of the horses. They seemed to steady the situation for a
moment, but only for a moment.

Suddenly William Henry Drayton, of the King's Council, leaped
to a bench. He held the crowd spellbound for more than an hour.
He spread before them the glorious records of the Roman Senate
and of the Long Parliament; each in its day had been a wise and
noble body, yet each had yielded to the people and had reversed itself;
so should the General Committee. Mr. Drayton, of the Ashley River
Draytons, out-Gadsdened Gadsden and the cheers could be heard
from the Battery to the Neck.

Down Broad Street, from No. 116, while Drayton was speaking,
strolled a familiar figure. It was that of John Rutledge. He had ridden
in on horseback the night before from Orangeburg and Edward
had explained the situation to him briefly.

As Drayton finished the crowd called for John Rutledge, who
spoke for about fifteen minutes. The members were threatening and
sullen, but respectful. Rutledge argued that the matter at issue "is a
trifle, and in these perilous times the principle of maintaining law
and order should be our first concern. No useful object is to be gained
if every decision of the General Committee is to be appealed to a
passing shadow of temporary feeling."

As usual he made an emotional appeal at the end, when he
cried, "What man is so craven as to shift his position from day to day
with what he thinks to be the drift of popular feeling! I ask you
to be fair with the Committee as you wish the Committee to be fair
with you. Abide by its decisions like honest men, and if you disagree
await the appointed time to register your disapproval, at the next
election. I urge you not to undo the good work we have already

established in the colony by taking into your own hands the affairs of government which can be better regulated by a more formal body. Let us not become the victims of rebellion within ourselves. You believe a principle is involved in the decision about these poor horses, and so it is, but the principle is not the integrity of the Association of the colonies. The principle at stake is the integrity of our own organization."

Rutledge received some applause, but it was not like that which greeted William Henry Drayton. Ballots were passed. The sub-committee, informally assembled, voted to rescind the permission granted by the General Committee to land the horses, thirty-five to thirty-four. By one vote the advice of John Rutledge was ignored for the first time in Charles Town.

At once a real question loomed, much more important than that of the horses. Thinking persons everywhere in South Carolina could contemplate little else. Was this the end of the triumvirate which had ruled their affairs so satisfactorily for fifteen years?

In the vote of the sub-committee only Rutledge represented the triumvirate. Colonel Pinckney, the chairman, already had signified his intention to withdraw from public affairs and was not present. He was heartsick with the rise of the "Liberty" tide. James Parsons was not far from death. These coadjutors always had acted as whips for Rutledge and, with them to assist, he never before had failed of popular support. If a historic point is to be noted to mark the end of the unofficial but practically absolute rule of the triumvirate in the affairs of South Carolina, the decision to expel the English horses may be said to mark the point.

It is the almost universal history of triumvirates that they come into being as a means of granting to a committee autocratic power which the society does not dare grant to any single individual. The second rule concerning these ineffective devices to bestow autocracy without concentrating it dangerously is that they usually result in the strongest of the three becoming arbiter of all.

So triumvirates often have preceded dictatorships.

9.

While Rutledge prepared for a long stay in the North, where it seemed the contest with the Crown must be settled, affairs in Charles Town became even more disrupted. The rule of the triumvirate apparently continued and in one episode, at least, Rutledge was reassured.

This was in the seizure of the royal powder magazine at Hobcaw, for which purpose Colonel Pinckney appointed a committee of five, With Drayton at the head. Drayton indicated he intended to do it clandestinely, and by surprise, as a secret military measure. Rutledge disapproved for there were no effective royal guards and such a move would have been only a gesture of defiance. The chief triumvir said the seizure should be made by leading citizens, unmasked, working at night to spare the feelings of Lieutenant Governor Bull, who held the royal authority, though without military aid or political support. Pinckney instructed Drayton to do as Rutledge suggested, and so it was done. However, during the action Drayton assumed the title of Captain, for which he had no warrant. This was reported to Pinckney and Rutledge and they decided to make no formal objection. They believed it was a bit of harmless ardor.

Pinckney was preparing to leave Charles Town for Florida "until it was all over." He was grooming as his successor his son, then twenty-four years old and already an avowed revolutionary. The father's instruction was, "Always remember that the first among us is John Rutledge."

Militia companies were being drilled, street boys were jibing at effigies of the King, and a spirit of militant rebellion had seized Charles Town. Nevertheless, on May second Rutledge sailed for Philadelphia and left Drayton in possession of the field.

The "shot heard round the world" already had been fired at Concord, and on May eighth, with Rutledge at sea, the news reached Charles Town. The effect was almost as if the King's troops had fired on South Carolinians. Drayton attempted military preparations at once and Colonel Pickney, in actual command, opposed him.

Arrived in Philadelphia Rutledge at first knew only of what had happened in Boston; it was not for months that he learned of the true state of affairs in South Carolina. During this period the thing which most concerned his restive and practical spirit was the vital difference between the authority of the Continental Congress and that of the Committee of Public Safety in Charles Town. Neither body had legal authority. In Philadelphia the Congress controlled nothing and could merely recommend; it had only a moral value. At the same time, in Charles Town, there existed that effective control, which he still possessed (or did he?) and which he had so completely wielded. What should he do? He endured the situation passively for nearly eight months.

In the second Congress Sam Adams and John Rutledge did not clash. In the union of the colonies, though it was still tenuous, their vital forces had been welded. While in the first Congress Adams had come to scoff and remained to pray, in the second he took the position that every other opponent of Rutledge took, sooner or later; he recognized a leader. Abandoning all thought that Rutledge was a King's man in disguise, he frankly turned to the South Carolinian for advice and accepted his direction in many matters of procedure, both legal and parliamentary, despite the fact that Rutledge at all times declared his ultimate object was "a reconciliation with Britain."

In Boston more royal troops were being landed; more fighting ships were enforcing the blockade; blood had been spilled at Concord and Lexington; thousands of embattled farmers were rising and pouring in. However, Massachusetts had no assembly, no organized military force, no government. Sam Adams had achieved his fiery goal. The people's revolution in Massachusetts was positively and spectacularly a fact, but now what? The Bay Colony asked the Continental Congress for advice.

Every delegate in Philadelphia, and especially Sam Adams, knew what had been done in South Carolina during the previous fifteen years where the southern colony had gone even further than Massachusetts in achieving independence and yet had done it deftly, retaining control of the machinery of government as well as of events.

They all knew that South Carolina had acted only "by advice of counsel."

Fortunately, South Carolina's attorney was now with them. Incidentally, he sent back home a message to the General Committee suggesting that some of the powder seized at Hobcaw be forwarded to the Boston rebels. This was done and for a long time it was only with South Carolina powder that the "armies" under Putnam and Ward were able to function around Boston.

By motion of Sam Adams a committee was set up to advise all the colonies on legal and parliamentary procedure. John Hancock, his political protege, was in the chair, and, at Sam's private suggestion, he appointed Rutledge to the head of this Committee on Government.

So the Committee on Government through its chairman, the first triumvir of South Carolina, advised Massachusetts what to do: "Send letters to prominent men in each section who shall choose, after conference with fellow citizens, representatives . . . who shall elect counsellors . . . and these acting as a Council shall take over affairs of government until such time as a government of His Majesty's appointment shall consent to govern the colony according to its charter."

This republican prescription was offered the land of the "folk motes." Prominent men were to supplant the town meetings. That is curious, but the incredible part is that Massachusetts adopted the "suggestion." The mountain had come to Mahomet!

Other colonies sought guidance and each received a similar "suggestion" from the Rutledge committee, which thus planted, from the extreme North to the deep South, its special republican formula.

Rutledge served on eleven committees. As head of the Committee on Government he performed a fundamental service by setting up in the established Union the embryo of state government.

The next most important committee of the Congress was that on Trade, later called the Committee of Ways and Means. The members of this were elected by secret ballot. Benjamin Franklin, already too old for vigorous activity, was elected chairman. The vice-chairman selected by the delegates individually and secretly was John Rutledge and he did most of the work.

However, none of these committees performed any act of interest comparable, in the light of history, with the selection of a Commander-in-Chief for the newly formed "armies." In this John Rutledge also guided the event.

Who should command the unorganized armed farmers and provincial militia slowly converging on Boston? That question was agitating every tavern and parlor in the thirteen colonies. The Congress hovered over it constantly. Nearly every colony had a candidate, most of them veterans of the French and Indian War, none of outstanding prominence. Sir William Johnson had died within the year or he would have been the most likely commander. General Timothy Ruggles would have been an almost certain choice, but, like Colonel Pinckney, he "could not stomach Liberty."

In the first Congress Adams had sought Gadsden, but not this time. As soon as the organization was under way, the committees at work and the business outlined, he sought John Rutledge and asked him whom he would suggest for Commander-in-Chief. Rutledge replied that his colony had only two officers of any experience, Colonel Pinckney and Captain Gadsden. He said he thought both were excluded because of age. Then courteously he asked Adams to suggest a man from Massachusetts.

Adams answered, "We have only Israel Putnam who is a fine soldier, but old, and—alas!—poor; and Artemas Ward, also a good soldier, but old and fat." Adams did not put in words, at once, what he actually had in mind. He wanted a rich, young, and handsome leader. He was not going to be led by any "wayside adventurer." It would not be good politics; he still was sensitive about his lowly political caste, a feeling which came from years of being denounced as "the ragged leader of a rabble." If Rutledge knew what was in the mind of his Boston colleague he did not express it.

At their third conference they agreed that they must have a non-political leader with some military experience, and preferably from a central point. From that agreement they proceeded by process of elimination.

A "central point" meant either New York, Pennsylvania, or Virginia. The military officers available in New York were too young and of insufficient background. Pennsylvania had no prominent candidate. That left Virginia.

The Congress had a delegate from the Old Dominion who could not be overlooked, for he had attended every session in military uniform—as an actor might place himself before the eye of a casting director. He had made no political speech and was extremely reticent in talking politics even in private; but he had been most definite in saying that he stood ready to raise and equip a regiment of Virginians, at his own expense, whenever necessary. He was a striking figure who looked more like a British general than any British general they ever had seen. Moreover, he was an aristocrat and very wealthy. He was George Washington.

These two political adepts—the indigent wizard from Boston and the leader of the American bar from Charles Town—reviewed his qualifications with extreme care. Were they aware that they were choosing a man to fill an immortal niche in history? Perhaps not. The choice was part of their work; they made it with caution and precision; the Congress being as it was, their decision would be final.

First, they questioned his military experience. This seemed of doubtful value. Washington never had won a victory in the field, never had commanded more than twelve hundred men; yet, after three defeats he had conducted successful "retreats"; and, in the face of losses that would have destroyed the reputations of most men, he had managed to come through with a halo.

However slight his military experience, the Virginian's imponderable assets were many. Rutledge and Adams listed them.

The first was geographical. Virginia was the most northern of the southern colonies and to give it command would probably assure support of the whole South. It was also the most populous colony and so local pride would unite home support, an essential in the beginning.

The second was political. Washington held no well-known views, and never having been identified with any theory of government, he was a political neuter and so had no enemies.

The third was social. He was a fox-hunting Virginia planter, and belonged to the most exclusive social group in the colonies except that of Charles Town. He would appeal infallibly to the snobbery of three million colonials and he might even impress the British enemy.

The fourth was military. As a general his curious facility in conducting successful "retreats" might be of special importance, for both Adams and Rutledge were seeking "long-term value."

The fifth was physical. His appearance was very impressive. As a type and symbol of human leadership George Washington, even in his obscurity, stood alone.

The last was psychological. He was open to advice. Judging from his record, he would not thrust himself forward. He had sat through several terms of the Virginia House of Burgesses and was now sitting in the second session of the Continental Congress without having expressed a political idea; and yet he had retained the respect and affection of his associates. This seemed proof that in a high place he probably would be "reasonable." Yet his character seemed incorruptible and his personality was clearly charming. To Sam Adams, who had fathered the Revolution in the North through emotional suggestion, and to John Rutledge, who had given it legally practical expression in the South, such a man seemed the best one available to carry their banner forward.

After six days of cautious, secret conference, Sam Adams and John Rutledge agreed that George Washington was the man they wanted. Yet they moved indirectly. Their chief object was to create an appearance of spontaneity in the choice of a general. And the nomination would have to come from the North; it would not be so effective if the South led in the proposal.

This put Sam Adams in a predicament, for he had many secret and conflicting commitments. In the chair was the vain John Hancock of Boston. Sam had nurtured and developed him as a figurehead to answer the charge that the rebels were composed of a "rabble of worth-less adventurers." The indigent revolutionary had wheedled and, on occasion had goaded Hancock, the rich importer, into taking his stand with "the rabble." He had written Hancock's speeches, had breathed courage into him when he was frightened, and had completed the conversion by finding political arguments to compel the "Indians" to hold their "Boston Tea Party," with its incidental result that a warehouse filled with Hancock's tea did not fall in price. Adams had been chagrined, in and after the first Congress, because Massachusetts had only poor men as delegates. He made sure that the Bay Colony sent to the second Congress at least one delegate who could wear a whole velvet coat and a richly embroidered waistcoat of his own.

Hancock *already* had raised and equipped a regiment of militia and was ready to do more. He looked upon himself as the logical Commander-in-Chief, for he was President of the Congress.

John Adams, the country lawyer from Braintree, had solicited legal work from the great Boston importer, but had been given only some minor jobs. So it was to Cousin John that Sam "sold" the idea of the Virginian as a general. Cousin John was known, in the Massachusetts delegation, for his irrepressible whimsy, and for being intractable. It was the morning of June 9, 1775, a pleasant day in Philadelphia, and the Congress meeting in Mechanics Hall had no pressing business on its agenda. So when John Adams rose and said, rather casually, that he thought they might consider the selection of a Commander-in-Chief he was promptly recognized. The Lesser Adams expanded a bit, declaring that the post was most difficult to fill, and that while some seemed to despair of finding the properly qualified candidate, he was confident that the right man was available, in their own body.

"He is the man," continued John Adams, "whom I now nominate, George Washington of Virginia."

The figure in uniform near the door rose hurriedly and left the room. John Adams's diary noted, "I never saw anyone's expression change as quickly as Hancock's changed."

John Rutledge seconded the nomination, but his words were not clearly heard. In the Massachusetts delegation there was evident division and in the Virginia delegation, right next to that from South Carolina, were vigorous protests. Before he sat down Rutledge moved for a day's adjournment to consider the important question in private.

By this prompt move Rutledge forestalled public knowledge of any dissension in Congress over the choice of a commander-in-chief. Only with an apparently spontaneous and unanimous front could union be achieved.

Sam Adams agreed to "look after" the seven northern colonies, while Rutledge canvassed the other six, during the one-day recess. Adams proved to have Massachusetts and the North well in hand, and the only real difficulty occurred in Virginia. Edmund Pendleton, the leader, was against Washington because he said it committed the Old Dominion to the defense of Boston. The other Virginia delegates agreed with him. Rutledge spent the evening with Pendleton and his associates.

The next morning Congress selected George Washington as the commander-in-chief of its "armies" by unanimous vote. There were no armies recognizing the authority of Congress; and Congress had no established powers and no money. Washington modestly accepted the dubious task and offered to work without salary, a proposition which Congress gladly accepted.

Before he left for Boston, Washington conferred with Rutledge. They were in complete agreement that their sole effort should be to restore the colonies to a definite place in the British Empire. Neither, at that time, believed in independence.

10.

A letter from Charles Town telling about Drayton's activities reached Rutledge as Congress adjourned for six weeks on August first. There was no vessel sailing for a week, so he traveled on horseback, a trip that took fifteen or sixteen days of hard riding, but he was thirty-six years old and in good health. He left Mrs. Rutledge in Philadelphia and plunged into the southern trail.

He had been gone from Charles Town about a hundred days,

during which time, in collaboration with John Adams, he had outlined the framework of state government for the separate states of the United States and had selected, in collaboration with Sam Adams, a commander-in-chief of its armies. He reached Charles Town in the midsummer heat. The air was unusually still as he crossed the Ashley. The Town seemed dead. No shipping was entering or leaving the port and local business was at a standstill.

A state of war existed—but not with Great Britain. The low country was arming against the up country. William Henry Drayton was in the saddle. He had no military training or experience, no more than John Rutledge had, yet he realized that if war came the military leaders would be the popular heroes. As soon as Rutledge had gone, he had secured a majority vote of the Committee of Public Safety giving him secret power to call out the militia at his own discretion.

Drayton had made two brilliant moves. In one he had seized the British mail, intercepting dispatches from the royal Governors of South Carolina and Georgia to General Gage at Boston. Drayton had counterfeited them, to give the impression that no succor was needed. Then he had seized a British ship with a big store of powder and brought it in to Charles Town.

As a result Drayton was looked upon by the Committee as its military leader, though Colonel Pinckney had not yet departed for Florida. Drayton proposed going into the up country, with a clergyman as companion, "to explain the need for homogeneity and to prevent the spread of sedition." The Committee agreed.

The Governor, Lord William Campbell, just arrived from England, had induced a large body of armed men under an officer named Kirkland to assemble in the stockade at Ninety-Six.

Drayton left Charles Town when he learned that Kirkland's "army" at Ninety-Six—about eighteen hundred men—had sworn allegiance to the Crown. The act was not warlike in itself, though its occurrence in the presence of the Governor was proclaimed defiant by the Liberty Boys.

About twelve hundred militia were assembled between the Ashley and Ninety-Six. Drayton called these to the new colors and they swore allegiance to the Committee of Public Safety in Charles Town. This was an exercise of his secret powers which he made without communicating again with the Committee. He had been sent "to prevent the spread of sedition" but shortly he addressed the troops, as their Captain and declared that if armed soldiers of the King advanced upon them they would shoot on sight.

This was the situation John Rutledge faced when he returned to Charles Town from Philadelphia. The war in South Carolina was about to begin; not between British regulars and provincials, but between rival South Carolinians. His constituents near Charles Town —many were from the vicinity of the Stono plantation—were about to fight his constituents from Ninety-Six.

Rutledge had no official position except as a delegate to the national debating society sitting intermittently at Philadelphia. The former triumvirate had disintegrated. Colonel Pinckney had been succeeded as President of the General Committee by Henry Laurens.

The chief peril facing the community was not any immediate menace from the Crown, and Rutledge felt that any chance the colony as a whole might have to win an eventual contest with the King would be vastly lessened if Drayton and Kirkland fought a pitched battle now. Could he revive the autocratic rule which he had held for nearly fifteen years?

It is extremely significant that the first night after Rutledge's return Laurens dined with him at 116 Broad Street. The delegate to the Continental Congress asked the President of the Provincial Congress, the title Laurens had inherited from Pinckney, to his private board for preliminary conference.

The tired traveler, apprehensive lest events had slipped beyond his control in the hundred days, found a Laurens he never before had known. That his business was paralyzed, that his ships were lying with sails furled in the harbor, that his income from export and import was stopped, seemed of no moment to him.

During Rutledge's absence, and upon election to his new office, Laurens had become converted to the revolutionary doctrine, and he had all the zeal of a new convert. At the moment he apparently was

ready to go as fast and as far as any Liberty Boy. Embarked on a
new adventure he was transparently elated.

Laurens' business was perhaps the most extensive and best-
organized then existing in America, yet he dismissed it with an ex-
pressive shrug of his French shoulders. He said he had intended to
retire; the threatened war merely gave him a good excuse; he had
more money than he knew what to do with; now he proposed to
devote it, and his life as well, to the cause of American Freedom.

As his guest talked Rutledge became calmer. Fate had dealt him
an ace. He had thought the retirement of Colonel Pinckney a calamity; but evidently it was turning out to be a blessing. He confided
to the new President his ideas about "Captain" Drayton and the ill-
advised military advance on Ninety-Six.

The following day President Laurens called a secret meeting of
the Committee. At his suggestion a messenger went before nightfall
to search for Captain Drayton with the Committee's instructions not
to fight.

Shortly afterwards Drayton returned with the militia and announced that the up country was "pacified," which was far from the
truth. However, the Governor's impending civil war was postponed.

Meanwhile Rutledge found the state of his business the opposite
of that of Henry Laurens. Instead of having less to do than formerly
he never had found such demand for his professional time. Many of
the important clients of Parsons and some of those previously
served by Colonel Pinckney applied to him to carry on their legal
affairs. The retainers from these new clients, added to his usual fees,
brought his income for the troubled year of 1775, during which he
gave more than half his time to public business, to its peak of more
than nine thousand pounds. No man of property in South Carolina,
royal, radical or moderate, would employ any attorney except John
Rutledge, if he could afford it. Rutledge was at his office each morning before six o'clock; in the "palace" he conferred late each night.

In the absence of his wife, his mother came in from the plantation
to live with him and to care for his children. He had had six, and
five were living, four of them boys. To accommodate them and the

necessary extra servants he had built an extra story at 116 Broad Street, and the house now rose nearly as high as Hugh's next door.

Sarah Hext Rutledge urged her son to work less and sought to gain his confidence, but he did not respond. She rather envied his wife, for she did not know that he confided nothing to Elizabeth either. Yet pride induced her to tell Hugh conclusions about John's activities which were only guesses, and not facts. When the brother repeated these fictions they added fuel to a flame already growing, for John had many Royalist clients and now it was whispered that John himself was a Royalist. Of these rumors he knew nothing for a long time.

John Rutledge had never confided in anyone, except James Parsons, and in him only a little. Now Rutledge was alone. He came into his intellectual maturity in his thirty-eighth year and sealed his heart and lips more tightly than ever.

The second week in September Rutledge took ship for Philadelphia. As soon as he was gone Drayton, who had learned how he had been thwarted in what he fancied was a chance to achieve a quick military reputation, induced the Committee of Public Safety to reorganize and elect a new President. Having no charter to guide it, the Committee was little more than a glorified Vigilante committee. On the wings of a swift gust of popularity William Henry Drayton superseded Henry Laurens.

At once Drayton tried to imprison Kirkland, who fled with the Governor and the Great Seal of the Province, to the sloop *Tamar* anchored in the harbor. He ordered Rangers to advance on bands of alleged "traitors," though traitors to what was not specified. He erected earthworks, purchased schooners, and sunk hulks in the channel. Then he took command of a ten-gun schooner, the *Defence,* and added to his title of "Captain" the loftier title of Admiral.

Without waiting for aggression, "Admiral" Drayton fired on two British armed sloops, the *Tamar* and the *Cherokee.* Acting with his orders, Fort Johnson also fired at the distant ships. As "Captain" he ordered troops drawn up on shore where they presented arms, while the shots were being fired. The British ships replied with a few perfunctory shots. No one on either side was injured. This, however, is accepted as the official opening of the war in South Carolina. The date was November 11, 1775.

Four days later John Rutledge returned with Mrs. Rutledge from Philadelphia on a sailing vessel. He went before the Committee, now functioning as a Congress in the state house, reported what had been done by the delegates to the Continental Congress, received public thanks, and then requested that he be relieved of his duties in the North.

William Henry Drayton was in the chair. A few days before the Committee had appointed a Council consisting of three, Drayton, Charles Pinckney, Junior, and Thomas Heyward, Junior. This Council had been granted secret dictatorial powers, Pinckney and Heyward, in their early twenties, were dominated by Drayton. It was, in effect, an attempt to set up a legally declared successor to the late triumvirate. The Governor was gone. Thus Drayton was now President of the Provisional Congress of South Carolina, Captain of its land forces, Admiral of its fleet, and, after dark, Dictator of its civil affairs.

At the suggestion of this Dictator, the Committee refused Mr. Rutledge's request to be relieved of his duties in Philadelphia. The chair suggested and the Committee resolved that his services in the Continental Congress were irreplaceable, and requested that he return at once or as soon as he could arrange his personal affairs.

II.

Rutledge had now reached his Rubicon. He advanced on Drayton with punctilious legality, which was executed in the Rutledgian manner by first turning his back. In mid-September he sailed for Philadelphia, alone. He could not confide even in Henry Laurens a plan which he had evolved. The merchant was always his loyal supporter, but he was not a successor to Parsons or Pinckney.

Shortly after his appearance on the floor of the Continental Congress Rutledge addressed the chair and said that it was the unanimous wish of his delegation that Congress should advise the colony of South Carolina as to procedure in the better organization of its own affairs. The chair referred this motion to the Committee on Constitutional Government.

The Committee on Constitutional Government, J. Rutledge, chairman, came into session and solemnly considered this proper request, as it previously had considered such requests from New Hampshire, Massachusetts, New Jersey, Delaware, and others. In this case it went a little further, however. It prepared a Resolution in which it "suggested" that "an orderly government shall be arranged in South Carolina, and that representative men shall prepare a written constitution which shall be considered the will of the people. . . ."

This Resolution being reported to the Congress by its proper Committee, received perfunctory reading, whereupon Congress unanimously adopted the Resolution, and referred it back to the delegation from South Carolina, where, naturally, it came to the hand of the chairman.

With this official Resolution in his pocket, Rutledge left Philadelphia abruptly. He did not again appear in the Continental Congress. He arrived in Charles Town early in November. His appearance made no apparent ripple in public affairs. The *Gazette* devoted three lines to his return. Ebon Hargrave, writing to a relative in St. John's, just before Christmas, said, "Mr. Rutledge returned from the North a month ago and is mummer than a Yemassee."

In his first report of what the delegation had done in Philadelphia the chairman made no mention of the Resolution of the Continental Congress on the subject of a more stable government for South Carolina. The congress accepted the report, and moved a vote of thanks to be delivered by the President in person. So, before an open meeting, to which spectators were invited, President Drayton addressed John Rutledge, who sat in the front row.

"Your constituents," said Drayton, "sensible of the propriety of your conduct, and of the benefits which, with the blessing of the Almighty, it is calculated to shed upon America, have constituted me their instrument as well to signify to you their approbation, as to present to you their thanks; and it is in discharge of those duties that I now have the honor to address you. In an important crisis like the present, to receive the public thanks of a free people, is to receive the most honorable recompense for past services, and, to deserve such thanks, is to be truly great. I know that it is with pain that such men hear their commendations, and, lest I wound your delicacy, when I mean only to do justice to your merit, I forbear to particularize what is already known."

Rutledge was then elected a member of the Congress. At once he asked to be relieved of his duties in Philadelphia, but Drayton adjourned the meeting before it could be considered. The next day, ignoring the request of Mr. Rutledge, the Congress unanimously reelected for the coming year its five seated delegates to the national body. Rutledge sprang to his feet and moved that the absence from Philadelphia for any reason of any delegate should not legally lessen the power of the others to represent the colony, if a majority was present. He moved for immediate consideration and the resolution carried. Now he was free; he could come or go at will.

For six or seven weeks Rutledge made no move. Still no one in Charles Town apparently knew anything of the Resolution of the Continental Congress advising a "more orderly government." There was no mention of it in the *Gazette,* nor had there been one in any northern newspaper. It had occasioned no debate and hardly any comment in Philadelphia; it was not controversial.

For the Christmas holidays Rutledge went to his mother's plantation and gave an "oyster roast," at which he fraternized with his constituents for the first time in years. Back in the Town early in January he spent all that month with his professional duties, and— in "sensing" the extremely critical situation.

Drayton was in sole command, for the displaced and discomfited Governor was in the harbor on the *Tamar,* conspiring with up countrymen and occasionally making a futile gesture of defiance at his late subjects. No royal troops were in sight and the two small royal vessels of war kept respectful distance. The only armed conflict was in the up country and that became steadily worse. The ousted Governor conspired with the Indians. To check this Drayton went out to meet the Cherokees and signed a treaty of peace with them in which he promised powder. He did try to deliver the powder, but too hastily and too carelessly, with the result that it was seized by the Royalists. Whereupon the Cherokees went over to the King.

When that happened Rutledge acted. It was on February 7. He presented to the Provincial Congress the resolution from the Continental Congress, suggesting "the establishment of a more orderly government" and "the adoption of a written constitution." He asked for the appointment of a committee to consider these suggestions.

Drayton, whose intelligence was, in many ways, of the first order, sensed something of the implications of the move, for the ground was shaking under his feet. The Rutledge motion carried at once and the President was obliged to appoint the committee. He named John Rutledge as a member only. In Philadelphia Mr. Rutledge might have been chairman of such a committee, but not in Charles Town, where the appointment depended on Drayton.

After three days the committee reported that it advised the "preparation of a written constitution."

The Congress was in an uproar at once. The majority still hoped and expected eventual reconciliation with the Crown. They looked upon themselves as English Whigs conducting a political movement within the empire, as had Hampden and Pym before them. Knowing this, and knowing that the former triumvir knew it and approved, Drayton could not fathom Rutledge's purpose. He felt there was a menace against his personal sway, but it was so subtle he did not know how to meet it, much less attack it; so he took no open stand.

Gadsden brought forth his extreme program which was no secret. In an hour's harangue he declared passionately for independence. John Rutledge replied, with unexpected vehemence, in a speech "of less than three minutes." He said that he abhorred the idea of complete independence from Great Britain. A violent wave of pent-up feeling was exhibited and he was cheered. Excitedly Rutledge cried, "I stand ready to ride post, by day and by night, to Philadelphia to assist in re-uniting Great Britain and America."

As he sat down the tides of communal feeling seemed to engulf him. He knew his people; he had accurately voiced their political opinion.

A motion to appoint a committee to prepare a written constitution was carried *viva voce*. President Drayton glanced over the room, and "without apparently seeing Mr. Rutledge" appeared about to name the members of the committee. Yet, before he could speak, the member from Christ Church moved that "in view of the importance of the exercise of a democratic process the selection be by the general committee, and by secret ballot."

Did Drayton's knowledge of history recall to him that in Venice the Doge, and in Rome the Pope, were so chosen; that a secret ballot taken in public body was the time-honored method of forestalling both personal power and intrigue? He had no coadjutor on the floor to assist him and he saw no way to avoid putting the motion at once. He did so and it was carried. Ballots were prepared.

By secret ballot the Provincial Congress chose John Rutledge to head a committee to draft a written constitution, with ten others to assist. Every man on the committee, except Gadsden, was accustomed to accepting the leadership of Rutledge, and even Gadsden instinctively leaned on him for legal advice. Three of the juniors—Pinckney, Middleton, and Lynch—were under specific instructions from their fathers to follow Rutledge.

The first draft was prepared quickly and it was then apparent for the first time that Rutledge contemplated establishing a republic on the soil of South Carolina. Henry Laurens, faced with signing on the dotted line, balked. Rawlins Lowndes and Thomas Bee refused to attend meetings, declaring they would have nothing to do with a step apparently so irrevocable, though the language of the proposed instrument was mild.

For six weeks the constitutional committee was unable to agree. All that time Rutledge carried on softly, revising and rewriting, persuading, pacifying, sifting opinion, never giving up his ultimate aim, nor his determination to secure unanimity. By the middle of March he almost despaired.

On March 21 fate played into his hands, when a vessel from

Savannah brought news of the Act of Parliament of December 21, 1775, declaring the colonies to be in a state of rebellion and authorizing seizure of the vessels and property of the colonials. Rutledge rewrote his prologue, incorporating a rehearsal of this arbitrary and violent parliamentary act. The committee unanimously approved and it was submitted March 24. It contained about three thousand words.

The South Carolina Constitution, as prepared by John Rutledge, set up the first independent legally defined government in America, and contained the embryo of the Constitution of the United States written eleven and a half years later. The essential features were:

The General Assembly, to be chosen biennially, was to be the base of all government and to come direct from the people.

The General Assembly was to choose out of its own body a Legislative Council.

These two bodies, Assembly and Council, jointly should choose a President, a Vice-President, and a Chief Justice.

The President was to be both Chief Executive and Commander-in-Chief of all military forces.

All money bills must originate in the Assembly, though the President would hold the veto power.

These five were the chief provisions. The most fundamental and revolutionary was that defining the powers of the President, for it is to this germ that can be traced the historic potency of the American presidency. No changes were made otherwise in the laws of the colony. There was a provision that if the Congress, as then existing, the Committee on Public Safety, adopted the Constitution it should go into immediate effect, but that to have final force it must be ratified by the people at the next election.

Debate on the Constitution lasted for two days. The chief objection was that it extinguished all authority under the British Crown. John Rutledge replied, "This instrument is only a temporary one. This Constitution will continue only until an accommodation of the unhappy differences between Great Britain and America can be obtained."

These sugared words won the moderates, who held the balance

of power, and the Constitution of the Republic of South Carolina was adopted.

Could they believe that if an independent government was once established the people would ever consent to give it up? Incredible though this seems from a distance, it was clear then, as well as later, that John Rutledge and a majority of his associates believed the "independence" would be temporary. They considered this written constitutional expression only an outward and visible recognition of a practical sovereignty which already they had achieved in fact. From that point of view it seems no more violent than the shedding by a chrysalis of its cocoon.

The Congress had demoted itself to an Assembly. Its first official act was to elect a President. Drayton, from the chair, asked for nominations. Foreseeing oratory, Henry Laurens moved that there be no nominations, but that they proceed at once to a secret ballot, and that the President and the Vice-President be selected on the same ballot. The motion carried.

On the first ballot John Rutledge led with thirty-eight votes; then came Henry Laurens with thirty-two, William Henry Drayton with thirty-one, and seventeen others scattered. For Vice-President 158 out of 162 votes were cast for Rutledge. The delegates, in secret ballot, differed widely in choosing an associate for the power and honor of the high place, but they agreed almost unanimously in wanting John Rutledge to stand close by whoever might be chosen.

On the second ballot Rutledge was elected President of the Republic of South Carolina by 153 out of 162 votes. Then the Assembly made it unanimous.

Thus the successor of George III in America arrived in the colonies. This was the first legislative act of sovereignty achieved on the soil of the new world: Charles Town, March 26, 1776, one hundred days before the signing of the Declaration of Independence at Philadelphia.

In his first address to the Assembly President Rutledge, after a formal acceptance, said, "I have always thought every man's best service to be due his *country,* and in her cause every moment of my time shall be devoted. I assure myself of the support and assistance of every good man in the *colony;* and my most fervent prayer to the Omnipotent ruler of the Universe is, that under *His Gracious Providence,* the liberties of America may be forever preserved."

He spoke, almost casually, of his "country" and of the "colony." He did not mention the "republic" or the "union." The only real change from a fifteen-year habit was in obeisance, which was no longer to His Gracious Majesty, but to His Gracious Providence. The language of his address seems naïve and it might be astounding if taken apart from the fact that all of the members of the Assembly believed that nothing had happened beyond accepting the "suggestion" of the Continental Congress, in "establishing a more orderly government." How that suggestion had come about did not appear. In fact, no one in Charles Town but the President of the Republic knew, for the records in Philadelphia were not then available in South Carolina.

Nothing less than the prestige of John Rutledge could have achieved this Republic with its written Constitution, accepted alike by Whig and Tory. Since his first appearance as an attorney Rutledge had been establishing confidence with the people. Over and over again he had stepped in front of them, spying out the new land, breaking ground, inventing new legal and governmental techniques, holding them secure to all their essential realities, and yet lifting them safely over the obstructions which troubled them. So far he had not failed. That he had created this "republic," a thing so abhorrent to many of them, so elusive even to those who had spoken in its favor, and had securely integrated it with an approved written statute, seemed to them no miracle. It was only another of John Rutledge's devices and it would see them through. If that was political magic then it was based securely on fifteen years of practical legerdemain.

William Henry Drayton did not record his thoughts or feelings during the period of the creation of the Republic. He must have been startled as the structure was erected before his eyes. He saw the Congress disappear and the Assembly rise in its place, composed of the very same men, without new elections. And there, in place of President Drayton, with his unlimited dictatorial powers, was President Rutledge, with specifically stated powers, for a definite period, and free, during that period, from any such clandestine electioneering as that which had replaced the circumspect Henry Laurens with the flamboyant Drayton. The whole procedure was so astonishingly legal, so well implemented with parliamentary and juridical tradition, that Drayton, barrister that he was, found nothing to say in opposition. The Assembly consoled him by electing him Chief Justice, which was the third prize, Henry Laurens having been chosen as Vice-President.

The first act of the Assembly, after electing officers, was to set the salary of the President at nine thousand pounds annually, based on the professional income of John Rutledge for that year. South Carolina placed its retention of legal counsel on a professional basis.

There was a difference, however. As an attorney Rutledge could and did insist that his clients pay in hard money, which meant Spanish milled dollars, pistoles, English spade guineas, French Louis d'or, or Portuguese escudos; all gold or silver. As President of the Republic he took his pay in script, and soon this was worth no more than what someone could be wheedled or forced into accepting for it.

Chief Justice Drayton relieved his feelings in his first addresss to the grand jury in which he declared "all men are created free and equal." President Rutledge drily objected to the unlimited breadth of the assertion, noting that it would be better to say that all men should have equal opportunity and equal legal protection. Nevertheless, he sent a copy of the address to President Hancock of the Continental Congress, and Hancock referred it to John Rutledge's successor in the Committee on Constitutional Government, Thomas Jefferson who with Benjamin Franklin and John Adams, was preparing a new declaration for consideration by the national Congress.

Rutledge had caused the powder to be sent to Boston in the same spirit in which he sent the "free and equal" phrase to Jefferson. Due to the caution and precision of his nature, which always avoided violence, if possible, he personally would not have used either, but the peril of the times indicated the need of explosives and he was willing that others have access to them.

As he prepared to go north in May to attend the Congress in Philadelphia, Edward asked John what should be done if a declaration of independence should be proposed, for it was known a strong minority was agitating for one. John reminded Edward that the Republic was only temporary, and that the belief of the Assembly was that "eventually an accommodation would be arranged with Great Britain." Edward assured John that he and his three associates were agreed in opposition to any open declaration, though each had been identified with the radical element in Charles Town. John's last words to Edward were, "In any event, do not break the union."

Rutledge was carrying on as President of the Republic of South Carolina just as he had carried on as a triumvir of Charles Town, only now he did it in the open. At last he had statutory warrant for the power he exercised.

During this period the Patriot King in London announced that "he would espouse no party but would govern like the common father of all his people." In practice, however, he identified himself with the Tories and attacked the Whigs with partisan violence.

In Charles Town, without announcement, John Rutledge actually did govern "like the common father of all the people." Though the Whigs claimed him and he was often on their side, the Tories flocked to him too.

Surveying the community, as President, he found that about half the people had no political opinions; they preferred to let things go along. If there must be a local ruler this group preferred Rutledge, but they were inarticulate and gave no reasons. They liked his scorn of titles, yet he seemed superior to them and they also liked that. They liked the legend that had grown up about him; they liked his conservatism and at the same time his youth and forcefulness. For them he was the symbol of Charles Town as they wished to see it.

The active ten per cent of Royalists were for him because he had never spoken against the King.

The moderates, with about thirty per cent of the voters, held the balance of political power and to this class Rutledge himself belonged by breeding and instinct. From this group always had come the initiative and effective leadership; their apostle was the new President.

Thus, while ninety per cent of the population was stoutly behind him, Rutledge did not oppose or neglect the remaining ten per cent who were the extreme radicals, those who wanted revolution. He courteously conferred with Chief Justice Drayton and frequently sought out Gadsden who was now a captain of the artillery. Each dined, on occasion, at his home.

However, the President's absorbing duty now was not political leadership, but the exercise of the executive function, and especially of that phase of it which he had insisted should be specified in the Constitution. He was Commander-in-Chief of *all* military forces. He must make ready for war.

There was no reliable census. An estimate made by Vice-President Laurens in a letter to the French Minister said that the population of South Carolina in 1775 was about sixty thousand whites and eighty thousand slaves. The highest estimate is a total of 175,000, of which about 105,000 were Negro slaves. Neither was there a reliable census in the other twelve colonies, but the total population of the colonies in the union is believed to have been about three million. It is important to bear in mind the ratio of these figures. They show that South Carolina, under Rutledge, had no more than five or six per cent of the total population of the American colonies, and that the *whites* of South Carolina composed approximately *two and one half per cent* of the total population of the colonies.

The highest potential fighting man-power of the Republic was not above seventy-five hundred men, many of these, especially in the interior, unwilling to join an army.

Working night and day for six weeks, Rutledge was able to marshal within a few miles of Granville's Bastion about seven hundred Charles Town militia, 1950 South Carolina regulars, 1972 country militia; a total of 4622 effectives from the Republic. There were also five hundred Virginians and fourteen hundred North Carolinians.

Here was a Republic with an army of 6522 men, a navy of three half-armed sloops; a Republic without negotiable money; captained by a provincial lawyer; isolated from the northern colonies by swamps and poorly charted seas. It was an obscure speck of civilization clinging to the flank of a continental wilderness, thrown into the pit against the chief power of the day; the Empire which had conquered Spain and Holland and France!

It is not surprising that John Rutledge, from the moment he held out his hand to John Adams in Philadelphia, clung tenaciously to the idea of union with the other colonies. That South Carolina was to give infinitely more than she ever received apparently never occurred to him. Nor was he prompted by any mystical dream of forming a future union. Self-preservation was motive enough. He felt it was obvious—at least it was obvious to him—that the only possible chance that South Carolina had of coming successfully through the approaching ordeal would be with the support of all the colonies.

In Philadelphia, after the selection of Washington as Commander-in-Chief and before he departed for Boston, Rutledge had participated in three conferences, which had been attended by Washington, Hancock, Franklin, Sullivan, and Sam Adams, with various others, who were the actual leaders of Congress.

In these meetings the strategy of the coming war had been evolved. It was articulated in action by Washington only after it had been expressed in words by others, particularly by Sam Adams and John Rutledge. Such was the Virginian's habit.

This strategy was simple and obvious, and Washington never altered it. All agreed the only likely way to baffle the great military power of Britain would be to compel her to scatter her strength along the vast coast and over the tremendous wooded interior, thus exhausting her and leaving her susceptible to surprise attack. They agreed the only hope lay in wearing down the military forces and in worrying the old country.

Rutledge wrote now to Washington that it seemed likely Charles Town would be attacked, and therefore he asked to have the best military commander available detached for service in South Carolina. At the same time he wrote to the Continental Congress, urging the immediate dispatch of the regiments and artillery promised.

Congress was dilatory, but Washington was prompt. He detached General Charles Lee (no relation to the Virginia Lees) from his forces and sent him to Charles Town. The Commander-in-Chief was giving his best to Rutledge, for he had written about Lee, "He is the first officer, in military knowledge and experience, we have in the whole army. I congratulate my countrymen upon his appointment."

Lee was thin, wiry, and indefatigable. Years before he had been a Lieutenant Colonel in the British army, but he was a soldier of fortune. At various times, he served with the Turks, commanded Cossacks, fought in Portugal, was aide-de-camp to the King of Poland, had assisted Frederick the Great, and came to America as its first important acquisition of foreign military talent. He had impressed the members of Congress who had given him not only his rank with pay, but also a present of a Virginia plantation. Washington called him Chief of Staff and so he was during 1776. The Commander-in-Chief spent hours in conference with him and was deeply impressed by his military advice which was, in many respects, sound. It would take a year more and the loss of the Battle of Monmouth with its resultant court-martial to show Washington what Lee really was, "a fuss-budget, a marplot, and the greatest bit of military nonsense that ever plagued a loyal army."

This opinion Rutledge formed independently in a few days, in spite of the prestige accorded Lee by the appointment of the Congress and the endorsement of Washington.

In their initial Charles Town conference, however, Lee conveyed invaluable information to Rutledge. The principal British force in North America, under Lord Howe, had withdrawn by ships from Boston ostensibly for Nova Scotia but in reality for New York whither Washington was moving overland with his army. Even then the two forces might be engaged. Lee had just come from New York which he had surveyed and in part prepared for defense by Washington. Howe had sent his ablest officer, Sir Henry Clinton, who was on his way South, to an unknown destination. Lee had seen Clinton at New York in May.

Lee revealed secret information to the effect that a fleet had been fitted out in England larger than that which invested Boston and able to transport more fighting men. There were to be thirty or fifty, maybe a hundred ships, mostly war vessels, carrying the largest and best guns then made and an army of twenty-five thousand men.

What Lee did not know, nor Rutledge either, was that the British fleet, under command of Commodore Sir Peter Parker, then considered one of the ablest sea officers in the service of the empire, had failed to pick up in Ireland all of its assigned army complement for transport. Crossed orders had sent two regiments elsewhere. Moreover, on the way across the Atlantic storms broke up the fleet's formation. Arriving on the American side Sir Peter Parker had been able to join up with no more than a third of the contemplated force. However, he was still confident that his ships and men would be sufficient. He was even more sure of this after he was joined by Clinton.

Parker's first objective was Norfolk and he lay off the Virginia Capes, waiting for reports from scouts, before deciding just where he should attack.

Rutledge was positive that Charles Town would be the final chief objective. Lee agreed. That would be any competent leader's obvious strategy—to attack the weakest military center and roll up the flank.

Caution, however, guided Rutledge in his initial steps and these were shrewdly devised to achieve a dual purpose: to utilize Lee's prestige, but to retain for himself actual military control. This control he would exert only in extremity.

Outwardly the President and the distinguished Major General seemed as one. Rutledge issued a proclamation, which he had posted on the walls of the Bastion and at The Corner, notifying the "citizens" that "the President placed in the esteemed Chief-of-Staff of General George Washington, Major General Charles Lee of the Continental Army, the support of all the armed forces of the Republic of South Carolina."

This seemed definitive. It satisfied everyone, including General Lee. The *Gazette* printed a long piece about his brilliant career, inferring that he had been responsible for the victories of Frederick the Great and that he graciously had consented to make a detour to South Carolina before re-joining General Washington and showing him how to conquer Lord Howe.

This news was a much needed tonic among a people depressed by ugly rumors that they were about to be wiped out by the combined British army and navy.

Lee heightened this favorable public impression by the intense and picturesque manner of his military activity. He set the troops at work, digging more trenches, erecting fleches, emplacing guns that existed as yet only in vivid hopes. He was up before dawn, was about long after dark, and he was democratic. He seized the spade from a slow worker and showed him how to dig; he drilled backward country militia and dazzled them with the smart display of a knowledge of the manual of arms; he even personally kicked a sluggard, and swore with open abandon, sparkling with odd obscenities which were novel to all and must, they thought, have come straight from London. He delighted the officers with whom he hobnobbed by his amazing capacity for liquor.

In short order General Lee became the idol of Charles Town. The entire community began to consider the threatened danger more calmly.

Then the British fleet appeared, apparently in good order, off the northern end of Charles Town's Long Island, later the Isle of Palms, about twenty miles from the harbor. Any previous doubts of its ultimate destination were now resolved. It dropped anchors and, with the leisurely military pace of the eighteenth century, proceeded to survey the prospect and anticipate the pleasure of devouring its prey. There seemed to be no chance that Charles Town, that picturesque, isolated metropolis of the southern seaboard, could run away.

Canoes slipped in and out among the anchored visitors, peddling vegetables and fruit, and bringing back fairly accurate reports. It was the largest fleet of war vessels, by far, that anyone in Charles Town, except possibly General Lee, had ever seen: more than fifty in all, including two first-class ships of the line, with fifty guns each, five frigates, and seven armed sloops. There were also transports and supply ships, and on these were above thirty-five hundred British regulars, professional drilled "lobster backs" straight from Whitehall, the most reliable troops of the empire, in personal command of Sir Henry Clinton who had with him Lord Cornwallis and General Vaughn. In addition to the regulars there were about a thousand marines and about twenty-five hundred sailors—seven thousand in all. Sir Peter Parker held sea command as Commodore of the Fleet.

On the second ship of the line, under protection of its fifty guns, was the Governor, Lord William Campbell. He was to be brought back to the state house and installed again in government as soon as the upstart President and the illegal Assembly should be cleaned out.

However, it took this force more than two weeks to traverse twenty miles, and the only physical obstacle was a sand bar which was readily negotiable at high tide.

The British moved slowly because they wanted to be quite sure there would be no mistakes this time. Both Clinton and Cornwallis had been present in Boston during the Battles of Lexington and Bunker Hill. They were high-ranking officers in the regular British military establishment and they were critical of Lord Howe, who had commanded so ignominiously in Massachusetts. That ignominy might be explained, they believed, by the fact that Lord Howe was illegitimate, though a cousin of the King, and because he had allied himself politically with the Whigs. It was professionally disgraceful for a soldier to dabble in politics. He had also spent the time he should have been with his troops in dallying with the fascinating Mrs. Loring.

Clinton and Cornwallis and Parker now were on their own and they intended to show how real soldiers and sailors, without any connections at court, should perform. They would have no mistresses in camp and no political sympathy with the rebels. This was to be solely a military exploit executed with dazzling certainty and success in the best British tradition. Their rallying cry among themselves was, "No more Bunker Hills!"

The shore-line approaches to Charles Town are marshy, but Clinton discovered that by landing at the far or seaward end of Long Island he could march on good land right up to within a mile of the Battery, except for the narrow strait separating Long and Sullivan Islands, and this, so his scouts reported, ordinarily held water only eighteen inches deep. Troops could easily ford it. Once across the strait they could march to within shooting distance of the Town, and a pontoon bridge could easily be thrown from Sullivan Island to the mainland.

Nearly half the population of the Town was made up of spies and these reported that the rebels had no more than eight or ten thousand pounds of powder and only about seventy big guns, widely separated. The British had over fifty thousand pounds of powder and two hundred seventy big guns. Naturally, they considered there could be no comparison between their gun-pointers—the carefully selected sharpshooters of the British navy—and the hastily impressed provincial pointers. The British gunners had practiced with armament, both in maneuvers and in actual battle, for years; the South Carolinians never had had occasion to fire big guns, except in rare salutes.

The prospective operation seemed comparatively simple under the protection of such a powerful fleet as Sir Peter Parker's. The question at last was one only of tactics: where should they strike first?

Decision on this tactical point held them up for days. It could not be reached solely from a military viewpoint. The ultimate object being political they must choose a conspicuous place in which to administer a paralyzing blow to these insolent colonials. The defeat must be ignominious, prompt, and in full sight of all.

Therefore, into conference with Sir Henry and Sir Peter came Lord William Campbell, now greatly emboldened by such substantial backing. If he had only had ships of the line and lobster backs from Whitehall behind him long before this! At last here was his chance to avenge, not only his own shame, but also the humiliations of his predecessors.

Sir Henry and Sir Peter heard, at first hand, how for more than fifteen years their viceroys had been rendered ridiculous by this "nest of scheming adventurers" in Charles Town. Up North in Boston there had been only rabble, but down here were "some gentlemen," only a little group; it would be easy to take its leaders.

Since the time of Boone these "adventurers" had treated royal governors "like scum." Lord William bitterly asserted that they had "shoved them around brazenly. Moreover, they were not open and boastful about it like the Massachusetts low-lives, but held their heads up and were so clever that not a Governor in the last four could do a thing in opposition. It all centered in that mealy-mouthed ring-leader, Rutledge, who had never uttered a word one could quote as being treason, and yet—now they called him President; He is so smooth that once he wrote a document—back in Stamp Tax time— that fooled the King Himself, God Bless His Gracious Majesty!"

Let Lord William get his fingers on Rutledge, and with proper British soldiers at hand to exert the royal will! For the past year the crowds had turned to look at this man as he passed in the streets as if *he* were himself a *king!* Had they looked that way at Lord William Campbell, properly alter ego of George III? No. The crowds had sneered at Lord William—behind his back, of course, but he knew it— "and only because Rutledge walked the same street."

There was a girl named Sally Izard, who lived only three doors from Rutledge. Lord William had married her, with fifty thousand pounds, but did that make any difference? "Neither her dot" nor his title "received the respect shown Rutledge, who has no real money and a poor wife—why, the man is but a barrister, a professional man; that is all!" Yet the people called his house the "palace" and the Governor's merely a "residence."

Thus Sir Henry and Sir Peter could readily see how this "designing, cunning traitor" had woven his spell. Let them put hands on him and Sir William would know what to do. They might, if they wished, accord Charles Lee the honor of shooting, for, after all, he had been a British officer, but—"for Rutledge it would be the rope."

After a most complete survey—political, military, social, personal, and topographical—to say nothing of the opening of many a bottle of Madeira, hock, and port, Sir Henry and Sir Peter, with Lord William's approval, decided that the point for attack which would answer all purposes was the rambling, half-built fort at the western end of Sullivan's Island, just opposite the Town.

The British studied it through glasses—this fort called Sullivan. They could see a platform built on bricks and above this, for about ten feet, walls of rough timber. This almost enclosed, though not quite for it was open at the back, a bastion sufficient to house a thousand men. It mounted twenty-four guns.

The walls that looked out toward the sea did not seem formidable. Parker asked what they were made of and was told palmetto. The South Carolinians had chosen it because it was the most available native timber from near-by swamps.

The fort was still in course of construction. Spies reported that the rebels were loafing on the job, that they were divided in counsel, that the emplacements were only half-manned, and that the whole bastion would never be put in proper condition.

Parker said to Clinton, "I can knock those walls down with one broadside from the *Experiment*." That was his flagship.

So the decision was confirmed. Sullivan was ideal, alike for the purposes of Lord William, Sir Henry, and Sir Peter.

If anyone questioned its military value, let him look at the location, as if in an amphitheatre, wherein all the harbor and all the Town could see plainly what a terrible whipping would be administered by the full force of His Majesty's strong arm!

Eagerly they waited for a clear day. Only on such a day could everyone properly see the terrible visitation of royal vengeance.

2.

Lee's activity became feverish as June wore on. He dashed over the eight-mile shore front repeatedly throughout the day. He kept relays of horses so that he could mount before the troops in a fury of energy and gallop off several miles, say a few words of sharp command, mount a fresh horse, and gallop back.

Rutledge was engaged in getting people out of town, seeing that transport was provided for them to reach the interior safely and that preparations for nursing were properly organized. Yet he kept an ear cocked and an eye open.

The first intimation to the President that his suspicions were justified came when he was told that Lee had ordered a regiment of men to march direct from the Town to Haddrel's Point. This route lay across a swamp in which the muck was waist-deep. Local officers protested, but, without personal examination, Lee insisted and the regiment was promptly mired.

Then Lee suddenly ordered a plank bridge thrown across from the main land to Sullivan's Island and impatiently insisted that one plank, with hand-driven short piles, was sufficient. A few tried the "bridge"; it sagged and they were thrown into the salt water.

Rutledge noted and said nothing. Then he got his third warning. This came when he met his boyhood playmate, William Moultrie, on Broad Street, about to go into Dillon's Tavern for a julep. Moultrie was the Colonel in command of Fort Sullivan and he told the President, without any surprise or resentment, that General Lee had ordered him to evacuate the fort.

This was on June twenty-fourth and the British fleet had been in sight for all of two weeks. It might be on them any day at any hour. No one had the slightest knowledge of how or where the attack would come, for no spies reached the Town from the British high command.

Rutledge, however, realized that the time had come to assert the authority he had held cautiously in reserve. How did he know the British would choose Fort Sullivan for the spot of honor? The answer is speculative. From a military point of view the place of attack was far from obvious. Commodore Parker easily might have led his fleet around Fort Sullivan, out of gunshot reach, and then have landed Clinton's troops safely at any one of several unprotected points, whence the advance on the Town would have been comparatively simple.

Why the British chose the hard way—except that, deceptively, it looked so very easy—has never been clear to technical military critics. Much ink has been spilled in the attempt to prove that the British commanders were stupid and bungling.

Lee said the British would not attack Fort Sullivan, that it was against military common sense. Cornwallis, later, said that that was his opinion, rejected at the time. Most military critics who have reviewed the situation agree that, professionally, Sir Peter and Sir Henry made a mistake.

Before the course of attack was outlined John Rutledge, alone, sensed what would happen. He arrived at his opinion without special information, or any conference, and it was against the apparent weight of military evidence, and in the face of orders of the former adviser of Frederick the Great and the current Chief of Staff of George Washington.

Rutledge told Moultrie, on the steps of Dillon's, the afternoon of the twenty-fourth, to go back to Fort Sullivan and stay there. This put Moultrie, the simple-minded and dutiful soldier, in a predicament. His superior officer, General Lee, had ordered him away; now his President ordered him to stay. Naturally, he protested, asking, ingenuously, how he could oblige Rutledge. His father, Dr. Moultrie, had been a medical colleague of Dr. Rutledge's. From earliest youth he and the President had been intimate. For a long time it had been "William" and "John" between them, but now it was "Colonel" and "Your Excellency." As they were in a state of war, the Colonel could not help feeling superior—just a little—to any mere civil servant, whatever his position.

Rutledge asked the Colonel to whom he owed allegiance. "To General Lee," said Moultrie. Why? Because—Moultrie hesitated—because the President of the Republic had placed all the troops under command of General Lee. Rutledge asked him how he knew that. Everybody knew it; wasn't it true? Rutledge insisted—*how* did he know it? Moultrie was obliged to admit he had not himself read the proclamation, but had taken it for granted. Then Rutledge asked if he was in the habit of accepting military orders from his superior except personally or in writing. No, said Moultrie and that settled it. Moultrie agreed that Rutledge, who was undoubtedly his Commander-in-Chief, had never personally or in writing ordered him to obey General Lee; he wanted to know what he should do in the future —defy Lee? Rutledge said, "No, obey him in everything, except in leaving Fort Sullivan; do nothing openly to destroy morale."

So Colonel Moultrie returned to Sullivan and took his siesta under the uncompleted bastion where the shade lay toward the west.

The next day Lee had himself taken in a canoe over to Sullivan. There he found Moultrie, sitting in the shade, with a julep in his hand, leisurely bossing the work of gun-mounting. The Colonel rose with difficulty, for he had the gout. He was fat and his paunch had been eased by unbuttoning his tunic, but he saluted. Lee wanted to know why Moultrie had not obeyed orders. The Colonel, remembering instructions, which were to avoid trouble, made excuses about the difficulty of getting boats. Lee made a rapid inspection, swore plentifully, and went off after repeating his orders to "move to the mainland, and leave only a skeleton force for vedette duty."

Lee was greatly annoyed by Moultrie. The General's idea of soldiering was to be excessively "busy" at all times, digging, building, mending, drilling. Moultrie had a different idea. He believed that manual labor was exclusively for "nigras," that a white soldier should hoard his energy and store it up until the enemy appeared and then fight.

On the twenty-seventh an informer whispered to Lee that Rutledge had gone over his head with Moultrie. Lee exploded in a rage and declared that he would seek Rutledge at once, that either the President would resign or he would.

However, Lee never faced it out with Rutledge. Upon reflection, evidently, he realized his insecurity. The South Carolina militia, of which Moultrie was an officer, had not been taken into the Continental military establishment and Rutledge was their constitutional Commander-in-Chief. The proclamation he had issued was not, in fact, officially binding on any of the militia. Practically, it had been done for political effect. Lee was too well informed and too shrewd to take Rutledge to task personally.

However, Lee was determined to get Moultrie on the mainland. Lee has been, repeatedly, accused of treason and branded as "the man who double crossed both the land of his birth and of his adoption." This is probably unwarranted. He was merely a petty man. Now he wanted his own way, and, to get it, he began to sabotage.

That evening, Lee conferred with Colonel Nash of the North Carolina militia and told him he wanted him to go the next day to Fort Sullivan and relieve Colonel Moultrie, and then to carry out the neglected orders of removing the garrison and dismounting the guns in the fort. He told Nash to come to him early the next morning and get written orders.

The North Carolina troops had been taken into the Continental Army, provisionally, and were under Lee's personal command. They would not obey the President of South Carolina. Moreover, Lee knew of the jealousy and antagonism that underlay most contacts between North and South Carolinians. He counted on this to cement his purpose.

As it was, that night of the twenty-seventh, as well as the next day, Fort Sullivan was less than half garrisoned. It might have held a thousand men; it actually housed, including officers, 435. It should have had at least twenty thousand pounds of powder; it actually had less than five thousand.

Lee was talking freely to Nash and to others, ridiculing Moultrie as "a half-baked country militiaman." He said loudly that the platform at Sullivan was "a slaughter pen" and that if the British ever started in on the fort they "would knock it about Moultrie's ears in half an hour."

This was repeated, on the evening of the twenty-seventh, to Moultrie by a company officer who had heard it in the Town that day. Moultrie, who fraternized with everyone including his subordinates, remarked, casually, "If that happens it will not be so bad. Then they will probably try to come at us pussonly and we can pick 'em off from under the ruins."

"I was never uneasy," Moultrie said, later, in his memoirs, "because I never imagined the enemy could force me to retreat. I always considered myself able to defend the post." That describes fully his military equipment. He did not believe anybody could lick him—certainly not the British navy, even if reinforced by the British army.

The President, too, had his informers and he heard late on the twenty-seventh, about the order to the North Carolina colonel. He wrote a note at once to Colonel Moultrie and sent it over to Sullivan's by special messenger. The commandant received it before midnight.

"To Colonel William Moultrie, in chief command of Fort Sullivan, Sir: General Lee still wishes you to evacuate the fort. You will not, without order from me. I would sooner cut off my hand than write one. J. Rutledge."

At dawn of the twenty-eighth Colonel Nash stirred himself briskly and before eight o'clock called on General Lee who was reading a report from the lookout at Granville's Bastion. This report altered the situation. General Lee told Colonel Nash to wait until another time for instructions. The twenty-eighth did not seem a propitious day to change commands.

It was a bright day, one of the longest of the year, in the first week of summer. There was a brisk breeze that filled the harbor with whitecaps, but the sky was clear. It was a great day for shooting; sights could be accurately leveled.

What changed Lee's plans was the sight of about fifty vessels, standing in past Long Island and approaching Sullivan's. The breeze favored them and they were spanking rapidly. By the time they reached the western head of Long Island more than half had slipped out and had dropped anchors. The remainder, the biggest, came on.

The drums and the Scotch bagpipes could be heard, piping to quarters. From the second floor of the Exchange, on the waterfront at the foot of Broad Street, President Rutledge could see, through his spyglass, the officers on the quarter-decks, in full-dress uniform, with gold epaulettes, red sashes, and huge tricorn hats with trailing black ostrich plumes. On the upper gun-decks he could see the gunners, swabbing the cannon, loading and priming. They were naked to the waist. The British fleet was coming in for battle.

Where would it strike? Lee watched from the foot of Granville's Bastion. Rutledge remained on the second floor of the Exchange for more than four hours. For days many who could leave Charles Town had been fleeing to the interior. Beginning with early dawn of the twenty-eighth still more escaped. Yet the waterfront was crowded. Thousands were huddled along the wharves and on the warehouses and on the tops of high buildings. As the day wore on and it became apparent that the Town was not to be shelled at once the spectators increased. Before nightfall, it was said, fully eight thousand persons, half soldiers, witnessed the battle.

Sir Henry and Sir Peter had been right in one forecast: a large audience was assembled and it had an excellent view.

Leading the fleet was a small ship, the *Thunder,* of a few hundred tons' burden. It was a bomb-thrower. About a quarter past ten the *Thunder* began tossing shells into Fort Sullivan.

A few minutes later the fort replied with four shots, at intervals, and dropped at varying distances, without effect. The *Thunder* persisted with regular and well-placed shots, all of which fell inside the works. From within the fort came no further reply.

Four random shots seemed the limit of resistance.

The *Experiment,* the flagship, flew a signal to her mizzen and the two frigates, the *Actaeon* and the *Solebay,* turned hard aport and headed in toward the fort. They were maneuvered neatly up within about fifty fathoms of the palmetto walls. Then the anchors rattled over the sides and the chains could be heard slipping through the hawser holes. As soon as the anchors "took" in the clay bottom of the bay half-nude sailors slipped over the side and attached springs on the cables. This was to pick up the slack as the vessels rode with the swell, and to hold them as near taut as possible, so as to give the gunners an emplacement nearly as sound as one on land.

The *Actaeon* and the *Solebay* had twenty-eight guns each, and each had two decks, but only half the guns could be turned on the fort. That made only twenty-eight effectives, half twelve pounders, half eighteen pounders.

Sir Peter decided that was not enough. So he moved in himself with the *Experiment,* and ordered the *Bristol,* the sister ship of the line, to do the same beyond the *Solebay,* and near the Town. This would add forty-eight more guns for the bombardment, half twenty-four pounders and half eighteen pounders, the heaviest armament then afloat.

It was now almost noon. There was a ghastly silence punctuated at intervals by the bombs, which, for an hour and a half, the *Thunder* had been tossing two a minute into the seemingly doomed fort.

Everyone could see what Sir Peter intended. He was taking no chances. He was going to give the fort everything he had—broadside after broadside. He would try literally to blow it out of the water.

Except for the first four futile shots the fort had been silent.

Then—just before noon—a two-pounder barked the signal for the first broadside. Seventy-two big guns were fired simultaneously at the log escarpment. As soon as the gunners could reload there was a second broadside. Then another.

Meanwhile, those on shore received a little hope. The fort was responding, though with only four guns. They went off at intervals, with a minute or more between.

Then Rutledge, watching through his spyglass, noted they were not the same guns. It would be four from one end of the fort; then four from the middle; then four from another segment; but always four.

Much more astonishing than the paucity of fire from the fort was the fact that the broadsides from the four warships did not "knock the walls down over Moultrie's ears."

Far from it. With several thousand shells poured in on the palmettos from a very close range the walls still stood. They sagged in two places, along the top, and there was one fair-sized hole, to be sure, but the palmettos did not give. No one knew until then that this wood absorbs heavy shot as blotters absorb ink. It is the reason why, since then, South Carolina has been called the Palmetto State.

The battle continued, uninterrupted, in that way, for about three hours—from twelve to three—before anyone at a distance began to notice things in the fleet—unexpected curiosities—and much more startling than those monotonous ill-spaced shots and the invulnerability of the palmetto.

3.

Moultrie made his dispositions in the morning as he saw the fleet coming in. His powder and shot were limited and he divided them up equally among the guns. The gun crews were placed close around the breeches and a first and second relief for each man was indicated—just in case—and these were separated on opposite sides of the fort. Then he gave out some bad news for the gun-pointers who were the seeded marksmen of the regiment. They were to ready the guns; that was all.

Twenty crews were to be at work constantly, readying the guns, but there were to be only four pointers. No one else was to point or fire unless one of these was incapacitated.

The four gun-pointers were Colonel Moultrie, Lieutenant Colonel Isaac Motte, Major Francis Marion, and Captain Daniel Hörry; four commissioned Frenchmen, the high-ranking officers. The trained pointers grumbled among themselves. Some claimed they were as good as Moultrie, Motte, and Hörry, each of whose records on the range was between .8 and .9. No one claimed to be as good as Francis Marion, a seemingly under-nourished planter from the woods, with an eye like a hawk. He was always conceded to be the best marksman in the Carolinas. It was said that he never in his life missed a shot.

As the fleet approached, the four passed along the line, "tendering" the guns, feeling with their hands in the breech blocks, weighing each parcel of powder cautiously, hefting each shell, helping ram the first ones into place, seeing to it the swabs were watered and waiting, and the fuses fresh. The Colonel did not seem to think that this sort of manual labor was a degradation.

When the *Thunder* tossed in the first shells and it thus became certain that Sullivan was to receive the conspicuous honor of attack, Moultrie ordered a response, from each of the four, "Just to feel for range."

Then the Colonel peremptorily ordered everyone to lie low. "Don't make a peep!"

When the *Solebay* and the *Actaeon* headed in and dropped anchors no farther off than the length of a city block suppressed glee pervaded the fort. This seemed incredible. Yet there was the enemy—right under the guns, and hooked in the mud.

Moultrie stoutly shook his head and ordered all to wait. He could see the *Experiment*, the fifty-gun ship, that old monster of the line, magnificent symbol of the might of Britain, hesitating. If he fired at the *Solebay* or the *Actaeon* she might be frightened off. In another half hour the *Experiment*, also, headed in, and then—Moultrie's cup of joy ran over—there was the *Bristol*, the second great ship of the line—the other fifty-gunner—going to place herself beyond the *Solebay* and yet in similar range.

The *Solebay* and the *Actaeon* fired first, and still Moultrie would permit no response, for the *Bristol* was not yet anchored and the *Experiment* was hardly in place. He wanted them all there, ringed around him, and *anchored*.

And so they were before twelve o'clock.

After the first broadside from the fleet Moultrie gave the word and the four pointers began their day's work. They fired singly but the effect was in platoons of four. And they passed from segment to segment as rapidly as possible. Four shots against seventy—four against a second seventy—repeated, over and over.

The loss in the fort was trifling. In all ten men were killed and twenty-two wounded. No pointer was injured.

In the British fleet it was different. "On the Bristol her scuppers ran with blood; her quarter-deck was twice swept of every man but her commander, who had his arm torn off and died a week later. . . . "On the flagship, the Experiment, the loss was worse, in all fifty-seven killed and thirty wounded, among them the Captain, who later died from his wounds, and the Commodore, Sir Peter Parker, who was twice wounded. The Solebay's guns were silenced and she was forced out of action. The Actaeon tried to get away and was nearly grounded. Half her crew was lost."

The chief casualty was the Governor, Lord William Campbell, who had been given command of the lower gun deck of the *Bristol* as "a signal mark of honor," and who died later of wounds received in the battle.

Moultrie had received an order from Lee, in the morning, to spike his guns and evacuate when the ammunition should be exhausted. By three o'clock his powder was nearly gone. He hastened a messenger to shore for more and ordered the pointers to fire only at ten-minute intervals. He felt that he was still under orders to Lee. The messenger found Rutledge who answered promptly with a barrel and a note scrawled in pencil, saying, "I send you 500 pounds of powder . . . you know our collection is not great . . . honor and victory, my good Sir, to you and your worthy countrymen with you. J. R. P. S. Do not make too free with your cannon. Cool and do mischief."

This arrived about four o'clock, as the *Experiment* began to list, and it was apparent Sir Peter was trying to get her out of the line of fire.

Just before five o'clock Lee arrived, by canoe, at Fort Sullivan, made a hurried inspection, and said, "You are doing very well. You may remain here, Colonel."

Moultrie saluted and replied, "Thank you, sir."

Meanwhile Clinton was unable to carry out his plans and make the passage between the islands because of an excessively high tide.

The next morning the fleet could be seen standing out to sea. All of Clinton's troops were aboard, with the wounded Commodore and the dying Governor.

That afternoon Rutledge sent fifteen hundred pounds of powder to the fort, with another note, saying, "If any of those gentry revisit you, you will not need any caution to spare your powder." He also sent a hogshead of rum from his own cellar.

Lee made a lengthy report to Washington in about four thousand words, with no mention of Rutledge. He praised Moultrie and Thomson. On the basis of this report, a few weeks later, the Continental Congress voted special thanks to Lee, Moultrie, and Thomson.

In the War of the Revolution there were three decisive battles wherein actual contest resulted in both immediate moral and military victory—and only three. They were Charles Town, Saratoga, and King's Mountain. Charles Town was the first.

Sir Peter and Sir Henry kept faith, if only ironically, with their secret rallying cry of "No more Bunker Hills." For, though Bunker Hill was for the Americans a moral victory, it was also a military defeat; when they were out of powder they slipped away and left the field to the British to whom the assault became a technical if somewhat tarnished victory. At Fort Sullivan, on the other hand, when the Americans were out of powder they remained, and the British ran away—and stayed away for three years. It was the news of Charles Town, received as the Continental Army was evacuating New York, which, as Washington testified, kept his army in courage during the monotonous series of disasters which befell it during the next year.

The day Sir Peter anchored the *Bristol* and the *Experiment* off-side Fort Sullivan—June twenty eighth—Thomas Jefferson brought before Congress in Philadelphia the revised copy of his Declaration. Benjamin Franklin had edited it finally the night before. When it was read, it stirred up such intense feelings that it was laid on the table for two days.

On July first the Declaration was brought again before the house, and an informal canvass showed Delaware, New York, and

South Carolina were against it. Two days later word came from Delaware that its Assembly had agreed. At the same time word came from New York that the outlook there was favorable.

This left South Carolina the only doubtful colony. The head of the delegation, John Rutledge, was detained at home and his brother Edward was in his place. Edward was appalled at his responsibility. He asked for two days to consider. This was granted.

Edward got his associates—Lynch, Middleton, and Heyward—together; they were four rich young men who thought alike and were of a type. For several years these four had been talking revolution. Now they were faced with the solemn responsibility of officially binding their colony—"the Republic"—to an irrevocable act.

The four agreed. They were against it. Each had the utmost respect and confidence in John Rutledge, their chief who was detained at home. Each knew that he had consistently declared himself to be against independence. Each knew that even when Rutledge submitted to South Carolina the Constitution which he had written, declaring for an independent Republic, he had told the Assembly it was only temporary and was to be supplanted later with an "accommodation" with Great Britain.

None of them knew, of course, that the week before in Charles Town the Governor had been slain, the English Commodore wounded, two captains killed, a ship sunk, Sir Henry Clinton foiled, and the British army and fleet sent reeling back across the ocean by the temporary government under the President.

For two days they consulted and hesitated. However, in John Rutledge's last words to Edward, "Whatever happens do not break the union," they found their solution. If South Carolina failed to agree to the Declaration of Independence, the Union would be broken.

Besides, argued Middleton, had not Jefferson closely followed the spirit of William Henry Drayton's address to the South Carolina Grand Jury, even to copying seven or eight of his phrases, and had not John Rutledge sent that address north to the Congress?

The next afternoon—July 4, 1776—Edward Rutledge announced

on the floor of the Congress that South Carolina would sign the Declaration of Independence. When they were assured that New York would come in later, the vote was ordered and was returned—unanimously.

At almost the very moment that Edward Rutledge addressed Congress, on the afternoon of July fourth, a different scene was being enacted in Fort Sullivan in Charles Town harbor. In the ruins of the palmetto fort on that first Fourth of July President John Rutledge was addressing the survivors of the battle six days before. He thanked Moultrie and his officers in the name of the Republic. He thanked the men. Then, taking from his side the sword which had been given him by grateful citizens two months before, shortly after his election, he bestowed it on Sergeant Jasper who had climbed down over the escarpment when the flag was shot from its merlon and had brought back the emblem under fire from the British ships. That was the only sword Rutledge ever owned.

4.

It took Edward five days to summon up courage to write to John the dubious news of the Fourth of July, and then he devised a double cushion for the shock. On July ninth he wrote for the Committee, reporting to its titular chairman, signing the letter with his own signature and adding those of Heyward, Middleton, and Lynch. The letter started off bravely, and irrelevantly, by announcing that the Congress had adopted a Resolution providing for provincial forces —this he knew was near the heart of his provident brother.

"Enclosed also," he continued, "is a very important Declaration which the King of Great Britain has at last reduced us to the necessity of making. . . . All the colonies . . . were united. . . ."

The latter half of the "report" discussed routine business. It was a "sandwich" letter, with announcement of the Declaration of Independence slipped in between "important" business. It was almost as if Edward had hoped John wouldn't notice the Declaration—for evidently he could not forget that the President was still hoping for that "accommodation."

The news did not reach Charles Town until August second—it was midsummer, with everything at a standstill. President Rutledge was not misled by the devices of his brother; he issued a call for a session of both houses of the legislature to begin on September seventeenth. Moreover, in violation of his customary aloofness from the public prints, he spread the news at once to his fellow citizens by giving out to the *Gazette,* the pertinent part of the "intelligence" from Philadelphia.

Charles Town went wild, apparently, with what seemed to be delirious happiness. Business was suspended for two days; bonfires were lit at many street corners; parades formed spontaneously and people everywhere were charged with excitement.

Superficially one might have thought South Carolina had reached its apogee, in that its long climb up from a savage wilderness through the promotional exploitation of the Lords Proprietors, and later of the Crown, had come to a joyous climax. The commonwealth was of age, free and independent.

The ruler in the "palace" had more to think about than bonfires and flamboyant speeches. He knew only too well that nearly every important family in the Republic was divided. Even among those openly declared to be Royalist there was usually at least one member who was either attending meetings of the Liberty Boys or declaring his sympathy with them. This division of opinion was not confined to one part of town. There was hardly a home south of Broad Street without its own civil war; the same thing spread throughout the low country and became even more virulent in the up country. Crimes had been committed because of it; many more were threatened.

The Pinckney family was a microcosm of the whole community. The Colonel departed the week the news of the Declaration arrived— dejected and unreconciled. Charles, Junior, *the* Charles Pinckney, remained, exalted with the prospect of change. In other families brothers killed each other; fathers disowned sons; cousins conspired to seize the estates of their kin.

President Rutledge met these intensities variously. To the Assembly, when it met, he transmitted the Declaration signed by its delegates and said officially, "May the happiest consequences be derived to the United States from the Independence of America who could not obtain peace, liberty and safety by any other means!"

It is not possible to pass over lightly anything that Rutledge is known to have said. He weighed and measured every syllable, every inflection, and yet his contemporaries often looked on him as an impulsive man. What he did *not* say was usually more interesting, and always more important, than what he did say.

Behind his utterance as he transmitted the immortal Declaration of Independence, one can feel a wary but courageous mind, hemmed in by a thousand insecurities, of which the greatest was the possibility that he might do or say something to weaken his own hold on his own people in this critical moment when prejudice was vividly alive and passion was high. He did not endorse the Declaration personally, tactfully avoiding thereby the wounding of the feelings of those he knew so well, like Colonel Pinckney; he did not even endorse it as President of the Republic of South Carolina, and so avoided unnecessary stirring of the swarming hornets' nests of disaffection.

Gently, but firmly, he led them all to that newly discovered mountain peak—the United States—a phrase fresh in the mouths of men. He said nothing of South Carolina, nothing of the rival feelings of distracted sons and fathers. He spoke only of the *United States,* nothing of what South Carolina must endure, sacrifice, discard, destroy, and mourn.

He held aloft the simple phrase, *The Independence of America.* Again, the accent was not on South Carolina, though it was the President of that Republic who was speaking, but on America!

With classic restraint, he told them, not that they must accept it for themselves, or because they liked it, but because "the United States could not obtain peace, liberty and safety by any other means!" It was not a gage of battle he threw down, but a breath of hope in strength beyond themselves—strength in the United States.

With these few words he left the chair to the Speaker, his brother Hugh, so the oratory could flow and the ten per cent of revolutionaries could expand in the state house, while he departed for the "palace" to prepare "medicine" for winning ninety per cent to the Cause.

This medicine was the war against the Cherokees.

Nothing could unite white men fighting each other on the frontier more quickly than an Indian menace. Fate operated for Rutledge again, just as it had earlier in the year when he was striving for unity in getting his Constitution accepted and news had arrived of the British Parliament's declaration of hostilities.

The Cherokees—inspired by British gold, powder, and the expert direction of John Stuart, the old Indian commissioner who had served the colony well for a generation, but who now had put all his skill, with the power of the Crown, behind his efforts—were loose on the northern and western frontiers.

The Indians were rolling down disastrously into the settlements on a front of between four hundred and five hundred miles in length. They ambushed, attacked, massacred with all the usual barbarities of Indian warfare, and several new ones added, for the redskins were never so fiendish as when allied with the whites.

Local militia had responded, though ill prepared, and met the massacre of white men and women by stealing in the night on Indian villages and destroying Indian women and children in their sleep. Through the forest "the parties pursued each other like wild beasts."

Defeat of the Cherokees became President Rutledge's major problem. After September he gave it his full time. He went into the field, examined the ground, made a temporary headquarters at Ninety-Six. He talked with the local militiamen. For the moment, he turned his back on all affairs of state in Charles Town and cooperated with the Governors of North Carolina and Virginia.

Rutledge's methods in handling this Cherokee situation were in contrast to those employed by Drayton the year before. Drayton had decided that the British menace, then only in prospect, required his chief attention, so he tried to handle the Indians incidentally, with his left hand, as it were, and he lost. Rutledge behaved as if there was but one problem in existence—the Cherokees. The problem was more than military; it was also one of unification, not only in his own state, but also in timing operations with those of the commands in North Carolina and Virginia.

A volunteer appeared who offered to make it easy for Rutledge to go back and attend to statecraft: William Moultrie, who had just been commissioned a Brigadier General in the Continental Army. This commission placed him beyond Rutledge's command, but Moultrie was generous; he offered to apply to Congress for the Cherokee detail if Rutledge would request it.

The President thanked his old colleague and told him he was needed elsewhere. Rutledge knew then—what other events later proved —that Moultrie was not a good Indian fighter. Indian fighting was a specialty. Only a frontiersman, born and bred and experienced, could hope to succeed at it. Nor was Rutledge deluded with the idea that he himself might become such a person by virtue of the power he held as President. He went into Indian country primarily to find the proper man. After nearly three months on the ground, in which he slipped surreptitiously from stockade to stockade, studying the methods and the people and talking with all at first hand, he made up his mind. Williamson, a Major of Militia, was the man, despite the fact that of the four other officers in the field one commanded more men than Williamson.

Rutledge made his decision at a dramatic moment. Williamson, with less than three hundred men, had made a brilliant sortie in the woods, had cut down a larger group of marauding Cherokees, had killed a number, and had taken more than fifty captives. The captives were brought to the nearest stockade, to be held as hostages. It was then discovered that thirteen of them were white men painted to resemble Indians.

This was a great catch. In conformity with the savagery customary on both sides Williamson ordered the thirteen hanged, with preliminaries. These preliminaries were "barreling," or laying a man naked across a barrel and drawing blood by tautening his bonds; "railing," which meant putting him astride a rail, with weights to his feet, so he would begin to split before the noose was applied; and "tarring," or immersing him nude in boiling tar before the final act. Williamson's men boasted they were not as savage as Indians; they would not run a captive through the gauntlet, or scalp him.

Rutledge arrived in camp the day before the appointed ceremonies. The President granted a reprieve.

The resolute Major protested vigorously. He said he was not vindictive, but only calculating and determined. He explained his idea of punishment to the Chief Executive. If these white men were not summarily executed, and with some preliminaries which could be talked about, he declared, other white men would not hesitate to follow the blandishments of Stuart and his British backers, but if they did get the treatment already ordered the news of it would spread throughout the frontier and would discourage others from following in their footsteps; if they were executed ignominiously and painfully, in sight of all, the Cause of the Republic would gain immeasurably.

It was the good old argument, quite established, and redolent of the times. Rutledge, the lawyer, the logician, did not condescend to argue.

Instead, the President took from his bag a blank commission, filled it out, and handed it to Williamson. Rutledge had appointed the militia major "Colonel, and chief in command of all the military forces on the frontier of the Republic of South Carolina."

Williamson was astounded, and, of course, delighted. Until then he had been troubled by conflicting authorities. He forgot, for the moment, about hanging captives, with or without preliminaries, but Rutledge did not permit him to forget. The President pointed to a clause in the commission which he had specifically inserted. The colonel could not execute, "or cause to be executed," anyone, without approval from the Chief Executive.

Williamson went about his business expeditiously, and fully vindicated Rutledge's confidence. His little force swelled to twelve hundred, within ninety days, to over two thousand. He built a stockade for his principal refuge and named it Fort Rutledge. Thence he went north, east, west; won battle after battle; and, finally, in a mountain ambuscade, in which he was caught by twelve hundred Cherokees and white Tories, fought his way out valorously, dispersed the enemy and drove them scattered across the line into what became Alabama. After that he lost no time in laying waste the planted and beautiful valleys of the Indians, destroying every settlement east of the Appalachians. The last remnant of Cherokees—about five hundred—finally fled to escape starvation and joined the Royalists in Florida.

The chiefs sued for peace and Rutledge negotiated the treaty which gave South Carolina all the lands beyond the Unacaya Mountains, or what later became the districts of Pickens, Greenville, and Anderson.

It was the most successful Indian war that ever occurred in the Carolinas, and one in which cooperation with North Carolina produced a unified strength of the two states, for North Carolina had an Indian fighter, General Griffith Rutherford, the equal of Williamson, and it was their harmonious collaboration that brought about the victory. Though Rutledge was the Commander-in-Chief in South Carolina, actually as well as nominally, he permitted the military laurels tc go to his selected subordinate.

The President retained, however, the pardoning power. He extended the reprieve he had granted the thirteen captives until the Cherokees had been subdued and then he granted them "political amnesty." The thirteen went free. And with them he pardoned Robert Cunningham, agent of Stuart's, who had been languishing for nearly a year in jail.

This act of clemency on the part of Rutledge has never been widely celebrated. None of his contemporaries, on either side, took similar action. Washington, Gates, Greene, Burgoyne, Cornwallis, Howe, Clinton, Tarleton—each, in similar situations, was obdurate. It was the eighteenth century; and man was inhumane to man. The humanitarianism of Rutledge was as calculated as Colonel Williamson professed his ruthlessness to be. Rutledge was making a political gesture to all the Royalists in the Republic; if they would come in and lay down their arms there would be no reprisals.

The effect, however, was different. The Royalists did not lay down their arms, and his old constituents in Ninety-Six, especially, were highly incensed when he freed Cunningham and the thirteen white "Indians." Elsewhere, throughout both North and South Carolina, he was severely criticized for weakness. The old tribal law was rampant —"an eye for an eye; a tooth for a tooth." Many hitherto devoted followers declared the new President must have softening of the brain to turn loose "traitors caught in disguise, and in the very act of stealthy murder."

As Rutledge entered the second year of his Presidency this was seized upon as his first major mistake and his clemency was utilized to undermine him politically. He had no open hostile opposition, then or afterward. He was too secure for that, but being in supreme power was also his weakness. He knew it, but the remedy was not apparent.

5.

The only man in South Carolina competent, in any degree, to match himself politically with Rutledge was the Chief Justice. Drayton had the ambition and the will.

The revolt of Ninety-Six over the release of the thirteen captives and of all the republicans over the pardoning of Cunningham convinced Drayton that the time had come to proceed with the operation of a plan he had devised for acquiring executive power. And John Rutledge, he thought, had shown him how to get it by constitutional means.

Drayton had learned another lesson from Rutledge—not to move directly. Drayton's hand was not seen openly in the agitation throughout the up country to disestablish the Church of England.

The Reverend Dr. William Tennant, a Presbyterian clergyman from a Congregational church in Connecticut, was the agitator who initiated the work. He was financed in part by the Chief Justice, himself a devout Episcopalian, who kept discreetly silent.

In the constitution Rutledge had written, nothing was said about the Church of England, but the statute laws in force as "Actes of the Assembly" were ratified. These laws recognized the Episcopal Church as the state religion, its ministers were paid as officers of the Republic, while many other grants to it were made that were given to no other church.

This was unjust. There were more South Carolinians outside than inside the Church of England. In fact, there were in 1777 only twenty Episcopal churches, and seventy-nine of other denominations in the Republic. The Reverend Dr. Tennant had good material to work with; he had a splendid personality and in the up country he found responsive audiences.

The damage to Rutledge was not so much in the direct agitation itself, as in its by-product, for word was rapidly spread that it was the President who stood by the Episcopal churchmen and all their works, because he was himself a Royalist at heart. This fitted in, also, with the allegation that he had pardoned Cunningham and the thirteen white Royalists in Indian disguise, not for humanity, nor for policy, but because he sympathized with their cause.

Neither Judge Drayton nor Dr. Tennant demeaned himself personally by uttering such malicious scandal, yet neither denied it. Dr. Tennant continued the attack obliquely, asserting that the laws must be changed to disestablish the Church of England, that the government must bow to the will of the people, and that there must be no more of this "left-handed alliance with the enemy." Chief Justice Drayton assented. President Rutledge said nothing in reply.

The campaign became excessively bitter, was conducted in an atmosphere of bigotry, and, paradoxically, sowed further the seeds of a rumor that Rutledge was an atheist. The slender justification was traced to his alleged willingness to have the First Continental Congress opened without prayer. Mr. Timothy had published an account of that episode in the *Gazette* as a means of protecting the reputation of Edward Rutledge, his intimate friend and supporter, and by way of explaining that Edward was only John's messenger, for the offer to Sam Adams had been delivered by Edward and had been well aired in northern newspapers and by many a stump speaker. The whole attack on the religious belief of John Rutledge was a prodigious whispering campaign, and was far reaching. If the up countrymen could be made to believe that the President of the Republic was also an atheist, cynically using the established church, it would be easier for Drayton to unseat him, for much as they hated Episcopalians they hated worse a man without any religious belief.

The facts about John Rutledge's attitude toward religion are clear. Toward the church as an institution he was objective, while at heart he was profoundly a theist. Religious belief sustained him at all times. Through this active middle period of his life his prayers, wherever known, bear marks of his individuality and were never the stereotyped phrases of ecclesiastic authority. He kept his mind free from prevailing dogma in religion as in all else, yet he did not consider the matter of church primacy important enough to stake his political career on it and he accepted the establishment of the church as readily as he later accepted its disestablishment. That he lived in the so-called age of reason affected him, if at all, only subconsciously. Deism, as a cult, was intellectually fashionable in England when he was there, and was believed in even by certain churchmen in good standing in orthodox Anglican circles, who thus developed a dual attitude toward religious belief, one for private solace and one for public ritual. Rutledge early adopted such an attitude as a solution of his own religious life. He was always a generous contributor to the upkeep of the church, but never permitted that fact to be utilized politically beyond the confines of the parish where the statute required that he hold membership. The fact that he never was even a vestryman in Christ Church of which he was always a member is eloquent testimony to his determination to separate religion and politics.

This unwillingness to discuss publicly any phase of the religious issue helped to weaken Rutledge's political position during the second year of his presidency. He did not realize how it was used to undermine him.

Through the spring and summer of 1777—after the Cherokee War was over—this agitation continued unabated, but in the fall of that year Drayton found what he considered even better ammunition.

In the winter the Reverend Dr. Tennant added a new issue to his ecclesiastical protest, and in this second appeal he was joined by others. He demanded that the Council be elected by the people directly instead of by the Assembly, as provided for in the Constitution.

Local debating societies picked up the question in the interior. The agitation was the origin of what became known later as Jeffersonian democracy, and its supporters pointed out the alleged nepotism of the system as it was practiced: there was John Rutledge in the Presidency; his brother Hugh was Speaker of the Council; his brother-in-law, John Mathews, who recently had married his sister Sarah, was Speaker of the Assembly; and his brother Edward was head of the delegation in the national Congress.

And none of these was elected by the people directly.

Nobody attacked the Rutledges personally. The system was wrong, said the opponents; they wanted the system changed. Hugh, as Speaker of the Upper House, was the center of the attack. He warned the President and sought his support. When the going was easy Hugh was one of the first of the Rutledges, but when the storms threatened he was glad to be John's brother.

Through January and February of 1778 the Assembly debated at length the formation of a new Constitution, without the slightest consultation with the Chief Executive, who, the members well knew, had an absolute veto on any possible act they might pass and who was also the chief authority in state and nation on constitutional government. First, they decided to do away with the Republic. South Carolina must be a state. Second, it must have a Governor instead of a President. Third, it must have a Senate instead of a Council, and the Senate must be elected directly by the people. Fourth, it must disestablish the Church of England. Fifth, provision must be made that a governor's veto could be overridden by a two-thirds vote.

Weeks were devoted to vain debates of other proposals. All were turned down except these five. They were written into a new Constitution which was adopted by the Assembly on March fifth and sent to the President with a request that he sign.

Rutledge knew what Drayton and his followers expected—that he would veto the new Constitution in the writing of which he had not been consulted. A veto would throw the popular measure back into the Assembly, and would place John Rutledge in the position of defying its will only twenty-one days from the expiration of his term on March twenty-sixth.

With Rutledge once manipulated into such a position Drayton planned to resign as Chief Justice and take the stump openly in support of the new Constitution, for in the preliminaries he had been merely a consultant. This would give him three weeks in which to achieve his object. The new Constitution already having been proven to be supported by a big majority of assemblymen, he expected to ride the tide into the high seat.

Rutledge got the bill at three o'clock the afternoon of the fifth, and at eleven o'clock the next morning appeared before the Assembly, in person.

"I have taken an oath," he said, "to preside over the people of this state according to the constitutional form of government agreed to and resolved upon by representatives of South Carolina in March, 1776, and later ratified by the people. That is our law and that is my oath. It is impossible for me, without a breach of this solemn obligation, to give sanction to the establishment of a different form of government.

"However, if I were not restrained by an oath, I should, nevertheless, put a negative on the bill because it annihilates one branch of the legislature, and transfers the right of electing that branch from the General Assembly to the people; and nothing is clearer to me than that we have no lawful power to do this. The legislative authority, being fixed and limited, cannot change or destroy itself without submitting to the people the constitution from which it is derived.

"The people, by that constitution, delegated to us the power of making laws, not of creating the means of legislative methods; and, there can be no doubt that if we have the authority to take the right of electing a legislative Council from that body in which the constitution placed it and give it to another we may not only do this but also the like with the right of electing members of the Assembly and a president, and vest also the election of both the Assembly and Council in another body than the people, and the election of the president in some other body than in the Assembly and the Council; and if we have the power to cut off one branch of the legislature we can cut off other branches, and invest the whole authority in some other body or person. These possibilities may seem here and now chimerical, but they are made real if we take the first step. It is the illegality which is the breach of the law; the eventuality is seldom foreseen."

Rutledge paused. So far he had not surprised them, though they did not grasp the significance of what he said. They had expected the veto, though perhaps with a little more flourish, not with such cool incision.

He continued calmly and reasonably, "Supposing, however, that we had the power to form a new constitution, I apprehend that the causes assigned for it are altogether insufficient. The bill recites that the present constitution was temporary only, and suited to the situation of public affairs when it was resolved on looking forward to an accommodation with Great Britain, an event then desired; but, that the United Colonies have since been constituted Independent States by the Declaration of the Honorable Continental Congress, and that it is therefore become absolutely necessary to frame a constitution suited to that great event.

"Admitting our form of government is but temporary it is to continue until that accommodation shall take place, until peace between Great Britain and America shall be concluded, though I do not hold that it must then be altered, and I think should not unless a better can be devised."

At this point Rutledge the Orator emerged. His voice rose; he became emotionally emphatic. "We still look forward to such an accommodation," he exclaimed, "an event as desirable now as it ever was, so that the situation of public affairs is in this respect the same as when the constitution was established, and though indeed since the Declaration of Independence the *style* of this country is somewhat altered, having been heretofore one of the United Colonies and being now one of the United States of America yet it exercised, and constitutionally, the same supreme power as it has since that period.

Such declaration, therefore, cannot make it necessary to change the form of government, nor can I conceive any reason which does."

The President's face seemed transformed with feeling. He had reached his wonted climax, or so they thought. He had cast his veto; he had given his reasons; so far all was according to plan—the plan of Drayton and his friends. His denunciation of the planned dictatorship was too subtle to be instantly effective; it would require his considered dramatic action for that.

However, instead of leaving the rostrum, Rutledge took his applause, for that never failed him in some degree, and waited. Then he continued, quietly again, in his drawing-room manner.

"The good of the people," he said, "being the end of government, that is the best form under which they are happiest, they being the fittest judges of what would be most productive of their happiness. And the people preferred the present mode of electing a legislative council to that which is offered for electing a senate, probably because it appeared more likely that persons of the greatest integrity, learning and abilities would be chosen by and from amongst their representatives when assembled, than by electors in their several parishes and districts, and it may have seemed incongruous that there should be two representative bodies, the less controlling the greater. The people also preferred a compounded, or mixed government to a simple democracy, or one verging toward it, perhaps because, however unexceptionable democratic power may appear at first view, its effects have been found arbitrary, severe and destructive. Certain it is that systems which in theory have been much admired on trial have not succeeded, and that projects and experiments relative thereto are of all schemes the most dangerous and fatal.

"The people, having adopted a constitution which seemed to them the most perfect, when it is not even surmised that any grievance or inconvenience has arisen from it, and where they are satisfied with and are happy under it (which I firmly believe they are) if we had the authority, I should conceive it neither politic, expedient, nor justifiable to change this form for another. Especially, I think the one proposed will not be better than or so good as what we now enjoy; and, whether it would be or not, is a speculative point which time only can determine."

Rutledge had been speaking for several minutes, becoming, as one account has it, "weaker and weaker." He was like a clock running down. He had had his emotional outburst long since. What made him continue? Only courtesy caused the assemblymen to listen respectfully —courtesy and curiosity, for no man could predict what Rutledge would say or do. There was a curious fascination about him, an element of surprise. His most quiet moment was usually the time to expect an explosion.

At length, he said, "I am not vain enough to imagine I can influence the Assembly in a matter so thoroughly debated, and, having given you my views with candor, it is only proper that I resign as President, which I do herewith!"

So he stepped down and walked alone from the chamber, through a hushed assemblage. "The members sat as if stunned." The Republic had no President! How could Rutledge resign—he on whom they had relied so confidently for sixteen, seventeen years—how *dare* he?

The Chief Justice had won, for the moment, but he was still Chief Justice, and a Chief Executive must be provided at once. This was the one thing on which Drayton and his followers had not calculated. They were armed only for opposition, while Rutledge applied to politics the principle of jiu-jitsu, forcing his opponent to defeat himself with his own energy.

As for the substance of the speech of resignation it would take weeks and months for them to grasp the fact in the thesis: that he had thought around them and beyond them in applying the basic principle of the Revolution, which was establishment of the considered will of the people as the source of all government.

This principle for which the war allegedly was being fought— and for which they all were staking their lives and fortunes—he constructively had placed behind the agitation of their pseudo-democratic reform—as a builder might sink a caisson through quicksands into bedrock—and had refuted their asserted democracy by impeaching the means of their assertion.

Of course they could not appreciate this at once. He did not use the language of debate in the Assembly. He spoke, rather, as to the high court of the ages, not to the political passion of Charles Town.

The reasons for his resignation—to them at the moment—were unimportant compared to its fact. To avoid anarchy they must elect his successor promptly. And who could be a fit successor to John Rutledge?

In the first startled surprise that was all they could consider, though under the surface ancient forces were battling for mastery of the first independently established government in America.

It was apparent to some that Drayton was moving to reestablish himself in a dictatorship which he had lost. He had successfully taken the first step on such a path in his clandestine control of the ruling caste, represented by his temporary majority in the Assembly. Now he proposed to reconstruct the constitution *in the Assembly,* without going to the people.

However, Drayton had to move with extreme caution and in observance both of tradition and of the new Constitution. He could not become dictator unless first he became President. And in John Rutledge's resignation he had been unhorsed in a wink, as it were. To stand for the presidency he would have to resign as Chief Justice, and if he did so his purpose would be unmasked. He could not think fast enough to meet this situation. Appealed to by a few friends to resign he said he would think it over. It then was too late, as Rutledge doubtless had foreseen.

That afternoon the Assembly elected Henry Middleton as President. He was at his plantation on the Ashley and when the news reached him that night he indignantly refused to sit in the chair from which John Rutledge had stepped down.

The next morning, "in the greatest confusion," the Assembly elected as President Rawlins Lowndes, whom Drayton had called The Great Procrastinator.

With the Republic thus restored to a semblance of order the Assembly passed a vote of thanks to the former President, sixty-eight to fifteen. That was the measure of Rutledge's strength the day after he resigned. President or not, he was still the leader of his people.

To console Drayton and properly to utilize his distinguished talents, the Assembly elected him, a little later, to the Continental Congress in place of Edward Rutledge. The Chief Justice had aimed at John's place, but he secured only Edward's.

In Philadelphia, the next year, as a member of the Continental Congress, Drayton contracted typhus and died. His career as it marshalled the forces threatening to achieve dictatorship in America, served as a foil to John Rutledge. If Drayton had not lived and worked as he did Rutledge might not have been driven to create his finest masterpieces of statecraft. But Drayton left potent influences behind him and with these influences Rutledge was obliged still to reckon.

THE Assembly adopted the new Constitution, without submitting it to the voters. Lowndes signed it as President, and the first act of the new State of South Carolina was to elect a Governor. Rawlins Lowndes was selected and, in his capacity as assemblyman, Rutledge voted for him.

New general elections were ordered at once and the sitting assemblymen were returned. A Senate was elected, for the first time. Two senators were allotted to the City of Charles Town and they were elected by the voters directly. From Mazyckboro, home of the artisans, mechanics, and other working people, the senator selected was John Rutledge, and as the same time he was returned, automatically, as assemblyman from Christ Church Parish.

In his dual role, Rutledge attended every possible session of each house. Governor Lowndes asked him to become a member of the Privy Council; he consented and participated in all its meetings, though modestly. He never forced his views, and he did not sulk.

Nobody attempted to answer Rutledge's argument against the new Constitution; he never repeated it, but returned to his law practice, which was not so good as before because of the upset condition of the times.

On January 11, 1779, Governor Lowndes faced an emergency joint session of the Assembly and Senate. The moment to meet great events with decision had come again.

Surveying the past three years, they realized that the first two of them, under the presidency of John Rutledge, had seen the Republic whipping the British in its front yard and the Cherokees in its back yard. With only script in the treasury, and little hard money in circulation, he nevertheless had managed to hold the depreciation at only about a third under the face value, and to this prices were quickly adjusted; business had picked up; a thriving trade had been established along the interior sea lines with the middle and northern colonies and even to the West Indies. Despite a half-hearted blockade, South Carolina had come back again into prosperity. The Republic was, beyond doubt, the most prosperous of all the colonies in that first two-year period and offered a striking contrast to the fate of the North.

News was slow in reaching Charles Town, but when it did come three to six weeks late, by way of Savannah, Antigua, or Halifax, it was mostly bad news. It reeled off a monotony of disaster, from the evacuation of New York to Valley Forge.

Fourteen months before, in October, 1777, had occurred the only engagement since the Battle of Charles Town which had actual military and political value. It was the second decisive battle of the war —Saratoga. Burgoyne had been caught, with all his army, between Arnold and Gates, in upper New York, and had surrendered.

For more than a year it had seemed that Saratoga had turned the tide. Again and again the people of Charles Town had been told the war was over; that the British could not go on after Saratoga, because the French were coming in.

However, in January, 1779, there was no visible evidence to the people of South Carolina that the French intended anything more than friendly gestures. And what was much worse—the British had gained time for a second assault. They sent more troops, more warships; they recalled the effete Lord Howe and put the war on a sound basis. At last they knew how serious this "revolt of the rabble" really was.

For more than a year Washington apparently had accomplished nothing at all. For weeks at a time no one could say for certain where he was. He made no attacks; he had given up the big cities; those who had seen his forces spoke only of rags and rusty weapons and of futile attempts on the part of the commander to enforce discipline by whippings and imprisonment which drove large numbers of his few remaining soldiers into desertion.

The people, if they could have been polled, both North and South, were utterly sick of the Revolution. A handful of privateers, gamblers, and leeches were rich and insolent; more than ninety-nine per cent of the people were much worse off than they ever had been. Their only prospect was enslavement if they lost, and nobody knew what if they won.

It was in this period that one observer in Philadelphia wrote: "O! Heavens! Grant us one great soul! One leading mind could extricate the best cause from that ruin which seems to await it for the want of it. We have as good a cause as was ever fought for; we have great resources; the people are well tempered; one active masterly capacity would bring order out of this confusion, and save this country."

That was John Adams, confiding in his diary, and with no thought of South Carolina, in 1777. And the situation grew worse, though the need continued the same.

That January morning of 1779 as the Assembly and Senate of South Carolina came together in joint session the members were reviewing, not so much the panorama of the whole war, as that of their own situation.

A month before a British fleet had appeared off the port, and had sent in a message, in courteous, but firm words, offering amnesty and peace, in return for which South Carolina only had to lay down her arms, and have again her preferred protectorate within the empire, to be maintained, of course, at the discretion of the Ministry in London.

This put Governor Lowndes, to whom the message had been addressed, in a customary flutter of indecision. He was tempted to hurl the message back indignantly—and he was tempted also to keep it and think it over. So he kept it and thought it over.

The third day the British captain sent in a second messenger. He wanted an answer at once. Lowndes, by this time, was in such distress he was unable to sleep and everyone felt sorry for him; he was haggard with the responsibility. Personally, he declared, and no one could doubt him, he "wanted to hurl the proper answer back in the teeth of the dastardly British," *but* there were weighty reasons which might lead to a contrary decision.

The Governor had conferred with the available members of the Privy Council, as was his duty and privilege. Four happened to be in the Town at the time. If only they had agreed, then he could have washed his hands of the responsibility, even if their agreement went against his own desires, but they did not agree. This made the situation intolerable for the harassed Governor.

Everyone wanted to know if John Rutledge thought this offer from the British was a proper "accommodation." Unfortunately, Rutledge was at the Stono plantation, attending to some business for his mother. Lowndes put a slave on a horse and sent him galloping off to Stono with a request for the privy councillor to return—on urgent official business.

That night Governor Lowndes and the Privy Council conferred at the "palace" with Councillor Rutledge. In a short time everything was made quite clear, and the next morning the British captain got his answer. It was a firm and clear-cut no.

As they assembled on the morning of January 11, the members of the joint session were obliged to consider first the urgent application brought to them by two swift travelers who had just arrived from Ninety-Six. These men claimed that the recognized assemblyman from Ninety-Six was not rightly elected; the man they declared to be the choice of their people was John Rutledge, and they stoutly demanded their rights. Pardoning the thirteen traitors might have been a mistake, but some were beginning to think it might also have been a virtue. They wanted John Rutledge—and no one else. This was no time, they said, "to trifle with nincompoops and second-raters!"

The senators and assemblymen were subdued. By common consent politics was suspended.

The grass was growing where the eager crowds had once milled about the base of the Liberty Tree. Drayton was gone. Gadsden talked no more; the "Lion of Liberty" was Vice-Governor now and impressed with the weight of his responsibilities. Edward Rutledge and Thomas Heyward, Junior, were enlisted as captains of infantry; Thomas Lynch, Junior, had perished at sea; the rich young men who had cried for independence and signed for it, had nothing to do now except forlornly to offer their lives; the Reverend Dr. Tennant had retired to a country parsonage. These men had sown the wind; who was going to reap the whirlwind?

The British naval captain had left his card at the front door of Charles Town a month ago. Now the British army was knocking at the rear gates. They had heard the night before that Prévost had crossed the Savannah River. Prévost was the new general the British had sent to command their southern department. He had landed—with an army of, some said, six thousand men, all picked lobster backs—safely outside the City of Savannah. He had taken the chief seaport of Georgia easily and, in less than thirty days, he had beaten down every resistance in the state itself.

So, for the first time in over a hundred years, South Carolina was the military frontier. She had nothing, on the south, between her and the enemy.

The day before Prévost and the British army had invaded South Carolina, and were reported as advancing. On that morning the enemy was no more than 216 miles from the shallow barricades even then being thrown up across the neck of Charles Town.

Governor Lowndes mounted the rostrum. There was no indecision about him now. Without any preliminary, he addressed the joint session.

"In our late elections," he said, "whereby we ratified the new Constitution, there came an end to our late provisional government, wherein I had acted as your Governor."

This was no resignation. He simply spoke of his executive tenancy in the past tense and stepped down by executive fiat. He had been Governor only eleven months and a week; and the Constitution called for a two-year term. Yet no one questioned the legality of the move.

"Your affairs will now," Lowndes went on, "in all probability be conducted more by arms than by councils, and their success, in a great measure, depends upon military ability and experience, and you should look to these qualities in choice of a Chief Magistrate. . . ."

"Rutledge!" yelled someone from the sidewalk, where crowds had gathered to hear what was going on. The contesting delegate from Ninety-Six shoved his gaunt way into the chamber from which he had been held until his credentials could be passed on. "We want John Rutledge!" he shouted. It was the cry of the frontier!

The chamber buzzed with suppressed excitement. No one could tell what was being said, but Lowndes rapped stoutly for order and went on: "There will be no nominations, but as has been established by precedent, we will proceed by secret ballot to the election of a Governor. The tellers will pass among you."

In a few minutes Lowndes received the report from the tellers and took his private glance, noting that three votes had been cast for him; all the others were for John Rutledge.

A hushed silence descended on the chamber, and on the street outside. Lowndes held up his hand. He was a small man, in surtout of dull maroon and bright yellow small clothes, and with a deeply powdered wig; precise, careful, something of a dandy. It was written of him that, "Nothing e'er became him like the serene and perfect timeliness of his taking off."

"The election," he said, smiling indulgently, "is unanimous. Our new Governor is John Rutledge!"

The Assembly and the Senate cheered, but in the streets where the crowds were waiting to hear the result, frenzied elation seized everyone.

Inside the chamber Lowndes administered the oath. Rutledge replied, "I will." The nearest member reached up to take his hand, eager to be the first to congratulate him. Others crowded in; Rutledge stepped down from the rostrum; everyone wanted to touch him; he was milled about the chamber, and when he reached the man from Ninety-Six, who had been able to get in no farther than the rear seats, that raw-boned constituent could no longer restrain himself. He seized the Governor and propelled him to the doorstep.

From the street many pressed forward, crying for Rutledge to come down to them and say something. Others complained they could not see; there was a babel of voices. In this confusion the man from Ninety-Six, elated as with a personal achievement, and as though to share his good fortune with all, placed his huge arms under Rutledge and lifted him up. Others joined, and in a moment the Governor was above the crowd, lifted up on a platform of strong muscles, while the cheering rang through the Town.

He was no longer merely the patrician leading them; no longer only the aristocrat qualified by delicate perceptions to administer from above. It was the only time, from the cradle to the grave, that the crowd had its hands on him. In this moment it was as if the spirit of the demos touched him and set him apart.

But they could not get him to speak. His public speech that day, when of all days they would have liked to listen to their greatest orator, was two words only—"I will."

2.

The enemy was to the south, but the next day at dawn Governor Rutledge rode north on Caesar, his white horse. He was headed for the most thickly settled section of the up-country to raise troops. There was only Moultrie to oppose Prévost, advancing from Savannah. The Assembly had been told that Moultrie had a thousand infantry; Rutledge knew Moultrie had less than six hundred. Six hundred against six thousand. They were South Carolina sharpshooters against British drilled regiments—but the outlook was not encouraging.

Somewhere in the western country General Benjamin Lincoln was operating, but all believed he was far to the north of Prévost, and probably in Georgia. He had the only real American army in the South at that time—three thousand to thirty-five hundred men; regular Continentals, in red coats that could not easily be told from the British uniforms. This army was mentally circumscribed with the whole artificial British manual of arms and its rigid training, which was as much a disciplinary goal to one side as to the other; physically it was oppressed with baggage wagons; professionally it was hidebound with affectation and title-hunting.

Lincoln had been under Gates at Saratoga. Everyone thought Gates and Lincoln had defeated Burgoyne, but the fact was that starvation and long distances, together with the quick movement of Benedict Arnold and his assistant, Schuyler, defeated Burgoyne, who, when he surrendered, had only six bottles of champagne left. One discerning writer said that "Burgoyne would have surrendered if Gates and Lincoln had been in China." As in the case of Charles Lee, South Carolina was deluded again by the military grandeur of a Continental general of rank and reputation.

Rutledge, however, was doubtful of Lincoln's military capacity. Lincoln had spent two days in Charles Town six weeks before. Rutledge never took long to make his estimate of a man. In the extremity, the Governor did what he never before had done—he took direct military action to the extent of going out personally to raise troops. At the same time, however, he dispatched two messengers by different routes to search for Lincoln.

Rutledge reached Orangeburg, then the second city in the state, and about two hundred miles north of Charles Town, that night. Local authorities met him and, by his order, sent out notices of public meetings the next afternoon and night.

Nearly every male in the town attended. They found recruiting sergeants in the entries and the Governor on the platform. A letter written by Jeems Denning to his brother in Mecklenburg, North Carolina, the following week, reported the event.

"Governor Rutledge," said Jeems, "spoke twicet and everybody was disappointed. It was hardly speechifying, but they say he does that for the Assembly. He only talked sense here, and twenty-seven joined up at the church and eighteen in the town hall."

In three weeks Rutledge raised six hundred militia by "talking sense." There were no commissioned officers available to drill them, so he undertook it himself, without a uniform or any weapon except a riding stick.

The recruits who had "signed up" were totally unused to any form of discipline; there were a few clerks, but mostly countrymen, who called themselves "farmers"; they rather gloried in the distinction; they felt dimly, but stoutly, they had middle-class virtue as opposed to the unknown vices of "the stuck-up planters."

Of one thing they were quite certain—"No one was going to tell them what to do!" They might admit that theoretically it was necessary to have officers in a war; practically it was all nonsense; one man was just as good as another, and maybe better. It was whispered about that the Governor who had come up there and talked them into it intended to lead them back to the big city on the coast, which they never had seen and which they sullenly resented. Apparently he made no progress at all as a drill master.

One afternoon, "the Governor's patience was sorely tried," as an old account quaintly puts it, and—"he lost his temper and struck a recruit with his riding whip." Just what provoked the blow is not recorded, but it was doubtless some deviation from accepted drill practice.

There was no apparent resentment, from the recruit or anyone else. Physical blows were common; they meant little enough. In fact, there was a tacit agreement everywhere that anyone in authority had the right to strike his inferiors.

After striking the soldier the Governor dismissed the company, and mounting Caesar rode to the house which had been provided for him near-by. Pompey was preparing his dinner. He had no secretary or aide, and no member of his family was with him. Alone in that wooden house in Orangeburg, Rutledge came to a momentous decision.

The controlling problem of the war was one of military technique; technique, in this case, was the whole problem. It was characteristic of Rutledge that he saw this, saw it swiftly, clearly, and then had the courage to act on it decisively.

In drilling his recruits Rutledge was only following the established military custom. He had seen Colonel Pinckney and Captain, now General, Gadsden doing it in Charles Town. Everyone in the Continental Army, from Washington down, had the same system, patterned, of course, on the British system, which the British had from other Europeans.

The general object of this system was to render soldiers in the mass effective to the will of officers. It was military totalitarianism in its eighteenth-century version, a perennial effort to rob men of their separate individualities so as to augment the power of their commander.

The system was effective with the British—to a degree—chiefly because their soldiers were mercenaries or impressed criminals. There was no possible social relationship between a soldier and an officer in the British Army.

Washington's whole military life was devoted to a futile effort to make the American Army conform to this pattern. He constantly complained of his difficulties and he never solved the problem. American volunteers would not stand for European regimentation. Washington tried the mercenary method of hiring, but that failed too. The number of desertions was scandalously large; sometimes over half of a command would slip off in the night and never come back. Washington tried court-martialing and shooting—more than fifty deserters were shot by Washington's order—but it made no difference.

Even the arrival of Von Steuben, a former drill master for the King of Prussia, changed the situation very little.

At Orangeburg, Rutledge was obliged to consider this problem officially. If he accepted it as incidental to his new duties he would become just another governor, or possibly, if he went the way of some other public officials, and accepted an obvious title reflecting martial glory, just another general. He had been chosen for his present post, in the words of former Governor Lowndes, because he was "a man of military experience." Actually the Battle of Charles Town was his sole military experience.

The "man of military experience" sat on his porch and thought it out, as the katydids and the mock thrushes were singing in the woods; with the rhododendrons and the laurel coming into bloom.

All his life Rutledge had been an attorney—for his mother, for Edward and Hugh, and his sisters, for Thomas and Andrew, and for such as the Cooke girl, and Dr. Haley and Colton Sparkins. Miles Brewton had left him with power of attorney and when Brewton was lost at sea Rutledge had to administer an estate of three hundred thousand pounds, with no restraining documents, and with only his conscience to guide him. Solomon Legare had trusted him with two plantations and a huge sum of money on call with a London broker in his own name to be an attorney for him while he enjoyed himself abroad. Laurens, the greatest merchant of them all, had turned all his holdings over to him when he went away, leaving him as his attorney; and he was that even now, while Henry Laurens was a prisoner in the Tower of London. These men and women had trusted him.

Now, however, he was the Chief Executive, duly elected; and the head of military forces, duly appointed; he was also the chief magistrate, with no one to review his decree. What should he do: follow the established military pattern or devise a new technique? The repercussion in his own mind of the incident of striking the recruit determined him.

Rutledge did not need to know the boy personally; the type was familiar. He was a frontiersman who could pick off a rabbit at three hundred paces and never miss, who could subsist for a week, if he had to, on a handful of parched corn and some rainwater. He would often be without shoes; his pants would have holes, he would have uncut hair, and be unshaven; he would be a boy of few words; yet would know how to take care of himself. No one could impose on him; he was a South Carolinian—an American.

Was this the sort of boy who could be whipped into an imitation of a European soldier? And, if Rutledge could thus create a miniature European army, could he perform a second miracle and overcome the British system with his imitation? Could he do this thing which Washington had tried to do more effectively than the Virginian, and succeed where he had failed?

Rutledge's reasoning did not employ such phrases as "public necessity"—"to save the state"—"in the interests of all we must sacrifice the individual."

He remained the logician, subdued by the virtue of his profession. A true attorney, having accepted an agreed retainer, puts aside personal motives, and proceeds to do for his client what the client cannot do for himself.

The next morning the Governor assembled the new companies in the Orangeburg square. Curious townspeople looked on. The troops had no uniforms; their arms were ill-matched, for each man had supplied his own; more than half were barefoot; a third had no head covering; the rest wore all manner of headgear, from colored tricorns to coonskin caps.

The Governor called them to attention. Then he called the name of the recruit he had struck the day before.

At first the boy did not respond, perhaps not believing his ears or perhaps fearful of another humiliation. Again he was called. Then he stepped in front of the ragged, uneven ranks.

Rutledge walked toward him and spoke distinctly, so that everyone might hear.

"My boy," said the Governor, "yesterday I struck you when I was not myself. I regret it and wish to apologize."

The tones were icy-clear. No one could be mistaken. More than a thousand persons heard it; the Governor—apologizing to a recruit.

Then Rutledge addressed the troops. "Tomorrow, at four o'clock in the morning," he said, "we will march toward the front. Meanwhile, assemble your baggage."

That was his last drill.

3.

If anyone in the Orangeburg contingent assumed that he could be intimate thereafter with the Governor, he was promptly undeceived. There was no back-slapping, nor any handshaking with Rutledge.

Moreover, the next morning he disappeared, leaving instructions with the sergeants for each company to choose its own captains and to proceed under these newly self-selected officers. He did not stop even to supervise the election.

He was gone—on Caesar—no one in the "army" knew where.

Rutledge went straight west from Orangeburg, until he reached a point fifteen to twenty miles beyond the Georgia-South Carolina border and there he found Lincoln and the Continental Army.

They were encamped in a pleasant little valley, with good water and dry ground on which to pitch tents. The General had both gout and rheumatism, and he complained that the low country helped neither. He weighed above three hundred pounds, of which a third apparently was in his abdomen. When he put on his tunic in the morning it required two orderlies to help secure the laces. But he made an impressive figure—in his vast tricorn hat and gold epaulettes, with a broad sash and an ornamental sword which Congress had presented to him for his great victory at Saratoga.

Rutledge rode into camp, without uniform, and was taken to him.

The Governor asked Lincoln what he was doing in a sparsely settled countryside, nearly three hundred miles from the British Army—and apparently going in the other direction.

They *had* been going in the other direction, Lincoln blandly explained. That was a week ago—when they received the first message from Rutledge. Since then the army had been coming down to the relief of Charles Town rapidly—at the rate of seven or eight miles a day. One day they had traversed fifteen miles, which was quite a record.

In the beginning, when they first left the vicinity of Savannah, Lincoln had detached about fifteen hundred men under a Colonel Ashe and had left them behind to "detain" Prévost, but this force had been dispersed. He had only just heard about it, but he was still bland and contented.

Meanwhile, Rutledge had realized why his standing was so low in the camp of the Major General commanding the Department of the South. His messages had not been given full weight for they had been signed, simply, "J. Rutledge," and Lincoln had supposed the Governor of South Carolina to be Rawlins Lowndes. Moreover, Lincoln, as military commander of all southern states, recognized Brigadier-General Moultrie as chief in command in South Carolina.

They were encamped in the State of Georgia! Rutledge might be Governor—fifteen miles away—but here he was merely a guest.

Rutledge had no time for nonsense. His last word from the southern front was that Prévost was cleaning up as he advanced, sacking the plantations, stealing the plate, taking off the Negroes, burning the houses, despoiling the women, impressing the men into military service, or hanging them if they resisted.

He communicated this to Lincoln and asked to see the roster of the Continental Army. It was shown him, under protest, but as a civility. The roster showed 2363 men.

Rutledge had also received, from spies, an accurate report of Prévost's force—it was twenty-six hundred men, second- or third-enlistment men, dependable professional soldiers. This he also communicated to Lincoln, who was surprised. He had been told, and believed, that Prévost had seven or eight thousand.

The fact was, the two armies—British and American—were remarkably well matched, both in numbers and in the stupidity of their commanders. An army of twenty-five hundred men was quite formidable during the Revolution. Several of Washington's battles were fought with forces no larger than Lincoln had at that moment.

Rutledge was obliged to postpone total application of the solution of the problem of military technique which he had decided upon at Orangeburg. The situation in hand indicated the use of the conventional military technique—and he thought he saw a chance to repeat the *coup de main* at Saratoga.

This plan he now laid before Lincoln. If the Major General commanding would condescend to hasten and close in on Prévost, from the rear, then Rutledge would proceed, alone, by inland routes, to

Charles Town, and there prepare the other forces, including those under Moultrie.

Thus, between them—Rutledge and Lincoln—the British would be caught in a trap, with an equal force before and behind; in front the fortifications of Charles Town and in back Lincoln's army. Burgoyne had bowed to a similar decree of fate. Perhaps it would be a sensational finish to the war.

Lincoln considered this sagely and approved—in principle. Then, as courteously as possible, but firmly, he told Rutledge he could deal in military affairs only with a military man—that meant with Brigadier-General Moultrie. The regulars had been in existence less than four years and their class-consciousness was already brighter than their blue-and-red uniforms.

Rutledge was not offended. He told Lincoln suavely that he well understood the military necessity, and then modestly related his own difficulties at Orangeburg, where he had raised six hundred militia. He also said he expected another six hundred or, perhaps eight hundred, waiting for him in Charles Town. Thus he could claim, even then, to have a force of fourteen or perhaps fifteen hundred, while Moultrie had, at most, six hundred. Moreover, the Governor had been *elected* Commander-in-Chief of all the military forces in South Carolina and there was the whole state for him to draw on. Rutledge was in a fair trading position.

After due consideration—Rutledge remained in camp for two nights and nearly three days, and there was plenty of Madeira in the baggage wagons—Lincoln became magnanimous. He agreed to accept Rutledge as a military equal—if the equality should be limited severely to the operation immediately pending. It would be all right if Rutledge should arrange the victory and let Lincoln have the credit with Congress and the country. Lee had got the credit for Fort Sullivan and Gates for Saratoga; now Lincoln thought he saw *his* chance.

Rutledge agreed.

In proof of the sincerity with which Lincoln kept his compact there is this entry in his order book, the next day: "The general [assembly] is to beat tomorrow morning at four o'clock, the assembly at half past four, and the army marches precisely at five . . . when the army marches commissaries' wagons and cattle on foot will fall in."

Two days later, here is further proof in the Order Book of the "intensity" and "determination" that attended Lincoln's "march on Charles Town":

"The inconveniences [he posted on all company bulletin boards] which must unavoidably attend an army encumbered with baggage are too obvious to require a particular detail. The general hopes the bare mention thereof will be a sufficient inducement for the gentlemen of the army to subject themselves to a temporary inconvenience which in its consequences may amply repay them. He thinks a portmanteau of necessary clothes, a case of liquor to a mess, and a wagon to fifty men, will curtail the line of wagons, without unnecessarily distressing the army."

So the Continental Army advanced, with heroic fortitude and sacrifice of its liquor. One day it advanced twenty-one miles.

The Governor arrived in Charles Town while the British were still seventy miles away. He found on defense two armies without counting his own militia. The more conspicuous, despite the fact that the other was Moultrie's, was the celebrated Polish Legion with its European commander, Pulaski, then at the peak of his military celebrity. Pulaski's Legion had marched in a few days before and was encamped on the Neck, just below Ashley River ford.

The *Gazette* had informed its readers of the already well-publicized record of their new hero. He was a son of the revolutionary leader, Count Joseph Pulaski, who had organized the Polish revolt against the Russians when their forces were of vast superiority. The son's many valorous personal escapades were detailed, as well as his latest in the Pennsylvania battles of Brandywine and Germantown, culminating in a warm letter of appreciation from General Washington. The residents of Charles Town experienced an upsurge of morale. For Pulaski was not only a general in the Continental Army, by appointment of Congress, he was much more importantly, through the recent death of his father, a person of authentic European title—Count Casimir Pulaski. For the moment this seemed to be all that the city required, and Rutledge was reassured to find the reaction to the foreign title even more vigorous than it had been to the merely military splendor of General Charles Lee.

The Governor found that Moultrie had been falling back before Prévost, never daring more than to try to pick off his advance guard, for he considered himself vastly outnumbered. Rutledge gave him the facts of Prévost's numbers—twenty-six hundred. Moultrie was agreeably surprised. Then he was obliged to reveal that he himself had no more than four hundred fighting men left. The others had left him as he retreated through country where many of them lived. When any soldier heard that his home or a neighbor's home was endangered, he would desert and go off to defend it personally.

Moultrie was helplesss to cope with this, yet, when he faced Rutledge, who revealed that he had assembled, under arms, from Orangeburg and elsewhere, 1618 men as state militia, he insisted that he be recognized as their commander.

Here was a repetition of the complication Rutledge had encountered with Lincoln. He was dealing with a continental officer and if he relinquished command of his militia to Moultrie he would no longer hold the whip hand as he had held it continuously during the first siege of Charles Town.

Rutledge's attitude toward his fellow townsman and boyhood companion was no different than it had been toward the Major General from Massachusetts. He prepared to trade, but before he even considered the terms he let Moultrie realize a few of the facts which apparently were obscure to the doughty soldier.

"How big is a legion?" Rutledge asked, for the nomenclature was new to them.

"I think," said Moultrie, "a legion must be at least a thousand men. A regiment is five hundred."

"Have you inspected the Polish legion?"

"Not yet."

Then Rutledge disclosed he had been to the Polish camp that morning before breakfast. There were 118 men, including Count

Pulaski and two Polish aides. The 115 legionnaires were Americans brought down from Maryland.

"Is not General Pulaski senior to you?" Rutledge asked.

This was a facer. Moultrie had been boasting about the Polish nobleman who had come to help them fight for liberty; they had met, but, through courtesy, the question of seniority had not been raised. Moultrie had felt he was dealing with an equal, a man with the same rank as his own, that of Brigadier, but he was also a Count and a visitor. It had seemed that hospitality should overlook the essential military distinctions. However, the South Carolinian saw the point now clearly. His own Governor could hardly recognize him as commander if his Continental senior was on the ground.

Moultrie bolted out to the Polish camp and in as short order as possible returned with Count Pulaski. He was greatly pleased. They had compared commissions. By virtue of his congressional appointment, Moultrie was the senior by eighteen days.

Pulaski was amiable about it. He saluted his superior officer and placed himself under Moultrie's orders. The two were sitting down to dinner with the Governor—not yet having resolved the prime question of whether Rutledge or Moultrie was in supreme command of all military forces—when a further complication appeared.

Colonel Harris was announced. Only half an hour before he had reached the Bastion with 250 men. His was part of the force of Colonel Ashe which Lincoln had detached in the Black Swamp, weeks before, near Savannah. Harris had managed to avoid the British Army and was on hand with his men in fair condition and ready to fight.

However, the Colonel was not ready to waive precedence. Being apprised of the moot point he contended that as he was on the staff of the Major General commanding the Department of the South he must insist on recognition of the seniority of his chief and of himself, ex officio, pending the arrival of Lincoln.

At his dinner table with Pulaski, Moultrie, and Harris the Governor revealed that one of his privy councillors, Thomas Bee, was pressing on him what the councillor considered a solution of the apparent *impasse* created by these various ranks, titles, and assumptions. Bee wanted the Privy Council to confer on the Governor the title of Generalissimo. He was arguing—Rutledge quietly dropped the bombshell—that Generalissimo Rutledge would outrank Major General Lincoln, Brigadier General Moultrie, and Brigadier General Pulaski.

Little as the officers relished this idea, still such a grandiose title, if Rutledge accepted it, would be only of importance in state affairs. No South Carolina title could outrank a Continental authority. As if he were meeting this objection Rutledge went on to tell them of the further solution of Colonel Laurens, who had suggested that if the Privy Council should name Rutledge Lieutenant General he was willing to ride at once to Philadelphia to ask Congress to confirm the appointment—his father has been the President of the Congress—and then to go to the Commander-in-Chief, on whose staff he was a favorite, to persuade Washington to give Rutledge command of the southern department.

The officers pondered. At that time there was no such rank as Lieutenant General in the American Army. Washington was a General and the next rank was that of Major General. However, there could be no doubt that if there was a Lieutenant General he would outrank any Major General.

Rutledge did not indicate his own position, though in fact he had rejected these proposals. He merely related the solutions offered.

The effect on Colonel Harris was salutary, for he announced shortly that he had decided to place himself and his command under that of the Governor, pending the arrival of his chief, Major General Lincoln. Apparently he had lively visions of Rutledge shortly superseding both and had no desire to drive him to extremity. Rutledge asked him if he would be good enough to give the same subordination to Moultrie. Harris was caught. He grudgingly consented.

Moultrie was elated. At last he was in command—almost. Pulaski was under him; Harris was under him; a new contingent of so-called Raccoons had arrived and was under him. There remained only the new recruits assembled by Rutledge. They certainly equalled and perhaps outnumbered all the other forces.

Through the dinner and afterward Rutledge did not again refer
to the subject of command, which he neither had refused nor yet had
given to Moultrie. Having received many evidences of the Governor's
favor and preference the commanding general decided it was not
tactful, at the moment, to pursue the matter of the militia.

4.

The next day the teapot tempest over rank and precedence was
forgotten when news arrived that Prévost was crossing Ashley Ferry,
only twelve miles to the north of the Town. Why Moultrie had not
met him on the west side of the Cooper River where they would have
had the advantage of water between the British and their objective,
no one explained; evidently it was more important to decide who was
in command. Now, however, Pulaski, at his own suggestion, took
his legion and some Raccoons, about three hundred men in all, attacked Prévost just north of the Town, and held him at bay throughout that day. It was a show of strength, anyway, and was enough
to set Prévost down and give the port another breathing spell.

By this time the city was in consternation. Fear and gloom had
settled much more deeply over all than in 1776 when the British fleet
had menaced them. It was less than half a mile between Moultrie's
lines near the race course at the north of the Town and Prévost's
vedettes, and late that afternoon word spread everywhere that *all* of
Prévost's army had crossed the Ashley. That explained why he had
not attacked earlier that day and why Pulaski had had such a comparatively easy time holding him. Surely—everyone believed—nothing
they had could hold Prévost on the morrow.

Moultrie could make a fight of it—he could die gamely, as everyone felt he surely would do, and then what? The inevitable sack of
Charles Town, a disaster the settlement had warded off for more than
a hundred years!

Rutledge was strangely dilatory. Communal confidence in the
Governor came almost to the breaking point that night. He was the
one on whom the people could always rely for that last essential ounce
of courage, so different from Moultrie's, for they knew there was an

unplumbed mental and spiritual resource behind it. In the final pinch he had never failed them before.

Now he was glumly indifferent. He went freely about the streets, which was not his usual custom. Everyone saw him and hounded him with questions. He only shook his head. Everyone asked him where Lincoln was. He said he knew nothing of Lincoln.

The word spread into every home and every bivouac that the Governor was fearful of the morrow, and, what was infinitely worse, that he had given up hope of Lincoln's arrival.

The moment dusk fell, singly and by twos and threes, and even by larger parties, the far-sighted citizens of Charles Town slipped through the lines, across the barricades or along the footpaths by one of the rivers, and cast their lots with what they believed to be the winning side. And they all brought the story to Prévost's ears that Charles Town was whipped; the Governor was ready to give up.

By midnight the British commander was in a glow of satisfaction; the metropolis of the south was all but captured. He retired happy, leaving orders for "general assembly" at four o'clock. He told members of his staff he expected to assault at six, and to be in the State House before noon.

Moultrie knew, within half an hour, what Prévost told his staff, for among the "deserters" were counter spies, who slipped back and forth. In fact, the fronts, of both armies, were sieves for spies.

Therefore, military secrecy seemed impossible. The moment either commander gave an order there was always someone to carry it to the enemy, promptly. On all the peninsula between the Cooper and the Ashley Rivers there was, that night, only one secret, and that was locked in the breast of John Rutledge; it remained secret because he told no one; not the garrulous Moultrie, not even a member of his Privy Council.

Moultrie had no sleep that night, for when he got the news of Prévost's plan to attack the next morning he believed he was in for the fight of his life; he spent the night going from post to post, steadying his officers, telling them what to expect and how to meet it.

About three o'clock he saw a light advancing from the Town, and angrily sent an aide to "see what fool that is."

It was the Governor. He had come out for a parley. It would soon be dawn and he had heard what was to happen. He asked what the last check-up of men revealed.

"We have twenty-two hundred," said Moultrie.

"I think around eighteen hundred," replied Rutledge, coldly. This was staggering to Moultrie, for he never knew the Governor to be wrong, but he protested, and then suddenly he asked if it was possible the Governor was not excluding the militia—the state troops he had raised personally. Rutledge was noncommittal.

Moultrie blurted out, "This is no time to divide authority, Governor. I think we ought to agree. Am I in command of the troops, or am I not?"

"General," said Rutledge, "as you are an officer of the Continental Army I am willing to place the militia under your orders, entirely, but only if you agree that in all parleys and possible capitulations with the enemy I am to have full control."

Moultrie had been worrying about his lack of authority over the militia. It was late to get it, in the very face of battle, but not too late, and he gladly accepted the conditions.

Rutledge continued with him and together they inspected the positions, from river to river.

About an hour later Rutledge said, "I believe Colonel Senf is right." Senf was the chief engineer.

"Right about what?" Moultrie demanded.

"The defenses. The fleches are badly built. The barricades will not hold an hour—they are no more than knee-high. There is not a bastion or earthwork on your whole front." This was only too true. Moultrie had had weeks for preparation, but he had wasted them.

It was then five o'clock. Dawn was beginning to break. Both armies were preparing breakfast.

"I think," said Rutledge, abruptly, "we had better send over a flag of truce."

It took some time for the Governor to persuade Moultrie that it was better to give up than to fight—better to save the women and children the horrors of being under the heel of an outraged and victorious enemy. Fighting was Moultrie's nature. Yet he gave in. "All right," he said, "send a flag."

"No," said Rutledge, "you send the flag."

The time apparently was getting short. They could look across the barricades and see Prévost's men being lined up, getting ready for the attack. Moultrie gave in to Rutledge and sent a flag to Prévost with this message:

"General Moultrie, perceiving from the motions of your army that you intend to besiege the Town would be glad to know on what terms you would be disposed to grant a capitulation, should he be inclined to capitulate?"

Rutledge and Moultrie, through their glasses, saw the effect of the messsage in the stoppage of activity on the other side. The Governor returned pleased. Townspeople crowding about noted his evident pleasure and learned the cause—he was going to surrender. Many were incredulous. Crowds gathered to expostulate. Some yelled derisively.

At eleven o'clock Prévost sent his reply—under a white flag. He "flattered himself he would be humane," he said, and, "if not all chuse to accept my generous protection they may be received as prisoners of war, and their fate will be decided later by that of the rest of the colonies."

Four hours was allowed for a reply.

By this time all the commanding officers had gathered. Rutledge solemnly led them to the "palace," where drinks and light dishes were served, and they discussed the situation. They argued interminably, and, as Colonel Laurens remarked later, "It was the only time any one had ever known Governor Rutledge to be so changeable. Positively he did not seem to know just what he wanted, but, whenever the council of war seemed ready to agree, he would say the word which put all in confusion again."

The wrangling was at its height—it was then nearly three o'clock, and the four-hour limit was about up—when a messenger came in from Prévost, protesting that Moultrie's men were at work on the barricades, and that if they did not stop he would call off the truce and attack.

Rutledge urged Moultrie to hasten a message back assuring the British general the work would stop. So it did stop. A few minutes later Rutledge said to Moultrie, "Send Prévost another message and ask him if he is satisfied. Make it courteous."

The second message was sent and shortly the reply came. Prévost was satisfied. By that time it was five o'clock. Rutledge told the council, "There are less than two hours left of daylight. He will not attack tonight."

At dawn the next day Moultrie sent his reply—at the dictation of Rutledge—saying, "Sir, I cannot agree to so dishonorable a proposal as contained in your favor of yesterday, but if you will appoint an officer to confer on terms I will send one to meet him at such time and place as you may fix on."

Prévost replied most promptly and discourteously by giving them two hours to make up their minds.

In the day of respite the officers had come together. Moultrie, Pulaski, Harris, and Laurens were agreed. They wanted to fight. Among themselves no one dared utter a suspicion which each was beginning to harbor: that Rutledge had lost his nerve. They felt they were not out-matched; they had forces nearly equal in numbers to Prévost and the advantage of interior lines and some fortification, even if hastily built; and their men would be fighting for their homes; they felt sure they could give a good account of themselves. And Rutledge was restraining them.

It was only nine o'clock in the forenoon. Rutledge had gained one day. What should he do to gain another?

When Prévost's ultimatum arrived, Moultrie got back his courage. He told the Governor frankly he would have no more of the negotiations and reminded Rutledge of the agreement that the executive should have control of parleys and capitulations.

The military officers stood aside—in the drawing room at 116 Broad Street—while Rutledge called the Privy Council into the library.

After a short time he had the consent of the Council, five to three, to the sending of a messsage to Prévost. Moultrie refused to have anything more to do with messages, so Rutledge induced Roger Smith and Colonel McIntosh to carry this one. They did so under protest.

Signed by Rutledge the message offered to Prévost "that he be permitted to take possession of the Town provided the state and harbor be considered neutral during the state of war, the question of whether it belonged to the United States or Great Britain to be waived until the end of the war, and that whatever was granted to the other states it should enjoy."

Gadsden and John Edwards, of the Council, protested. Gadsden rushed from the "palace," proclaiming that the Governor had become craven and was surrendering them all and calling on all good soldiers to resist with their "lives and sacred honor." Behind the fortifications they erected a bench for him and he orated in his most exuberant manner, in full sight of the British lines. And word was carried over even as he talked—word that the civil command and the military had quarreled, but, above all, word that there was still good hope of surrender.

Thus, though his given time had not been met, Prévost still waited.

Edwards, the privy councillor, wept at The Corner, crying, "Are we to give up the Town without a fight!" Word of this, too, was carried to the enemy and was received as soon as was the Governor's message, carried by the lugubrious McIntosh and Smith.

Prévost's answer was prompt and decisive. He was well aware, he declared, that the Governor had merely civil authority. *He would deal only with the military commander!*

It was three-thirty in the afternoon. Rutledge called a final conference, this time with the military officers. Moultrie, Pulaski, Harris, and Laurens faced him in his library. He seemed "almost absent-minded" as he related "casually" what had happened and gave them Prévost's message.

Moultrie, at last fully aroused, stoutly faced his Governor. "Do you mean," he cried, "that you still insist you want me to give you up as a prisoner of war?"

Rutledge quietly replied, but without looking at him, "Yes."

Moultrie glanced about for support. He reassured himself that Pulaski, Harris, and Laurens were at one with him. Then he exclaimed, with as little vainglory as possible, "I am determined not to deliver you a prisoner. We will fight it out!"

Colonel Laurens shouted, with all the pent-up delight of his twenty-three years, "Thank God! We are on our legs again!"

The four saluted and departed.

Rutledge looked at his watch. It was five-twenty. He had gained the second day.

All that night Moultrie and the others feverishly prepared for what they believed would be the inevitable attack at dawn. As the light came they gazed anxiously at the British trenches.

They were empty. Prévost had departed in the night. At that moment more than half of his command was across Ashley Ferry and all of it was over before nine o'clock.

Lincoln had sent a letter the day before to Rutledge, telling him he was only twenty-four hours away. It had been intercepted by Prévost. Lincoln was only twelve miles from the Ferry when he sent the letter. If Prévost had not heard from Lincoln in writing while he was negotiating with Rutledge, his army would have been "Burgoyned."

Rutledge uttered no word of complaint. When Lincoln entered Charles Town, two days later, with his army—after "resting" the final twenty-four hours—he was hailed as a deliverer.

The British did not stay away so long this time, yet it was 1780 before they came back. Thus, for another year Charles Town was spared—by advice of counsel.

5.

Sir Henry Clinton had been in supreme British command for more than a year—the same Clinton who came with Parker in 1776 to make an easy conquest of Charles Town. He was the ablest of the British generals, the only one who did anything that might be called original thinking in the solution of his problems.

And yet—Clinton was but an agent of the King. In 1779, George Hanover was absorbed with winning in America. He might with some justice have placed the blame on North and Bute and the others who had so badly advised him, but he had taken the responsibility in the beginning; he did not shift it now. Many writers have tried to do this for him, but George III never attempted it for himself.

He looked to Clinton to retrieve what had been lost, to devise a way to hold the colonies. Clinton had the King's money and all the King's power behind him. There was no default in the final contest. It had to be fought to a finish on its military merits.

Clinton knew what good strategy the Americans had devised in Philadelphia in 1775, when Washington, John Rutledge, Sam Adams, Benjamin Franklin, and the other congressional leaders had agreed to avoid the British armies, as much as possible, and wear down the invader by keeping away from him.

Washington had been singularly faithful to that policy. For more than two years now the British had not been able to engage him, even in a skirmish. Clinton knew as well as Washington did how ragged the rebel army was, how ill paid, and how discontented. But when the British general advanced, Washington retreated. The American was always nimbler than his opponent.

Moreover, Clinton felt that even if he should actually capture Washington and all his army, he still would not have won the war. He realized he was fighting not just an army but a whole people. He decided that the only way was to conquer and subdue one section at a time, and so proceed from colony to colony. It was not a new idea—conquerors had been doing it for thousands of years—but it was new for the British in this war.

The question was where to start. Of the thirteen colonies the British had pacified and fully occupied only Georgia. Clinton's reports said that the people of Georgia had welcomed the occupation and that they seemed to be mostly loyal.

Logically South Carolina was the next. Moreover, the possibilities of loot there were attractive. So Clinton cast the die; the fate of America should be decided in South Carolina.

In December, 1779, a little less than four years after his first voyage in the same direction, the British commander sailed south from New York.

Late in January Rutledge was in the back country when word first reached the city of the approach of Clinton with his fleet and army. While a messenger was dispatched to reach the executive the General Assembly, February 3, 1780, fearing it might have to disperse suddenly, passed a resolution with only two dissents, "Herewith delegating to John Rutledge, Governor and Commander-in-Chief, and to his Privy Council, power to do everything that to him and to them appears necessary to the public good."

Thus, in violation of the Constitution he had written, without his knowledge and in his absence, John Rutledge was made dictator. The period during which he held this power is the only period in the history of the United States, or of any one of them, when any man was legally dictator. Under this grant he held all power, including that over life.

The Privy Council, in 1775, in the colonial period, in granting secret powers to Drayton, actually had used the word dictator, while in 1780, under the union, the Assembly of the State of South Carolina avoided the word, but openly voted the fact.

It was fitting that Clinton should be matched with Rutledge at the finish, because each was the most representative champion, in the realm both of ideas and of competent administration, of the respective sides.

Clinton had learned his lesson, he thought. He would have no more frontal assaults and he would take greater care by advancing more slowly. He knew he had only Lincoln to oppose him—"an obese tombstone"—with poorly drilled and badly provisioned troops.

His report on the Governor was: "Rutledge is a barrister who thinks only of the ways of the law courts, and is so lacking in spirit and military knowledge that the least corporal in his militia can ride over him."

When Clinton landed his army thirty miles south of Charles Town—February 11, 1780—the blockade was complete. The Town was cut off by sea. The Georgia frontier was closed and so was the western frontier. Thus three sides were gone, and the way into North Carolina was nearly impassable due to an unusually heavy series of rains.

Lincoln was in military command with one gouty foot wrapped in bandages. Gadsden drilled but had lapsed once more into silence. Moultrie was vigorous; for the first time he worked hard on the fortifications. There was a new Colonel Pinckney—the young Charles Cotesworth.

They all did what they could, but it was no use. Clinton had twelve thousand men, well fed, with plenty of ammunition and supplies, and a fleet of thirty supply ships for constant replenishment. Lincoln had less than four thousand men. Powder was low, and food was lower. The price of a pair of shoes in the city was seven hundred dollars. Yellow fever appeared, and smallpox threatened.

Rutledge issued a proclamation calling on the country militia to come in to defend Charles Town. None came. The hot season was approaching, and they would not come to the Town.

Then a British fleet of seven war vessels appeared and sailed calmly by Fort Moultrie, giving it a wide berth, as Parker might have done four years before. They joined Clinton at Wappoo on James's Island.

Clinton was leisurely, and certain. It was the first of April before he crossed the Ashley River. Then he did not cut off the Neck at once. He waited. Perhaps he wanted to spare his men, for the Town was starving as it faced the fate so long avoided.

On March 29, 1780, the Assembly was even more deeply frightened than it had been in February when it first granted dictatorial powers. It was about to scatter in all directions and it "delegated until ten days after their next session to the Governor, John Rutledge, Esq., and such of the Council as he can conveniently consult, a power to do everything necessary for the public good, except the taking away of the life of a citizen without a legal trial."

The dictatorship was thus confirmed, but limited. Rutledge still had supreme power over property and the liberty of citizens, but power of life and death, which he had held for fifty-four days without exercizing it, was taken from him.

The first grant, loosely, had extended the power to the Council; the second grant concentrated while it limited the supreme authority, making it more flexible, but defining it more sharply. The first grant of power was made by the Assembly without Rutledge's knowledge; the second he wrote himself.

Rutledge's voluntary self-deprivation of the dictatorial power over human life may be traced to several sources. For one thing, he lacked the predatory instinct. He had slaves to hunt for him; there were soldiers to enforce his will; he directed generals to realize his considered policies. Yet, personally, he never killed, wounded, or even harmed any life, human or animal.

Shortly before, however, in Orangeburg, an enemy bullet went through his coat. This emphasized how narrow was his hold on his supreme office; and someone else might not be so lenient, for the records show that during his presidency of the Republic he pardoned at least eighteen condemned to death, as well as the thirteen white "Indians" 'taken at Ninety-Six, and a later ninety who had been sentenced to stand before a firing squad.

From the beginning he had seen the essence of his problem as being that of unity. Even union with the northern colonies was a secondary requirement to unity among his own people, and that essential union, he decided, could best be advanced by practicing clemency as a major policy.

On April 1 Clinton crossed the Ashley River, but only with a small detachment, and occupied the northwestern approaches, though the Neck was still open.

Again the Assembly met. The members knew it was for the last time. Only a third of the legislators were present. Gadsden took the chair. He was lugubrious, making a virtue now of taciturnity, perhaps in imitation of Rutledge who was saying nothing.

They discussed conditions. The only question was—how long

could they hold out? Several were in favor of getting Clinton's best terms and surrendering at once, to save what they could. John Rutledge entered, unexpectedly.

Rutledge stood in the well just below the rostrum where Gadsden stood and announced a decision he had just made. He intended, he said, as soon as night fell, to leave the city. His canoe, with eight rowers, was waiting, he told them, underneath a wharf on the Cooper River. It would carry him to the Patey-Boone plantation where he had sent his mother several weeks before.

The dictator turned to the presiding officer and addresssed him as Governor Gadsden, and advised him, as well as all the others, to leave the city while it was still possible. At once there was an explosion, led by Gadsden.

The Vice-Governor proclaimed that nothing could induce him "to desert the city of my birth and the residence of my loved ones, and the treasure house of all I hold most dear. If in the course of human events. . . ." It sounded as if he might have been preparing it for days.

Rutledge listened politely, and then, without a word, started out. A hubbub rose. A member from the Peedee district blocked his path, and demanded assurances that if the Governor reached safety he would not again pardon "traitors." He cried, loudly, that the "spirit of our defense is petered out because you have poured on us from the sewer all the cut-throats we have caught." Rutledge made no reply, but kept on, though slowly, for "members were crowding the aisles and he could not go rapidly."

This only made the up-country member more angry. He shoved his way more closely to the Governor, who ignored him and was chatting with some friends among the other members. The man from Peedee ripped a piece of lace from his jabot and threw it in Rutledge's face, and "challenged him, on the ground that the Governor thought himself better than the men who made him dictator, and that his manner was insulting."

Instant quiet came to the stormy chamber. Here was the South Carolinian's badge of courage—the duelling code, instant leveler of all ranks, the acid test which no man could refuse and still hold his head high. In Savannah, only shortly before, the Governor of Georgia, Button Gwinnett, in the Assembly chamber, had been challenged by General McIntosh and, the next morning, had been killed. Those who recalled it had difficulty in remembering what the quarrel was about. However, when the Georgia Governor was gone there departed from that state a vital spirit of resistance and the British conquest was rendered so much easier.

Did those in the Assembly chamber at Charles Town think of that in this tense moment? His friends had reason to think more of Rutledge's aversion to personal combat, of the fact that he did not use either firearms or steel weapons. He had never even taken a fencing lesson, a strange fact for the place and period.

Two members offered themselves in place of the Governor, and to satisfy the honor of the challenger. A few moments had elapsed during which the challenged "Dictator" said nothing. When his friends offered to take his place on the field of honor he restrained them with a gesture. Everyone, including the man from Peedee, was quiet.

Rutledge surveyed them. "His blue eyes narrowed and when he looked at one it was if a sharpshooter had 'lined' him. He had been shoved and his wig was a little awry, and under its white powder could be seen his own hair. He looked like a fighting man—everyone stood as if in fear, or it may have been in awe—because it was known he had a terrible temper. . . . His lips were very white and when he spoke his voice was not pleasing."

"If I offer myself to your bullet," he said, "and am destroyed I would be a party to a crime which would haunt you through life. If I destroy you I would neither absolve myself nor enlighten you. Therefore, sir, I cannot accept your challenge."

He stopped abruptly, as was his wont. The Chief Magistrate had spoken. Habit, and instinctive recognition of the judgment of their selected leader swayed them. The man from Peedee walked alone, as the other members said farewell to their "Dictator."

That night a party of Tories in the employ of Clinton and living in the Town, watched hour after hour near the canoe tied up under the wharf in the Cooper River. At dawn, exasperated, they pounced on the Negro rowers, seized them and rushed them off to British headquarters.

It was too late. Rutledge, shortly after midnight, had ridden safely through both lines, on Caesar. Nobody was looking for him on horseback. Before nightfall of the next day he was safely at the Stono plantation, with his wife and children.

6.

Clinton closed Charles Town Neck the next day, but the bird had flown. He said he cared nothing about the Governor. Those in the North—DeWitt Clinton of New York and Jonathan Trumbull of Connecticut—had given him no trouble; he did not anticipate anything different in the South. His objective was the destruction of all *military* opposition. Why should a civil governor's escape annoy him?

However, the British commander had some warning—a premonition of the fate which was riding on his flank—for he sent a platoon of soldiers with a trusted lieutenant to Patey-Boone. Spies had reported the Governor's announcement in the Assembly, that he intended to join his mother.

The lieutenant returned with a prisoner—Mrs. Sarah Hext Rutledge. The General received her graciously, and offered her tea, which she refused. He offered her a glass of wine, which she also refused. He offered her a glass of cognac; she drank the cognac.

The General asked Mrs. Rutledge what had become of her son. "I do not know," she replied, "and, if I did, do you imagine I would tell you?"

"No matter," said Clinton, "we will capture him soon."

She quoted scripture, "Let him boast who putteth the harness off, not him who putteth on the harness.'"

He assigned a separate cottage for her use, and, after he captured the city—Charles Town fell May 11, 1780—permitted her to live in the "palace" and ordered that the belongings of her son be respected.

Clinton paid his respects to Mrs. Rutledge one day in the "palace."

The widow's idea of her son surprised the conqueror. She often spoke of "the sovereign." Clinton thought at first she meant George III; she undeceived him; she meant John Rutledge.

The mother of "the sovereign" of South Carolina insisted that Clinton "must" release some of her women friends at Christ Church Parish, with whom the British soldiers were making free. The General offered to favor a particular friend or two if she would designate them, but she claimed it as a right that they all be freed at once, stoutly declaring that if the positions were reversed her son would do as much.

Clinton would not concede the "right." Mrs. Rutledge gave in to the extent of "asking for the favor" of the release of two irreproachable girls of excellent family who were thus saved from indignities which drove other gentlewomen to suicide.

Though Clinton was the most humane of the British generals yet from the moment he set foot on South Carolina shores, he saw to it that every bit of negotiable movable property, which included plate, coin, china, furnishings, produce, wine, liquors, and the like be brought to central depots. The first item in such personal property was slaves.

These were sent to Barbados, St. Eustacia, Jamaica, and Havana where they were sold and the proceeds returned. The same procedure was followed with the stuffs seized. Everything was systematically converted into cash—at great sacrifice of real values, necessarily, under the pressure—and placed in a common account to the credit of the "army of occupation." Finally, it was "equitably" dispersed.

A statement of the amount realized in South Carolina was three times asked for in the British House of Commons but was never given, though it was asserted privately that a Major-General's share amounted to four thousand guineas, and that every common soldier of the twelve thousand received above fifty pounds.

Clinton later excused his conduct, when under fire in Parliament, by saying that the expedition had come by sea and was therefore a naval exploit, and was entitled to the proceeds under the accepted booty rule of the British Navy.

There were two Major Generals, Clinton and Cornwallis, but Clinton got two shares, as was his established right under the "booty rule," one for his rank, and one as viceroy of the marauding expedition.

As soon as possible the commander liquidated everything, especially the prisoners, whose care annoyed him. Lincoln and Moultrie were paroled, with most of their men. Gadsden refused parole and was sent to a dungeon in Florida where he remained for two years, studying Hebrew. Some of his followers regarded him as the only true hero of the Revolution.

Subordinate commands were sent out, in all directions, as much as two hundred miles. All returned reporting that no armed forces remained intact. Clinton was greatly pleased. Within sixty days he had completed his "conquest" of South Carolina and he so reported to the Ministry in London. Apparently Clinton had adopted a sound and workable theory of pacification. Now that he had South Carolina, to add to Georgia, and since the states adjoined each other, it rendered the whole situation in North America extremely promising for the British.

The next step was to conquer North Carolina, where reports indicated there was little to stop him. After that came Virginia which had, scouts said, only two meagre regiments of militia, with local commanders of no experience in meeting drilled troops. In Maryland and Delaware there was said to be even less prospect of opposition. After repeated conferences with his intelligence staff Clinton decided that the British, with a little luck, should be able to pacify and occupy everything up to Philadelphia, where they were already in possession, by winter.

Then, the following year he felt confident he could make his final moves and complete his job. Before spring he expected to have Washington "bottled up" north of Pennsylvania, cut off from his Congress and the big cities. From that point the plan required that Clinton should close in on the American commander, county by county, state by state.

It was a good plan—a scientific policy of territorial occupation, as opposed to the previous hit-or-miss strategy pursued by Lord Howe. Clinton, too, was relying on drilled regiments, but his object was to subdue the people.

It does not seem to have occurred to him that the people could defend themselves, or strike back. Before he left Charles Town Clinton had word of the royal approval of his plan. He expected an earldom as a reward. A grant of the title would be a certainty for the man who could do in North America what Clive had done in India.

Clinton had been handicapped through his career because he was a younger grandson of the Earl of Lincoln. This conquest would make him as much an Earl as his brother and the inevitable military decorations would lift him even higher. The eight thousand guineas of booty would enable him to enjoy his new title. The frugal General had not dissipated his share of the loot; and he hoped he would not have to buy his title from Parliament, but that the King would grant it in return for military exploit. He sailed from Charles Town for New York July 11, 1780, and left Cornwallis to carry on.

Cornwallis had inherited an earldom; he was a Constable of the Tower, a Lord of the Bedchamber, and husband of "the very wealthy Miss Jones." He was a career man, and this was merely another job for him. He went about it with the best lights he had, a plodding example of the prevailing military mode.

While Charles Town was enduring for the first time in its life of more than a century the bitter degradation of being under a despoiler's heel, the Governor of South Carolina, who held the delegated legal power "to do all necessary," hastened north. He spent only a night at Stono, with his family, and then took the road to Charlotte, which was called by the British "the hornets' nest" because it was a Whig center. There he found General Rutherford who had recently assembled fifteen hundred volunteers. The North Carolinian promised to march south.

However, as soon as Rutledge departed for the North, Rutherford broke up his force and sent it variously to different spots to guard his own border.

In Richmond Rutledge presented the case of South Carolina and its appeal for help to Governor Patrick Henry, and received promises, though nothing definite. Henry told him that there were available in the whole State of Virginia only about twelve hundred militia. As soon as Rutledge had gone Governor Henry emulated the policy of the commander in North Carolina, though he arrived at it independently; he split up his force and sent it out to "guard" strategic points along the border.

Both Rutherford and Henry knew that Rutledge was on his way to the national Congress for aid and both felt that was where South Carolina should look. After only a day and a night in Richmond, he pushed on to the village of Baltimore, the new capital of the United States.

Nearly all the thirty-five hundred inhabitants of Baltimore, he discovered, resented the fact that the Congress of the United States had come among them. Of its fifty-six delegates only thirty-one or thirty-two were present. Some of the others never had come and a dozen or more had recently gone home, being unable to get credit for board any longer.

Rutledge found his brother-in-law, John Mathews, delegate from South Carolina, living in a boarding house, which was reluctant to allot a room to the traveler—until he displayed a Portuguese gold piece.

Several members of Congress had had their horses turned out of stables because they could not pay for their keep, and Congress itself had just been served notice that unless it could pay for the rent of the hall it was using, it could look elsewhere, for the owner would not accept Continental paper.

With two English guineas which Rutledge gave him, Mathews proceeded to buy three thousand dollars in Continental currency. He could have had more if he had held out for it, he declared, but, as a member of Congress, he felt it his duty to be moderate.

Rutledge learned now, at first hand, what a slender reed he was relying on when he looked for help to "the United States of America." It lacked not only money; its prestige was in the dust; its authority extended only to the few officers whose titles it had created. The union was, in fact, a rope of sand. Only the idea still lived.

Hardly a week went by that a letter was not received from Washington filled with bitter complaints about what Congress did *not* do for him. They did not send him men; they did not pay his troops; they did not devise means of getting his supplies.

Mathews revealed to Rutledge that Congress was as heartily tired of Washington as Washington was of Congress. Nearly half the members were fully persuaded he was a military misfit, and they wanted to replace him. A cabal among them had been organized in favor of Horatio Gates who, they claimed, had won the only decisive victory of the war. (The first Battle of Charles Town had been forgotten.) Mathews said he rather expected that within a few weeks Congress would place Gates in command.

Rutledge had intended to go to Washington for a personal conference. He found that the Commander-in-Chief, with his army, was in the upper Hudson River Valley. A trip to him would require several weeks. Anxious to return home, the Governor instructed Mathews to go in his place, and to ascertain, privately, two things: whether Nathanael Greene was really responsible for the American victories two years before at Trenton and Princeton and, if so, what his methods of fighting were.

In three days the "Dictator" found out what he could expect from Congress. It was not possible to get money, men, or supplies. He might get a commander; but he wanted something better than Charles Lee or Benjamin Lincoln. Moreover, he had a definite idea of the type of commander he wanted. He had decided on the method of victory; now he must choose the personnel.

As Rutledge started for home word came to him that Washington had detached De Kalb to command in the South. This did not hearten him, though he wrote a formal letter of welcome and promised cooperation.

General Baron De Kalb, a German of noble birth, was, next to Von Steuben, the best example in America of the Prussian idea of discipline, to which Washington was now thoroughly devoted.

Washington wrote to Rutledge that with Von Steuben as his Inspector General and De Kalb in command of the most perilous detail of the moment—the southern front—he felt confident. De Kalb passed through Virginia a few days ahead of Rutledge on his return trip. He was more successful with Governor Henry than Rutledge had been. A Continental military title, especially when added to a title of foreign nobility, was impressive, and De Kalb had been permitted to take with him as he proceeded south one of the Virginia regiments. In North Carolina he added another, from Rutherford, and, as he crossed the border of South Carolina, the Baron General was met by a hastily formed contingent of raw local troops.

Rutledge had taken a long hard trip and came back with nothing. De Kalb arrived at Richmond with a single aide and when he reached Eutaw Springs in South Carolina he had a force of twelve hundred men. The prestige of the United States might not be sufficient to pay rent for a hall in which Congress could deliberate in Baltimore, but it was enough to induce Virginia and North Carolina to help South Carolina when direct appeals had failed.

Rutledge now was seeing the first local fruits of the union. The people in each colony, almost without exception, disliked the other colonies; yet the *union* was to them a cabalistic symbol of strength; they believed it could save them where they could not save themselves and they seemed to overlook the fact that they themselves formed the component parts.

The chief problem of the "Dictator" in South Carolina was to utilize for his own people this new and potent force which he had done as much as anyone to create. The old divisions still challenged his authority; while the new allegiance challenged his tact and ingenuity.

The Governor rode Caesar into Eutaw Springs, set up his capital there (by tying his horse in front of the inn), and did what he could to induce recruits to join De Kalb. The German proceeded to drill and harry his army—twelve, fourteen, or sixteen hours a day.

Then an official letter was delivered to the Governor from the Congress, notifying him that a new Commander-in-Chief had been appointed for the Southern Department, Major-General Horatio Gates. He was requested to give full cooperation. And what of De Kalb whom Washington had appointed to the same post? On arrival Gates answered that neatly by making De Kalb his Chief of Staff.

A letter from Mathews told Rutledge that Congress had taken military control of the nation from Washington, though not yet openly. A very small majority was not entirely convinced of the ultimate wisdom of the step, but had agreed to follow the cabal to oust Washington if the "Victor of Saratoga" should prove his capacity in the Carolinas. They had appointed Gates to the most important command of the moment without the courtesy of even notifying Washington. Now all Gates had to do was to whip Cornwallis and he would be recognized as chief of all the American armies.

Rutledge wrote a letter to Gates, pledging assistance. He received no answer. Gates was too busy. The Governor wrote a second letter. Weeks later he received a perfunctory reply. Gates had heard something about the methods Rutledge had employed with Charles Lee; he did not propose to have anything like that happen to him. This was to be a great victory, and he wanted sole command and sole credit. It was gossiped in Continental Army officers' messes that Rutledge was a "hard" man to deal with. His conduct in both sieges of Charles Town was held against him. The Army claimed the victories were won despite him.

Gates brought with him from Maryland and Delaware nearly a thousand men. To these were added De Kalb's force and the recruits Rutledge sent until the army of the south had about twenty-seven hundred men. The Victor of Saratoga and the Prussian Baron were drilling and maneuvering these troops near Camden when Cornwallis suddenly appeared.

The British earl, who knew his business when it was conducted along the familiar lines, had made successive forced marches from Charles Town, with a compact force of two thousand lobster backs. He attacked Gates from two sides at once, broke up his army in a few hours, and dispersed or captured its chief units. De Kalb was killed and Gates ran away. The Victor of Saratoga rode so hard he destroyed two horses under him and did not stop until he reached Hillsboro in North Carolina, nearly two hundred miles away.

That was the end of the Gates cabal in Congress and the beginning of the final phase of the military career of John Rutledge.

The military lessons of Camden were not necessary for the "Dictator"; they only confirmed what he already knew. Camden proved again that America could not expect to win the war by fighting pitched battles with forces formed and utilized in imitation of the British. Gates had been ranked by many, including Congress, as equal to or the superior of Washington in military skill. De Kalb had technical equipment equal to that of Von Steuben, who was the recognized chief of all drill masters. Yet both had been wiped out.

Even among the thirty impatient congressmen who were evading landlords in Baltimore the discretion of Washington was appreciated. He had not won any victories, but, at least, he had not been destroyed or ignominiously defeated. Even when driven back he had retired in fair order. He made a retreat look like an achievement, and so it was. No one ever avoided defeat more gracefully.

Yet—the time had come when avoidance could no longer win. If there were not a positive victory there would be a positive defeat. No one expected Rutledge to solve this problem, to win this essential victory. No one looked to *him* for it. If it had not been won no one would have blamed him. Though he occupied the key position no one recognized it as such. As he went about his work this obscurity became, perhaps, his greatest asset, for it enabled him to proceed through various channels which became essential to achieve the result.

These were three channels: the new American military technique; clemency as a considered and persistent public policy; and the moral force of the conception of union.

To do his work well, the "Dictator" "made himself of no reputation and took upon himself the form of a servant."

7.

Clinton had not announced his intention to reduce a whole people with a trained army. Rutledge was even more secretive in his resolve to conquer a formal British army with the people. Yet therein lay the terms of combat.

Cornwallis, like Clinton, depended almost abjectly on spies, and in their employ the British enjoyed the advantage. They could pay more; their promises were more tangible; they had the pick. Rutledge avoided doing anything which the omnipresent spy might report to the enemy as indicating military resource; he wanted no revised estimate of his importance; he wrote few letters; he did not live formally. His carriage, which he used only when he wanted to call attention to his office, was his sole state appurtenance.

After Camden Rutledge learned of Cornwallis's statement that he had completed his conquest of South Carolina and was ready to start north if no actual army became visible at once.

The "Dictator" thought to fortify this enemy decision, which would at least get Cornwallis out into the open, by himself leaving the soil of the state. This he did ostentatiously, by driving in his carriage, with an outrider fore and aft, to Hillsboro in North Carolina. Now the state had no army to defend it; no civil government to uphold it; perhaps the invader might leave his fortifications.

Cornwallis intended to do so, following a final consolidation of his forces in Charles Town. Arrived there, he found General Williamson—the same whom Rutledge had elevated and inspired to whip the Cherokees three years before.

Williamson informed Cornwallis that Sumter, the most ardent disciplinarian in the state, having personally escaped the rout at Camden, had assembled several companies which he was training. This training proved to be their undoing, for, with Williamson's information, Cornwallis managed to have Tarleton surprise and overwhelm Sumter and, again, Sumter barely escaped with his life. Now, finally, all drilled military opposition was wiped from South Carolina soil by the British.

Proud of his new importance, Williamson accepted as partial pay the title of Brigadier General in the British Army, and—the old account reads—"then sold out his new masters and sold information to his former friends from a doubly tainted source."

However, Williamson did not consider himself tainted, for he had served Rutledge earlier with the definite agreement that he would fight "only Indians." He never had professed hatred for the British; and never had subscribed to the Declaration of Independence. He always declared he had heard John Rutledge deliver a speech of loyalty to the King, and that he would never believe that "a man like him kin turn his coat."

Now, flaunting his way proudly about captured Charles Town, in the uniform of a British Brigadier General, and hearing that the mother of his former commander lived in the "palace," he called upon her. Mrs. Rutledge did not discuss politics; curiously she was interested only in the military, and she flattered the frontier chieftain. Ingenuously, he told all that he knew, which included the plans of Cornwallis.

Though most of her slaves had been seized and sold to help swell the British booty, the widow had been permitted to retain a few of her own selection. From these she sent one to Patey-Boone plantation, ostensibly for provisions, but he went on, up the Wando and eventually reached Hillsboro. Thus the "Dictator" established a pipeline for information from his old capital to his new. Slaves carried the messages verbally.

Leaving his carriage at Hillsboro, as a sign that his headquarters was in North Carolina, Rutledge rode back by night on horseback and personally carried to Francis Marion, then camping obscurely on one of the islands in the Santee, the information that Cornwallis was to send an advance train of wagons, with some prisoners, and heavy baggage, north along the Peedee.

Marion's military unit never had appealed to the Governor for supplies. Its members lived off the land—and the rivers—"finding" themselves as they went along. They made their own bullets and, sometimes, their own gunpowder. Their bayonets, made from saws out of the mills, were razor-edged, for Marion's men were noted for an aversion to taking prisoners alive.

The size of Marion's force was determined by the available guns. When Rutledge arrived Marion had only twenty-four assorted rifles and muskets. Accordingly his "army" numbered twenty-three soldiers —twenty-four with himself.

Anyone tempted to judge this an inferior force must be informed that the sole rule of its commander in choosing and in retaining his men was that percentage of hits in shots must be a hundred. In Marion's force a man might miss roll call; he might appear without a tunic or shoes; he might be persuaded that an order to "present arms" was an invitation to give away his accoutrement; he might sleep all day or be detained at a neighborhood cock fight for a week-end without leave, and receive therefor neither reprimand nor even any comment. But let him miss a shot and he was no longer in "the army." Marion would take away his gun and call in another partisan; there were plenty waiting for the call. Nor did Marion make any attempt to teach a soldier how to shoot. They had to come to him perfect shots, and there was no greater distinction than to be "one of Marion's men."

Rutledge went with Marion and his men when they raided Cornwallis's wagons. He saw them spread out separately along the side of the road through the swamp, apparently without orders from their leader, and then ambush the British, not by signal, but in eccentric rotation. Within half an hour every British officer was picked off by sharpshooters, and all but one was killed. Marion's men had only three rounds of ammunition left, but it was enough. They started the action with twenty-four guns; they took forty-eight from the bodies of the dead.

Soon Marion's army numbered seventy-two. As Rutledge rode out of Marion's camp one of the men asked the commander, "Where is the seat of government of the state now?" "In the saddle of the Governor," Marion replied.

This raid on his baggage wagons caused Cornwallis to stop for another week or ten days. Spies reported that Marion had only two dozen men; this could not be an army; certainly not enough to justify the Earl in altering his plans for a triumphal progress northward. The Earl decided to wipe out Marion. He sent Tarleton on that detail. "Bloody" Tarleton took six hundred mounted men, a double legion, who could travel in a unit through the swamp trails forty to fifty miles a day.

The next two weeks were vital, for if Tarleton had accomplished his object Cornwallis would have departed for the North without serious opposition.

Tarleton picked up two of Marion's men the second day out, and finished them with the rope; he was not dealing with soldiers, but with "rebels," "outlaws," and "traitors." A few days later Marion took seventeen of Tarleton's men, and hanged them. The "Swamp Fox" did not excuse his conduct by saying the redcoats were traitors. When Rutledge called him to account, Marion declared he could not spare the powder to shoot his captives; the rope could be used more than once.

Twice Tarleton caught sight of Marion; once he saw his heels, and again he saw the "Fox" as he sat lunching by the side of the road —the lunch consisting of parched corn carried in a handkerchief. The British Lieutenant Colonel thought surely he had the South Carolina Colonel this time and closed in swiftly, with a large mounted troop. Even as he charged, however, Marion's sharpshooters, concealed near-by, began picking off the leaders, and the British were demoralized. Tarleton's arm was broken by a musket ball.

The next day Marion took the musket from the partisan who had only broken Tarleton's arm, and called in another to take the place of one so incompetent.

When Tarleton returned to Charles Town, with his arm in a sling and one man out of every five dead or missing, Rutledge, writing to Mathews, laconically noted the "turning point in history," saying only, "Marion reports the loss of eleven men in Tarleton's raid." Cornwallis again postponed his own departure.

When he left Marion's camp Rutledge rode direct to Sumter's, and found him drilling. Rutledge protested at the drill; Sumter said it was the only way to discipline an army. Rutledge pointed out to him that twice he had been whipped while maneuvering with formal military units. Sumter seemed to see no fault in the system; he had an incessant energy and he had imbibed the prevailing military dogma.

At last Rutledge hit on what appeared to be the only way to dissuade him; the "Dictator" offered to commission Sumter as General (he was merely a Colonel) but on one condition—that he drill no more. Sumter agreed. The commmission was issued in the fall and meanwhile its prospect was disciplinary.

As the Governor said later, his situation was not unlike that of the national Congress—"The only thing I had enough of was paper to write commissions on."

News of the prowess of Marion spread through the state like wildfire and Rutledge utilized it. He held up the "Swamp Fox" as a soldierly model. He found that Pickens had been raising companies and going through the usual motions, not unlike those of Sumter. The "Dictator" induced Pickens to keep his men in virtual disbandment, never subject to discipline, but always ready. His task was rendered easier when he could point to Marion's success.

He worked on other neighborhood leaders in the same way. Success was easier with them as Rutledge was only encouraging the others to follow their natural inclinations; Sumter and Pickens were exceptions. Rutledge kept in touch with the headquarters of Cornwallis by means of his slave pipeline to Hillsboro via Patey-Boone, and knew every plan that Cornwallis made before he put it into effect. Cornwallis had almost forgotten that Rutledge existed.

The summer of 1780 passed and when the leaves began turning in the fall, Rutledge learned that a crisis was impending. Cornwallis had overstayed the time agreed on with Clinton when the supreme commander departed for New York. Then both had believed that South Carolina was conquered. Now there was just enough opposition to cast some doubt. Cornwallis had defeated the main army; Gates had fled; De Kalb was killed; Sumter had been routed; there was no national commander on the scene; there was no army to oppose him.

However, there doubtless did exist five, six, maybe seven, groups of armed "rebel outlaws"; none large; but none defeated. The worst of it was that each of these groups seemed to have the same answer for Cornwallis's campaign of terror. When one of his detachments went out, caught a few "rebels" and hanged them, according to instruction, one of these bands would descend, usually by night, on a camp of redcoats, and—ignoring the "Dictator's" instruction—hang a few of them, with personal indignities added. To Cornwallis the hanging of "rebels" was justifiable routine, but the hanging of redcoats was a more serious matter. He decided to put a stop to it at once.

Rutledge heard of the British decision, almost as soon as it was made, and knew that his policy was to be supremely tested. He heard that Cornwallis was sending out Colonel Ferguson, his most trusted subordinate, to make the rounds of the state and subdue all the various bands of rebels as he found them.

The moment for the start was chosen when it was known Marion was out of the state, for the Swamp Fox had gone to North Carolina with some prisoners. He later complained that it was only his conformity to the clemency policy of the "Dictator" that denied him the privilege of assaulting Ferguson on his foray.

Ferguson had about fifteen hundred men; nine hundred were Tories who had been under British discipline for many months. It was a well drilled and handled army, as formidable a unit for its size as then existed. Ferguson was a professional, a martinet, bold, resourceful, and a bit of an inventor. He had devised two improvements for the service rifle which Whitehall had approved. Cornwallis favored him greatly.

As Cornwallis's secondary army started, Rutledge sent out his calls. Sumter and Pickens were too far away to come in time, as was Marion, so his three best-known commanders were unavailable, but he got word to the North Carolinians, Sevier, Cleveland, Shelby, and to Williams. These—with Colonel Campbell of Virginia—met Rutledge one hundred fifty miles south of Hillsboro, and held a conference lasting only three hours.

Williams (Colonel James Williams, not to be confused with General Andrew Williamson) had first met the "Dictator" the previous fall, at Ninety-Six. His father, a mountaineer, had been seized by the local commander—the same Colonel Sevier with whom he was now fighting side by side and had been thrown into jail with two other suspects. The three were told they would be tried in the morning for treason. All expected to be hanged.

The son talked with the father that night through the window of the jail. The mountaineer urged young Williams to ride out after Governor Rutledge who had been in town only the day before.

The son, who had no faith in anything but his own prowess, declared he could raise as many men as Sevier had and wanted to shoot it out. But the father prevailed. Young Williams went for Rutledge and managed to get the Governor back in Ninety-Six the next morning.

Rutledge gave Sevier a chance to prove his case by appointing the trial for noon of the same day, when he appeared as magistrate, selecting a local man as defense attorney and picking a jury of twelve. None had ever before been in a court room. Rutledge heard the evidence, instructed the jury, and, as a result, the elder Williams went free.

That made a republican of Williams. If Sevier had executed his father he would have been fighting for the British, but he raised a company of sixty mountaineers and offered them to Rutledge, who commissioned him Captain. Within a year Rutledge twice elevated him, first to Major, and then, by midsummer of 1780, to Colonel, with eighty men in his command.

Rutledge and Williams talked for half an hour after the general conference had disbanded.

8.

By the time Ferguson was ready for his foray, at the end of September, 1780, nearly everyone in South Carolina knew that Williams was the favorite of the "Dictator." He seemed to combine more of the soldierly qualities Rutledge was looking for than any other. He did not utilize drill, discipline, formation, nor did he favor any particular style of fighting; he liked open attack as well as an ambush; when he found an enemy detachment he would swarm over it like a flood. He worked fast and surely. And he was not vindictive, which helped to establish him in Rutledge's confidence.

Williams's force was called a regiment, but in fact it was a posse; each man a captain without commission. As the force became established and grew, it was never defeated; never gave ground; and Rutledge spent more and more time with it. Rutledge rode with Williams for long periods at a time. It looked as if Williams would be the man selected to rout Cornwallis.

Any Carolinian who enlisted had the right to choose his commander; that was custom stronger than law. Through the late summer it could be seen how the wind was blowing. Men coming to offer themselves for service asked, "Kin I fight with Williams?" Williams's force jumped from eighty to 340 men in six weeks.

Many of them were from North Carolina, and, toward the end, more than half of them, a fact indicating how state lines were broken under the menace of the enemy as well as through the tactful pliancy of the Rutledge regime. Men who could have served with Shelby, Sevier, or Cleveland, North Carolinians, or with Lacey, a South Carolinian, chose to follow Williams.

At the end of their talk south of Hillsboro the Governor wrote out a commission for Williams as a Brigadier General and gave it to him with careful instructions. Three days later Rutledge commissioned Sumter a Brigadier General, thus fulfilling his promise, though the "Gamecock" was junior to Williams.

The instruction to Williams was to keep his commission in his pocket, a secret; he was to bring it out and use it only in the event of a disputed authority; he was to defer, in the coming action, to Colonel Campbell of Virginia.

Thus Rutledge picked Williams to be the actual, and, if need be, the nominal commander in the coming battle, while he was to operate in careful observance of the military disorganization which the "Dictator" had cultivated. If Rutledge's technique was to prove itself in its major test it must appear to rely solely on individual initiative. The Americans were to appear to fight as a people. The enemy was not to know, nor were the Americans to realize, that they were guided by the will of an unseen military coordinator.

Ferguson's army was largely mounted; as a whole it moved with the mobility of cavalry; and shortly it was winding through the passes of the mountains in the northeastern part of the state. Ferguson learned, when it was too late, that he would not have one, but five "armies" to fight. In combined numbers they were about equal to his —fifteen hundred men.

This did not alarm him; he was told the Americans were disorganized and had scant ammunition. He had plenty; and his force was disciplined to respond as one man to his whistle. However, he maneuvered for position and was cautious. He was near King's Mountain and he managed to emplace his troops well on its lower plateau.

The British commander believed, and apparently with good reason, that he had all the advantage. He was on a secure height; the attackers would have to come up to him; he had equal numbers, and, of course, his troops were professional. The British had two hundred rounds of ammunition for each man; the Americans, on the average, eleven rounds each.

In accord with his instructions, Williams sent a rider to Campbell, asking for orders though in fact he had arranged his forces so their neighbors from North Carolina and Virginia should have the posts of honor. Twenty minutes before they went into action the rider returned with the Virginian's final command: "Fight the best you know how."

It became the order of the day: "Fight the best you know how." Cleveland repeated it to his men. Williams had no time for speeches —he assigned himself to the most perilous and most exacting post.

The British Army was attacked—as the official report recorded— "by five gangs of rebel outlaws." These were the commands headed, respectively, by Campbell, Williams, Sevier, Cleveland, and Shelby. Williams managed it so that two each of the four Carolina commands should be on opposite sides of the plateau, with Campbell asssaulting the front.

The Americans swarmed up three sides of King's Mountain, beginning at the front and then working back, flowing over like a modern caterpillar, and in unison strangely coordinated for "gangs of outlaws." Without formation, apparently merely under common impulse, "the embattled countrymen rose, like the storied dragon's teeth, out of the very earth, aroused magically from every hole, from behind each tree."

The men on both sides knew they were fighting with halters around their necks. On neither side did they expect, if captured, to find mercy. Each man of the three thousand engaged fought with bitter desperation.

Their high position proved to be a disadvantage to the British. The attackers, all woodsmen, were accustomed to shooting *up*hill at game, which often ran for cover to high land. Moreover, in *down*-hill shooting, unless a man is well trained to it, there is an optical illusion which causes an elevation of sights. Without being aware of it the British suffered from nature's handicap, refraction.

The Americans shot so true that many British corpses were found with one eye open and a bullet through the other eye. Ferguson fought coolly and with courage. The superior marksmanship of the Americans was incredible to him. In an hour two-thirds of his force was destroyed. As he saw his responsive companies, alert and obedient to his whistle, melt under the lead hail of the "outlaws," he called to the survivors to follow him up the mountain. Escape there still seemed quite possible; and if he could escape with even a portion of his command, at least a complete debacle could be avoided.

But as he turned he found himself facing Williams, who had led his men around Ferguson, up the higher portion of King's Mountain, above the British, and was coming down! The Mountaineer had managed the battle consummately, and the moment had arrived for a perfect coup de grace.

Yet Williams held his hand. One of his followers felled Ferguson. Remembering his instructions about clemency, Williams lowered his rifle and advanced towards the fallen British commander, saying he need not fear surrender and offering fair treatment. With his last strength Ferguson fired his last bullet, as a fresh contingent of Americans loosed a paralyzing volley.

The two bodies were found close together, that of the chief support of Cornwallis and of the chosen champion of Rutledge. In Williams's pocket was found his commission as Brigadier General, obediently withheld from knowledge of his companions.

It was an example of the ideal of the new Americanism in pure essence, perhaps never surpassed in significance.

The battle was a complete British rout. The entire stand of fifteen hundred rifles, with their precious ammunition, was seized, and less than two hundred men escaped into the near-by forests. The British lost thirteen hundred out of fifteen hundred; the Americans, one hundred and fifty out of fifteen hundred.

Ten of the captives were hanged. Twenty more were condemned and the ropes were around their necks when the Virginian, Colonel Campbell, whom the others recognized as chief, learned of the commission found in the pocket of the dead Williams.

Suddenly the neighbor realized the tact of Rutledge, who had denied himself the credit of a victory, and the selflessness of his modest deputy, who had given the honor to the Virginian and insured it with his life. Campbell stopped the executions.

King's Mountain was the third and last decisive American victory in combat in the Revolution. The battle was a military classic; in planning, in execution, and in effect. Its repercussions were almost incalculable. The result, dramatic and complete, told Cornwallis, Clinton, and all of Europe and America in the clearest language what to expect.

The people were unconquerable. Without military training, man for man, they could defeat, on the field of battle, the best-trained troops from Europe. That was the lessson—quite simple, and, until then, unbelievable.

The Revolution had been struggling for six years to accomplish something like this. It was foreshadowed from the beginning, but, for various reasons, it had never quite come off before. At Concord and Lexington the new note was struck, and the courage of the minute men proven, but Concord and Lexington were skirmishes *and* retreats. Bunker Hill, like Charles Town, proved the capacity of the undrilled soldiers, but they fought behind emplacements, and from Bunker Hill they retired. Washington's battles were fought with drilled troops in imitation of the British and were largely losing encounters. This demonstrated, for the first time in terms conclusive and admitting no dispute, an authentic shift of sovereignty. At King's Mountain the Common Man—the Individual American—was enthroned.

9.

The Battle of King's Mountain was fought October 7, 1780. Cornwallis decided to remain in Charles Town. He was in a confused state of mind; snow would soon be due in the North.

The Rutledge coach and four remained in Hillsboro, across the border, still advertising that South Carolina was without any government. However, Caesar bore the Governor back and forth incessantly.

Once the "Dictator" spent the night at Patey-Boone, only twenty miles from Charles Town; he arrived after dark and left before morning. The next day a slave, under a white flag, entered the city, with a message for Cornwallis who was living in the Miles Brewton house. The Earl was puzzled by the message, whose source was unknown. He kept the messenger five or six hours while he discussed it.

Standing on the street the slave managed to relay to several people the news of King's Mountain—five weeks after the event. Until then no one in Charles Town, except the high command, knew of the British disaster. Thus, under flag of truce, Rutledge spread his news, the imponderable more valuable to him now than armies.

While the people in arms were in contest with Cornwallis for the military control of the state, Rutledge fought the British for the political control. The war, he knew, could not be won actually in the end, without first winning public opinion.

The British played into his hands with their campaign of terror. This he answered with his policy of clemency. Rutledge anticipated another leader, in another civil war; like Lincoln, he saw in clemency its double political value: that of breaking down immediate resistance and of rendering less deep the wounds that later would have to be healed.

Rutledge made it a habit to be on hand, whenever possible, after each battle; there were more than fifty within a year, never involving

more than a few hundred, and usually only a score or two. Rutledge
was ready to reprieve or pardon the Tories or Loyalists condemned.
To some his long-continued clemency seemed to gain nothing, to
weaken the prestige of the government, and to bolster the British contention that the state had no government.

Yet many, who were wavering on the fence, wondering which
side to join—for the state always had been divided in feeling—found
at home, among the women, the convincing argument: " 'Dictator
John' don't stand fo' it—an' he's th' state o' S'uth Ca'lina."

The moral attitude of Rutledge began to soak into them—the
essential justice of it. Many a story kept alive by word of mouth
entered the folk-lore of the people, who were transferring their hopes
from that mythical king across the sea to the nearer, and more tangible relief, "Dictator John."

As 1781 came around all this was bearing fruit by uniting the
people. The up-country men were beginning to feel that they were all
South Carolinians, not Englishmen.

The devastation of Charles Town had something to do with it.
They had hated the big city, but now it was lower in the dust than
any of them, and the Governor was with them, the "seat of government in his saddle."

Rutledge became "the best recruiting sergeant South Carolina ever
had." He would ride into a town, alone, throw his bridle over a hitch-
ing post, step to a bench in a public square, and begin speaking without ceremony—if advance notice had been given a band of Tories
might have seized him. Everyone would gather around. He would
answer questions and talk, back and forth, informally, seldom staying
more than an hour. Before he left, every able-bodied man present
had come forward and offered himself.

Getting supplies was the Governor's hardest job. He did what he
could for each of his generals and colonels, but it was not much. He
made another begging trip to Philadelphia and came back with seven
wagons filled with assorted clothing.

Locally he commandeered anything edible that he could find.
The country people hid their provisions when they saw him coming.

In December, 1780, Nameby Caton wrote to his brother Caleb, from a farm on the Pocatoligo Road.

"One day last week," wrote Nameby, "Ma saw Dictator John coming up the road, an' hustled me an' Josiah to cover the corncrib. He set with us for supper, an' told us how Marion's doing fine, an' then he sayed how the army needs corn terrible. So I showed him the corncrib, and he tuk most the corn, too, an' made me an' Josiah tote it to town next day. Ma blessed us out terrible."

The Governor had to take food from the people, for the army, but how could he pay for it? He had "the power to do all necessary for the public good," and this included, naturally, the power to issue and control money, but the issuance of promises to pay by the state, in the form of paper currency, had long since lost its value. Five years before, when he was President of the Republic, the credit of South Carolina had been much better than that of the United States; now it was lower and the United States currency was "not worth a Continental."

Every governor from Massachusetts to the Carolinas faced a similar problem. Only one made even a temporary solution; Rutledge issued the fiat of the state that indigo should become a medium of exchange. This did not affect his personal fortunes, for the lands he owned which were planted to indigo were in possession of the enemy.

Indigo came in little cubes, half an inch square, and was worth about two dollars a pound. The Governor declared that the customary cube should be accepted in payment for public and private debts in the amount of one shilling.

People went about with pockets lined with cubes of indigo, for hard money had practically disappeared. The Governor commandeered large stocks as he found them and issued in payment the state's promise to redeem them "after an accommodation has been reached with the Government of Great Britain."

The use of indigo as money conflicted with the use of ammunition, which had been popular before the Rutledge fiat. "Three bullets for a cube of indigo" was not readily altered to "a cube of indigo for three bullets." The "Dictator" made no attempt beyond that of moral persuasion to enforce his decree. For a while both bullets and indigo cubes were mediums of exchange. Finally, the fact that the state had issued promises to redeem payments of indigo outweighed the backing of ammunition, which was solely intrinsic, and indigo ruled as South Carolina money.

The use of indigo money became extremely popular. It persisted in remote settlements in the hills, many years after the state rescinded the Rutledge fiat.

Rutledge's problem with his military command was not unlike his money problem. Mathews had reported to him that Nathanael Greene, on inquiry, appeared to be worthy of the reputation he had gained, that he was willing to subordinate himself—he had never had an independent command—and that he did not favor the imported disciplinary measures.

Rutledge instructed Mathews, after securing the approval of the delegates from North Carolina and Georgia, to go in person to Washington and request the assignment of Greene to command the Southern Department.

Washington complied at once and has often been credited by historians as, in that act, "making the most brilliant decision of his career." It was "brilliant" because, unlike so many of his military decisions, it brought success. Three times before Washington had sent generals to South Carolina—Charles Lee, Benjamin Lincoln, and Baron De Kalb; Congress had sent Gates. Each of these four was now liquidated. The Governor had chosen none of them and so at last Washington was only too eager to comply with a request from Rutledge.

South Carolina's Commander-in-Chief met Greene beyond the Peedee. The Major General had only one aide. He greeted the Governor cordially and at once they established harmony, which often thereafter was tested severely, but never actually broken. There was a great deal of jealous derision, especially among the friends of Sumter, who never forgave Rutledge for not securing the appointment of their champion to the chief command. On the whole, however, the South Carolinians were cordial to their new overlord.

Greene was a Rhode Island Quaker. His father did not believe in education, pleasure, or war, so Greene had read all the books he could find, enjoyed the theatre, and reveled in a military career. He boldly declared, to those in close touch with the Governor, that he subscribed to the art of war as endorsed by Rutledge.

The Governor issued requests to all South Carolina forces to recognize Greene as Commander-in-Chief. The requests were written and issued directly, with no apparent political reservations, and yet the situation held reservations. The South Carolina commanders, Marion, Sumter, Pickens, and the others, had to look to their Governor for promotion.

As soon as Greene was actually the military power, removed from Washington, supreme even above the Governor, and, for the first time in his life, independent, he began to reveal the customary military pattern. He gave orders for concentrations, for drills, for extended outposts; all of which orders, naturally, were relayed by spies to Cornwallis.

Rutledge hastened to Greene. After a few days parley the orders were rescinded. The army, now "Continental," again played possum and became, in effect, partisan.

Again Cornwallis sent Tarleton out and this time at Cowpens the savage young Lieutenant Colonel was soundly thrashed by a force under General Daniel Morgan. Cornwallis made light of the defeat, which, reported in the North, furnished six months' supply of "moral meat" for New England. Cornwallis could not afford to admit any military meaning in Cowpens; he wanted desperately to report the final conquest and go North for the long-delayed meeting with Clinton. To facilitate that Rutledge was striving to hold Greene in leash.

As the war rose to its climacteric, Rutledge saw that the available American forces could be driven in for the kill and he was more alert than ever to retain actual, though he cared nothing for the nominal, control. He wanted only victory and he felt sure it could be had in only one way. His mental attitude then can be summed up in the words of Clemenceau, who, in a similar situation, said, "War is too important to be entrusted to the experts."

To complicate the situation Washington sent Von Steuben to assist Greene, and shortly the villages and farms of Virginia resounded with the harrying of the Prussian drill master. First De Kalb; now Von Steuben. Washington was susceptible to formalized military men. Already he was favoring Henry Knox, the Boston bookseller who learned the art of war from the texts on infantry, cavalry, and artillery he sold the officers of General Gage and who later became Washington's first Secretary of War. Knowing this weakness of the Commander-in-Chief Greene, when he was Washington's Quartermaster-general, had the habit of going about with a volume on tactics in French by Turenne, which he absent-mindedly left once or twice in Washington's tent. Washington could not read French; neither could Greene.

However, Greene had too sound a military sense actually to rely on the ability of Von Steuben to raise and train quickly an effective army. He only used the German's European reputation in striving, over the "Dictator's" head, to impresss Sumter whom he knew to be partial to the technique of drill, and whom he wanted under implicit, direct command.

Greene and Rutledge always agreed on the main objective: the destruction of Cornwallis's army. That held them together—that and their inescapable need of each other. But how should they reach their main objective? There were only two ways—by annihilation or by attrition. Greene, with Turenne in his pocket—by this time he had a translation between the lines—and Von Steuben in Virginia, wanted to do it in the grand manner; Rutledge insisted it be done by attrition.

In the late spring of 1781 the Earl posted his official announcement on the bulletin boards of the barracks of Charles Town: "The expeditionary force of H. M., the King, under personal command of His Excellency, Major-General, Charles, Earl Cornwallis, will break camp and depart. . . ."

The slave pipeline carried the news north swiftly. Rutledge had it within two days. Cornwallis was taking his army with him, leaving only a garrison in Charles Town. He would have about four thousand men, plenty of ammunition and supplies, and a commensurate wagon train. He never travelled without being fully and properly equipped.

The Governor spread the news to Marion and Sumter as he started to confer with Greene. The Swamp Fox spread his force along the roads beginning about sixty miles from the Town. The third day out Cornwallis was attacked by Marion, but never in force. He sent detachment after detachment after the Fox, but none ever saw him, and only one of Marion's men was taken. Sumter was recovering from wounds, but he started to assemble his followers.

Greene was preparing for a set battle when Rutledge reached him. A check-up of his forces told the commander of the Southern Department, he reported to Rutledge, that he could equal the numbers of Cornwallis. He already had under him troops from Virginia, Maryland, North Carolina, and Delaware. These, combined with the South Carolinians—he was counting on Marion and Sumter—prompted him to believe he could be a match for Cornwallis. He wanted to fight it out in one maneuvered formation. When the test came he was reverting to military type.

The problem which Rutledge, for South Carolina, faced and solved, the State of North Carolina had avoided by appointing a Board of War whose function it was "to take from His Excellency, the Governor, the burden of making decisions of military moment." As a result there was neither unified command nor concentrated military power in North Carolina, and the most that was accomplished was to drive one of the state's best officers, Davie, into Greene's commissary department. At the same time it both complicated and intensified the necessity existing in the situation for Rutledge to solve the problem for both states, whose vital interests were one; and this he had to do not only without authority in North Carolina but in constant threat of failure in both states for lack of it.

Lacking authority to command, Rutledge set himself to persuade Greene not to try a pitched battle. He recalled the episodes of Gates and of Lincoln. A defeat now of a Continental army would be an irretrievable disaster. The thing to do, Rutledge urged, was to continue the war of attrition.

Though, of course, he could not know it, Rutledge was securing the base of that legend that the "palmetto soldier" could lick ten men. So he could, but only when the Palmettan was loose and the ten confined in the artificial restraints of drilled maneuver. Rutledge saw this clearly, but Greene apparently could only see that on paper he had about as many men as Cornwallis—or would have if Marion and Sumter would join him. Greene lacked neither courage nor audacity, but he would make no discount for the tested and proven superiority of Cornwallis in his own métier.

Rutledge had a strong hand to play; his two aces were Marion and Sumter. Marion would not come out of the swamps voluntarily and place himself under command of a "no'then'r," nor would his legal commander, Rutledge, issue an order to that effect. Greene sent a message urging Sumter to join him. Sumter went the other way to marshal his men. It was clear his imperious fighting will resented an outsider.

Greene appealed to Rutledge and Rutledge smoothed things out— but not too well. "I shall be glad that you continue," the Governor wrote to Sumter, "to give Gen'l Greene and myself the earliest intelligence—" The tact as well as the emphasis in the "—and myself" was lost neither on Sumter nor on Greene.

Sumter's commission from Rutledge as Brigadier was dated October 6, 1780, the day before Williams was killed at King's Mountain, and it antedated Marion's commission as Brigadier by several weeks, so, for the final year of the war, he was the senior officer in South Carolina, and conscious of it with Continental officers. His commission from Rutledge antedated Morgan's from the Continental Congress and he refused to accept orders from Morgan; he did not refuse those from Greene, but only "failed to get" or delayed implicitly obeying those he did not like. When Morgan and Sumter clashed Rutledge smoothed things out—by referring Morgan to Greene. In the final analysis Sumter belonged to him.

Greene was double-faced, or even triple-faced, about the methods of the South Carolina commanders. He wrote to Sumter, paternally, striving to argue him out of continued "partisan strokes," which he called "only garnishment for the table." (This was the very thing Rutledge continuously insisted on.) It was galling to Sumter who had had so much trouble with Rutledge, and such a terrific beating from Cornwallis, for fighting the year before as Greene was advising now, in 1781. His answer is not of record, for Sumter knew how to answer, as well as to obey, with inactive silence. At the same time Greene was writing this to Sumter, he wrote to Marion praising the methods of the Swamp Fox, which were never anything but partisan, or, as a later age called them, guerrilla. At the same time to Rutledge Greene alternately opposed and accepted the principle of the partisan warfare; opposed out of hearing and accepted in conference.

All of this was known to Rutledge, whose espionage system was much superior to any other, on either side, and who already had survived his Charles Lee and his Benjamin Lincoln. Fortunately, he had more competence to deal with in Greene, but the great problems were still there: the problem of getting personal military rivalries to work together in harness and the greater problem of keeping the Continental officers away from old-world military formulas. They were copying Europe—and Europe in a bad model, at that—when their best chance to whip Europe was to follow an American pattern.

While Rutledge and Greene were debating this problem—the conference lasted for five days—a slave arrived from the South bearing to Rutledge an intercepted letter from Cornwallis addressed to the Ministry in England. The letter had been seized en route to a British warship by a sloop off the James Island Inlet.

"I am surrounded," Cornwallis complained, "by inveterate enemies and timid friends . . . these rebels will not stand up and fight like gentlemen. . . ."

That letter and Marion's assertion of the individualized principle of warfare, backed by Rutledge's strategy and the obvious fact that both Marion and Sumter were subservient to Rutledge, caused Greene not to attack Cornwallis in formation.

So His Excellency's complaint seemed justified. The Americans sniped from behind trees and boulders; they would rush out of the swamps in small groups and would be gone before the British could see how many they were.

This had come to be expected from Marion and his men, but when the British got through the lowland swamps and into the dry land of the up-country they met a real disappointment. They were now in the presence, as spies accurately reported, of an officer of the national army, whose reputation had spread even to England and who bore a commission equal to Cornwallis's own, that of Major General. Yet he sent roving bands of men, the kind Williams had organized, to swoop down on the redcoats and harry them.

There was something so improper about it that Cornwallis was shaken to the core of his professional code. He longed to be up North where he could deal with—even if he could not fight—Washington, who at least was gentleman enough to maneuver troops in formation and give a soldier the prospect of something solid into which he could sink his teeth.

Day by day as Cornwallis' army advanced—week by week as it crawled north, the British faced one incessant skirmish; the Americans gave no rest, night or day. A few ragged rebel outlaws would dart out of the wayside and kill a few redcoats and be gone before one of them could be caught. By the end of six weeks it began to tell on the British morale—and His Excellency knew it.

He was glad to be turning his back on it all, but the rebels would not let him depart peacefully. They offered him a battle on the banks of the Great Catawba River. He was preparing himself when suddenly they disappeared and were off across the raging torrent, and taunting him from the other side; and, as he made himself comfortable for the night, not trying to ford the stream in twilight, another "gang of the devils" raided him from the rear, broke up his wagons, and ran off with half of them.

"They were not like white men; they were savages," the Earl commented.

Then, no sooner was he across the Great Catawba, two days later, than a swift sortie was made on his flanks from what seemed to be an impenetrable swamp. A few non-coms were picked off; it was strange how the sharpshooters specialized in officers. Cornwallis personally directed two of his best platoons, the reserve grenadiers, to chase down the "savages," but they disappeared in the swamp.

His Excellency stopped for a week, to repair damages and to count his losses, which proved to be astonishingly high, and suddenly there seemed to be an answer to his prayer. Directly in front of him, with a file of soldiers drawn up across the road and reliably reported by scouts as only a mile and a half away, was Major General Greene, U.S.A., the opponent of proper rank to engage a British Major General.

Cornwallis was immensely cheered. The drums beat. The fifes shrilled. The platoons responded magnificently and stood at attention, three deep across the sandy South Carolina road. At last he was to be rewarded. He sounded the charge. And then—when the redcoats reached the place where Major General Greene had been there was only the sight of barefoot mountaineers running away. The British pushed on bravely when, suddenly, from behind trees, out of the bushes, sharpshooters—no one could tell how many—picked off the non-coms.

An army cannot stand that sort of thing indefinitely.

Perhaps the worst episode of that whole campaign came after Cornwallis had crossed the state line into North Carolina and found that the South Carolina technique did not stop at the state line. The North Carolinians also apparently were devoid of the rudiments of military knowledge. Combined, the men from both states, worked on a system, in relays. They would not let the exhausted troops sleep, nor would they let them come in contact with any considerable body of rebels. It was like a nightmare.

Then Rutledge lost his control, for Greene's army was in North Carolina, with only one South Carolina officer, Huger, under him and with most of the South Carolina men fighting under North Carolina command. Greene succumbed to his complex and proceeded to annihilate Cornwallis at Guilford Court House. It looked like a good chance. The British and Americans were of about equal number and the Americans had a superiority in guns of three field pieces.

Each side fought well; each side lost about the same number. When it was over the British had the field—and claimed a great victory. So it might have been except that their losses were irreplaceable, and Greene was not another Gates. He withdrew undismayed and in good order —to South Carolina.

Again fate placed the cards in the hands of Rutledge. Greene complained to him that the cause of his retreat from Guilford—he would not admit defeat—was that he got no cooperation from the North Carolina commanders. He had been complaining about the same thing in South Carolina, but he had not had such a whipping in South Carolina as he had at Guilford. Greene was a voluble complainer, both in correspondence and verbally, but he never sulked. He had emotional depressions and often seemed on the verge of quitting, but examination of his military orders reveals that this never reached the point of defeatist action. He had mental resource and his political skill was apparent to Rutledge. Greene knew how to flatter, to underplay vanity and overplay pride, to balance rivalries, and, withal, he was a good tactician; his chief weakness was the one commonly prevalent, a desire for military glory.

Rutledge utilized Greene's weakness. While the officers on his staff were trying to persuade the Major General to hasten after Cornwallis—toward Virginia for there would be the decisive action of the war—Rutledge, whose power with the Continental officer lay primarily in his understanding, revealed to Greene that if he did go to Virginia he might lose all chance for individual glory, for Washington might be there, and then what would Greene be but a secondary officer? To make it even more attractive for Greene to stay in South Carolina Rutledge said he would place all of his officers—Marion, Sumter, Pickens, and the rest—directly under orders to Greene. This latter might not have been so convincing to Greene, for Rutledge had given similar orders before only to have them at least liberally interpreted, but now the "Dictator" offered to make it practically effective by going North himself. When he could not be reached Sumter and Marion would have to obey Greene without evasion or delay. As it happened they both resigned sooner than obey Greene—but that was not apparent for some time.

Greene decided to stay in South Carolina. That *was* the decisive *decision*. "With Hannibal at the gates of Rome it was carrying the war into Africa." No matter what might happen in Virginia Clinton's grand strategy was stalemated.

Rutledge went North and called on Washington. Greene advanced on Carthage—i.e., Charles Town—by way of Hobkirk's Hill, Eutaw Springs, and way points, with losses and discouragements, but he advanced. The Continental army, Southern Department, was intact —H.Q. in South Carolina. The "Dictator" was absent, but he was "doing all necessary." Von Steuben raised fifteen hundred Virginia militiamen and drilled them copiously. North Carolina uttered a draft. South Carolina's "recruiting sergeant" was not there; he uttered no draft. What he lost in numbers and in paper strength he more than gained in fact, for "man for man the rank and file were physically and intellectually superior."

Cornwallis managed to cross North Carolina and get to Wilmington. He reported that he had "cleaned up" the South. It was much later that Clinton sneered, "What! with 700 men left out of 3,000?" However, the organizations were still intact; His Excellency was unscathed; the army was undefeated. They had not had a real defeat— not since King's Mountain—this was only a calamity they could not sense. By the rules of the only game they knew they had won.

With relief the British redcoats pulled themselves out of the swamps and into the green fields of Virginia, and entrenched themselves beside the cool waters of the York. Beyond, to the north, they expected clear sailing to Clinton's army. Instead, they saw the stout sails of De Grasse; the French fleet arrived at Yorktown as Washington marched in.

Here was the chance Cornwallis wanted: warfare as written in the books. Now he could meet, in regimental formation, the Americans who never in such formation had defeated the British in pitched battle.

But, should he make a stand-up fight of it—the kind in which he was proficient? *Could* he—with the bowels of fortitude sapped from his soldiers back there in the swamps? On the shore appeared the fat French admiral, waddling like a duck.

Suddenly it came to the British army that its will to win had gone during the nightmare!

Cornwallis, in calm judgment as a responsible British general at a supreme crisis in history, faced a solemn decision. From his cul-de-sac he saw the French sails drawing alongside the rebel army. Yet the "sac" was not closed; there was one way of retreat; the way whence he had come.

But he could not face those Carolinians again; each man a general, each sharpshooter a sovereign!

No. The war had been settled, man to man, in the swamps. The surrender at Yorktown came without a contest.

CHARLES TOWN became Charleston, by resolution of the Assembly, early in April, 1787. With a letter and an elision they wiped out the monarchy. Thomas Pinckney was Governor. Thomas was the law partner of Edward Rutledge, the nephew of Colonel Charles Pinckney, the brother of General Charles Cotesworth Pinckney, and the cousin of Charles Pinckney. The Rutledge-Pinckney dynasty was pretty well established. John Rutledge had been the first Governor (with an interregnum under Rawlins Lowndes), his brother-in-law John Mathews, the second, and here was the third.

> . . . no one came from the sod
> The Pinckneys talked only to Rutledge
> And Rutledge spoke only to God.

The up country was champing at the bit and claiming it deserved more, including possession of the capital of the state, which was still at Charleston. The site on which its successor, Columbia, rose was then a cotton field, partly timber, where, in the acorns, the owner, Mr. Taylor, pastured his razor-back hogs. The whole world had changed, sovereignty had been moved from one continent to another, but nothing essential had changed in the Palmetto State; the commonwealth still revolved around a tricorn hat that moved daily with almost mathematical regularity along a thousand yards of Broad Street in the old Town.

Since 1784 John Rutledge had been Chancellor Justice. They called him Chancellor, a title, if he must have a title, he preferred above others. Practically he was the Chief Justice, and there was no appeal in the state from his decision, nor elsewhere, for that matter, as there were no national courts and the tie with the old country was broken.

Following his governorship, from 1782 to 1784, Rutledge had served as a delegate to Congress. Thus, since his election to the Continental Congress in 1774 he had continuously occupied high office, either as delegate, governor, president, or chancellor. Since his election as President of the Republic, eleven years before, he voluntarily had relinquished his leadership of the bar and had made no attempt to practice law. After the war, he might have moved to New York where the rewards for highly specialized legal talent were now the greatest in America, or to London where they were greater financially. For all his experience he was only forty-eight years old, in good health, and at the height of mental power.

The salary of the chancellor was twenty-five hundred dollars annually, and Rutledge's contentment with that hardly could have been due to financial security, for his estate was involved and he was dwelling, like most of his contemporaries, in financial shadows from which he never escaped. The new state of Franklin, presently to be called Tennessee, had given him twenty-five thousand acres of land on the Elk River as its recognition of his efficiency in the Revolution, but this land was never more than a tax burden. From time to time, in a very poor market, he sold pieces of real estate, including much of his city property in Charleston, to satisfy insistent creditors.

Although he still lived in the "palace" his complement of slaves was much reduced and his social activities were extremely restricted. His name and that of Mrs. Rutledge appeared rarely in the social columns of the *Gazette*. His guests were confined to a few intimates. He did not frequent the places where he would meet those of his own class. There were no more "oyster roasts" on the plantation.

Edward and Hugh, as practicing attorneys, were making much more money than John received as a salary, and in the life of the community each attracted more attention. In 1784 Governor John Mathews, Sarah Rutledge's husband, had named one of the principal north and south streets of Charleston "Rutledge," and when the delegate to Congress thanked him for the honor Mathews replied, curtly, that the street was named not for the former governor, but for the wife of the incumbent governor.

In many ways John Rutledge seemed to be fading out of the Charleston scene; he was already becoming a legend. He was, as always, following his natural bent. Apparently unconscious of any change in status, either professional or social, he lapsed back into the ways he had established when he first arrived from London. There was a bigger job ahead of him than any he had yet undertaken, and in this period he prepared himself for this task. He avoided taverns, other people's houses, and all exclusive society. Yet he was far from being a recluse.

For three hours of the day, from ten to one in the morning, he attended Court, but he never took the Court with him away from the court house. He did not believe in "paper work" nor in "book study." As chief jurist of the state, from whose findings there was no appeal, he established a record which never otherwise has been equalled in a high court in any English-speaking country since the days of Francis Bacon. Through a period of two years his docket was never held over for a single night.

Rutledge was usually courteous in listening to counsel even if the argument was protracted, but he never delayed decision. To those who protested he replied, "Delayed justice is injustice." He was averse to writing and when he did write revealed a somewhat slovenly habit formed during the war of not finishing sentences, and of not using the proper grammar. He usually announced his decisions orally from the bench and let the clerk enter merely a phrase, such as "Judgment for plaintiff" or "Petition refused." Yet, a contemporary account says, "Litigants were always satisfied because when he delivered judgment he illuminated the causes of action and the reasons for his opinion so impartially that even the loser was satisfied he had justice."

Rutledge ran his Court magisterially. One morning he was late; the clock in near-by St. Michael's registered 10.45. Someone objected to his lateness. The Chancellor took out his watch, laid it before him, and announced, "When this court sits it is ten o'clock, and no other hour." However, he was dictatorial only in trifles.

Every afternoon, weather permitting, he could be found on his bench at the Corner, ready to chat with all who approached. In the evening—every evening—he went to the Exchange, at the foot of Broad Street, frequented by factors, merchants, and ship captains who came and went at the rate of two to a dozen daily.

A ship captain usually carried power of attorney and when he reached his port of call bought and sold cargo as if he were sole owner; at sea he also had power over life. So he was carrier, purveyor, sales-man, autocrat; and, because of the political complexity, ambassador of industry and commerce. And he enjoyed talking about what he did and had to do, cautiously, to trusted intimates, for his calling involved everything:—property, quick turnover, life, death, and—smuggling.

Thus the only efficient newsmen of the time were these ship cap-tains; the Exchange was their club; the only outsider among them— except merchants and factors, their employers and partners—was the Chancellor. There, in the evening, he kept his finger on the pulse of the swiftly changing world outside, just as in the afternoon, at the Corner, chatting with members of the Assembly, planters, travelers, workmen, he kept in touch with the Town and the up-country. He was as close to his own people as a modern precinct captain; he was as well informed about current events outside as a modern managing editor.

No other man in Charleston knew as did Rutledge what was going on. At the Corner he realized that the *Gazette* was only mirror-ing the reactions of its constituency when, after informing its readers rather pompously that the confederation of the thirteen states was facing bankruptcy, it conveyed the impression that this was a "foreign" matter of only academic interest. That was the way most of those who stopped to talk with the Chancellor under the magnolia seemed to regard the situation. They were put to it enough to struggle out of the hard times that followed the war without worrying too much about that distant entity known as the United States.

At the Exchange he got the same story, but from a different angle. Through the skippers he sensed the temper of the North, more intense than that of the South. Also, he got its relativity. He realized at the Exchange more concretely than at the Corner, that the Federal

Congress, which was a part of him, for he had served in it off and on from the beginning, was only a laughing stock to everyone.

It all centered in the fact that the United States could not levy taxes or custom duties, while the several states, individually, had these rights. Massachusetts, for instance, had custom houses; so had Virginia; there were none in New York or Rhode Island; in other states the situation varied, from year to year, from product to product. The problem for each skipper, on each voyage, was to know where to sell his cargo to best advantage, and how. Boston might seem to offer the best market, but if he could save enough on custom duties Providence might provide the better entry. Though he might have a cargo for New Jersey or Connecticut, New York usually knew how to make it more profitable for him to anchor off Manhattan Island. Though Virginia was the most populous state and offered the best market of all he often sold the Old Dominion through Baltimore, for Maryland claimed the Chesapeake, and the duties were stiff in Norfolk and on the south shore of the Potomac.

Rutledge saw how these mariners regarded Virginia, Maryland, New York, New Jersey, Pennsylvania, and Massachusetts as separate nations—component parts of the United States in name only. France and Spain and England were European; Virginia, Connecticut, and South Carolina were American. The difference lay only in the hemisphere; practically they were two congeries of nations.

England was in the same position as a Charleston ship captain to take advantage of the situation. By picking her ports of call she could "sell" America free; then, by levying duties on American import and by granting access only to British ships, she cut off the whole English market from all the states. Many a ship captain said the old country was better off in commerce and navigation than before the war. Moreover, she could openly discriminate now between the states and owned shops in key cities, through subsidized merchants who, with duty-free products, readily undersold native dealers. So American business in imports was ruined.

Inherent in this situation was a professional ignominy especially galling to the man who had struggled for many of his best years

against the degradation of the courts as typified in the reign of Charles
Shinner. Charleston shippers were looking on smuggling as legitimate
business. That the whole thing might be purified at its source apparently did not interest them; they were practical men and must live
from day to day. The only way, they felt, for them, or for their alter
egos, the ship captains, was to buy English goods as Englishmen, or
through English agents, in the West Indies and bring them in, duty-
free, as Americans. When the ships were caught, as they were on
occasion, the owners naturally sought counsel; the principals were
respectable; they had much of the ready cash in circulation; so they
employed the best legal talent.

Herein could be found one reason Rutledge did not care to practice law, for the members of the South Carolina bar were coming
to the place which the members of the New York and Boston bars
regarded as normal—the euphemistic defense of smuggling; this was
a necessity from which Rutledge and his former colleagues had been
immune. He never appeared in any Court to defend a client against
penalty for evasion of customs, though the practice, cloaked, of course,
in legalistic quibbling, was becoming "honorable." To have raised his
voice against the general condition would have been useless. He, and
all of them, were in the grip of something that was dragging them
to depths lower than any previously imagined.

The worst of it was, John Rutledge realized, that the idea of the
United States was dying out. The attitude of the *Gazette*—supercilious,
speaking of the Federal Union almost in the past tense, as something
historic and evanescent, but hardly a going concern—correctly interpreted the feeling of the community. So he did something dramatic.
When his seventh child, a boy, was born the Chancellor named him
"States" Rutledge.

This strange act created hardly a ripple of interest. The older
regime—his own class—spoke of it as an oddity; none of them would
do such a thing. His former constituents, in St. Phillip's Parish, mostly
mechanics and artisans, who had elected him Senator in the days of
the Republic, held a meeting and applauded the Chancellor for his
"fine sentiments." Others said it was sentimentality. After a few weeks

it was forgotten as a futile protest against the trend of the times, though States Rutledge carried the nominal flag all the forty-six years of his life.

The Chancellor said nothing to explain or to accentuate, while he avoided the public agitation about rebuilding the structure of the nation. He hardly could avoid knowing that John Adams had written a book about it; that a young man named Madison in Virginia . was vying with young Charles Pinckney in writing and talking suggested panaceas in the possible form of a new Constitution, something with teeth in it to replace the old Articles of Confederation; that Washington in seeking a road to the Ohio where he had acquired large tracts of land found Pennsylvania isolationism balking inland development, while the public waterway of the Chesapeake, in his front yard, was claimed intensively as its own by both Virginia and Maryland, that these selfish antagonisms and many other factors had aligned the chief public figure of America with the forces seeking a new deal; that Alexander Hamilton had suggested a meeting in Annapolis to consider "waterways"; that there was talk of expanding the personnel and the purpose of the proposed convention. It was the old familiar night-crying of the clans. Rutledge had heard it before through a quarter century, back before Stamp Act time. The only difference was that heretofore a foreign foe had aroused them; now it was something more insidious, even more alarming, if less tangible.

It was characteristic that Rutledge consulted no one. All the other public figures—Washington, Franklin, Adams, Jefferson, Hamilton, Madison, Wilson, Jay, King, Dickinson, and many others—were writing letters to each other, or to the gazettes, or were making speeches or manipulating the political wires. Rutledge knew them all, had been intimately associated with most of them; but he was cut off from them as if he did not exist. He had never consulted anyone but Parsons; and him only a little; Parsons was dead. He alone knew that he had appointed himself a committee of one on the state of the Union.

However, there was a John Rutledge who was persona grata and conspicuous at the moment. He called on John Adams in London; the American Minister treated him with extreme cordiality and respect;

he attended a dinner party of English noblemen and when someone spoke slightingly of George Washington he indignantly and eloquently delivered a eulogy that still exists; became the guest of Thomas Jefferson in Paris where he discussed anthropology and the science of government at great length; and when he left carried on a spirited correspondence with the American Envoy; returning, he stopped at Mount Vernon and slept the night in a bedroom adjoining that of the General; it was said that "his views as to reforming the government of the former colonies were highly worthy and would have done credit to a much older man." He was only twenty-one—John Rutledge, Jr. He attempted one useful function (for us); he kept a diary. It contains very few direct clues to John Rutledge, but if this were a work about John Rutledge, Jr., it would be invaluable. Later—much later the son became a United States Senator, a General, and he killed a man in a duel, thus supplying the deficiencies in his father's career as a Southern statesman.

The pertinent query here is: what did John Rutledge favor as a possible new Constitution for the United States? Up to this period—early 1787—this was a complete mystery, if, indeed, he knew positively himself; his views as to what might or should form a Constitution were as unknown at that moment as were his views as to independence in 1775.

Yet the crisis had been steadily rising since 1783. Among those in Charleston who stood forth conspicuously the most vocal was Charles Pinckney. He was now only thirty; eleven years before he had been one of William Henry Drayton's colleagues; with Drayton and Thomas Heyward, Jr. he had composed the abortive triumvirate which had made its bid for sovereign power; nineteen-year-old Pinckney (while his Royalist father was broken-heartedly preparing to leave forever the land of his birth) had been one of the committee of eleven headed by Rutledge which prepared that first of American constitutions.

In 1780, when Rutledge was granted autocratic powers by the Assembly, with the sole check of, "with the advice of such members of his Privy Council as he may conveniently consult," he saw to it

that Charles Pinckney, then twenty-three, should be one of his councillors. When Clinton closed in on Charles Town, Councillor Pinckney
escaped with the Governor, but shortly afterward gave himself up to
the enemy and was interned for the duration, while his cousins,
Charles Cotesworth and Thomas entered the Continental Army and
emerged from the war with commissions, one a Major General, the
other a Brigadier.

After the war Charles Pinckney picked up the leadership of the
bar of Charles Town where John Rutledge had dropped it. His chief
competitors were Hugh Rutledge, General Charles Cotesworth Pinckney, and the firm of Rutledge and Pinckney (Edward and Thomas),
but the important clients preferred to have Charles Pinckney—if they
could get him. That his professional income should be three or four
times the salary of the Chancellor did not lessen his feeling of superiority over the man of whom his father had said, "Never forget that
John Rutledge is the first among us." Young Charles did not see why
a Pinckney should be second to any Rutledge.

Charles Pinckney read French, Spanish, Italian, and Latin, and
his addresses bristled with classical allusions, just as had William Henry
Drayton's before him. He could be winning and ingratiating and
had great charm, yet he dressed flamboyantly and his personality was
aggressive. Some unknown called him "Blackguard Charlie" and this
was resented by his followers, but the phrase went into use, somewhat affectionately and with apologies—"to distinguish him from
Charles Cotesworth," the serene and courtly.

That Rutledge did not assert himself, a characteristic that increased with time, for mastery of his contacts, both political and
intellectual, was now more than ever below the surface, was in itself
a challenge to Charles Pinckney. Those who remembered the situation of eleven and twelve years before, when William Henry Drayton
had just returned from London and had pitted himself against the
established primacy of John Rutledge, felt that another such contest
was now being established between Pinckney and Rutledge.

This contest was not defined, for they as yet had not been aligned
over principles, and how could any man in Charleston oppose John

Rutledge? Several had tried it—from Gadsden to Drayton to Pinckney—but none had ever come to a show-down. Rutledge apparently
was unaware of any contest; but Pinckney would not let others forget.
When Young Charles referred to the war-time governor he called him
"Dictator John." His intimates knew that Rutledge did not like to be
called dictator, but Pinckney would not let the word die.

Charles Pinckney was at this time a delegate to the Continental
Congress, sitting for the moment in New York, and when he traveled
in the North he sometimes referred to "the Constitution I wrote for
South Carolina." Late in 1786 he had been made by Congress Chair-
man of a Sub-Committee to draft suggestions for amendments to the
Articles of Confederation.

Early in March, 1787, a fashionable audience in Charles Town,
containing many members of the Assembly and their ladies, listened
to proposals concerning a remodeling of the Articles of Confederation,
under which the Union nearly had fallen apart. Neither Chancellor
nor Mrs. Rutledge were present, and the principal address was by
Charles Pinckney, who told his hearers in detail just what he thought
should be done. Indeed, he had been offering elaborate panaceas, in
public and private, for several years.

This conspicuous rostrum furnished Pinckney his final opportunity to publicize himself on the subject, for the Assembly was about
to select four members to represent South Carolina in the proposed
Federal Convention called for Philadelphia the coming May.

Already there was in full bloom a "Charles Pinckney party," and
its brilliant, egoistic, and militant leader boldly told its members that
he felt he should head the delegation to Philadelphia. Even today,
though he has been in his grave for five generations, there are partisan
followers of Charles Pinckney in South Carolina who cherish in their
hearts any advancement of his reputation.

·The Chancellor made no bid for the chief place, though he sat
each afternoon at the Corner and chatted with the members of the
Assembly as they went to and from the state house; since his first
election to the Assembly in Christ Church parish, at the age of twenty-
one, he had never asked for any votes and he had never announced

himself for any office. In the present issue no one made a speech for him, no one knew positively that he had any specific ideas as to what should be done, and he was committed to nothing; yet the Assembly selected John Rutledge to head the South Carolina delegation.

Three others were selected: Charles Cotesworth Pinckney, Charles Pinckney, and Pierce Butler. A month elapsed before they were commissioned and during that time members of the Charles Pinckney party said that their leader was the second choice of the Assembly "and nearly the first." When the commissions came Charles Cotesworth Pinckney's name was second and that of Charles Pinckney third. They were signed by the Governor, Charles Cotesworth's brother, Thomas.

Two days later Rutledge received his three colleagues at dinner and they spent the evening together in the library at 116 Broad Street. They could see from the western windows the rose-covered brick wall and, next door, the big yard covered with magnolia petals. Far back in the yard nestled tiny St. Andrew's Hall. In that hall seventy-four years later the Articles of Secession which started the War Between the States were signed. However, the structure of the States had to be built before there could be any effort to tear it apart. Now, after dinner, Charles Pinckney handed a bulky manuscript to John Rutledge. The Chancellor opened and read aloud: "Notes—draught and suggestive outline—Constitution of the United States of America—by Charles Pinckney."

The former Governor handed the manuscript back to its author and asked him to read it. Pinckney read. His audience of three lawyers, all Temple bred in London, might have felt the presence of the mighty shades of Francis Bacon, John Locke, Simon de Montfort, Coke, Sandys, Eliot, Hampden, even John Milton, for Pinckney had imbibed them all. He had gone further, back to Justinian, to Cicero, to the tyrants of Syracuse, and to the Greek republics. Yet he had been shrewd enough to depart from his customary flamboyant style. His draft was in the style of the South Carolina Constitution which had been written by John Rutledge in the economical English of the King

James Bible. Though nothing creative had been added, it was, in fact, a first-rate research job.

The Constitution of the United States, as it stands today, has sixty components. Of these sixty twenty-nine appeared in that first version as written by Charles Pinckney. It was an embryo, containing practically half of the final document, though it was the obvious and the inchoate half.

Charles Cotesworth Pinckney, who in later years was twice a prominent presidential candidate and who had the impartial qualities of a chief executive, generously applauded, with no specific comment. Pierce Butler, who had been chosen because it was believed he had noble English blood, a little out of his element, was the only one to offer changes; he offered two. Rutledge listened and said nothing; he was sphinx-like.

Finally Charles Pinckney demanded the opinion of the chairman. The other two were also eager for him to speak. He had dominated the courts and the law practice too long for any man engaged in such an enterprise to be content until he had spoken.

Rutledge said he would reserve the privilege of further study, but that he would like to ask Pinckney to present his draft to the convention as the South Carolina plan. By preparation and by splendid audacity Pinckney had taken the play from their traditional lawgiver.

Two days later Rutledge sailed for Philadelphia.

2.

When George Washington arrived in Philadelphia, by coach, on May 13, 1787, he was driven to "the genteel boarding house" of Mrs. Mary House at Fifth and Market Streets. While his luggage was being placed in the room he had reserved, Mr. and Mrs. Robert Morris appeared and personally pressed their invitation, previously presented, that he stay with them during the Convention. He accepted this invitation and ordered his luggage to follow him, while he walked with his hosts through a cheering crowd up Market Street, little more than a block.

Morris's house, east of Sixth Street on Market, was the finest private residence in the city. It was of brick, three stories high, with three windows on the first floor front and four windows on each of the upper floors. A vacant lot on each side was devoted to gardens. The main building was forty-two by fifty-two feet; there was a separate kitchen and wash-house in the rear, and stables to accommodate twelve horses. The General was taken to the second floor front and half of the stable room was allotted to his use. He had five coach horses and a riding mount.

The General's first act, after being settled, was to walk down Market Street. People gathered from blocks around to shake his hand, to cheer and to gape. He was amiable, so his progress was slow, but finally he reached his destination four blocks away, below Third Street, in the district that had been fashionable for residence twenty years before, but where business was now crowding out private houses. One residence remained, set back from the street, in a commodious yard, with a long walk leading around the side, to a huge mulberry tree in the rear. Washington turned in here, the crowd remaining cheering in the street, and called on the President of Pennsylvania, Benjamin Franklin, who was eighty-one years old.

Three days later Franklin gave a dinner to the twenty-one members of the Convention who had arrived (not yet enough for a quorum) and Washington sat at his right hand. The small talk turned on the accommodations available in the city, for it was hoped that sixty delegates in all would appear and already the two principal hostelries—the Indian Queen and the City Tavern—were "turning them away," while rooms at Mrs. House's were at a premium.

On May 18, John Rutledge arrived by boat and was met at the wharf by a messenger from James Wilson who bore a letter inviting him "because of the unprecedented tax on the facilities of our excellent taverns" to become his guest.

Rutledge accepted and for the first three weeks of the Convention lived at Wilson's house which was diagonally across Market Street from the Robert Morris residence. When Mrs. Rutledge arrived, as she did by a later boat, he joined her at the Indian Queen.

The Wilson residence was only a little less impressive than that of Robert Morris. It had gardens only on one side; the third floor was "merely an attic"; the stables could accommodate only eight horses. The structure, however, was newer than the Morris's house; it ranked as "one of the most aristocratic" in the city; Wilson had moved into it a few years before from a far less pretentious residence in the old part of town near the Franklin homestead. He had become the most sought after lawyer in Philadelphia; among his clients were Benjamin Franklin and Louis XVI. Coming from his native Glasgow by way of London, only twenty-one years before, he was now recognized as the leader of the American bar, as Rutledge had been before him. In another year George Washington would be handing him five hundred guineas in gold for the privilege of having his nephew, Bushrod Washington, "read law" in his office, and this at a time when the General was so hard pressed that he was pleading with friends to lend him money to pay taxes. In the days before the war, when Rutledge was practicing, Wilson had been his correspondent in Philadelphia.

The close association of these two men is one of the most significant facts underlying the history of the Constitutional Convention. Intellectually they complemented each other. Rutledge was a jury lawyer; Wilson an office lawyer who seldom appeared in court and who never had been on the bench. Moreover, as he often admitted himself, Wilson lacked practical political instinct; he was not a mixer, yet he possessed the very qualities, and they were essential, which Rutledge lacked.

Rutledge had inspirations, "as by a lightning's flash," but often he was inarticulate in written expression; and he was impatient with details, which was in profound contrast with his patience with essentials. This was accentuated by his lifelong aversion to "book learning."

Wilson was erudite, cautious, exact, and yet extremely sympathetic with his colleague's insight and grasp of practical affairs. Rutledge would leap at a decision instantly and then would turn to Wilson to show him a way to carry it out. Technically, they worked together, hand in glove.

Politically, they were also in contrast. Wilson, the bookish man, who dreaded intimate contact with his kind, was the type known to us as a liberal; he discoursed learnedly and theoretically on expanding political rights from the base. Rutledge, in intimate touch with the ordinary citizen, skeptical of the abstract, divinely concrete, was more a conservative. Wilson spoke eloquently of the people's rights; Rutledge, taxed with the current apprehensions that the Convention would ignore personal rights, answered curtly, "We are here to conserve property."

Psychologically, Wilson replaced Gadsden in the Rutledge milieu. The Philadelphian possessed the erudition, mental discipline, and professional contact lacking in the Lion of Liberty, but in sympathies, in leaning toward the "demos" and in basic articulation of popular desires, he resembled Gadsden. Rutledge opposed—up to a point, and often only for the purpose of understanding. Wilson was his mental sparring partner.

Wilson favored immediate concentration on those liberties that later were enumerated in the Bill of Rights, which Rutledge favored as the first ten amendments when they were specifically proposed. However, in May of 1787, with Wilson and others, Rutledge took the position that they had fought and won the war for the Bill of Rights, which was irrevocably established, being assured in each state; and that now there would be no rights, personal or otherwise, if they did not define and properly expand, where need was, the powers of state and of national government. Wilson wanted to liberate man; Rutledge said man had been liberated and that now he would be again enslaved unless they united the states and established the nation.

These, and other arguments, mutually stimulated Wilson and Rutledge. Neither was an extremist nor irreconcilable. Rutledge had the enormous advantage of no previous commitment. He could accept or reject anything, and still be consistent, for he had no obviously known record of political crusade to confront him—if he wished to change his mind, or if politics required it.

Wilson was a liberal, as Rutledge was a conservative, only in trend of character. They "gave and took"; at heart they were one. In effect, they could be compared to a well-selected team in a modern law office, in which one assembles the decisions and prepares the briefs, while the other argues them before court and jury.

While the two keenest legal minds in America were coming together on one side of Market Street, across the way, under the Morris roof, the financier and the General were exchanging the amenities, but only in gracious formality. Neither ever broached discussion of the political realities surrounding them. Washington was not in the habit of discussing politics and his host made no effort to draw him out. Intellectually, they lived solely on the surface, hoping to guide, if possible, and equally willing, if necessary, to follow the event.

At the same time the other delegates were foregathering, and no center was more important than the establishment of Mrs. House. Charles Pinckney, arriving from New York, where he had gone from Charleston to attend to some duties at the Congress, took a room there and sat at the common table with George Mason, Edmund Randolph, George Read, James Madison, and others. On the second floor the rooms of Mr. Pinckney and Mr. Madison adjoined.

Madison was tight-lipped, but Pinckney would talk to anyone he considered important enough and who would listen. George Read wrote his fellow delegate in Delaware, John Dickinson, "I wish you were here. I am in possession of a copied draft of a federal system intended to be proposed, if something nearly similar shall not precede it." This was the plan Pinckney had read in Charles Town to his three associates in the South Carolina delegation. Through Edmund Randolph, who had participated in its preparation, Read knew of the Madison plan. This "secret" of the interesting parallels between the two proposed systems became further known. In Mrs. House's, at the taverns, and elsewhere the assembling delegates discussed them. Pinckney eagerly canvassed the delegates for his plan and he usually received attentive respect. Once, in the hall adjoining the rooms which they severally occupied, Pinckney caught Madison and "orated" to him at length about his "system." Madison merely acquiesced by nodding his head.

Meanwhile, the date set for the opening, May 14, had been postponed because not half the delegates had appeared in Philadelphia.

Travel was slow and there were many uncertainties connected with the approaching event. The coming together of a small body of men, with not very specific powers, seemed to many a futile gesture in the face of the peril which faced them on all sides.

If it had not been for the presence of the two chief personages in the states—Washington and Franklin—few would have taken the Convention seriously. As it was, public judgment was merely suspended. The general belief was that the Convention was just another "congress." For twenty-two years or since the Stamp Act Congress at New York in 1765, America had been having congresses. The prevailing belief, shared by the vast majority, was that a congress could do nothing, and solve nothing. In fact, the United States at the moment had a congress which for four years had been beating from town to town searching for a home. Not once had all the elected members been assembled together, and all the time a large proportion had been shuffled about from lodging to lodging; many of them could not pay rent and the states which sent them did not pay it for them. There was no way, nationally, to raise money, pay bills or command respect. If a boarding-house keeper in Baltimore, Trenton, Philadelphia or New York had no respect for members of Congress who could expect France or Spain or Great Britain to accord them any respect?

While many of the delegates prepared themselves through tentative discussion of the plans brought to them by the representatives of the Continental Congress and of the Annapolis Convention, for thus Pinckney and Madison ranked, respectively, in general estimation, George Washington went out to tea, dined, inspected near-by farms, attended the theatre, church services, and concerts. Wilson and Rutledge, however, postponed the social amenities as well as any close consideration of the proposed Constitution; they were absorbed with problems of political strategy.

These were only two of the twenty-nine members who opened the Convention on May twenty-fifth—eventually fifty-five were present— yet they were, practically, from the beginning, the key organizers, Wilson was, in a practical sense, a political amateur. He had tried, several times, to organize political campaigns in Pennsylvania, but never had met with success. At the moment, his intimacy with Franklin, whose whole confidence he enjoyed, made his influence with the Pennsylvania delegation paramount. His distinguished abilities as writer, speaker, and attorney had led to his selection as delegate to this Convention; he had also represented Pennsylvania in the Second Continental Congress where he had signed the Declaration of Independence. Now he was in a place of great strategic advantage, but he was in troubled waters, and he was not too sure of himself. The services of a master politician were required now before the first "statesman" could be heard effectively. So Wilson clung to Rutledge.

There were no cliques organized, no parties, no factions, no caucuses. Yet all these characteristics of conventions existed in embryo in Philadelphia in 1787. There was New York to be "handled"; Massachusetts to be "placated"; Pennsylvania to be "held"; Connecticut to be "understood"; the Deep South to be "kept in line"; Virginia to be "controlled"; New Jersey to be "decentralized"; and the smaller states to be "satisfied."

In that prologue to the Convention, held in the home of James Wilson, with only two men present, the grand strategy of "the most important convocation of men ever to come together on this continent" was set up and agreed upon. This agreement did not concern the component elements of the Constitution itself, which subject was being discussed avidly at the taverns, at Mrs. House's boarding table, and elsewhere; it concerned solely the method and means of arriving at effective consideration of a Constitution.

Rutledge pointed out at once that their controlling problem was to find some way that arbitrarily would limit internal dissension. At this point he was not interested in any opposing strategy that might arise in the Convention. He did not reveal to Wilson that he had any specific proposals of his own to foster. Their mutual opponent, he said, and their only serious menace, was chaos. The delegates had no specific warrant from the state legislatures and assemblies which had appointed them. And if it became known what Rutledge and Wilson, and the others who were in sympathy with them, were about, what they planned to do, every imaginable force of dissension would be loosed. Many of the delegates would be so distracted that they would be unable to continue. If that menace was not controlled in advance, the Convention probably would break down before its labors could be concluded. They must have a fair chance. Before the United States could be saved from chaos the Convention had to be insulated from its threat.

Wilson recognized the menace but was frankly at a loss for a solution. On the other hand, Rutledge's experience and instinct had prepared him for such a situation as this. There was no other man in Philadelphia who had been for years anonymous ruler of a commonwealth without being directly answerable to any constituted authority, nor any other who had been obliged to subordinate such authority to generals appointed to protect his people who, nevertheless, had to be taught the rudiments of their own craft.

Rutledge said that a town meeting was out of the question. The proposed Constitution could be an open covenant only if it was not arrived at openly. Though it went against the grain with him Wilson was obliged, under the circumstances, to agree. Rutledge then submitted his plan to safeguard the Convention.

The solution of the former triumvir from old Charles Town was to have the delegates agree, in advance, that during the Convention not a word of what went on behind the doors of Independence Hall should be repeated outside. The public should be kept absolutely in the dark about what was going on until after the Convention adjourned.

Wilson was impressed. He was willing to join Rutledge in trying to have his device adopted, but Rutledge was too canny to submit his idea directly; he realized that the name of "dictator" hovered over him. He suggested that Wilson consult Franklin.

The aged President of Pennsylvania was being tormented by an avalanche of neighbors, henchmen, and constituents, all of whom wanted to know what the newly assembled Convention planned to do. Many were demanding to be reassured that dark plans were not afoot to take their "liberties" away from them. All manner of rumors were afloat. The old talk of monarchy was in the air. Every suggestion made—reasonable or otherwise—was seized upon and bandied about.

Franklin leaned heavily on Wilson for advice and had come to trust him completely. Also, in the First and Second Continental Congresses, as Chairman of the Committee on Trade, he had come to trust the judgment of his Vice Chairman, John Rutledge. So now when his attorney presented Rutledge's solution of the obvious menace —which incidentally offered an easy way for the amiable old man to avoid endless explanation—as being their joint proposal, Franklin pounced upon it and accepted it eagerly, though it was directly contrary to his lifelong preachment and practice concerning the proper way to conduct public affairs.

George Washington called while Wilson and Rutledge were present. Franklin, "with almost childish delight," told the General of the proposed "oath of secrecy," as he called it.

Washington, it might be supposed, would be more likely to accept such an idea than Franklin. It was essentially a military idea and the habit of Washington's mind was military. Moreover, his chief military successes were based on the use of secrecy and surprise; yet the General hesitated. He asked for time to consult his colleagues.

Two days later, however, Washington notified Wilson that the Virginia delegation was unanimously in favor of the "oath of secrecy." That practically settled it. When the Convention assembled on the twenty-fifth, its first act was for each of the members to bind himself not to utter, outside the hall, either verbally or in print, any word which might convey any information as to what was being said or done. They went even further. They agreed that no one, during the lifetime of the members, would reveal what happened in the Convention, except for the formal publication they expected to authorize.

Thus the Constitutional Convention was held behind closed doors. Armed sentries paced the walk before the Hall. No one, except delegates, was permitted near the scene. Two of the delegates were appointed, spelling each other, to accompany Benjamin Franklin wherever he went, and to nudge his elbow if he spoke carelessly, for the old man was garrulous and sometimes forgot his oath. One day a written notation of his speech dropped in the hall, was placed on the desk of the presiding officer, and Washington, reading it, gravely admonished the carelessness of the delegates. He left the paper on his desk, saying its owner might find it there, after all were gone. No one ever claimed it.

With the creation of this integument of secrecy, Rutledge took the step which probably spelled the difference between success and failure of the great "experiment."

In the choice of a presiding officer Washington, naturally, came first. It was planned that Benjamin Franklin should nominate him and John Rutledge second him—the proposal from the North supported by the South. However, on the opening day Franklin was indisposed, so his place was taken by Robert Morris, who made the nomination. Rutledge then made his seconding speech, a very short one. The election was unanimous. Then Morris and Rutledge escorted Washington to the chair, where he faced the twenty-eight other delegates present.

Two days were required for the organization of the Convention and the establishment of its rules with selection of officers. On the third day the curtain rose when Washington recognized first Edmund Randolph, who presented the Virginia plan, which had been prepared chiefly by James Madison, though with the assistance of several others, including Randolph himself and George Mason.

Immediately Charles Pinckney rose and presented the South Carolina plan. When the Pinckney and the Madison plans were compared a most astounding similarity was discovered. Of the twenty-nine components of the final Constitution which Pinckney first read to his state colleagues in Charleston, and, later, to the Convention in Philadelphia, twenty-seven were to be found in the Madison plan and the two differences were on minor points only.

Madison had access to the same works which Pinckney had perused. Both were scholarly men. Both had read the early records arduously, had studied the various state constitutions which had been enacted up to that time in America, and had made the necessary eliminations.

Later William Paterson presented the New Jersey plan. It differed from the Madison and Pinckney plans chiefly in its accent on state rights, but twenty-one of its components were identical with those of the first two plans.

The Convention was now ready to begin its work. These plans had to be broken down into elements before they were offered, piece by piece, for consideration.

In accordance with his well-established parliamentary method, Rutledge remained quiet on the sidelines for a long time. He was weighing and studying his problem. Other men came to the gathering to air their views and exchange them, to see what could be obtained for the things they held dear. But this was only the lesser part of Rutledge's purpose. The ruler was dominant in him. He knew the temper, the strengths, and the weaknesses of such assemblages. Each was a challenge to his sense of mastery. It had been so with him in all the deliberative bodies he attended since his first appearance in the Assembly of South Carolina. Invariably, he had emerged in control.

From the first day of this one he let Charles Pinckney appear as the protagonist of South Carolina. The second day Charles Cotesworth Pinckney was on his feet with an address and, a little later, Pierce Butler. Of the twenty-nine delegates present the first week eighteen spoke before Rutledge was heard, and then he was forced to speak by a remark of Benjamin Franklin's.

It was on June first, the sixth day, and the question of a national executive was before the house. Pinckney was heard, with others. Then there was a long pause, and the chair was about to put the question when Franklin remarked that the question was of great importance and that he wished the gentlemen would deliver their sentiments on it before the question was put. He looked directly at the South Carolina chairman.

Though Franklin, because of his infirmities, held aloof from the inner manipulation of the Convention, he had so much political awareness that he was conscious of what was going on under the joint direction of Rutledge and Wilson and this was an effort to smoke out the South Carolinian.

Rutledge responded graciously. He "spoke softly" and declared himself on the debated point. What he felt eventually about each of its parts is best seen in the Constitution itself, for there is his finally considered opinion, rectified by the compromises he made on minor points to secure the major purposes which he held paramount.

The delegates were discussing the components of the proposed Constitution; for the moment, Rutledge was more concerned in analyzing the components of the *Convention* itself. He knew that unless he could correctly assess the motivation of the other fifty-four men who eventually composed it and then organize them politically, any of his opinions, or all of them, would have the force only of his single voice.

3

Most of the delegates believed they were separated from each other chiefly by sectional lines and state groups. Bluntly, it was said the chief issue was "state rights against federalism." The fact that each state was, practically, a separate nation with separate interests had long fostered this belief and it was so much reiterated that it became a cliché dominating nearly every mind. It was an idea that persisted for generations, and that still persists in part.

John Rutledge saw that the situation was more complex than that, and yet more readily soluble than it might have been if the delusion about it had reflected the actuality. He found there was a double cleavage in the membership of the Convention, dividing it into groups overflowing state lines completely. The first cleavage, which was vocal, divided them all into two natural political groups which might have been called by names then unknown to American politics—"liberal" and "conservative." These groups were without organization, publicity, or other articulation, yet balance of power might lie with either—unless the second cleavage intervened.

This second cleavage—the "money" issue, to use an easy phrase—was the vital one. We will encounter it later, when we arrive at the establishment of the actual control of the Convention.

Rutledge was naturally a conservative and the "conservative" interests looked to him instinctively for support. He did not have to cultivate them. Rather, he allied himself openly with the "liberal", group, which was led by James Wilson and which included Franklin and Dickinson. Political instinct dictated this alliance and it was a formidable one. When the liberals accepted his "oath of secrecy" and seemed delighted with it, he was planted well within their ranks. Dickinson, the scorner of intrigue, always a friend of the Chancellor, had not changed in twenty years, and while he had always favored having a property qualification for voters he readily, forgave Rutledge for insisting that there be no such qualification for *voters*, but only for *office holders*. Dickinson said this was a quaint idea and only proved Rutledge to be more liberal than any of them. Wilson was the original champion of the copyright clause, giving special rights to authors and inventors. "To protect the labor of the intellect is the noblest prerogative of government," he declared. It was a new idea to Rutledge, but he accepted it and naturally pleased his Philadelphia colleague by doing so; Rutledge's education on this point was an incidental fruit of their friendship.

These, and other exchanges, occurred in the initial stages of the Convention. It was through them that Rutledge and the "liberals" became intimately acquainted and interdependent. A web of mutual reliance was woven among them, so that they became accustomed to "accommodating" each other—before the real test arrived. These skirmishes made it possible for them to consider the only problem which dangerously separated them—the "money" issue.

Meanwhile, Alexander Hamilton, who had been largely instrumental in bringing about the Convention and who knew his way about politically, arrived in Philadelphia and began canvassing the delegates. He had expected easily to dominate the Convention, but he discovered even more clearly than had Franklin, the alliance between Rutledge and Wilson and all that it implied; he perceived that he would have little chance to control, despite his favor with Washington, who refused to participate in the actual negotiations. The thing that convinced Hamilton of the seriousness of the Rutledge dominance was the fact that the Chancellor had practically deserted the South Carolina delegation, giving over its floor leadership by default to Charles

Pinckney. Instead of deceiving the New York delegate, this influenced him to announce that he had prior business in Manhattan.

Hamilton had a program, which if it had been adopted, would have meant a monarchy for America in due time. His was the traditional dictator's policy, for such was his inherent nature, but when he realized the existence and the composition of the Rutledge-Wilson cabal he felt it was impregnable and he bolted. After the Constitution was agreed upon by the Convention, however, he decided that half a loaf was better than none and became its most effective salesman to the nation. Meanwhile, though he observed his "oath of secrecy," which he took with the others, his action created uncertainty, so much so that within a few weeks his fellow delegates, Yates and Stirling, also departed, leaving New York without representation.

Sectionally this reduced the pattern of the Convention practically to that which underlay both the New York Congress of 1765 and the First Continental Congress of 1774. New York was out, Virginia became the figurehead, and Pennsylvania had ceased to hold the balance of power, for the arrival of fresh delegates had shifted the balance farther North; the vital force of union had to come, if at all, from an alliance between New England and the Deep South.

This brings us to Roger Sherman. For eventually the organization of the *components* of the *Convention* came to three men, Rutledge, Wilson, and Sherman. In their hands, circumstances combined to place controlling power. Together they ruled. For the first month Rutledge ignored Sherman, who was antagonistic to him in the beginning, though the Yankee was as quick as Hamilton or Franklin to sense what was taking place.

In the earlier congresses Massachusetts *was,* practically, all of New England. But now Sam Adams was ill; John Adams was in England; none of the Massachusetts delegation, headed by Governor Gorham, was of any particular mentality or acumen.

In 1787 Connecticut moved into the spot held by Massachusetts in the earlier congresses. In the Constitutional Convention Connecticut *was* New England, by virtue of three very strong men, Johnson, Ellsworth, and Sherman.

Roger Sherman towered above them all. Incidentally, he was one of the oldest present, being sixty-eight. He now held the parliamentary key previously held by Sam Adams. His native force of character caused both Massachusetts and Connecticut to follow his lead. Politically he was always willing to trade two or more weaknesses, however impressive, for one strength, however minor it might be. He was born a very poor boy, earned his living as a cobbler, studied law over his bench, and elevated himself to the highest legal position in his state by sheer application. He was the delegate of constituents who did not own slaves, never drank, swore, played cards, went to a theatre, or talked politics on Sunday.

Here was the man to whom John Rutledge had to "sell" the slave trade. That is what it came to, after all the other organization had been completed. If Rutledge and Sherman could agree the *United* States could be assured.

Rutledge's attitude toward slavery therefore became a vital factor. It was through his skillful guidance that the issue was kept under control in the Constitutional Convention. Though it was fated almost to break the Republic in two during the next eighty years, *the slavery issue was used by Rutledge to bind together the basic agreements in the Convention.*

Because he asserted on the floor at Philadelphia that "if the Constitution abolishes slavery South and North Carolina and Georgia will never sign," he is often referred to as the chief parliamentary protagonist of slavery in his day.

The exact opposite, however, is the fact. There is no record that he ever *defended* the morality of slavery as an institution. Rutledge was too canny an attorney to permit himself to be maneuvered into a position where he had to defend the *morality* of slavery.

Concerning the essential justice or the *ultimate* practicality of slavery, Rutledge was always cautiously silent. When he came to maturity his mother owned about two hundred slaves; at the beginning of the Revolution he personally owned around sixty; at the time of the Constitutional Convention he owned twenty-eight; when he died, thirteen years later, he owned one.

This record of personal ownership of slaves is not unlike that of the Virginians, Washington, Jefferson, and Madison, each of whom owned fewer and fewer slaves as the years passed, and for the same reason—experience taught them that slavery was economically unsound.

Rutledge's brother-in-law and supporter, John Fauchnaud Grimké, was the earliest abolitionist in the South. His daughters, the nieces of John Rutledge, Angelica and Sarah Grimké, became celebrated as militant abolitionisis during the early days of the movement. Rutledge's wife, Elizabeth, devoted to her brother and his family, gave up all her slaves before she died. John, silently and strongly devoted to his wife, could not have greatly disagreed with her, in principle. Rutledge's chief client and close friend, Henry Laurens, passed from being a trader in slaves in early life to being a theoretical abolitionist, though he never politically advocated the point.

Rutledge, *in feeling,* shared Laurens's attitude. He asserted on the floor of the Convention, "Morality and religion have nothing to do with the slavery question; it is solely one of economics." Despite the furious opposition, led by George Mason of Virginia, himself a slave owner, Rutledge forced the acceptance of this dictum.

However, this final mastery of the Convention came to Rutledge only through Roger Sherman. The canny Connecticut trader was one with whom Rutledge could talk "horse sense." Both were practical men.

The crisis came in the fifth week of the Convention, during the last days in June. "The first month we only came to grips," wrote Daniel Jenifer of Maryland to his wife, "and the second month it seemed as if each day we would fly apart forever, but we didn't—we jelled."

They "jelled" in Rutledge's rooms at the Indian Queen on the evening of June 30. It began with a dinner at which Rutledge entertained Roger Sherman in the taproom,—apparently a casual little meeting, but on it hung the fate of America.

Preceding this dinner the Convention had been living through its most ponderous sessions, in an atmosphere almost of futility. Somehow they seemed to be talking in circles. The largest amount of time was devoted to the subject of an executive, his nature, duties, and length of term. The executive was an amorphous subject, largely theoretical; nobody cared intensely about it. Not a state would have walked out if its views on the subject of a chief executive had been disregarded.

The second most absorbing subject, judged by extent of comment, was the federalism-versus-state-rights issue. This did arouse bitter feeling. There were always at least three states, sometimes four and once five which threatened to walk out if that issue was not settled *its* way. Because of this acrimony the idea has always persisted that "state rights" was the crucial issue in all that occurred behind the closed doors of Independence Hall.

Two issues went deeper: the slave trade and regulation of the maritime carrying trade. From the standpoint of practical politics both were economic problems. Separately each vitally affected the commercial lifeblood of a large section. Together they practically determined the income of the states; they composed the "money issue" which, as Rutledge realized, actually controlled the Convention.

On both of these issues South Carolina held the key because on each Rutledge had taken an extreme position from the beginning and had held it consistently. He had said, and had secured a majority vote to back him, that the Constitution must ignore the issue of slave importation. Also, in the beginning, he had secured approval of a motion that navigation acts must be ratified by a two-thirds vote of the Senate. That was his shrewdest move, his chief parliamentary ace.

By "navigation act" was meant legislation that would control the carrying trade by sea. England had controlled the carrying trade of America through her navigation acts, which had made her the premier nation of the world. New England aspired to emulate her.

New England was the ship-building and ship-operating center of the new world. Though few ships were built south of the Chesapeake, the South demanded freedom to contract for the transportation of her products (and her slaves) in the best market, even if that might be in England.

This was the sand in the molasses for Connecticut and Massachusetts. All else that was discussed—state rights, human rights, executive rights, judicial rights—was superficial compared to this. Thrifty New England minds were appalled at the idea that the South might hold the key to commerce.

So Roger Sherman, who three weeks before had said he had no use for John Rutledge, came to dine with him in outward amity, as his guest, that night of June thirtieth.

It was said of Sherman that he was "as fitted for a polite dinner party as a chestnut burr is for an eye stone." His face was corrugated and gnarled; his hair hung unkempt over a wilted collar; he had a sharp protruding nose, shrewd but dreamy eyes; and he usually held his left fist cocked and clenched, while his right hand grasped his left wrist, even at dinner. When he spoke the knuckle of the left fist would be shoved out grotesquely as if about to hit someone. John Adams described him as "an old Puritan, honest as an angel." His puritanical honesty had caused him to agitate during the war for an agreement from all the states to abstain from cock-fighting, horse-racing, and play-going. He had been told that it was hopeless to propose this in South Carolina, where the Governor was a confirmed theater-goer and also owned a race horse. Memory of this was not erased.

Rutledge now held two aces. Sherman knew exactly what he wanted and where to get it, yet that "strange New England cant" which William Pierce, delegate from Georgia, noted, ran through all he said, publicly and privately.

Rutledge, always at his best at a small dinner party—practically all of his great diplomatic achievements were accomplished amid Georgian silver and French napery—speaking the pure English that comes from the University of Dublin, put the awkward Connecticut jurist at ease. This time the South Carolinian did not serve Madeira, or offer long-handled clay pipes filled with Virginia leaf. There was no smoking and no drinking.

The southern Episcopalian asked the northern Congregationalist to say grace. Roger Sherman bowed his head and prayed for ten minutes. They ate, and then they settled the slavery question—for seventy-six years.

The deal was simple enough. The South—that is, the Carolinas and Georgia—would give up its claim to a two-thirds vote on the navigation clause if New England—that is, Connecticut and Massachusetts—would oppose any immediate effort to abolish the importation of slaves. As five states could carry the Convention, this meant final solution of both the "money" issues. A time limit of thirteen years already had been proposed for the importation of slaves. Sherman was generous enough to offer to extend this to twenty-one years. Rutledge accepted and then assured his guest that the South wanted New England to have her carrying trade.

That was all there was to it, except that Sherman asked the one question he was privileged to ask—What about North Carolina? For weeks North Carolina had been showing tendencies of aligning herself with Virginia and Pennsylvania, for in population she was already third in size. It looked as if "bigness" and not "money" issues would influence her vote. She had been standing with the federalists as against the state-rights group. How would North Carolina stand now? Could the Chancellor "deliver" his neighbor, notoriously jealous of South Carolina?

Rutledge was prepared for this question. When the evening was only half over Hugh Williamson, head of the North Carolina delegation, was announced. He confirmed the fact that he already had been persuaded by Rutledge. North Carolina would change her vote on the two-thirds vote in the navigation clause in consideration of New England's agreement that slave importation should continue for twenty-one years.

However, more than three weeks were consumed in debate before the votes were recorded, which indicates how secretive the "traders" were with their "deals." Rutledge remained silent on the issue all that time. If he possessed a sense of humor, and whatever humor he had was of a dry and ironical sort, he must have been deeply amused as he watched anti-slavery Virginia fight it out with Connecticut as the militant *champion* of "black ivory." The Virginians, George Mason and Edmund Randolph, both slave owners, were vitriolic in denunciation of the slave trade. Then pithy Roger Sherman rose and remarked that he did not see the difference between a slave and a horse. "Both are property, aren't they?" he asked.

This remark brought about what has often been termed "the most inspiring moment of the Convention"—the celebrated oration of George Mason of Virginia against the slave trade, source material for abolitionists for the next two generations. He reviewed the hideous traffic, laid it originally at the door of Old England, and then in his peroration tacked it down securely on New England. "I lament," he cried, "that some of our eastern brethren have, from a lust of gain, embarked in this nefarious traffic."

Puritanical Roger Sherman's square jaw shot out; his clenched fist dug into his neighbor, Oliver Ellsworth, a much more polished speaker, but his twin in thought and action. Ellsworth, who, after George Washington, was in appearance the most impressive man in the Convention, rose. "I have never owned a slave," he said, "and so cannot judge of the effects of slavery on character." He looked at Mason, the eloquent abolitionist, a slave owner.

Then Ellsworth squared his huge shoulders and went into the fight. "Virginia," he continued, "is, I believe, even more vulnerable than New England in this matter. She is already a breeder of slaves for sale in the plantations of the lower South. Is this the explanation of the Old Dominion's hostility to slave ships? Is it because the African traffic is hurting its business? Is the importation of slaves from a foreign land interfering with a prosperous home industry? Slaves multiply so rapidly in Virginia and Maryland that it is cheaper to raise than to import them, while in the rice swamps foreign supplies are necessary. . . . Shall we be unjust to South Carolina and Georgia?"

Virginia, especially in the persons of Mason and Randolph, was unreconciled. Mason declared he "would cut off his right hand rather than put it to an instrument that does not abolish the slave trade." Randolph was with him—for the moment.

Then Roger Sherman said he thought it better to have the slave trade for twenty-one years than to lose three states to the union, which was stating a half truth so it appeared whole. He said nothing of New England's gain of the carrying trade.

While the debates in the Convention proceeded ponderously, day by day, the treacherous political undercurrents were always menacing. Just before the senate clause, which was Roger Sherman's device to give the small states an equal voice with the large, was voted on, Rutledge faced what seemed, at the moment, a final crisis. Sooner than be obliged to "knuckle under" to little states like Delaware and Rhode Island, Virginia and Pennsylvania seemed ready to bolt. The large states regarded this setting up of a Senate as the height of injustice.

James Wilson, calling the situation appalling, brought about an informal gathering at his home of a dozen delegates from the "big" states to decide what should be done. Rutledge came, uninvited.

Everyone present recognized in Rutledge the strategist who had brought about the situation they all faced, for his "deal" with Roger Sherman on the slavery trade and navigation issues had been instrumental in turning North Carolina away from her alliance with the other "big" states. He had studiously avoided being tagged as a "state rights" man, nor was he consistently so, yet he was in fact their political enemy and, for the moment, triumphant. Though against him on the issue, Wilson, his trusted friend, asked Rutledge to speak. The Chancellor saw that if the men present persisted in the views being expressed the states they represented would bolt and end the Convention.

Rutledge spoke, it was said, "in a manner quite unlike his known parliamentary method." He made no positive assertion whatever. He merely suggested that each man present look into his own heart seriously and ask what was the paramount necessity with all at this grave moment. "It is not accommodation?" he continued. "I can assure you, gentlemen, that I have been obliged to sacrifice much that I have held dear. However, when I have been tempted to reduce our joint actions to a nullity by consulting only my own desire I have said—'is it not better that I should sacrifice one prized opinion than that all of us should sacrifice everything we might otherwise gain?'"

This one speech, "softly uttered," turned the tide, and saved the Convention. The "big" states decided to bow to the inevitable.

On the twenty-fourth came the decisive vote—five to four. The same vote was recorded on the slave-importation clause, on the navigation clause, and on the Senate clause which decided the state-rights dispute.

Again the Union was saved by the narrowest possible margin.

4.

The Convention, apparently, had composed its chief differences. For two months it had been torn in the storm of controversy, and all but rent asunder. Now it was calm and intact. But nothing was yet written; no specific resolution had been agreed upon. For sixty days the delegates had explored each other's minds, for seven, eight, and once eleven, hours a day in the hall; and evenings and Sundays, in the taverns, homes, and rooming houses. They had whispered, implored, shouted, defied, inveigled, and verbally assaulted one another; they had traduced, intrigued, and traded; and they had voted, on the proposed Constitution, bit by bit. Yet—where were they? No official record had been kept of the votes, as it had been agreed on the first day of the Convention that the members should not be bound by them, because they might change their minds. Which of them had changed his mind, about what, and why? The final organizer, the moderating genius who could bring them all to book would have to be politically clairvoyant and if he were adept enough in a subtle tilt of the scales he might impose his own will on history.

A motion was made that a Committee on Detail, which would be the Drafting Committee, should be selected.

Washington looked over the room. He asked how large a committee was desired. The motion came from King of Massachusetts that it be five. It was carried. Washington—as well as everyone else —realized that these would be the men who would actually construct the Constitution. They would be guided, naturally, by what they knew to be the sense of the Convention, judged by the proceedings of the sixty days, and their work would be subject to later ratification. Yet here was august responsibility. There were fifty-five men to choose from, and a fifty-sixth, the only paid employee, the secretary, Major William Jackson, who, from the time the Convention was first proposed, had ingeniously set himself to secure the secretarial post. It had been assumed that he would keep minutes, but now it appeared he had not done so. He had been only a repository for papers and for the keeping of an account of the names and dates of delegates attending, nothing more than a sergeant-at-arms. He excused himself from the onus of not having made minutes by referring to the conspicuous and untiring efforts of the delegate from Virginia, Mr. James Madison.

Mr. Madison weighed about one hundred twenty pounds, was quite sallow in complexion, wore tight clothes, and was possessed of indefatigable energy. In addition to writing the Journal of the Convention in longhand, which is one of the greatest feats of reporting of all time, he spoke from the floor in support of various propositions —which included twenty-seven, or nearly half of the sixty components of the Constitution—and appeared thus *oftener* than any other member, except Gouverneur Morris. In all, Madison spoke 174 times. James Wilson spoke 142 times, though these included forty appearances for Benjamin Franklin. In physical activity there were no *two* men in the Convention as busy as James Madison alone.

As stage manager, Mr. Madison also excelled. Possibly remembering how George Washington had dramatized himself to the first Continental Congress as an available Commander-in-Chief of its new armies by appearing in full uniform, Madison set himself before the Constitutional Convention as the possible drafter of the Constitution by taking a seat, slightly elevated, directly below the President, and facing the other delegates. Here, on a desk before him, he scribbled in his journal and from this spot he could step down one pace, turn, and address the chair. So he became, after the President, the most conspicuous of the fifty-five.

Madison had no official position as secretary or historian. He proposed to his own Virginia delegation that it might be desirable to keep a record of the debates for their own reference and the members readily agreed. When he chose his seat to face the Convention he explained to others his purpose and his became an accepted though unofficial function. The fact that it conflicted with the Convention's first official act, the "oath of secrecy," Madison evaded by saying that nothing he wrote would be published or shown during the lifetime of anyone present. This promise he strictly kept and the contents of the Journal were unknown for fifty years; after his death his widow sold it for $30,000 to the nation. Ever since then Madison's Journal has been the principal source of information about the forming of the Constitution.

Madison's entire activity, before the Convention, during it, and, especially in the preparation and the revelation of the Journal, is a masterpiece of suggestion that he wrote the Federal Constitution. He never said so. He only permitted it to be inferred. In fact, the Journal says, in effect, exactly what is written here. That Madison was the Father of the Constitution was not asserted, directly or indirectly, by any other of the fifty-four men in the Convention.

When it came to a choice of a head for the Drafting Committee everyone knew what was needed: a man who could reduce to writing, in legal phrase, the until now inexact agreements which loosely bound them, and yet astute enough to leave out those assertions which might drive them apart. This man who wrote the Constitution would have to be an original thinker, and a constructive statesman able to seize and to express every important lesson which had been learned by the era in which they lived, and which had been discussed, though only tentatively, by the present Convention. Also, he must be a practical politician who would realize that it was useless to present a document which could not command the immediate suffrage of a majority of the people. More—and here was the invisible requirement which no one dared express—he must be of such vision that while he solidly constructed the present he would leave the document open for the future. He must close no doors. No theorist would do;

only demonstrated practical efficiency in statecraft could be considered. No one identified with any specific advocacy, no self-aggrandizer would do; they could consider only a selfless man.

There was no opportunity for conference or for political "deals" or for trading. The Convention had gone beyond that point. No nominations were made; they proceeded at once to the secret ballot, which the rules agreed upon the first day designated as the method of choice of committees.

John Rutledge was first choice, as he had been in 1775 in Charles Town when he wrote the Constitution of the Republic of South Carolina. The men who knew him best, who had observed him at first hand through sixty days of strife and compromise, and who knew his record, not only as a war-time executive, but also as a delegate to similar conventions for twenty-two years, entrusted to his chairmanship the preparation of the momentous document.

James Wilson was the second choice and Oliver Ellsworth of Connecticut the third. Ellsworth was chosen instead of Roger Sherman because he was recognized as having views identical with Sherman's, while it was believed he had more "literary" ability. In effect, the triumvirate which ruled the Convention—Rutledge, Wilson, and Sherman—were named by its members to formulate the ultimate expression of its will.

This triumvirate, composed of men from South Carolina, Pennsylvania, and Connecticut—the Deep South, the Middle Atlantic, and New England—had never operated by conference, either open or secret. This rule, though informal, was effective.

Two others were added, each a governor of an important state: Randolph of Virginia and Gorham of Massachusetts. The character of this committee sufficiently attests the character of the forces which were in control.

The Constitution was written in ten days—from July 26 to August 4, though nothing was done either the first or last day. Thus, there were eight days of actual labor, including one Sunday.

The committee worked night and day. Only one man was present at every session—John Rutledge. The others came and went. The original drafts are in the handwriting either of Randolph or Wilson, but the corrections, and the changes, mostly of vital import, are in the hand of Rutledge. Some of the sessions were in Independence Hall. Others occurred in the home of Wilson and on Sunday three members of the committee met with Rutledge at the Indian Queen and worked with him there. His mind hovered over every sentence, every syllable.

At the first meeting of the Drafting Committee, on the morning of July 27, in Independence Hall, Rutledge, as chairman, drew from his pocket a parchment, which had never been referred to in the Convention or by any of its delegates outside, and read it aloud.

It was a replica of the constitution of the Treaty of the Five Nations (the Iroquois) of 1520. Rutledge read what the Indians had written more than two and a half centuries before: "We, the people, to form a union, to establish peace, equity and order. . . ."

The chairman made no speech. He merely read the dry, quaint, and archaic words of the Indian parchment. The inference lay in the act. Pinckney, Madison, Paterson, and the others had gone back through England and Greece. The fruit of their research lay to hand in the documents on the table. They would be utilized. But for the first brief moment Rutledge was saying to his committee, in effect: We are American, of this soil and none other.

This prologue was very brief—it occupied but a few minutes. Then Rutledge took up the Articles of Confederation and picked from them items on which all readily could agree.

They had everything to go on—of course—and nothing definite. The action of the Convention, during its prior sixty days of debate, was in their memory for guidance, but the whole subject—and what broader subject could there be than the government of man—was fluid.

In surveying the facts about the writing of the Constitution one wonders at the legends which have surrounded it, especially the one attributing its actual preparation to that vague group of men known as The Founding Fathers. One might as well attribute *King Lear* and *Hamlet* merely to the Elizabethan age. True, the plays were written in that period; true, their origins and components were old material and were lying about for any passerby to seize and express. But it took one individual, a great artist, to bring them to book.

Now the Constitution, though formed of materials known to all and contributed by very many, found expression through the medium of one man, John Rutledge. To paraphrase Emerson, "He was selected by the Convention as the lens through which it would read its own mind."

A few days before he was selected to head the Drafting Committee, Rutledge had said, on the floor, "As we are laying the foundation for a great empire we ought to take a permanent view of the subject and not look at the present moment only."

He did put the "permanent" view in the Constitution. However, he was cautious and exact in rendering homage to the politics of the day. He kept all the bargains, diplomatically covered the slave-importation issue with weasel words which would not alienate his own people, and avoided anything which would prevent New England from securing her beloved carrying trade. He put in Roger Sherman's invention, the United States Senate; he defined the three principal departments, the executive, the legislative and the judicial. He adequately but succinctly defined the four great essential powers: the boundary question, the guarantees of a republican form of government, taxation, and commerce. He leveled the bogey of state barriers against interstate commerce; he arbitrarily included the highly disputed exclusive right of the government to coinage—Had not his fiat when he was Dictator made money out of indigo?—but, as a final answer to all who objected, there was the ever-ready possibility of a constitutional amendment if other methods of establishing money values proved to be more popular.

In fact, to all objections, there was always that open door—the amendment. It was the permanent cushion over the springs of state—the power to change by the people's will. Anything could be done—not by the sword, but by the vote.

When it came to the executive clause, Randolph and Wilson wanted the chief of the nation to have very little power at any time.

At the moment Randolph was in contest in Virginia with Patrick Henry for political control of the state. Henry fought eloquently against all central authority and Randolph meekly avoided contest with him (in Virginia) on this point. When Randolph, whom the chairman in Philadelphia asked to prepare the first draft of the Constitution, came to the powers of the executive, he quibbled, giving the executive only limited authority over the state militia and otherwise "paring his nails," as Henry on the stump was urging should be done.

Rutledge boldly and simply crossed out this limitation of authority and gave the Chief Executive complete military authority in time of war. He knew what it meant not to have it. The "man of military experience" had not survived for nothing his two sieges of Charles Town and that last year of the war, in which he had had military responsibility without full authority. Whether or not he foresaw 1861-1865, 1917-1918, and 1941-, it was the former "Dictator" of South Carolina who placed in the Constitution the means whereby the President of the United States, in time of war, becomes the military dictator of the nation. His personal alteration of the first draft was never materially changed.

Nowhere in the document are the words nation or national used, and yet between every line and into almost every syllable is breathed something to create national power. This astounding indirection of expression is essentially Rutledgian. He had the faculty of making a simple assertion in plain language, seemingly quite innocent and irrefutable. Yet it contained a hidden power far transcending the direct postulate. He brought this faculty especially to the "powers of the President" clause.

However, this gift for understatement has its most profound expression in the clause that probably was nearest to Rutledge's heart— the judiciary clause.

The one complete novelty in the Constitution is in the establishment of the judicial department. Seemingly, on first reading, the judicial department is only one of three, but the potentiality of placing it above all is there.

Why is the Constitution not more explicit on that point, which,

The Randolph-Rutledge draft of the Constitution; from the Colonel George Mason collection in the Library of Congress, Washington, D. C.

RUTLEDGE   RANDOLPH

The Executive

RUTLEDGE	RANDOLPH
	1 Shall consist of a single person
Governor of the United People and States of America	2 who shall be elected by the legislature by joint ballot
	3 and hold his office for the term of seven years
By ballot in each hav'g a Negative in the other.	4 and shall be ineligible thereafter
	5 his powers shall be
	1 to carry into execution the national laws
to be Commander-in-Chief of the Land and Naval forces of the Union, and the Militia of the several states	2 to command and superintend the militia
	3 to direct their discipline
	4 to direct the executives of the states to call them or any part for the support of the national government.
shall propose to the legislature from time to time by Speech or Messg such Meas as concern the Union	5 to appoint to offices not other wise provided for by the constitution
	6 to be removable on impeachment made by the House of Representatives and on conviction of malpractice or neglect of duty before the supreme judiciary
No increase or decrease during the term of service of the executive.	7 to receive a fixed compensation for the devotion of his time to the public service the quantum of which shall be fixed by the national legislature and to be paid out of the National Treasury.

(The above reading of the script is the one offered by Dr. Max Farrand in *Records of the Constitution.*)

Here is the origin of the constitutional powers of the President. The first writing, (right) uses the ideas in the Madison plan, and is that of Edmund Randolph, later (1789) the first Attorney General of the United States. Corrections (left) are in the hand of John Rutledge. They were not thereafter materially changed, carrying through the Wilson and Morris drafts into the adopted document, where they remain. Note Rutledge's definition of the executive as "Governor of the *People and States*"; this was later changed, while the idea as embodied in basic law remained in the later paragraphs. If the Randolph draft had persisted the President would not have, in time of war, his present military power.

A. The executive

Governor of the
united People & States
of America:

1. shall consist of a single person;
2. who shall be elected by the Legislature
3. and hold his office for the term of seven years,
4. and shall be ineligible thereafter.

5. His powers shall be
   1. to carry into execution the national laws
   2. to

   to direct the executives of the states to

   5. to appoint to offices not otherwise provided
      for by the constitution
   6. to be removed on impeachment,

   of Treason Bribery or corruption
   7. to receive a fixed compensation for
      the devotion of his time to public service
      the quantum of which shall be settled
      by the national legislature
      to be paid out of the national
      treasury.

+ the commander in chief
  of the Land & Naval forces
  of the Union & of the Militia
  of the several States
  shall propose to the Legis, &c from
  time to time by speech or message such
  Meas as concern

A no increase or decrease during
the term of service of the
Executive.

so far as Rutledge was concerned, is the one, next to the wartime powers of the executive clause, of chief interest? The answer goes into the temper of the times and the records of the Convention. It was one of Rutledge's most delicate tasks to grasp the meaning of both, and, despite both, still to register his will.

On the subject of judicial power the tension was at all times high, the decision as to how it was to be treated very close. If the subject had been left to a popular vote, by itself, no state would have passed the clause which eventually was ratified as an integral part of the whole document and which still stands unchanged. No one knew this better than John Rutledge. The unruly temper of the former colonials on the subject of court authority and of the expense of legal procedure, he knew well and considered as uninformed and unreasonable. Remembering Shinner, he was satisfied that every objection to the propriety of judicial authority as a final repository of power could be met by "improving the personnel of the magistracy." "Give us good judges and we will have good rule," he once said in the South Carolina Assembly.

In the debates in the Constitutional Convention Rutledge uttered no word about judicial power, though the subject was well aired by others. Benjamin Franklin, for instance, made a stout attack on the proposition that the high court might void Acts of Congress. He said he resented such an idea, "as giving into the hands of a limited number of selected judges the power to overrule the considered acts of the direct representatives of the people." Rutledge sat ten feet from the aged mentor and made no comment. Perhaps he reflected that Franklin had said, earlier, "I submit my ideas, which may not meet approval, and which I may be persuaded to change." Rutledge himself had made a similar remark, but in public expression he was not so naïve as Franklin. He knew, in general, exactly what he wanted and in this he had the advantage over nearly all the others. Certain basic ideas—chiefly those as to the powers of the President and of the judiciary—he would not change, while others, on the navigation clause and the length of the presidential term, he held for trading purposes.

John Dickinson was one of Rutledge's close friends who did not even know the South Carolinian's mind on the subject of the judiciary. He attacked on the floor the idea of giving the court the power to void Acts of Congress. Rutledge made no reply to him. Mercer and Bedford also made known their objections, which were similar. Elbridge Gerry and Luther Martin spoke up in favor of supreme judicial power. Rutledge listened to them all and said nothing.

Finally Charles Pinckney took the floor. The others did not know just how John Rutledge felt on the subject, but Pinckney knew and his deep personal antagonism came into the open, even though only his fellow South Carolinians realized it. With his flair for popular appeal and his instinct for opposing the entrenched "old dictator," he delivered a brilliant and fiery address against giving the judiciary the power to review legislative acts. Every member of the Convention listened attentively. There was no applause because it was one of the rules of the Convention that no speaker should be applauded, but Charles Pinckney might believe that he had driven his point home and won it, for no one made any response. John Rutledge sat absorbed and said nothing.

With this debate and the temper of the people back home to consider, the Drafting Committee, at last, approached the Judicial Clause. Here was the key to the Constitution; here was the "tune" that would set the march of history. The third, the judicial, clause, which contains only four hundred words, is the essence of John Rutledge. All else in powers of government had elsewhere been closely specified and limited, with due and exact regard for stipulated checks and balances, and then, with an uncanny economy of words and with an ease utterly belying the gravity of the act, Rutledge granted the final authority, the ultimate power, to the appointed judiciary. After cautiously distributing power everywhere else, he gave the authority to a single group of men to undo all else. That was his own private view of the correct repository for ultimate power. It happened, also, to be the Iroquois view; they gave final power to the elder sachems. Yet the judicial clause would not be in the Constitution as it is if John Rutledge had not believed in the final competence and in the

The Wilson-Rutledge draft of the Constitution, from the Wilson papers in possession of the Historical Society of Pennsylvania, and here reproduced (in facsimile) for the first time. Reproduction is with permission of the Historical Society of Pennsylvania. (Wilson wrote first on the right, using half the page; Rutledge re-wrote on the left half of the page.)

RUTLEDGE	WILSON
to the Legislature of state of the Union.	He shall from time to time give information of the State of the Nation to the Legislature. He may
such measures as he shall judge nesy. & expedt.	recommend matters to their consideration, and may convene them on extraordinary occasions. He shall
In case of a disagreement may adjourn them to such Time as he shall think proper.	take Care to the best of his ability that the laws of the United States be faithfully executed.
It shall be his duty to provide for the due and faithful exec. of the laws.	
—to the best of his ability.	

(The above reading is the one offered by Dr. Max Farrand in his *Records of the Constitution*).

This is part of one of thirty pages in the Wilson-Rutledge draft, and is chosen because it indicates clearly the characteristics of the two men who wrote it; the translucent impersonality of Wilson and the sharp, definite mentality of Rutledge. The persistence of Rutledge in this draft of giving to the Executive the power to propose "such measures as he shall judge nesy. & expedt.", which amplifies and sharpens his editing of the prior Randolph draft, indicates not only his own determination, but offers a profound commentary on this origin of one of the chief sources of Presidential power.

Note that the grant of power to the executive to adjourn Congress in case of disagreement to such time as "he shall think proper", (in Rutledge's hand) is not in the Wilson draft (nor was it in Randolph's). It appears in neither the Madison nor Pinckney plans.

The Wilson-Rutledge draft of the Constitution. Reproduced by permission of the Historical Society of Pennsylvania. It was not photographed until 1942 for use in this work. The reading is transcribed from that given in *Records of the Constitution* by Max Farrand.

RUTLEDGE	WILSON
Assign any part of the Jurisdiction above mentioned except the Trial of the Executive — to — inferior —	The Legislature may distribute this jurisdiction in the manner and under the limitations which it shall think proper among such courts as it shall constitute from Time to Time.
Judgment in Cases of Impeachment shall not extend further than to removal from office and disqualify to Hold and Enjoy any place of Honr Trust or Profit under the U. S. But the party convicted shall be nevertheless liable & subject to Judl Trial and Punishment according to the Law of the Land.	Crimes shall be tried in the state in which they shall be committed, and the Trial of them shall be by jury except in cases of Impeachment.

This page is chosen chiefly to give a visualization of the drafters of the Constitution at work. The holograph record tells its own story. The minutiae of the entire ms. of thirty pages, together with the earlier Randolph-Rutledge draft, may be studied in detail in the library of the Historical Society of Pennsylvania in Philadelphia, Pennsylvania, and in the Library of Congress, Washington, D. C. The format of both Randolph and Wilson drafts is similar, in that the right half of the page was used for the initial articulation of the assigned writer, while the left half was reserved for the final revisions of the Chairman of the Drafting Committee.

reliability of conscience of the selected magistrate. He assumed that they should, could, and would be a succession of John Rutledges.

James Wilson wrote the first draft of the judicial clause, giving it a much more exact definition than exists in the final document. Rutledge deleted this forthright expression, declaring it was not discreet to define the powers of the Supreme Court too carefully. Randolph, not averse, said that would please the opponents of court power; he meant such delegates as Benjamin Franklin and Charles Pinckney. Wilson remarked, cynically, that the courts would assume all power unless it was specifically denied, whether granted or not. To this Ellsworth was quite agreeable, and both Gorham and Randolph withheld definite opposition, in presence of the unity of the ruling three.

So the judicial clause stood, with its profound Rutledgian possibility, while history has verified Wilson's perception of its ultimate meaning. It took more than a hundred years for the courts to define just what John Rutledge meant in writing the judicial clause as he did. If he had been more explicit the Convention would not have passed, nor would the people have ratified, the Constitution.

On August sixth the Drafting Committee submitted its report. It was printed on seven folio pages and a copy was placed in the hands of each member. Then the debates began all over again and lasted for another six weeks, though they did not again reach an *impasse*. In late August, Madison says, "John Rutledge complained of the tediousness of the proceedings. He spoke of the impatience of the public and of the extreme anxiety of many members to bring the business to an end."

Another Committee was selected, one on Style, it was called, to prepare the final draft. This final draft differs from the Rutledge draft only in arrangement and in the addition of some qualifying and, presumably, some decorative phrases. On September seventeenth it was adopted.

The document achieved through "the lens of the convention" had been set and framed and was ready for its long life.

O<small>N</small> J<small>ANUARY</small> 1, 1789, John Rutledge took the oath as Chancellor of the Southern District of South Carolina. The nation was in its first and most terrible depression. Charleston was almost as near financial exhaustion as it had been when Clinton was camped across the Neck. The pay of the Chancellor was two thousand dollars a year. Two years before this was only a fraction of a first-rate attorney's income, but, as conditions then existed, no attorney in the state could earn half that amount.

In New York, on April 30 of that year, George Washington became the first President. Shortly afterward he began making appointments, first of his Cabinet, then of others. Through the summer he was asked repeatedly what he would do about the Supreme Court. He replied that he considered those appointments the most important of all; he would have to wait. He did, in fact, come to them last.

A few days after his inauguration Washington marked a drawer in his cabinet in his study on Cherry Street "sup'r ct." Into this he placed names and recommendations, whenever received. The drawer had no lock and he was in the habit of opening it and spreading the items in front of callers and bringing up the subject for comment, while he would listen to the arguments about the various candidates.

In September it was known to members of his cabinet and to others intimate with him, that the choice for Chief Justice had narrowed down to three men: John Rutledge, James Wilson, and John Jay. Wilson was still regarded as the ablest "office" lawyer in America. Eventually, however, Washington decided to eliminate Wilson from consideration for the high office because he believed that the Chief Justice must be a man not only eminent as a lawyer, but also with an important administrative and political background. This was the idea he had received from Rutledge himself during the Constitutional Convention. The choice was now between Rutledge and Jay.

John Jay had never tried an important case in court. For over twenty years he had occupied political positions, as an appointee of his father-in-law or of his uncle-in-law, and had been elected only to his last place. His state was coming to be known as Empire and held the seat of government, though it was not yet the most populous nor even the wealthiest. He had been one of the seven to write the Constitution of the State of New York, but had not been chosen to attend the Constitutional Convention. His political availability lay in the fact that he was, at the moment, Governor of New York.

Washington asked the opinion of John Adams, who was then Vice-President. Adams said, "If ability is to decide, take Rutledge—if politics, Jay." The President, the Secretary of State Jefferson, and the Attorney General Randolph, all were southerners. There were obvious geographical objections to giving the Chief Justiceship to another southerner, especially to one whose state contained less than three per cent of the white population of the country.

In October Washington sent his nominations for the Supreme Court to the Senate. They were promptly ratified. John Jay of New York was Chief Justice; John Rutledge of South Carolina, first Associate Justice; James Wilson of Pennsylvania, second Associate; Richard Henry Harrison of Maryland, third Associate; and John Blair of Virginia, fourth Associate.

However, several days before he sent in these nominations he wrote a personal letter to John Rutledge, notifying him of his nomination, well in advance of the others, to be sure Rutledge would get the news first from Washington himself.

In his reply to the President Rutledge said, "Your personal letter to me is so polite and considerate I feel it would be ungracious to refuse."

The only other remark he is known to have made is, "At least I have had as much court experience as Jay." The new Chief Justice had had almost none.

Rutledge received five quarterly payments of salary from the

United States Treasury as Associate Justice of the Supreme Court. The pay was thirty-five hundred dollars a year. He presided over the first circuit court established.

In 1791 he resigned to accept the office of Chief Justice of the Supreme Court of South Carolina.

In June, 1795, Rutledge was hearing a case in Charleston when he received news that John Jay had resigned as Chief Justice of the United States. He adjourned court and at once wrote a letter to George Washington, saying he would be willing to accept appointment to the place vacated by Jay. He sent the letter by his own slave.

Washington received Rutledge's letter in Philadelphia. It was summer. Congress was adjourned. The President told his aide to hold the slave who brought the letter. Four years had elapsed since he had chosen Jay; Philadelphia had supplanted New York as the capital. Did he remember that night in 1775, when the First Continental Congress was considering choice of a Commander-in-Chief for its armies, when only the deft words of John Rutledge had plucked from his own neighbors their reluctant votes? Or did he recall the message Rutledge had sent in 1780, asking for Greene to command in the South, culminating in his own easy checkmate at Yorktown? Had not the South Carolinian handed him both his great opportunity and his supreme victory? Or did Washington recreate in his mind's eye those four hot months in Philadelphia in 1787 when a new world was being molded? Who could interpret the Constitution better than the man who wrote it?

However much of this he may have thought Washington came to the point quickly, for "the instant he received the letter the President made out a commission appointing John Rutledge Chief Justice of the United States, ad interim." The slave started on his return journey without even sleeping in Philadelphia.

Rutledge served as Chief Justice four and a half months. The yearly salary was four thousand dollars and there is in the Treasury a duplicate of the one voucher paid him—for one thousand dollars. He presided over two sessions, wrote one opinion, and delivered another orally.

Sir

Having accepted the Office of Chief Justice of the United States; I resign to your Excellency the Commission of Chief Justice which I held, under this State.—

I have the Honor to be, with great respect and Esteem. Sir,

Your most Obedient Servant

J. Rutledge

July 29th 1795

His Excellency
The Governor

This letter was addressed to His Excellency, Arnoldus Vanderhorst, Governor of South Carólina, by John Rutledge and is here reproduced for the first time, with permission of the present owner, Mr. Arnoldus Vanderhorst, of Charleston, S. C., lineal descendant of the eighteenth-century governor. Mr. Vanderhorst, who is President of the St. Cecelia Society of Charleston, said of it to the author, "I have often studied this letter to learn if I could utter its context in any better form, or if I might eliminate any phrase or even a word. I could not. It is both a social communication (for Mr. Rutledge and my great-great-great grandfather were neighbors in Christ Church Parish) and a state document. As either it is impeccable. Here it is, two in one."

It happened that this four and a half months coincided with the agitation concerning the Jay Treaty with Great Britain, in which stipulation for the final withdrawal of British troops from United States soil, the definition of boundaries, and West Indian agreements were made.

Rutledge was appointed July first, but without any public announcement. The terms of the Jay Treaty became public July second and the fury of opposition from Boston to Charleston was such that nearly every popular leader spoke against it. Thomas Jefferson, who had resigned from the Cabinet, became the chief leader of the opposition and Alexander Hamilton, Secretary of the Treasury, made it his business to see that the Treaty should be ratified. Hamilton's first success lay in convincing President Washington that, whatever anyone thought of the terms of the Treaty, ratifying it was better than the alternative, another war with Great Britain.

While this political alignment was in process of being defined and while the air was filled with the first bitter recriminations, a public meeting was held at Charleston. The first speaker was Charles Pinckney, who was highly incensed by the Treaty. His cousin, Thomas Pinckney, Ambassador to France at the time, and formerly Ambassador to England, had been replaced by John Jay as a special ambassador to negotiate the Treaty and Charlestonians believed that their local favorite could have done much better than the New Yorker. This added fuel to the flame. A crowd hung Jay in effigy.

John Rutledge appeared unexpectedly at this meeting. The news of his new appointment had just appeared in the *Gazette* but the fact that the Chief Justice of the United States was addressing them was not their primary concern nor his. They felt they were listening to him as their own leader and those who heard him were rewarded, for it was said to be "the first time in years he let himself go." Many of the younger generation who often had heard about the eloquence of John Rutledge now were able to understand why the earlier generation had considered him its greatest orator.

Rutledge spoke for more than an hour. He took the Treaty apart, line by line, section by section, and demolished it. That speech, later printed, became a bible for the campaign being waged throughout the states by opponents of the Treaty, including Jefferson and his followers. Yet the printed words, strong as they are, do not reveal the fire which one auditor reported as "sufficient to raise the tombstones in the nearby graveyard." Read in the cold light of a later day (and especially in the light of the denouement) this attack on the Jay Treaty appears as the able, uncompromising advocacy of a vigilant and informed political opponent, quite devoid of judicial restraint. It remains as a *curiosa* of political spellbinding by a Chief Justice, equalled only in judicial tactlessness by some of the diatribes later delivered by John Marshall, *after* he had been confirmed as Chief Justice.

Never before had Rutledge made a serious error in his sense of timing. His dual personality previously had stood him in good stead and the orator in him had appeared only at behest of the competent politician. Now, for the first time, he was indiscreet. He ignored the fact that he was Chief Justice only ad interim, and that to be secure he required the confirmation of the Senate. That he spoke impromptu on an important issue, contrary to habit, can be accounted for only on the score that he did not anticipate the national platform his words eventually reached. He was near the Corner, in St. Michael's Church and, he assumed, among friends and neighbors.

Throughout the summer and fall of 1795 the campaign for and against the Jay Treaty absorbed the political attention of the country. In August the Treaty was ratified by the Senate, which might have been considered ominous for Rutledge, for it showed the temper of the controlling body on the issue.

However, the Senate excepted the important article on West Indian trade. The President signed the Treaty and then objection was made that it could not become law until the House of Representatives should ratify. This was a constitutional quibble, but Great Britain seized the indicated advantage and refused to be bound by the Treaty until the final barrier should be removed.

Thus the fight became more bitter than ever. It was not, in fact, until the following spring that the House of Representatives finally did pass the measure and then it was ratified by only a single vote. All that winter the issue was in most serious doubt and on it Alexander Hamilton had staked his political fortunes.

The leader against the Treaty in New York was Aaron Burr. Though later Burr and Jefferson were to oppose each other in deadly political combat they were, in 1795, together against Hamilton. Each quoted John Rutledge as his leader and did all he could to secure the confirmation of the Acting Chief Justice who, by his public assertion, had placed himself in the anomalous position of opposing the administration, for both Washington and Adams were now committed to the Jay Treaty in every detail.

On December 10, in the Senate, then in its eleventh session, "a motion was made to consider the nomination of John Rutledge as Chief Justice." Consideration was postponed to December 15.

In those five days Alexander Hamilton carried on an industrious lobby among members of the Senate, alleging that Rutledge was insane. He had three exhibits:

First, a letter from a bystander in Charleston who said he had heard the Acting Chief Justice denounce the Treaty and that "Rutledge talked like a crazy man." In noting this comment from a political opponent it is recalled that Ramsay reported Rutledge's first court advocacy at the age of twenty-two, as being "like a tropic downpour," and that John Adams, in 1775, when in skeptical review of his purposes, noted in his diary, "John Rutledge talks so rapidly, the words pouring from his mouth, that one cant tell what he says."

Second, Hamilton showed a clipping from a newspaper in Norfolk where Rutledge had recently held court, saying, "The court was adjourned for a day because of the illness of the Chief Justice who was unable to attend."

And, third, a clipping from a Rhode Island paper containing an anonymous letter from an alleged contributor in Charleston, using much the same language that was used in the letter shown the senators. Later it was learned that Hamilton was part owner of the Rhode Island newspaper.

That was all the evidence. No senator talked with Rutledge personally while the question of his confirmation was before the Senate. No medical report was asked for or received.

On December 15, to quote the archaic words of the executive journal of the Senate, "On motion the senate resumed consideration of the message of the President of the United States, containing the nomination of John Rutledge to be Chief Justice of the United States, and, on motion, to advise and consent to the nomination, it *passed in the negative,* (yeas 14, nays 10.) the yeas and nays being required by one fifth of the senators present."

2.

For the thirty-five years from Christmas Eve of 1760, when Rutledge stepped from the ship that brought him from England, to this December of 1795, he had not suffered a major defeat. He had been deflected; often he had had to bide his time; but his first irrevocable reverse was at the very end, when his important work was done.

At this time Rutledge was often ill and sometimes had to remain in bed for several days at a time. He had kidney stone and he had also an ailment, little understood in his day, which even lacked a name until an English physician named Dr. Bright (born in 1827) diagnosed it. Since then it has been known as Bright's disease.

Men like Rutledge, of consistently repressed emotions, are often subject to such kidney ailments. To self-control may be attributed his physical deterioration as he passed the age of fifty-five. Medical ignorance during the period in which he lived is also to blame. He was never "mentally unsound" unless such a phrase might be used to describe his condition in the moments of angony when he suffered from his illness.

*   *   *   *   *

In 1796 he was again in Charleston, a practicing attorney, living on Broad Street. Elizabeth, his wife, had been dead three years; his mother four. He had had ten children; six were living, four married; yet he was alone.

His office was in the same place, near Church Street, across from the Corner. The port did not have the business of the old days—

New York had supplanted it. When he first came to practice there were only twenty attorneys at the bar of Charles Town; now at the bar of Charleston were more than sixty, with very little businesss to divide among them. Moreover, the chief merchants, the great planters sought other counsel now.

They were proud of him, however, and pointed him out—as they did the broken stump of the Liberty Tree. He was a legend among them—in many ways he was becoming a myth. Though alive, he was dead.

Sometimes he was addressed as "Governor," or as "Judge." In his later years he never responded to either. He then accepted two honorifics only: "Mister" and "Esquire." Not together, however. Once a letter addressed to "Mr. John Rutledge, esquire" was handed him; he refused it, saying he knew of no such person.

The times were extremely hard. For years he had been accumulating debts and paying little or nothing. Piece by piece he disposed of all but three parcels of real estate and these were so overburdened with taxes the state finally took them over. Now, when he was down, the vultures gathered and threatened him with imprisonment if he did not get money for them.

Imprisonment for debt was commonplace. General Moultrie— who had recently been governor of the state—was seized and lodged in jail because he could not pay the notes he had signed during the Revolution to get food for his soldiers.

John Rutledge, however, enjoyed a curious immunity. He received dunning letters from various attorneys—some he knew and some he had not met; he replied courteously, though without payment. Yet no one ever served a summons. There was not an attorney in Charleston who would employ a deputy sheriff to tap John Rutledge on the shoulder. He walked freely among them.

One day a caller appeared to him unexpectedly. It was James Wilson, now first Associate Justice of the Supreme Court of the United States and traveling on circuit. He was surprised to learn of the immunity his old associate enjoyed and revealed that in Philadelphia he was not so fortunate. During the war he had speculated heavily in lands and he had long been insolvent. There were judgments against him and he expected never again to set foot in Pennsylvania. If he did, he ran the risk of being arrested and thrown into prison. The first Associate Justice of the Supreme Court of the United States was a fugitive from Pennsylvania justice. Even then his creditors were securing extradition papers, whose service he barely escaped, shortly after, in Edenton, North Carolina, by dying.

Rutledge took Wilson to call on Moultrie at the jail on Magazine Street. They found the General enjoying himself on the warden's porch next door; he had the freedom of the town and lived well at the warden's expense. There was only one drawback: the jail closed at ten o'clock at night and Moultrie made it a point to observe the rules and be "at home" not later than ten. He invited his guests to dinner and the three ate and drank at the warden's table.

After dinner Moultrie revealed an embarrassment. He had been given tickets to the theatre, around on New Street only a block and a half away, and had invited the warden to be his guest.

Rutledge and Wilson urged Moultrie and the warden to go along to the theatre, while they sat on the porch, for it was a pleasant, moonlit night. There they were found talking when the General and his host returned, just before ten o'clock, so as to get in before the jail closed for the night.

Moultrie was disappointed. It was a good show, he said, and he had seen only two acts. There were two acts more, and he held the return checks in his hand. So Rutledge proposed that he and Wilson take the checks, see the rest of the show, then return to the jail the next day to report on the last two acts. They did.

When elections for the Assembly rolled around in December, 1797, somebody in Christ Church Parish suggested that they should send John Rutledge to Columbia to represent them. There was a meeting in the vestry room of the church to consider it and an objection was made that "the Old Dictator is getting cloudy in his mind—he may not have more than one good day a year—we should have a younger man."

Someone leaped up and cried, "We don't want anybody else than John Rutledge—let's send him up there for us—suppose'n he does have only one good day in a year—he'll do more for us that day than all the rest of the Assembly can do the whole session—if they're at their top every day."

An account of this was written three years later. The only record of Rutledge in the Assembly is that he served during 1798 and 1799, but what he did is not revealed, for the sponsors of acts were not recorded. The account concludes; "So they did and he did."

This final official episode in his career seems to resolve conclusively any question of his sanity. No man "of unsound mind" would be elected by his neighbors to represent them officially in a law-making body. Those who knew him best trusted him the most.

While Rutledge was serving this last term as assemblyman James Iredell, of North Carolina, who had been appointed to the United States Supreme Court as an Associate Justice, came to Charleston to hold court.

On May 8, 1798, Judge Iredell wrote to Mrs. Iredell, "I am told Mr. John Rutledge is quite recovered. He was from home when I arrived, but called on me yesterday evening, when I was unluckily from home."

On May 11 Judge Iredell wrote to Mrs. Iredell, "Mr. John Rutledge has repeatedly pressed me to stay at his house, which however I have declined as I have previously engaged lodgings. . . . Mr. Rutledge is perfectly recovered and of such high spirits that he, and another gentleman and myself, outsat all the rest of the company at a friend's house, till near 11 o'clock. He remarked, with surprise, that I never swore, which seems to be an equal proof of my former sin and present reformation. He himself and most of the gentlemen here swear a good deal."

In a letter dated May 12, Mrs. Iredell heard from her husband again, for he wrote in apparent eagerness to report, "I am to dine today with Mr. J. Rutledge, who has invited a number of other gentlemen. This week, I am told, is the first time he has broke from his retirement—"

Then, in a fourth letter, this one dated May 18, from Statesbury, S. C., Mrs. Iredell received a final, and to us graphically satisfying report from the traveling justice, "I left Charleston on Monday," he wrote, "and spent a delightful day at Mr. Roger Smith's, only about nine miles from town, on Ashley River, and by far the handsomest place I have seen in the whole state. This gentleman is married to a sister of Mr. Rutledge's, and has a very large and agreeable family. Mr. Rutledge came out with me, and we had other company from town specially invited. Mr. Rutledge has lived so much in retirement that, though very fond of his sister, and the whole family, they had not seen him for a long time; and it was truly affecting to witness their meeting, and how happy they all seemed to be. Mr. Rutledge himself was in the highest spirits the whole day, and prolonged his stay as long as he could. . . . Considering that Mr. Rutledge has lived totally recluse before my arrival, his attention, his friendship, I could almost say his affection to me, was conspicuous to a remarkable degree."

To the very last Rutledge kept his office in the same place and spent his afternoons at The Corner and his evenings at the Exchange. Some of his married children wanted him to live with them, but he sold the residence at 11⁵ Broad Street and took a room at Dillon's. Now and then he visited some friend for a week or two.

One of his sons was being suggested as the next United States Senator. The children resented the way their father shambled about. One complained, "he is as common as an old shoe," for Rutledge would not foregather with his class. Seven male members of his family were Masons, but he never was. Neither was he a member of St. Andrew's Society, nor of St. Patrick's, to both of which Edward belonged. He had never joined the Library Society. The records of St. Cecelia's are lost, but it is believed he was not a member of that exclusive organization, either.

John Rutledge was not a "joiner." He was what the French call "a type." There was just one like him.

One day, in his sixtieth year, he stepped from St. Michael's—he liked to go in there for a half hour of quiet meditation—to meet James Fraser, the painter, then a twelve-year-old boy.

In his reminiscences, Fraser recalled, "Mr. John Rutledge, of Revolutionary celebrity, who was a very old man then, but very erect, happened to meet me near the church whilst the judge and sheriff and a few officers of the court were crossing over from the court house. Seeing this scant and motley procession he asked what it meant. I told him they were going to hear a session's sermon, when he observed how differently it had been conducted formerly, when the judges in their scarlet robes, and the lawyers also robed, and all the attendants of the court, proceeded in great form to the church. When I told him I wanted to be a painter he described for me how the wigs were held down and how the lace jabots were made. This meeting is further impressed upon my recollection by his offering to walk up with me to Gen. C. C. Pinckney's house to show me Stuart's portrait of Washington recently sent here, which he accordingly did."

This is our last authentic glimpse of him as he traveled into the shadow. He was still interested in human beings; and he was still interested in technique, even when the calling was another's.

Edward Rutledge was elected Governor of South Carolina at the end of 1799, the week after George Washington died. He began his term in January of 1800. A week later his heart failed and he died at his desk.

There was a state funeral for Edward. They laid his body in St. Phillip's churchyard, near the outer fence, and placed a high ornamental stone above it, and an eloquent inscription of his achievements. He had been a commissioned colonel, a signer of the Declaration of Independence, and Governor of South Carolina. The stone also proclaimed that 'the almighty' (in small letters) doubtless would care for EDWARD RUTLEDGE (in large letters).

Six months later, in the home of the Episcopal Bishop, the Reverend Dr. Smith, John Rutledge died. He was buried obscurely in St. Michael's churchyard, under a slab of sandstone bearing only this inscription:

John Rutledge
June 21, 1800
aged 61 years.

Under the earth, perhaps six or seven feet, it is believed that a silver plate on top of the casket may contain the date of his birth, which otherwise is unknown.

EPILOGUE

In the 1830's Alexis de Tocqueville, the French savant who was preparing a volume on the workings of democracy, came to the United States to study its American manifestations at first hand. He asked at once about the identity of the author of the Constitution. He was told that Jefferson had written it.

The Frenchman knew that Jefferson had been in France while the Constitution was being written. "I do not mean the Declaration of Independence," he said, "that was but a gesture—a *succès d'avocat* —I mean your title, your patent—who prepared that?"

So they told him the accepted legend: the Constitution had been written by "The Founding Fathers," and they gave him a list of names, beginning with Washington and Franklin.

"This is ridiculous," replied de Tocqueville, "such an important product of the human entity, one of the most idiosyncratic documents ever emanating from the human brain, can have but *one* authentic father. Who was he?"

De Tocqueville was referred to the archives, and he studied them, including Madison's journal of the Convention, the notes of Judge Yates, and the few other sources then available. Finally de Tocqueville exclaimed, "There is no mystery about it—the authorship of the Constitution is quite clear—a man named John Rutledge wrote it. Who was he?"

Nobody in Washington knew much about him. Having an instinct for logical definition, and holding as sacred the verified sources of historic events, de Tocqueville journeyed to Charleston. He knew that Rutledge had survived the Federal Convention by thirteen years and imagined that he had spent most of that time telling his children and grandchildren all about it. He supposed that they would be full

365

of traditions and memories and that he would reap a rich harvest for his book.

In Charleston de Tocqueville found all the available Rutledges —quite a number were living—but not one could give him any of the information he sought. In fact what he told them was news, apparently. He was astounded. Finally he declared to one of them, "But there is no doubt that your grandfather is the authentic author of the American Constitution. How can you be so indifferent?"

The reply was, "It may be quite true, as you say. Dictator John did many remarkable things, but . . ."

De Tocqueville gave up.

Among his own people, as elsewhere, there developed a sort of conspiracy of silence concerning the reality of Rutledge's contribution to history. Looking through the printed pages that came from South Carolina, one finds in a century only occasional comment; yet when such a comment does occur, it is strangely poignant.

There is, for instance, William G. Simms, generally considered first among South Carolina writers. In 1854 he delivered an address in Brooklyn to "defend the memory of John Rutledge," but that was in the North. Ten years before, in his *History of South Carolina,* he had written, "John C. Calhoun became a worthy successor of the illustrious John Rutledge, though as an orator not so eloquent. . . ." It required courage in the South in the 1840's to compare anyone, living or dead, to Calhoun.

Then there is *The Bench and Bar of South Carolina,* by John Belton O'Neall, a standard volume dedicated to state pride. It quietly records: "Few men ever lived the equal of John Rutledge, and none will ever live to excel him." Then the writer retreats into silence as if he feared contradiction or protest.

Elihu Root once said, "There are mighty few men important enough to warrant inclusion in any historic study of American statesmen, and to know who they are you would have to wait a long time after they are gone."

Why has it taken so long to resurrect the life of John Rutledge and to assess its meaning? There are definite reasons.

One of them is sectional jealousy. South Carolina had less than three per cent of the white population in the Revolution, and she has produced since even less than that percentage of the historians. New England, assisted by Virginia, New York, and Pennsylvania, has been writing the histories. America is conscious of Bunker Hill, Valley Forge, and Yorktown, but is largely unaware of Charles Town and King's Mountain.

Yet sectional preoccupation is perhaps the least of the reasons this name has been obscured so long. Most of the records are lost. There are known to be in existence today not more than two hundred and eighty documents containing the handwriting of John Rutledge, and this writer has discovered nearly half of these. The official journals of the Assembly of South Carolina recording the events of his most important years are unavailable. Practically all the letters to him from every important man of his time have disappeared.

Superstition also played a part in the suppression of Rutledge's fame. That the Senate of the United States had not confirmed his appointment to the chief justiceship was explicable, even to some of its own members, only on the score that Rutledge was "mentally unsound," though this was neither in the record nor the fact. But madness was a familiar charge in those days. Two of the senators who voted against Rutledge's confirmation, each at the time an intense administration partisan, were John Marshall and Oliver Ellsworth, each later Chief Justice. Of these men, Thomas Jefferson, among others, for years seriously contended that John Marshall was mad, while Oliver Wolcott, and others, asserted stoutly and often that Ellsworth was mad. When Ellsworth heard of Wolcott's charge he was in England; he called on George III, who at the time was truly pathologically mad, and later wrote home to tell how tea was served to "the two madmen." Political pamphlets still exist that were written to "prove" that George Washington was mad. In that age frustration in political polemics often resulted in the accusation—nor was that age alone in the practice. In the case of Rutledge, the action of the Senate coincided with an attack of physical illness, in itself somewhat mysterious at the moment, though far from destructive mentally, and at once the eighteenth-century superstition about mad people descended upon his name. It was then widely believed that if one were mad his name should not be mentioned. This impalpable prejudice enveloped the memory of John Rutledge in the minds and speech of his own generation and of that immediately following, those who knew most about him. Even while he still lived and the evidence of his alertness and soundness was before their eyes men calmly proceeded to bury Rutledge alive, with all his deeds.

Religious prejudice assisted in the process. Rutledge suffered in reputation from several species of religious bigotry. Some despised him because they believed him an atheist, a much more terrible word of reproach in his day than it is now. Others hated him equally because they believed he tried to retain the Church of England as a state religion in South Carolina. Still others, in the church, condemned him because he had not continued the state establishment of the church. The writer has been surprised to find that more people seem to be interested in the religious phase of Rutledge's life than in any other. He has several letters imploring him to satisfy the correspondents that John Rutledge was not an atheist. Generally, it may be noted, that while the Irish have produced all manner of men, good and bad, they are not apt to produce unbelievers: anti-clerics on occasion but not atheists. In his faith John Rutledge was a theist and there was never any argument about it; also, he was a sincere, though (by his own design) inconspicuous member of the church in which he was born and died. Also, he helped place in the Constitution of the United States the clause which forbids the application of any religious test to citizenship. Despite all this, during his lifetime, and in the generations following when his reputation was being forgotten, the intensities of religious narrowness were visited upon his memory with unmerited severity and with far-reaching effect.

When it came to identifying him with the writing of the Constitution, the nineteenth was a poor century for that—in the South, as de Tocqueville discovered. Throughout that bitter period before, during, and after the War Between the States, it was not very likely that men would assert in South Carolina, much less look for proof, that a

South Carolinian had woven the strands of union so cunningly strong that they never could be torn apart.

And yet all of these reasons for Rutledge's obscurity—sectional jealousy, lost records, superstition, religious prejudice, and the intense preoccupation in itself of the Lost Cause—were but secondary, really. The prime cause was John Rutledge himself. He willed that his deeds be largely anonymous. He not only neglected his own fame; he practically forbade it. It never could be said of him, as it has been said of Washington, Jefferson, John Adams, and Hamilton, among others, that "his eye was on posterity." The man who avoided titles, who never signed his name even with those titles which clearly belonged to him, who, after his first stand for the Assembly at the age of twenty-one, asked for only one place, that of Chief Justice, and then was so negligent of his security in it that he flouted sponsors and, when they refused him, uttered no word of protest, was not the man to spend any part of his life explaining himself. He was like a force of nature; he acted, he was gone, and that was all. His attitude toward posterity was the same as it was toward the citizens of Charles Town. Let others look to the records and memoirs, portraits and monuments. That was not his concern.

Modesty, however, was not the cause of his persistent and, it may be said, triumphant anonymity. Nor was it persisted in solely for efficiency. Instinct, training, logic—and his own inner self—combined with the circumstances of his milieu to compel him to suppress his ego and, thus, eventually his fame.

The psychology was super-normal. Rutledge became, very early, in effect, husband and father, and when he became, as a very young man, the new triumvir, instinct led him to·expand his family to include the whole town, on political terms which compelled anonymity. Eventually, as he became dictator, his family embraced the state. Through it all John Rutledge the man did not change. He remained the elder of all, anonymously, while, for the state, he shrewdly used anonymity to increase his political powers.

In the war the character of the man still did not change, while the area of his responsible influence expanded and became more complex. The attitude, begun as a youth with his blood kin, extended in his young manhood to the city-state, now expanded to take in everyone and everything required to conserve and protect his own.

Only by realizing this can the unique fact in the political life of John Rutledge be understood, that literally he had no opponents. This began in his own family; each member, at one time or another, tried to compete or to contend with him. He suppressed none, opposed none, and, practically, improved and magnified each. The same thing happened, in communal affairs, with Gadsden, Drayton, Moultrie, and others. They were merely his larger family. When one or another seized advantage that seemed dangerous to the communal life Rutledge managed the situation so that the values of the contenders— such as Gadsden's appeal to the masses, Drayton's eloquence and audacity, and Moultrie's fighting heart—should be utilized while they were curbed and directed. And when he felt obliged to hold one of them down, momentarily, he managed the business indirectly. The same principles were observed when his rule went beyond his own borders. The law of his life was so established that he operated with Washington, Adams, Greene, Lee, Lincoln, Sumter, Marion, Wilson, the North Carolina commanders, and all the others, as he had with Gadsden, Moultrie, Drayton, and the members of his own family. By practically eliminating himself, and especially the celebration of his acts, while retaining his prestige and authority, he vastly multiplied his power.

Thus integrated psychically, fully mature intellectually, ripe in years and in wisdom, widely experienced, he approached the Convention that invented a structure for an entirely new civilization when it prepared a bible for the future governmental life of mankind.

That his approach and his control were politico-military seemed to him necessary in the circumstances and, however much they may be criticized as a means, common sense has chosen to look rather at the result. With Rutledge the Constitutional Convention was planned and executed like a battle. It began with the *coup d'état* of the "oath of secrecy," in which the fortress of chaos was isolated and seized; it then proceeded, step by step, to the final assault that rose from the exaction of the Powers of the President Clause and that culminated in the writing of the Judicial Clause; it went almost methodically, triumphant from first to last, "according to plan."

Yet this masterpiece of political strategy, possibly the most superb in history, comparing its hazards with its achievements, was, after all, but a setting—a cloak for the ultimate achievement. Within it could operate, in secret calm, with his accustomed authority, the father of the city-state, the obscure but powerful architect of the Revolution, who had no opponent on that floor, but who wanted only to give the best, and most harmonious expression to the talents of Wilson and Pinckney, of Madison and Randolph, of Hamilton and Paterson, of Franklin, Sherman, Ellsworth, Martin, Mason, Dickinson, Morris, and all the others. Thus, while functioning like an irresistible force of nature, he acted as the guide and counsellor of "that group of demigods."

There were three indispensable men in the American Revolution, taking the whole period, from 1760 to 1789, and only three. Many others were useful and important, but they might have been replaced; remove any of these three and the drama could not have been enacted as it was. They form a human trinity; each intensely individual; each utterly different from either of the others; each indispensable alike to the others and to the total achievement.

First, there was Sam Adams, stirred by his dream of a new world; the originator, the revolutionary; a crusader; a mind with a single track and a sole idea, splendidly tooled with Yankee cunning and thrifty mastery of the folk mote; nothing in his life wasted and all thrown into that blazing obsession to pull down any foreign throne erected on these fresh shores.

Yet, with only Sam Adams to lead, there would have been a revolt, but there would not necessarily have been a Revolution, and certainly there would not have been a United States as we know it.

Second was George Washington, the arch bridging the way from the inspired revolt to the achieved Revolution, patient bearer of the burdens of multitudes, symbol of courage and faith. Yet, if there had been only these two leaders, there still would not have been what we know as the United States of America.

Any achievement is composed of three elements: the desire, the will, and the energy. A complete act cannot be achieved without combination of the three; and, it has been said, the greatest of these is the energy to organize and express the other two.

The man of energy was essential. When the War of the Revolution had bogged down someone was needed to supply more than a desire for independence and the patient courage to stand out for it. Someone had to devise the technique for victory; someone had to climb down into the stalled works and touch off the vital current which would release the pent-up power. Then, when the Revolution was accomplished, but when all the old order was in ruins and nothing had been erected to take its place, a man was required with unerring constructive statecraft, totally selfless, who could achieve a structure that would carry its spirit into the future.

That man was John Rutledge.

CHRONOLOGY

1739, September. Birth of John Rutledge in Christ Church Parish, South Carolina.

1758–60. Barrister-at-law, Middle Temple, London, England.

1761. Member of the Commons House of Assembly from Christ Church Parish.

1763, May. Marriage of John Rutledge and Elizabeth Grimké.

1764–65. Attorney-General of South Carolina.

1765. Delegate to the Stamp Act Congress in New York. Writes the memorial to the House of Lords.

1770. Writes charter for the College of Charles Town.

1774. Delegate to the First Continental Congress.

1775. Elected delegate to the Second Continental Congress; but does not serve long.

1775. Governor of South Carolina.

1776. Elected President of the Republic of South Carolina after writing its Constitution.

1778. Resigns from the office of President.

1778. Elected Governor of the State of South Carolina.

1780. Granted dictatorial powers by the Assembly.

1781. As commander-in-chief he causes the defeat of the British army in the South.

1782–83. Delegate to the Continental Congress.

1784–91. Judge of the Court of Chancery of South Carolina.

1787. Chief of the South Carolina delegation to the Constitutional Convention.

1787. Chairman of the Drafting Committee in the Constitutional Convention.

1788. Leads ratification of the Constitution in South Carolina.

1789–91. First Associate Justice of the Supreme Court of the United States.

1791–95. Chief Justice of the Court of Common Pleas and Sessions of South Carolina.

1795, July. Appointed Chief Justice of the United States by Washington.

1795, December. After presiding over one session of the Supreme Court, his nomination is rejected by the Senate.

1798–99. Member of the South Carolina Assembly.

1800, July 18. Death of John Rutledge in Charleston.

NOTES AND SOURCES

I. THE CLAN

The general background extends to these authors listed in the bibliography: Dalcho, Drayton, Duane, Fiske, Fraser, Flanders, Hartley, Henderson, Hewatt, Jones, Leiding, McCrady, McMaster, de Chastellux, Pinckney, Rivers, Salley, Simms, Smyth, Ravenel, Ramsay, Rhett, Wallace, Waring, Webber, White, and Whitefield. As standard historians of the state special reliance is put in this book, as elsewhere, in General McCrady and Dr. Wallace. However, at all points, original sources are sought wherever possible, and these include *The South Carolina Gazette.*

Mss.: the wills of Hugh, Thomas, and Francis Hext in Probate Court, Charleston; vital statistics in the church vault in Christ Church Parish; files for years 1732 to 1760 in Court of Ordinary (Common Pleas) (Charleston); memorials of the proprietary and royal governments (Columbia).

In searching the genealogy, after consulting the records of the South Carolina Historical and Genealogical Society, including various publications in its magazine, notably H. A. White's "The Rutledge Family in the Making of South Carolina" (1906) and Mabel L. Webber's exhaustive study of the descendants of Dr. John Rutledge (1930), this writer sought Miss Webber, then the guiding spirit of the Genealogical Society in Charleston and long considered a final authority on South Carolina genealogies. She was confined as the result of an injury which not long later brought death, but she reviewed her records, with stimulating courtesy, and painstaking reference to her ingenious files. A great genealogist, endowed with vivid imagination and keen sympathy, Miss Webber used both only to suggest possible sources while she held sternly to inexorable rules of documentary authenticity. She seemed to glow with an impersonal intensity as she related her continuous interest, covering more than twenty years, in the records of the Rutledge family. Aside from the main outlines of her study, incorporated in this text, she confided that she believed that the only lineal descendants of JR then living were three ladies, with residence in Greenville, S. C., that other surviving descendants of Doctor John are through Edward, that even these are extremely few, so that all others in the United States named Rutledge (extremely numerous) are of other origin; that in upper South Carolina before the Revolution there lived two brothers named, respectively, John and Edward Rutledge (not related to the family of Doctor John), and that these brothers are the ancestors of numerous living persons of their name; that Ann Rutledge of Illinois, identified with Abraham Lincoln, was not related to the family of Doctor John; and that, while she could trace the Hext family successfully into Wales, she had been unable to trace the Rutledges into or beyond Ireland. Later the writer determined the Irish and French background of JR through the Irish Genealogical Research Society of London, England.

The family anecdotes are from Ramsay, Simms, and Flanders, while the legendary material is augmented from personal conversation with Miss Eleanor Wragg and Mrs. Edmund Fedler, so-lateral descendants, and the family of W. C. Wolfe, of Orangeburg, S. C.

The subject of Nicholas Trott has long been a specialty of Mr. Theodore Jervey, President of the South Carolina Historical Society, who conveyed personally some of his unpublished conclusions. These, with data in McCrady, were checked through the Memorials. Professional association of the two men is established by comparison of clients of Andrew Rutledge with those of Trott when he was out of office as shown in the files of the Court of Ordinary.

II. THE TRIUMVIRATE

The sources of Book II are: First, the general bibliography, which includes the works of, especially, Ravenel, Snowden, Jervey, Fraser, Heyward, Salley, Phillips, Sellers, Schlesinger, Quincy, de Chastellux, Rhett, Simms, McCrady, Wallace, and Wertenbaker. The "order of chivalry" quotation is from Thomas Waring in *The Carolina Low Country.*

Second, what may be called the "anecdotal volumes": Flanders, Hartley, Ramsay, and O'Neall.

Mss. sources are third, and include the Pinckney papers in the Library of Congress, the diary of John Rutledge, jr., the Rutledge family papers, the Laurens papers in the Long Island Historical Society library, the Langdon Cheves and the Barnwell papers in the Charleston Library Society's library, provincial messages to the Crown, and the files in the Court of Ordinary in Charleston. Also, letters in possession of Mr. Arnoldus Vanderhorst of Charleston, S. C., were consulted.

Fourth, *The South Carolina Gazette,* which paralleled in publication the mature life of JR. Data about editor Timothy are from *Benjamin Franklin* by Carl Van Doren.

Fifth, personal reminiscences of Mrs. Edmund Felder and Mr. Langdon Cheves. Mrs. Felder, a descendant of Dr. John Rutledge, possessed a collection of manuscripts and personal belongings of JR, and had a distinct and vivid sense of him, though she was in the fifth generation. Mr. Cheves (aged ninety) is the grandson of the Speaker of the House of Representatives who succeeded Henry Clay in the administration of James Madison and who, as a boy, knew JR as an old man. Mr. Cheves, sitting at the window of his home overlooking the Battery in Charleston, told what he remembered having been told by his grandfather. It was the nearest to living personal contact that this writer had with his subject.

The material thus gathered is here dramatized (but in no important detail fictionized) and presented as a continuity, in which color is always secondary to factual accuracy.

The writer had no opportunity to do research in England or Ireland for data concerning JR's three formative years there. The report of his activities attributed to him in the third person is composed, largely, from data in Flanders, Ramsay, and O'Neall.

The episodes of the greeting of JR by the members of the bar of Charles Town and of Greenland's going down the bay are from Flanders. The latter checks with the plea in JR's writing filed in the Court of Ordinary in 1761.

Eliza Pinckney, in her letters, notes that JR "wore court mourning on his return." The description here is checked from official orders of the Court Chamberlain.

The physical description of JR is a composite, arrived at from various sources, including his portraits, and in part from deduction, as there is no satisfactory contemporary description, a fact in itself challenging later assertions that he was "heavy" or "tall" or "large." The most informative account this writer has found was written four years after JR's death by E. S. Thomas, who saw him only in later life and who said, "he looked like any well bred gentleman who would easily be lost in any crowd."

This, plus the fact that contemporaries did not refer to any physical characteristics must be weighed cautiously. His qualities were noted, not his person. Except for his red hair (usually obscured by a wig) he had no outstanding feature, though Mrs. Pinckney comments on "his always sunny nature." Perhaps the hair accentuated this impression. The Trumbull portrait (1791), painted when he was fifty-two and at the top of his living, indicates a slender person; the early miniature shows him positively thin. There is abundance of evidence that he enjoyed eating and drinking and had the best available of both; he was not athletically inclined, nor was he sedentary; he was never corpulent. Though only peripatetic still he was a man of action. The color of his eyes and hair is determined through a miniature by Ramage formerly in possession of Mrs. Edmund Felder, painted in JR's youth. His brothers and sisters were brunettes; he was the one redhead among seven; and it is a Rutledge tradition that each generation has at least *one*. Evidently he liked this distinction for in his early years he avoided wigs, but their use later, especially in official life, precluded casual notice of his hair. (In this connection, it may be noted that Washington, Jefferson, and Hamilton were also redheads.) JR's approximate height is determined from the length of the casket containing his body, which is six feet overall; making necessary deductions for lumber, lining, shrinkage of the body in later life, etc., gives one a fair idea.

The anecdote of the swearing-in costume of JR stems to the contemporary letters of Mrs. Eliza Pinckney, while that of JR's tossing his last coins to his mother with the exclamation that he started "penniless" is from Flanders, who noted that he had corresponded with surviving members of the Rutledge family.

The oyster roast is neither a composite nor fiction. The *Gazette* notes that JR gave an oyster roast attended by neighbors in the Christ Church Parish; the Laurens papers reveal the order for supplies; the *Gazette* gives the date of an announcement of JR's candidacy as that of the roast; the rest is the writer's deduction. Technical data concerning the roast itself is largely from Mikhel's *Rumbling of the Chariot Wheels.*

The question might be raised: "Did JR depart from South Carolina custom in offering elaborate food and drink to secure votes?" Yates Snowden records similar instances. This is the only known instance in JR's life in which he spread himself to this extent. The need was great and the remedy heroic. Afterward he scorned such devices, though early in 1776 he gave a less ample "roast" for constituents. Henry Laurens and Gabriel Manigault, in the decade preceding the Revolutionary War, annually "received" constituents, and at these receptions served hard-liquor punch. In 1775–76 William Henry Drayton frequently "entertained" in this fashion for the "commonalty," but by that time JR was above it and confined himself to dinners for close associates. In the earlier period (the 1770's) Richard Henderson moved from Virginia to "the purer air" of Kentucky "to escape the degradation of political life in which candidates give liquor and food in exchange for their neighbors' suffrages." The "candidates" who so "degraded" themselves (in Virginia) included Patrick Henry, Edmund Randolph, George Mason, and George Washington.

The avenue of live oaks where JR served his oyster roast still stands, as do the slave houses then (1761) owned by Mrs. Rutledge, though built in 1730.

In the Charleston County Court House a little cubicle, newly built in the rear, and up a few steps, is called, affectionately, by research workers, "The Plunder Room." The largest space, and the most accessible, is devoted to papers from the period of the War between the States. Next, and across, is the space for "ante-bellum" papers. (That period, too, has many devoted students.) In the far corner, neglected, are the pre-Revolutionary documents, tied in bundles with half-inch tape, each bundle labeled with a year-date. The bundle marked "1761," caked with dust, contains presumably all the papers filed in that year in the Court of Ordinary (Common Pleas) of the province of South Carolina. The writer came upon that bundle with trembling expectancy and eager haste which might seem absurd if one reflects that it had probably lain there untouched for more than a century and three-quarters. However, he felt adequately rewarded when he opened, one after the other, the pleas in the Guerin, the Crotty, the Hörry-Moncrief, and other cases, each obviously in the handwriting of JR, and each as clear, as legible as if it had just been written, for his early writing is careful, distinct, each letter well formed, and quite in contrast to the writing of later years.

This bundle of papers marked "1761" in itself tells a comprehensive story of the old Town. And it seemed so casual to find them there! The writer remarked to the County Clerk in charge, Mr. Wallace, that it was lucky they had survived the historic cataclysms in Charleston. "They got by Clinton and Cornwallis, all right, and Sherman, too," he said, "but their closest shave was that day we built this mezzanine and took them for a week to a room in the Timrod Hotel next door and the boy who was to watch them left a lighted cigarette on the table and went out to lunch." It seems easy to predict that the time will come when all those documents will be microfilmed, processed, and guarded in a manner befitting their priceless character.

The winning by JR of the "first breach of promise suit in America" has been always a high point in his hitherto brief biographies. It is noted by Flanders, O'Neall, and Hartley. However, it has not been noted that he had *two* breach of promise suits in his first year of legal practcie. It was supposed by Flanders and the others (relying apparently on tradition) that the Greenland case was the important one, as these earlier writers identify "the carpenter who went down the bay" with the "case that landed JR at the head of the bar of Charles Town in his first year." It was so only indirectly, as search of the files in the Court of Ordinary marked "1761" and "1762" revealed. The quotations are from the pleas in the handwriting of JR, and are here published for the first time, after 181 years.

Flanders and others assert that JR "never" lost a case at law. On this point every available record has been checked in the Courts of Common Pleas (Ordinary), Admiralty, Probate, and the later Supreme Court (all of South Carolina). JR practiced nowhere else. The Hörry-Moncrieff case in 1761 (his first jury trial) appears to be the only one he ever lost. His leading cases, beginning with the Cooke-Lennox, are analyzed and described in this work; those not mentioned specifically are omitted because they lack apparent dramatic or political interest. The "story" of every case is taken from the original papers.

In the bibliography are two indirect references to the fact that Charles Town was ruled by triumvirs. William Henry Drayton said, referring to an episode in 1775, that "it was the first time in many years in which the people of the city dared to go against the advice of those who ruled them." Josiah Quincy said (1773), "It is common knowledge that three men, all lawyers, determine everything of moment." No one before this writer ever named them publicly. This writer calls these three the "triumvirate." They were not so known contemporaneously. Why this situation has been ignored is a commentary on the inertia and artificiality of the time and period, which harbored the classic pattern of the triumvirate that precedes a dictatorship, and was preparing the people and the civilization to go down the path to arbitrary government.

The description of the house JR built (and lived in so long) is first-hand, through the courtesy of the present owners, Dr. and Mrs. Harley P. Lindsay, and the assistance of Mr. John Mead Howells, an architect who reconstructed for his own use a near-by residence. Mr. Howells pointed out the original construction and the latter additions such as the top floor and the iron balcony in front.

The Sparkins and Mangin case pleas in JR's hand are on file in the Charleston County Court House; they have never been published verbatim before. The latter is supplemented by Gadsden's indictment of Shinner in his Memorial to the Governor as submitted to the House of Lords.

The episodes concerning the Chief Justice and the Governor overlapped in point of time, over a large part of the decade of the 1760's, but for the sake of unity in telling, and as this is not a history but the picture of one man's life in relation to his times, the incidents that bear on the story of each office have been separated, though in fact all were inseparably mingled. The interpretation is this writer's.

III. THE FIRST AMERICAN CONGRESS—NEW YORK

The view of the Stamp Tax here adopted has become a consensus in the past generation: see Guedalla, Woodward, and Hockett, among others. This "long view" of the Stamp Tax has not before been applied specifically to South Carolina. It enabled the writer to make this interpretation which does not follow any previous local pattern, though it checks factually with McCrady and the *Gazette*. The fascinating and wholly absorbing underlying conclusion is that JR (almost alone among leading contemporaries) saw the Stamp Tax, its origins, and the motivation of its implications, as historians saw it only after a century and a half.

The sources of this book include: Mss.: The Thomas Addis Emmett Collection of Autographs and Letters of the members of the Stamp Act Congress in the New York Public Library, being sixty unpublished letters; the Laurens Papers in the Long Island Historical Society Library, and the Rutledge Family Papers.

Bibliography: *A Journal of the First Congress of the American Colonies* by Henry Cruger; *The Book of America*, published by the Massachusetts Historical Society; *Authentic Papers from America* and *A Vindication of the American Colonies* by James Otis; *Iconography of Manhattan* by I. N. Phelps Stokes; *Social New York under the Georges* by Esther Singleton; *History of the City of New York* by Martha J. Lamb and Mrs. Burton Harrison; *Colonial Days in Old New York* by Alice Morse Earle; *Colonial Days and Ways* by Helen Evertson Smith; *New York, Old and New*, by Rufus Rockwell Wilson; *DeBowe's Review;* Ulrich Phillips' *American Negro Slavery;* the Correspondence of William Pitt; Redpath's *History of the United States; The Protest in the House of Lords Against the Bill to Repeal the Stamp Tax; On William Pitt's Speech* by William Hicks; and two magazine articles, "The Stamp Act in British Politics" by W. T. LaPrade in the *American Historical Review* and "The English Stamp Duties" by Edward Hughes in the *English Historical Review*.

Newspapers: South Carolina Gazette, New York Weekly Post Boy, Niles Weekly Register, the New York Mercury.

The sources for the study of Samuel Adams here, and elsewhere, are in volumes with his name in the title written by John Chester, William Vincent Wells, Samuel Fallows, L. B. Vaughn, Ralph Volney Harlow, and James Kendall Hosmer.

No previous writer has asserted that JR caused George III to repeal the Stamp Act, though contemporaneously it was attributed both in England and America (and variously) to Gadsden, Lynch, Dickinson, and Otis. In his address on James Wilson published by the Philadelphia Law Academy (*circa* 1906) Burton Alva Konkle says that Wilson, who had been in London during the period shortly after the repeal of the act, sought to ally himself with Dickinson when he arrived in Philadelphia because (he believed) "Dickinson had written the resolution of the Stamp Act Congress which had apparently caused its repeal." Otis protested later that the Memorial to the Lords, on which he said he had collaborated, had been written by JR without using material Otis suggested, notably quotations from Coke. The Memorial to the Lords, to one familiar with JR's legal papers of the period, has also the internal evidence that makes it distinctly Rutledgian.

The fresh reading of history here is the crediting the Memorial to the Lords with changing the King's mind. It must be remembered that the King, despite his industrious snooping, lived largely in a vacuum, and knew of affairs only what his trusted ministers desired him to know. He never saw the Memorial to the Commons, written by Dickinson. It was not because of Dickinson's Memorial, but in spite of it, that the Commons eventually acted. Pitt's Correspondence confirms what Redpath says: "That Lord Rockingham took to the King the Resolution to the House of Lords submitted by the Congress of the American Colonies." This was at the moment when the non-importation agreements were causing riots in London. Of these riots the King knew, as he knew of the American riots over the Stamp Tax. However, he was a very stubborn man and force was ineffective with him. What caused such a stubborn man to change his mind so readily? If the evidence were only circumstantial it should be conclusive that it was this masterpiece of advocacy which happened to reach its goal at the opportune moment.

IV. THE CONTINENTAL CONGRESS—PHILADELPHIA

Bibliography: Histories of the United States by McMaster, Bancroft, Redpath, Fiske, and Woodward; of South Carolina by Simms, Drayton, Ramsay, Snowden, McCrady, and Wallace; biographies of Sam Adams by Wells and Hosmer; Irving's *Knickerbocker History;* Van Doren's *Benjamin Franklin;* Fraser's *Reminiscences;* Journal of the Commons (S. C.); works of John Adams (especially diary, autobiography, and letters to Abigail); *Delegates from South Carolina to the Continental Congress* by A. S. Salley, Jr.; Journal of the Continental Congress; *Extracts from Votes and Proceedings of the Continental Congress* (Phila., 1774); *Secret Journal of the Continental Congress* (1820); *Letters from Members of the Continental Congress* published by the Carnegie Institution; *The Continental Congress* by Edmund Cody Burnett; *Conduct of Delegates to Congress* by Samuel Seabury; and *Parties and Controversies in the Continental Congress* by B. M. Dale.

Mss.: Emmett Collection of Autograph manuscripts of members of the Continental Congress, New York Public Library; four hundred and fifty documents; family papers of Rawlins Lowndes, Langdon Cheves, and Yates Snowden; letters of Edward Rutledge to Joseph Reed; and files of Court of Ordinary, Charles Town, 1770 to 1775. A plea in equity (County Court House, Charleston) drawn by Hugh Rutledge in 1803, asked for an accounting from the heirs of Edward Rutledge. It was presented before a Court of Equity where Hugh was sitting. Change of venue was granted and the plea denied. However, it reveals much concerning the inter-family relationships of John, Hugh, and Edward.

Anecdotes: O'Neall, Flanders, and Hartley.

Newspapers: *South Carolina Gazette; Pennsylvania Gazette.*

The family papers of Rawlins Lowndes contain two letters leading to this writer's conclusion in reference to JR's growing political influence after the Haley trial. The *Gazette's* reports reveal the partisanship of Timothy for Edward Rutledge and, despite that, his controlled respect for John, which evidently was a discreet journalist's registry of a consensus. In dramatizing the Haley trial itself the writer has put in the first person what is reported in the third person in the sources noted.

In 1770 Lt. Governor Bull noted (Wallace) that "the Bar of Charles Town consists of thirty members while most of the business is conducted by five or six lawyers." Who, besides Parsons, Pinckney, and Rutledge, could get important business? Examination of the files in the Court House show that the leading lawyers in order of *importance of clients* were John Rutledge, James Parsons, Charles Pinckney. The fourth was Hugh Rutledge, the fifth John Mathews (later the husband of Sarah Rutledge, sister of JR).

The statement that "no other leader in the colonies during those critical years held a place of such power and responsibility as he [JR] did" is based on an estimate of the known history of the period, plus the source material noted here and previously in this work, all of which the writer is judging *a priori.*

What men in America held continuously important political power *and* responsibility in that period (1760 to 1775)? Only four come to mind: Samuel Adams, Sir William Johnson, Benjamin Franklin, and John Rutledge. Each was a pioneer but in his own way and each came to his own place uniquely. Each left an impress, yet variously, according to the character of each. However, Johnson died in 1774; Adams had political power with little direct responsibility; while Franklin had personal influence and the power that went with it indirectly, but practically no direct responsibility. JR was the only man then in America (1775) who had organized and continuously controlled at its source the actual ruling power of an established key community. Incidentally (or perhaps significantly), JR's professional income topped that of every other American Colonial of that period. And what other man removed a Chief Justice while he "manipulated" successive governors? Comparisons, usually, are fruitless as well as odious, but in this case they clear a way to a perception of a core of history. For here, in origin, we see something at work that was to enter the American scheme and leave there a pattern of the coming sovereignty.

John Adams provides the most voluble authentic sidelight on the Continental Congress, though he wrote (1816) in response to a request for aid in collecting material about that event, "of all the speeches made in Congress from 1774 to 1776 . . . not one sentence remains, except a few periods of Dr. Witherspoon . . . in plain English, I consider the true history of the Revolution . . . lost forever, and—that nothing but misrepresentations or partial accounts of it will ever be recovered." This was written forty-two years after the "First Congress." However, Adams did not consider his own diary or his letters to his wife Abigail, nor the multiple other sources, then obscure, which painstaking modern research would assemble in the coming century. Evidently he had in mind a series of reports such as now are made in the *Congressional Record.* However, if such a report (official) existed as exists, say, of the 77th Congress, it would be only one of the sources for such an account as that herein.

The speech of Thomas Lynch was reported in the *Gazette* in the third person; this writer has put it in the first person.

Dr. J. G. deRoulhac Hamilton, sometime Kenan Professor of Government in the University of North Carolina and Director of the Southern Collection at Chapel Hill, is of the opinion "that John Adams had more to do with the outlining of the state governments than John Rutledge." There is no record of the work in committee in the Continental Congress. What part was borne in the Committee on Government by its chairman, John Rutledge, and what part by its member, John Adams, must remain largely a matter of conjecture. We have no "works in ten volumes" by John Rutledge as we have of John Adams. The question remains: who contributed most to the outlining of state governments, the "country lawyer" from Braintree whose annual income was around a hundred pounds, or the leader of the American Bar who required a hundred pounds to look into a case. The member or the chairman?

While all factual statements in this section extend to the mentioned original sources, the arrangement and interpretation is by the writer. Never before, to his knowledge, has anyone described what to him seems the obvious contest for sovereignty between JR and Drayton. William Henry Drayton, who wrote his own reminiscences of these events, and his son, John, who edited them and added his own "history," never refer to John Rutledge as an opponent. Yet to this writer the contest of JR and Drayton recalls the "story" of Pompey and Caesar, with Roman intensity and for similar stakes, if in little, and with quite an opposite significance to the broad whole story of man. The contest was carried on legalistically and in the rarefied atmosphere of colonial politics as if with the artificial punctilio of a duel. Both opponents were gentlemen of the period; neither admitted that the "affair" existed, nor discussed it. Each scorned to indulge in political personalities, for such was not the vogue. There is not a line in the handwriting of JR, nor a word traceable to him indicating that he knew what he was doing, or, indeed, that he was doing anything with feeling or with purpose; there exist only those inescapable and irrefutable records of the Continental Congress and of the Congress of the colony and the Assembly of the Republic (or 'colony' as it persisted still in calling itself) of South Carolina. Personally, however, the contest was typically Rutledgian, for JR permitted only principles to be involved, while all concerned participated in the fruit of the victory.

Dr. Wallace notes that New Hampshire, chronologically, was the first colony to accept the advice of the Committee on Government of the Continental Congress, on Nov. 15, 1775. However, new officers were not elected, an independent government was not set up, sovereignty was not established, nor did the action (of the Granite Commonwealth) occasion contemporary stimulation in the other colonies. The complex and confused facts are set forth in E. S. Stackpole's *History of New Hampshire* in Chapter VII, written by William Henry Twitcher.

The advice from the Committee on Government of the Continental Congress to New Hampshire, was to "proceed in the manner to which you are accustomed," and this was done. When the same committee came to South Carolina the advice was "to adopt a written constitution," which also was done.

As an instance of how textbooks have ignored both the Rutledge primacy in the Committee on Government of the Continental Congress, and the South Carolina Constitution, which is the parent not only of all constitutional government in America but also is the embryonic source of the centralization of presidential powers in the United States, there should be noted a work entitled *Sources and Documents Illustrating the American Revolution and the Formation of the Federal Constitution,* selected and edited by S. E. Morison, Professor of History, Harvard University. Through the nineteen thirties this work was utilized as a textbook at Harvard. It lists as the first Constitution in America that of Virginia, adopted June 29, 1776, three months and three days after the adoption of the South Carolina Constitution. Nevertheless, the same work reproduces part of a letter from John Adams to his friend, James Warren, in Boston, and dated Philadelphia, April 22, 1776, saying, "The news from South Carolina has aroused and animated all the continent. It has spread a visible joy and if Virginia and North Carolina should follow the example it will spread through the rest of the colonies like an electric fire." In a footnote explanation Professor Morison notes, "The Provincial Congress of South Carolina on 26 March, 1776, had adopted a constitution for that 'colony', elected and set up a government independent of all royal authorities."

A reason for not including this first Constitution of South Carolina in such a work as that of Professor Morison is that it still retained a nominal "colonial" adherence, while the *state* Constitution of South Carolina was not adopted until 1778, long after Virginia and other states were functioning under their separate Constitutions. This is a legal technicality which may be argued adequately and with which this work is not concerned.

The chief point here (the fresh reading of history) is to be found in the life and work of JR as it was reflected in the Constitution. This section reveals how the career of Rutledge was dramatized in the Constitution of the South Carolina Republic. This would be a curiosity of some moment if it were unrelated. Its true significance is found only later in the story of the writing of the Federal Constitution.

V. THE REPUBLIC

Bibliography: *Memoirs of the Revolution* by General William Moultrie, of which the only perfect copy seen by this writer is in the Library of Congress; *The Record of the Moultrie Centennial in Charleston in 1876,* as published by the *Charleston News and Courier; The Siege of Charles Town, with an account of the Province of South Carolina,* being diaries and letters from Hessian officers from the Von Junkkenn papers in the William L. Clements Library, translated by B. A. Uhlendorf. *Gibbe's Documentary History of South Carolina; Diary of Lady William Campbell* (Sally Izard); the histories of Drayton, Ramsay, Simms, McCrady, Wallace, McMaster, Redpath, and Bancroft, as well as of Botta and Rhett; Green's Revolutionary War; Garden's *Anecdotes of the Revolution;* Lossing's *Field Book of the Revolution; Letters of George Washington* as edited by Jared Sparks; Woodward's *Washington;* Sir Henry Clinton's *Narrative of The Attack on Sullivan's Island; Some British Soldiers in America* by Walter Harold Wilkin. The official reports of the battle of Charles Town are in the *Jounal of the Continental Congress.*

Sidelights are in *Russell's Magazine* (Charleston), Vol. 4; the *Southern Review* (Charleston), Vol. 1; *Origins of Jeffersonian Democracy in South Carolina* by John Harold Wolfe; *History of Upper South Carolina* by John H. Logan; the *History of North Carolina* by Archibald Henderson; the Colonial and State Records of North Carolina; the South Carolina *Gazette;* the *Commons Journal* of South Carolina; the sketch of Andrew Williamson by Anne K. Gregorie in the *Dictionary of American Biography;* and the Revolutionary Diary of William Lenoir as published in the *Journal of Southern History* with notes by Dr. J. G. DeRoulhac Hamilton.

Mss.: the Cornwallis section of the Clinton papers (University of Michigan); letters of Edward Rutledge to Joseph Reed; the John Rutledge papers in the Charleston Library Society's library; the documents relating to the Cherokee War in the Southern Collection, Chapel Hill, N. C.; and the Yates Snowden Collection in the University of South Carolina.

If it is felt that more attention is paid to the effort of South Carolina than to that of North Carolina in the Cherokee War (in which both states were deeply involved), it must be noted that this is a study of JR and not primarily of any war. The records show that one thing he did not do was to seek military glory for himself, nor yet for his state. If he had been eager to accent his own state he might have secured for his boyhood friend, William Moultrie, the federal command which would have brought North Carolinians under dominance of a South Carolinian. Rather, he proceeded tactfully and sensibly to utilize the best talents in both states, by deference often, so that even if he lost political strength in South Carolina he did not lose his chief objective—the defeat of the Cherokees.

There is record (Lossing) that a bystander near Granville's Bastion on June 28, 1776, overheard JR command a soldier to take powder to Fort Sullivan, and that forty years later he still remembered the tone of the voice. "It sounded," the account states, "as if it would enter the soldier and tear him apart if he hesitated one second." The emphasis here is that the *tone* existed in memory of a bystander for forty years.

The listed historians, except Drayton, give the credit for victory at Charles Town to General Lee and Colonel Thomson, to whom the Continental Congress awarded medals, following Lee's report. William Henry Drayton, the only historian here listed who was present at the siege, says, "The credit for the victory was due to no person, but should be accorded to Almighty God." The quoted estimate of Charles Lee is from Woodward's *Washington*.

Except for the *South Carolina Gazette* and the Journal of the Commons, none of the printed sources for chapter five were written until long after the events recorded. Ramsay is the earliest (1785) and, curiously, is the one which gives the most sympathetic and liveliest picture of JR. All the others were written when JR's reputation was in almost total eclipse. That Rutledge resigned as President of the Republic for the purpose of foiling Drayton is this writer's interpretation based on an analysis of the official documents and the formal records.

VI. THE REVOLUTION

Bibliography: *The Clinton-Cornwallis Controversy;* Tarleton's *History of the Campaigns of 1780–81 in the Southern Province of North America; Strictures on Lt. Colonel Tarleton's History* by Roderick McKenzie, Lieutenant, 71st regiment; Steadman's American War; *Letters of George Washington* edited by Jared Sparks; *Journal of the Continental Congress;* Colonial and State Records of North Carolina; Journal of the Commons of South Carolina; Gibbes' *Documentary History of South Carolina;* Gordon's *History of the American Revolution;* Botta's History of the American War; the histories of South Carolina by Ramsay, Drayton, Hewatt, Rivers, Simms, McCrady and Wallace; the histories of Upper South Carolina by John H. Logan and John Landrum; Memoirs of the War of '76 by Henry Lee; *History of Georgia* by McCall; histories of the United States by Bancroft, Redpath, Fiske, McMaster, and Woodward; the Washington bibliography (containing more than a thousand items of which this writer has examined around a hundred, including the works of John Marshall, Washington Irving, Henry Cabot Lodge, William Woodward, Rupert Hughes, and Stevenson and Dunne); the *Life of Horatio Gates* by S. M. Patterson; Moultrie's *Memoirs;* the *History of North Carolina* by Archibald Henderson; *History of Orangeburg County* by A. S. Salley, Jr.; Flanders' *Life of Rutledge;* Garden's *Anecdotes;* Johnson's *Traditions; Benjamin Lincoln* by F. Bowen in the Library of American Biography; Count Pulaski by W. Spencer in the *Georgia Historical Magazine;* Pulaski's Legion by R. H. Gordon in the *Maryland* Historical Magazine; Guedalla's *Fathers of the Revolution; Miscellaneous Publications of the State of South Carolina,* covering the years 1780–81, as edited by A. S. Salley, Jr.; lives of Francis Marion by James, Simms, and Weems; and the life of General Thomas Pinckney by the Rev. Charles Cotesworth Pinckney.

There is coming into being a separate bibliography of King's Mountain, whose birth may be dated 1881 when Lyman Copeland Draper published *King's Mountain and its Heroes,* a monumental piece of research and a contribution to southern history by a native of Wisconsin. Until then the Battle of King's Mountain was little more than a fading legend, a colorful fight of secondary significance only, obscured by Cowpens and Yorktown, though James Bryce had commented on it in his *American Commonwealth* and

Bryce was never interested in a battle unless its relation could be tied in positively to social and governmental trends. Following Draper's publication, Theodore Roosevelt treated King's Mountain feelingly in his *Winning of the West* and McMaster considered it with particularity in his *History of the American People*. So, in its second century, King's Mountain began to live. On its Hundred and Fiftieth Anniversary (1930) President Herbert Hoover stood beside the historian of North Carolina, Archibald Henderson, on its battlefield and sounded the official keynote that indicated that some day it might rise in popular esteem even to the eminence of Bunker Hill. The modern bibliography, consulted by this writer, is now of respectable size and includes, in addition to the above: *The King's Mountain Men* by Katherine K. White; *The King's Mountain Baptist Association Record* by Deacon John R. Logan; *King's Mountain* by Hugh Carpenter; the notes on the letters of Isaac Shelby by J. G. deRoulhac Hamilton; and the studies of James Wilson and Isaac Shelby by Archibald Henderson. To these must be added the original source material in: the McKenzie-Clinton-Cornwallis-Tarleton controversy; the *Memoirs* of Colonel Hill, an officer under (the then) Colonel Lacey; the *Diary* of Allaire (one of Ferguson's officers); *The Affair at King's Mountain* by dePuyster (the extreme British view); the life of General Lacey by Dr. M. A. Moore; J. G. M. Ramsey's *Annals of Tennessee;* the papers of John Rutledge in *Russell's Magazine;* David Ramsay's history; *North Carolina in 1780-81* by David Schenck; life of Isaac Shelby by Archibald Henderson in *North Carolina Booklet;* a sketch of the life and career of General James Williams by Archibald Henderson in the *Raleigh (N. C.) News and Observer*, March 25, 1928; *General Joseph Graham and His Revolutionary Papers* by W. A. Graham; a sketch of James Williams by the Rev. J. D. Bailey (Cowpens, S. C., 1898); *Records of the Moravians of North Carolina; Papers of Archibald D. Murphey of North Carolina;* and the *History of the Presbyterian Church in North Carolina* by Dr. George Howe.

The bibliography for the last year of the war also includes: the lives of Nathanael Greene by the Hon. William Johnson, Dr. C. Caldwell, William Gilmore Simms, George W. Greene, and Francis Vinton Greene; *Greene's Retreat* by D. H. Hill in the *North Carolina Booklet;* General Daniel Morgan's Original Report of the Battle of Cowpens; *Russell's Magazine,* Charleston, Vol. 4; the *South Carolina Historical and Genealogical Magazine,* Vol. 11; *Annual Register,* for 1781 (London); and the *Charleston News and Courier* for May, 1881.

Mss.: the papers of Rawlins Lowndes and of Henry and Colonel John Laurens; Order Book of General Lincoln in the Renne Collection at Athens, Georgia; Letters of Thomas Bee; the Langdon Cheves and Barnwell Collections; letters of John Rutledge (in New York Historical Society Library's Gates collection and in the library of the Historical Society of Pennsylvania); collections of the South Carolina Historical Society; the Clinton Papers in the Clements Collections, Ann Arbor, Michigan; the Sumter Collections in Summerville and in Charleston, S. C.; the collections of the South Carolina Historical Society (partly published); the collections of the North Carolina Historical Commission, Raleigh, N. C.; the Southern Collection at Chapel Hill, N. C.; and the Thomas Pinckney section of the Pinckney papers acquired by the Library of Congress in 1939 and never before then available; the John Rutledge letters (only in part published in *Charleston Year Book* of 1899), in the Charleston Library Society library; and the Mss. section of the Renne Collection in the library of the University of Georgia, at Athens, Ga.

Personal Reminiscence; Mr. Langdon Cheves and the family of William C. Wolfe of Orangeburg, S. C.

The house in which JR lived in Orangeburg (in 1779 and later) still stands and was visited by this writer (1937). It is in the fields about a mile outside the city. As an instance of the persistence of local tradition, which is skeptical of the written record, the present owner remarked, casually, to this writer: "On that porch is where John Rutledge won the Revolutionary War." "How did he do that?" was asked. "By thinkin' out the only way it could be done," was the answer. The incident of the whipping of the recruit is authenticated by Simms and Johnson. The latter says that it occurred during the siege of Charles Town to a man still living in 1835 (Johnson wrote in 1851), but an account by John Laurens places it in Orangeburg a few weeks earlier, with the soldier unknown. It is the Laurens account which evidently Simms accepted; taken with the tradition still existing in Orangeburg it seems more credible.

The unpublished Order Book of General Lincoln is the most helpful original source for Chapter Two. Another contemporary source is Moultrie's *Memoirs*, written in the year following the death of his chief and when there was "none to do him reverence." All the components of the episode of this second siege of Charles Town have never before, to this knowledge, been assembled. The genius of Rutledge revealed in the first siege was much more severely tested in the second. And never before has JR been treated in an account of this second siege as the central and dominating figure. This fact is not merely a curiosity, but a profound commentary on the man, his method, his purpose, and his meaning.

General Lincoln is the only source available now who wrote contemporaneously, from day to day, and this is the first writer to have access to the general's Order Book, which came into the possession of the late Mr. George W. Jones (Renne), who willed his important collection to the University of Georgia at Athens, where it became available to students in 1937. John Laurens wrote shortly after the siege, from notes made in part during the event, and it is his version of the proposal to Prévost that is usually accepted, though it is not complete in his hand and was finished by his father, Henry. (See McCrady, Vol. III.) Bee wrote after the war. Ramsay (published in 1785) wrote almost contemporaneously, and while not present knew the chief personages. Moultrie wrote about twenty years after the event (published 1802) at a time when JR was in total eclipse and when he, himself, part of the time in jail, was hounded by creditors. Though he was suggestible and in events acts under the tutelage of JR there was always an intellectual chasm between the two and with JR gone and discredited Moultrie (the writer) became a medium for the martial braggadocio of the period, though the honesty of his doughty nature prevents a basic falsification. Moultrie is an essential witness of events whose significance he never grasped. So is Lincoln, pompous almost beyond belief. Their very gaucheries, intense but transparent, confirm the elusive realities with which JR struggled.

The historic point, at issue continuously from the beginning to the present time, centers in JR's proposal to Prévost. Was it justified? Was it honorable? Because of it many have condemned JR, though this condemnation remains with his own people. The Continental Congress received a report; the matter was well aired at the time nationally; JR was not even criticized in the North for his proposal of capitulation.

A typical anti-JR view may be found in the *Anecdotes* of Alexander Garden (1828) who said, "The fatal act of Governor Rutledge's life, which should consign his name to infamy, was the pusillanimous offer to the British General Prévost." Garden was a major in the Continental Army and a year after the siege was aid on the staff of Nathanael Greene. General Greene's relations with JR, judging by the documentary record, were twice strained but never broken, but this comment, after his death, by his aid, makes one wonder if there was not developed, during the Revolution, what might be called today "a Continental Army complex" toward JR. One must consider the whole record and remember Charles Lee, Horatio Gates, William Moultrie, and Benjamin Lincoln, as well as Nathanael Greene, with all their aides and satellites, and the esprit de corps they developed. Boil down the history of the whole period and refine it and to the top comes one ultimate question: Who won the Revolutionary War, the Continental Army or the technique organized and pointed by JR?

Ramsay (by profession a physician) writing nearly forty years *before* Garden wrote, and with personal knowledge of JR, calls the offer of capitulation a *"ruse de guerre."* It is baffling that he does not enter into details, but neither did William Gilmore Simms, two generations later, and, as an historian, he takes the Ramsay view. So does McCrady (1901), with tantalizing modifications.

To this writer, after examining the original sources, including the newly discovered Order Book of General Lincoln, and noting the treatment of the various historians, none of whom saw JR except as *one* of the actors in the drama, and the prey of a situation rather than its master, the conduct of JR in the Second Siege of Charles Town had a triple aspect.

Though it was not the most important aspect consider first the *legal*. It must be noted the original Ms. of the proposal of capitulation is lost. The best reliance is on the report of Colonel Laurens, aged twenty-three, without legal training, and frankly disapproving of the proposal. It may well be that Laurens missed a phrase or unwittingly twisted one, or even omitted a sentence—and what could not a lawyer like JR do with phrases and sentences? However, after all, the exact wording is not so important as it has been said to be. JR did send an offer of capitulation. Laurens, Moultrie, Ramsay, and Bee, as well as Prévost, agree on that. The criticism, however, is not of the offer, per se, but of the terms. JR offered to lay down arms if Prévost would then consider South Carolina as a neutral, and at the same time agree she should share the fate of the other colonies later. Putting aside the question of Prévost's power even to consider such a proposition, consider what this lawyer was asking for his client. His client was whipped (or so it seemed he must be assuming, though the facts he knew to be different) and yet if the conqueror accepted this proposal he would be frustrated in his conquest, for, under international law, as laid down by Kent, and recognized by Great Britain, a neutral port could carry on all accustomed business, except in munitions of war, with *both* contestants. Then, in addition, JR proposed that when hostilities were over South Carolina should share the fate of the other colonies. He certainly had his tongue in his cheek when he wrote that. However, to the soldier, especially the artificial soldier of that period, it was a bit of legal legerdemain wholly obnoxious. JR could not take any of them into his confidence. The soldiers saw it at its face value only, and not as a move in a game, a proposal impossible of acceptance as it was astounding to deliver. If Prévost had been simple enough to agree, JR well knew that in due time his superiors would disavow the agreement. He expected, probably, a counter proposal. In any event, time would be gained, and that was all JR was playing for.

The second aspect is the *military,* and that doubtless controlled. If the proposal of capitulation was a *ruse de guerre*—and this writer cannot conceive it as being otherwise—the question at once arises: how did JR know it would not be accepted out of hand and that he would thus be in the equivocal position of having negotiated a separate peace for South Carolina, thus breaking the Union? He had two good reasons to know it would not be accepted; he had well advertised to the enemy that he did not have full military authority (in this act converting his chief administrative and military liability into a diplomatic asset) and, even more important, he—and he alone— knew just about how near Lincoln was and just what his military alliance with Lincoln was. Inviolate silence about Lincoln seemed to him essential in the circumstances. JR did not know, of course, that Lincoln was so stupid as to send him written notice of his position, but neither was he himself stupid enough to depend solely on Lincoln for military information. Judging by his forethought evidenced in a later campaign he probably had his own slave pipeline into the up-country, and even white counter-spies as well. Military lines were not closely drawn. So, without regard for the inter-national legal aspects, practically JR could utter his proposal knowing it was in truth a *ruse de guerre,* made solely to gain time.

The third aspect is *personal.* In uttering the proposal of capitulation, and all that went with it, JR had to act the part of apparent fear, when others (in uniform) were bustling about in simulated bravery. He also had to depend on a legal technicality to preserve the consistency of his devotion to the national Union, thus inviting, from skeptics, an impeachment of his chief life-work. So he had to risk and perhaps sacrifice his reputation for integrity and courage. Apparently he did not hesitate, if indeed he even considered the hazard. He threw his reputation into the fiery furnace of his towns-people's derision and the Continental officers' scorn. Whatever he lost his main objective was achieved—Charles Town was saved and the Union preserved.

Bancroft was the first national writer to maintain that the Revolution was won militarily in the South, but in his editions published after 1857 this point of view is softened. McMaster, in the eighteen nineties, returns to it somewhat. It was not until the twentieth century that the general view here presented was well considered, especially by Woodward and Guedalla.

The picture of Rutledge as the key figure in opposition to Clinton is presented here, it is believed, for the first time. The grant of dictatorial power to JR has always been something of a mystery. This writer owes the beginning of his interest in JR to the plaque on the gatepost at 116 Broad Street, Charleston, stating that the mansion is the former residence of "The Dictator." The plaque is authorized by the Charleston Historical Commission. After consulting the obvious sources, such as Meriwether's sketch in the *Dictionary of American Biography,* Flanders' life, etc., the writer sought the offi-cial State Historian of South Carolina, Mr. A. S. Salley, Jr., widely recognized as a final authority on the old records of his region. Mr. Salley asserted positively that JR was "never dictator and there is no legal authority to use that word in connection with him." So the issue was joined (at least in the mind of this writer). The State of South Carolina says no; the city of Charleston says yes. The text herein was prepared after consulting the sources noted above (and considerably more). In fact, as must be obvious, the word "dictator" hovers over the whole subject of JR. At first, to this writer (before the diverse and obscure sources had been explored), it seemed that if there was an American "dictator" in that period he probably was like one or another of the petty Italian dictators or kinglets of the time. Such was the view, for instance, of Rafael Sabatini, who gives a highly fictionized picture of JR in his novel, *The Caro-linian.* Without setting forth the historic facts or articulating their apprehensions it has been, apparently, to prevent the spread of such notions that the guardians of the South Carolina shrine have frowned upon efforts to identify JR with dictatorship. For instance, this writer sat all one rainy and very pleasant afternoon, before a fire with Mr. R. Goodwin Rhett in his study above Mrs. Rhett's "Pirate Den" opposite St. Philipp's church, in Charleston, while Mr. Rhett read aloud his history of Charleston then in mss. and since published. Possessor of a distinguished name, once Mayor of Charleston, former owner of the JR home at 116 Broad Street, Mr. Rhett treats the dictatorship episode in the customary casual manner. This writer asked if he had ever given any close study to the actual terms of the dictatorship and Mr. Rhett replied, "I never thought it very important." Mr. Salley, the State Historian, thinks it is important, and the basis of his flat denial that there is any authentic record of the grant of autocratic power is in his explanation that the original journal of the Assembly was taken by the British from Charles Town when they evacuated the city in 1781; it has never been found, though Mr. Salley believes that it may be in the Tower of London, where other records taken at the same time have been found. The journal published by the State of South Carolina is a *copy*, never to his mind adequately authenticated. From that copy the Statutes of South Carolina (of that period) have been in part officially recorded. From those statutes and that copied record (with their official connotation) the two quotes of the grants of dictatorial power in this chapter are taken. However, the second grant (March 29, 1780) is the most often noted in the various histories named in the biographical sources. The first grant (Feb. 3, 1780) had been ignored. This is a characteristic euphemism with which the whole subject of the dictatorship has been treated continuously. The separation of the two grants, with a study of their origins and implications (to this writer's knowledge), has never before been attempted. That JR wrote the second and not the first is this writer's deduction, not only from the fact that the *Gazette* states he was not present in Charles Town early in February, but also from the internal evidence. In that second grant is the second step (the first being in the Constitution of the Republic of South Carolina) in the growth of the organic law which finally centered in the Powers of the President Clause of the Federal Constitution. Again, if this episode were unrelated, it would be, perhaps, merely a curiosity, or, at most, one of the rivulets flowing into the great stream that eventually formed the centralized force of the American republic. However, it is not unrelated; nothing connected with JR is unrelated. What he did in Charles Town in March, 1780, leads directly to, and is a part of, what he did in Philadelphia in July and August in 1787.

The key to the true story of the final military phase of the war is in the revelations of the British officers responsible. Fortunately they quarreled, and at great length. Clinton, Cornwallis, Tarleton, and a minor officer (but an illuminating one), Lt. McKenzie, are fully on record. They told all—all they knew. They are professional soldiers and an established type of professional which gives them certain solid qualities lacking in their Continental American brethren of the period. They are the universal soldier type, like Caesar, Turenne, Von Moltke, Lee or Grant, in that they saw and analyzed a military problem solely as a military problem. After reading their letters, their evidence, their controversial works three conclusions readily arise: (a) the empire gave its last ounce of military strength and skill to win the war; (b) in 1780 the British high command looked on the North as already conquered and on Washington as a negligible figurehead; and (c) they all professionally were frankly puzzled by the *technique* of the southern opposition. That it was a *technique,* a military asset of the most alarming proportions, Cornwallis, especially, recognized. All of them, however (Clinton, Cornwallis, Tarleton, and McKenzie) pay tribute to it, and nowhere more than when they blame each other for not solving it. Nothing else in the American situation seriously concerned any of them.

The Battle of King's Mountain was fought on South Carolina soil within a very few miles of the North Carolina line, and by men from both states, with the "Old North" state perhaps having the preponderance. Therefore, this campaign was a severe challenge to JR's military coordination. He had to contend with state as well as individual jealousies and rivalries. That the North Carolinians and the Virginians resented the recognition by JR of his favorite Williams as his coordinating representative is proven by a letter to General Gates (still in nominal command of Continental forces) written October 4, 1780 (two days after the conference at Hillsboro and three days before the battle) and signed by Cleveland, Shelby, Sevier, Hampton, Campbell, Winston, and Hambright, and asking that Gates appoint a commanding officer to be over them. It is significant that Williams was not a signatory. The appointment was not made. No Continental officer was at King's Mountain or in any part of the preceding operations. It is the interpretation of this writer that the real commanding officer was JR.

In tracing the military career of John Rutledge and in coming to his conclusion that the Dictator was responsible for the strategies, including the military technique, that controlled the battle of King's Mountain this writer has followed the advice of General Wavell, who has written, "If one wishes to understand the military strategy of a given situation let him not study the histories or the books on strategy but let him rather consult the biographies, memoirs, the letters and the other writings of those who participated." It is out of the memoirs, lives, testimonies and letters of Clinton, Tarleton, Cornwallis, Graham, Mills, Lacey, Shelby, Campbell, Moultrie, Thomas Pinckney (then on the staff of Gates), Thomas Sumter, Allaire, and the contemporaneous writers, Ramsay and Ramsey, that this writer has perceived the operation of that prescience with its tenuous will, the fluid yet exacting control of that sympathetic dynamism. The lower terrace of King's Mountain was the arena where, though personally they never met, Clinton and Rutledge, with all they represented, the Old World and the New, the past and the future, met and had it out, and settled the issue—in a single hour.

Shortly after he was appointed Director of the Southern Collection at the University of North Carolina (Chapel Hill), and when he was only beginning to assemble that greatest array of southern source material in existence (now consisting of more than one and a half million original manuscripts), Dr. J. G. deRoulhac Hamilton heard that "a great cache of John Rutledge" was about to be released in Charleston. That was long before the State of South Carolina by appropriation had commissioned Professor Meriwether of the State University to collect important old manuscripts. Dr. Hamilton recalls, "I went at once to Charleston. I found the place was out on Calhoun Street. There Miss Marie Rutledge, the only living lineal descendant (except two sisters) of the Revolutionary Governor was giving up her home, preparatory to moving to Greenville. Had she any old letters or manuscripts? Yes, she said, and led me to the stable in the rear. On the way she told me that only the day before she had opened the boxes and barrels. I hardly dared ask her how many, but I did. She said, off hand, "About twenty." You can imagine my excitement. Twenty boxes and barrels of John Rutledge! Why, everything in known existence from him could be put in one small box! We arrived at the stable and she pointed out the containers—filled with *powder!* The boxes and barrels had been in the damp basement for fifty years, she said. There was not one single legible remain; every letter, every document sifted to nothing at a touch."

Very likely, in that collection of dust were the papers the Dictator received during 1780 and 1781, for it is certain he received many letters from every important leader of his time, and few remain. He himself was not a voluble correspondent, not when one considers that the writings of George Washington had filled thirty-seven volumes up to the time when the government temporarily suspended publication (in 1939); that John Adams' ten volumes are less than half that is known to be by him; and that even Nathanael Greene wrote enough to fill three volumes, and mostly from the battleground of the Carolinas in the last year of the war. (Where did Greene find the time?) Of course, it seems likely that whatever papers of Rutledge's were lost in the Calhoun Street cellar were *to* not *from* him. Yet this book, as much as any other part of this work, has held close to the original sources—as Wavell advises—to the "biographies, memoirs, letters . . . of those who participated." The bibliography mentioned "has been honored more in the breach than in the observance." And the sources of this book are not from JR, though two of his letters are invaluable clues. Why is it that none of these histories and biographies traces to JR the supreme guidance of that final campaign through the Carolinas? The Bostonian, Bancroft, while seeking appointment in the cabinet of a southerner, Polk, readily wrote that the Revolution was won in the South, though when the Civil War came and he retired to the North, he and his publishers excised the credit. That it was won in the South would not be seriously disputed today, perhaps. But that Rutledge guided the winning of it, in dictating the technique of its decisive engagements and in selecting the commanders to win them and then in performing practically the function of the commander-in-chief, has heretofore escaped the attention necessary to link all the known facts together. Why? To this writer there seem to be chiefly two reasons: first, because the technique of the warfare, which was primarily responsible for victory, has not been definitely analyzed as being *planned,* and, second, that practicaly all writers on the subject have devoted their attention to celebrating the prowess of the field commanders: Was it Washington; was it Greene; was it various raiding diversions in the North; was it Sumter or Marion; or who? Was it, perhaps, Cleveland, Sevier, and Davie as is sometimes claimed in North Carolina? Was it Shelby, as thousands in Kentucky believed for many years? Was it Sevier as many Tennesseeans believed? Or did the British default? Or did it just happen? Was it, perhaps, an act of God?

The winning technique was not just "partisan," or "guerrilla," or "bush-whacking" warfare. It was infinitely more than mere civilian sniping. It had coordination, but was so designed that it gave the maximum effect to the prowess of the individual, a cumulatively greater effect than any system of totalitarianism ever devised, and so it stands in the pre-dawn of the modern epoch. This text reveals the story as a first-hand narrative might.

To arrive at a logical basis this writer sought first the English sources. He found what to him is a key to the whole problem in the Annual Register (*London Magazine,* 1781) in an anonymous contribution written months before Yorktown. "Most of these actions," said the Register, referring to the 'war in America,' "would be considered in other wars as but skirmishes of little account, but these small affairs are as capable as any of displaying military conduct. * * * It is by such skirmishes that the fate of America must necessarily be decided." Six years later, before the House of Lords, Clinton attested that it was so decided. Cornwallis agreed with him and added, *"It seemed to be planned."* These experts were not interested in any political fortune in America; they were not concerned in Fourth-of-July orations; they were not striving to boost one section of the country at the expense of all the other sections; they were merely a pair of professional soldiers, with their reputations at stake, conducting an honest post mortem. If they had disagreed we might pause, but, though antagonistic to each other, when testifying on this main point they agreed. To this mind, therefore, theirs, from a military viewpoint, is the whole story.

JR, alone in America among those in high place, saw it from the first and saw it continuously; and, fortunately, fate cast him in a key spot where he could compel, by various means, the effective operation of this technique for victory. His was "the still small voice of authority," not heard above the din at the time, but actually felt, which ruled the event.

Where southern writers comment on the activities of JR in curbing Greene and Lincoln and Lee, as a rule, they attribute them to "state pride." McCrady, for instance, a writer usually laudatory of JR, says of his interference with Greene, using Sumter as a check, that it was due to "jealousy." Let us examine this "jealousy" explanation, which appears in Johnson, Garden and McCrady, while the "state pride" phrase extends elsewhere whenever JR is mentioned by historians. How could there be jealousy in JR, or even state pride in the sense meant? Had he not asked for Lee, the first Continental officer Washington sent him? Did he not himself pick Greene? Did he ever claim credit for himself or his state? He knew he had to have a Continental officer. There was no other symbol of Union to hold South Carolina and her neighbors together for attainment of a common goal. And politics dictated the choice of a northerner for this post. For the same reason that Sam Adams wanted the southerner, Washington, to command around Boston,—so that Connecticut, New Hampshire, New York and other states near-by would work together harmoniously—JR wanted a northerner to hold the Carolinas, Virginia, Georgia, and Maryland together.

It is chiefly in the Sumter letters, containing some from JR, and many from Greene and Marion, that one may read the story of the Dictator's finesse, firmness, and vision; to these must be added the many Greene letters in the General's later biographies, and the few extant from JR in the library of the Charleston Library Society. If, reading these letters, one keeps in mind the key supplied later in London by the British officers the true inside story becomes transparent and irrefutable.

Through all these letters one feels that impalpable cloud which was John Rutledge's most absorbing menace (second only to the obvious one of Cornwallis' army); the hold which the old-world military formulae had taken on the Continental Army. JR sensed —he knew—that technique would win that war (or lose it), just as technique has won or lost every other important war in ten thousand years of human history. Though his letters often appear to be casual and incidental one may see in practically every phrase a military order, in almost every casual reference a statesmanlike prescience. Reading all the letters of that period (and nothing else to distract the attention) brings one astonishing incidental reflection: *JR is the only one who never complained*. Greene utters a constant stream of complaint—against subordinate commanders, against the people, against the Congress, against conditions, against practically everything. Sumter was well named "The Gamecock"; he lived in a constant state of offense with almost everyone. Marion was a little king, in his way; in his bailiwick he was master, yet he growls against Greene, against Sumter, against JR. As for Washnigton he was, perhaps, the chief pessimist of all; his writings are cluttered with complaints against—his army, the people, Congress, various commanders. In one man only was there calm—no personal feeling or outcry. He was the master—of himself, of others, and of the event. He accepted the burdens and bore them without complaint. He played politics, with the highest and the meanest—but with his other hand, as it were; intellectually and spiritually he was a ruler.

The mystery of who originated the idea of Greene's turning his back on Cornwallis for the final campaign has never been solved. No one to this knowledge has suggested it was JR. Colonel Lee, who was on Greene's staff, said, in his memoirs, that the idea was from "another than Greene." While otherwise he was not modest he left only an inference that he himself suggested it, and his son then made the full claim. It was largely to upset this claim that Judge Johnson devoted himself to Greene's memory. The debate of Lee and Johnson over this point was acrimonious and divided feeling, especially in the South, for two decades or more. There was something worth contending for, for that decision proved to be the high peak of Greene's career and one of the most creditable military episodes in American history. As the speaker at Greene's funeral said, "This was one of those strokes that denote superior genius and constitute the sublime art of war. 'Twas Scipio leaving Hannibal in Italy to overcome him in Africa." Curiously, Greene never committed himself. He never said that he originated the idea or what caused him to adopt it. A letter from Greene to Lee, made public after the death of both, saying that Lee advised the march South was the chief support of Lee's son in his contention, but the letter reveals that the subject was one which Greene had submitted to Lee for consideration. The fact that Lee agreed with the unknown originator may have tipped the scales in Greene's mind or only confirmed his judgment, but, as General McCrady, after reviewing all the evidence (which fills volumes), says, "We think it is conclusive that with whomsoever this plan of campaign originated it did not originate with General Greene." Then where did it come from?

Here is a résumé of the circumstances which weigh with this writer; when Greene made his decision Rutledge had just returned from Washington's camp and shortly he made another journey to the Commander-in-Chief, and, as Greene and Washington had independent commands (similar to those of Grant and Sherman) the practical co-ordinating factor had to be Rutledge, and yet, considering the complicated inter-state and inner-state jealousies to be met, the Dicator was obliged to exert his influence anonymously. It might have been extremely embarrassing to him and to the cause if it were known in North Carolina, faced with imminent peril from the enemy, that Rutledge induced the national commander to stay in South Carolina.

Point number two lies in the fact that Greene's letters reveal that his heart was not in "carrying the war to Africa." For the first six or eight weeks he protested against it constantly, every few days and while he was leading his army south. This was while JR was in the North, out of the state. Reading Greene's letters of that period one is irresistibly drawn to the conclusion that he was doing something against his desire, something to which he was only in part persuaded, something against his nature, but something he could hardly avoid doing. He could have changed his mind and have gone the other way at any moment, yet he kept on—"into Africa." Something powerful kept him to his course.

The third point is in a comparative study of the contrasting military natures of the two men, Greene and JR. Greene was basically an exhibitionist; he liked to go forward, to be up in front, to attack; and he was in constant difficulty because of this; here is the only instance in his whole career in which he actually turned his back on the enemy and went the other way; he was never at any other time a profound strategist. On the other hand, the maneuver was JR in essence; almost always—in law, in statecraft, in military art—he seemed to leave the field to his opponent, while he marched to the rear to assault some weak point which in the final analysis proved to provide the key to the action.

Fourth, and most conclusive, is the duty, both legal and moral, that lay on JR to induce Greene to march South rather than North after Guilford Court House. If he had not been present, if the conditions mentioned had not also existed, Greene's decision might have been a coincidence, but JR was there and to assume that he did not have a voice in the decision is to assume that he shirked his duty "to do all necessary." It is also to assume that he lacked the vision and insight and will to make such a decision; while his previous record in the war shows the opposite. He had taken actual though never nominal command in a similar situation at the first siege of Charles Town; he had acted again, in varying but essentially similar circumstances, at the second siege; again, at King's Mountain, he had reached out subtly and pioneered a way to victory. Would he not repeat his characteristic strategy when the war came to its final stage? JR is of a piece—all of him. He employed no codes to cloud or conceal his thoughts or desires in writing; he had a better cloak—silence.

Greene took responsibility for that campaign and carried it through, as the records tell, with fine success; thus, of course, he deserves the credit he has been given, no matter who gave him the idea.

VII. THE CONSTITUTIONAL CONVENTION

The bibliographical sources for the first chapter of this book are in the Journal of the Commons of South Carolina, the Journal of the Continental Congress, and the contemporaneous issues of *The South Carolina Gazette,* as well as in the histories of South Carolina by Ramsay, Drayton, Simms, Snowden, McCrady, and Wallace. Printed anecdotal material is from Flanders, O'Neall, Hartley, Fraser, and the diary of John Rutledge, jr.

Mss.: the records of the Courts of Common Pleas, Admiralty, and Chancery, and the registry of deeds (containing real estate transfers) in Charleston; ms. in possession of the estate of Mrs. Edmund Felder reveals the land gifts to JR from the state of Franklin. The episode of the reading of the Pinckney version of the Constitution derives from the Charles Cotesworth Pinckney section of the Pinckney papers in the Library of Congress.

For the chapters covering the Convention itself, Madison's Journal is the primary source. However, the notes of Robert Yates, the Pierce reliques, the McHenry diary, the autobiography of William Few, the David Brearly papers, the General Information of Luther Martin, and the letters of Alexander Hamilton, Rufus King, and Oliver Wolcott, add contemporary sidelights that have assisted in developing the picture for this writer. In addition he has consulted: *The Writings of George Washington* as edited by W. C. Ford; *The Records of the Federal Convention* by Max Farrand; *The Writings of James Madison* as edited by Gaillard Hunt; *The Works of Thomas Jefferson,* edited by P. L. Ford; *Correspondence of John Jay* as edited by H. P. Johnston; *The Works of James Monroe* as edited by S. M. Hamilton; *The Works of Alexander Hamilton* as edited by Henry Cabot Lodge; *The Letters of Richard Henry Lee* by James Ballagh; *The Letters of Joseph Reed; The Life of Oliver Ellsworth* by William Garret Brown; *The Manuscripts of Robert Morris* by Henry Holmes; *The Life of Elbridge Gerry* by James Austin; and *The Autobiography of Charles Biddle.*

The general bibliography includes: *Annals of Philadelphia in the Olden Time* by John T. Watson; *The Law of the American Constitution* by Charles K. Benedick; *The Colonial Mind* by Vernon L. Parrington; *Diary of Jacob Hiltzheimer; The Book of the Signers* by William Brotherhead; *Sources of the Constitution of the United States* by C. Ellis Stevens; *Catechism of the Constitution* by Lewis Cruger, as well as *The Statesman's Manual* by the same author; *Patriots Off Their Pedestals* by Paul Wilstach; *Life, Journal and Correspondence of Manassen Cutler; Documentary History of the Constitution; Elliott's Debates; History of the United States* by Edward Channing; "James Wilson and the Constitution" by A. C. McLaughlin in the *Political Science Quarterly;* and *The Life and Times of James Madison* by W. Cabell Rives.

Concerning the Pinckney draft there is a separate bibliography which has developed largely in the past half century. The first hundred years of the Constitution was the period of glorious myth, when it was assumed that the document had spontaneous birth from "that group of demi-gods," to use Jefferson's phrase. Then, beginning with the first discovery of the early consignment of George Mason papers (1881), and following on through a series of discoveries of documentary source material, through more than thirty years, a reasonable, realistic basis for concrete knowledge of the making of the Constitution has been assembled. That part of it should be concentrated on the Pinckney draft is a curiosity attested by the bibliography, which includes volumes noted on that subject by Bemis, Bethea, Meigs, Nott, Owen J. Roberts, Hannis Taylor; as well as pertinent sections of the works by Charles A. and Mary R. Beard, Max Farrand, J. F. Jameson and Charles Warren. *DeBowes' Review,* Vol. 34, also has a pertinent item about Charles Pinckney.

There is an extensive separate bibliography of interpretation of the Constitution, in which those volumes touching on the origins and consulted by this writer include works by Atwood, Bancroft, Charles A. and Mary R. Beard, Beck, Bowers, Bryce, Burns, Carson, Cruger, de Tocqueville, Farrand, Ford, Gibbs, Guedalla, Hamilton, Hendrick, Hunt, Jameson, "Justinian," Konkle, Meigs, Roberts, Taylor, Warren, and Webster.

In mss. the writer has consulted five important collections: the documents from signers of the Constitution in the Pierpont Morgan Library; the Rutledge family papers in the Historical Society of Pennsylvania; and the Madison, Mason, and Pinckney collections in the Library of Congress. However, there is also a sixth, more important to the present quest than any other. That is the collection of Wilson papers in the library of the Historical Society of Pennsylvania.

The Wilson collection (1500 items) constitutes a mine of information about the writing of the Constitution as yet insufficiently explored. These papers were not known to be in existence for a full century after the Federal Convention. Then one day an elderly lady, Miss Margaret Hollingsworth, modestly brought to the curator of the Historical Society of Pennsylvania a packet of documents from the estate of James Wilson, of whom she was the last lineal descendant, and asked that they be "kept" for her. On Miss Hollingsworth's death, a few years later, it was discovered that she had willed the collection outright to the Society, together with many more. Even then their priceless character was not revealed for a number of years, until an examination by Dr. J. F. Jameson (1901) discovered that they included the final draft of the Constitution in the handwriting of James Wilson and John Rutledge. Dr. Jameson, and later Max Farrand, made factual record of the direct evidence, without venturing on any interpretation that would effectively penetrate the existing nebulous impressions about the preparation of the Constitution. The handwriting of John Rutledge was identified, but that it meant anything beyond the obvious fact that he was, as Hannis Taylor promptly said, "a bold and slovenly scrivener," was not suggested. In fact, so little has the Rutledge relation to the document been considered that it was never reproduced in facsimile until this writer asked to have it photostated. It was then locked away in an unnamed vault "for the duration," and the Director of the Historical Society of Pennsylvania consented that it be temporarily submitted to a photographer so that a part of it could be reproduced in this work. The writer remarked, "Do you realize that you possess the most important document in America?" Mr. Reitzel replied, "We know it, but I am not sure that we realize it."

Burton Alvah Knokle has had access to the Wilson papers in the preparation of a five volume life of James Wilson, not yet published, but otherwise the Wilson Collection has not had seriously intensive attention until this writer sought it, inevitably, to pursue his study of JR.

In his study of the Federal Convention the writer has observed the same rule he set for himself in estimating the war; he has confined himself, eventually, to the personal records, letters, reminiscences, and biographies of the participants and of those who had contact with them.

The historicity of the Convention has its three dimensions. The first was in the flat; the reportorial job of Madison and his contemporaneously unknown colleagues, Yates, Pierce, Few, Brearly, Martin, Hamilton, Lee, Read, and McHenry. Perusal of these gives one a fair idea of what happened in the open. However, it is chiefly a running account, and in each case biased, for checking one with the others has proven that none was infallible, not even Madison, who, for the first century after the Convention stood as the final authority. Nor do any of these unofficial reporters alone take us behind the scenes in any constructive sense.

The second dimension of the historicity (called here, for convenience, the upright, for it reaches high as the heavens) goes into the illimitable field of the sources of the components of the Constitution—quite a different thing from the creation of the covenant itself. In this second dimension the larger part of the bibliography of the Constitution (more than four thousand volumes) is, for the purpose of this study, practically unusable, for it goes into the whole story of man's world-wide and age-old attempt at constitutional government.

It was in the confusion and profusion of this literature that Madison was established as "the Father of the Constitution," because he had assembled in his plan such an imposing array of the components actually used, and, also, because of his conspicuous activity. In opposition, Pinckney was set up, with similar endowment, but in the same spirit. It may never be determined exactly what was contained in Pinckney's first draft, nor is Madison's absolutely certain, for both are lost. This writer does not consider the details very important and uses in his text a consensus of the estimates of Meigs, Warren, and Jameson. The chief point here is that neither Madison nor Pinckney invented anything basically important, even though each is granted his extreme claim.

Madison has, from the first, been in the established position of accepted authority, but the Pinckney claim is more colorful, perhaps because there is an intense realization on the part of all scholars and students of the period that the making of the Constitution has been more shrouded in mystery than any comparable event in modern history. The uncertainties surrounding the Pinckney draft feed but do not solve that mystery.

None of the Pinckney advocates—and he has had at least five very determined ones —has been more ingenious than Hannis Taylor who, in his huge volume, *The Origins of the American Constitution* (1913), attempted to prove by the then newly discovered Wilson documents that Peletiah Webster, a Revolutionary economist and pamphleteer in Philadelphia, was the inspiration of Charles Pinckney, who gave no credit to his mentor, and who then, by some hypnotic power unexplained by Taylor, induced John Rutledge to be his representative on the Drafting Committee. Taylor's work appeared to celebrate the forgotten Webster, though acceptance of his theory required one to believe that a single radical economic theory dominated the making of the Constitution. This theory has fallen by the wayside; and so have all the theories of the making of the Constitution which depend on a thesis that it was controlled by any one section or interest or group. It is only recently that the idea that the Constitution was established primarily to conserve property has been overruled.

The third dimension of the historicity of the Constitution is in the round, and so perfects the first two, the flat and the upright. This takes one into the realistic, rationalistic account of the actual making of the great document. The word "making" is used advisedly, for the writing of the Constitution was merely its incidental literary expression. The "making" included the writing, as well as the development of the various plans—the Madison, the Pinckney, and the Paterson plans—and very much more. It was, literally, a third dimension. Politics dominated at every point; and every phase of politics: local, sectional, regional, national, and international (though the latter least of all); yet statesmanship in its true meaning had to overshadow politics. And—above all that—came a requirement that can be called only generalship. In a concrete sense the making of the Constitution was a battle. It had to be conducted like a battle and it was.

As this third dimension of the historicity of the Constitution contains the most important phase of JR's activity it is, for this study, paramount. It is documented chiefly in two major collections, the Mason and the Wilson, the first containing, with many other papers, the first draft made by Randolph and annotated by Rutledge and the second containing innumerable letters, and other documents, as well as the final draft by Wilson with the basic and controlling changes by Rutledge. These holograph records supply the essential keys. It is necessary, however, to glean carefully the straw to be found in the bibliographies of the first two dimensions. Clue to the only pole of conflict in the Convention—the opposition of Rutledge and Sherman—is in the letters of Oliver Wolcott; it is confirmed in the confidences given late in life by Oliver Ellsworth. Note of the dinner Rutledge gave Sherman is in the *Massachusetts Centinel*. A foreshadow of the Rutledge-Sherman rapprochement is in the Yates Notes, published in 1828, twelve years before the Madison Journal was published. Take these facts—clear enough when they are brought to light, though ignored for more than a century and half—and combine them with the superficial accounts of the Madison Journal, and the underlying strategy of JR becomes apparent. Then all else fits into that pattern.

Though it was a battle there was no obvious strategy for JR to overcome. He did not have an opponent like Sam Adams as he had in the First Continental Congress. His opponent was chaos. His problem was similar to the one he faced the last year of the war, when he grappled with local rivalries, inter-state jealousies, and the ambition of diverse generals as well as the enemy, while, subconsciously, as it were, he solved the essential problem of military technique. Psychically it was the same experience over again—but in a unified orbit and in an intellectual sphere.

Why has JR's part in the making of the Constitution been so long ignored? (This is its first serious appraisal.) The answer lies in the oath of secrecy. The agreement to conduct the Convention in this manner made fame the first casualty. JR kept his oath and went to his grave without a word of revelation; he left no papers. Neither did Roger Sherman. George Washington wrote at least 100,000 words during the Convention and about its activities in the form of diaries, letters, and reports. He was the chairman; he was present at every session; he was intimate with practically every important member; ultimately he was the official custodian of all records; he must have known what was going on; *but* he took the oath of secrecy, and not a syllable ever escaped from him, before or after death, as to what actually went on at the Convention.

Then we come to the others. If they all had been as discreet as these three guiding spirits we might never have known the facts and the truth. Madison, who began the technical violation of the oath, though he always claimed and believed it was not an actual violation, was so conscious of the oath that he resisted all appeals, even forty years after the Convention, to make public his records, and permitted them to be known only after his death. Wilson evidently believed himself faithful to the agreement, but his papers which finally saw the light more than a century after his death reveal nearly everything; at least they give definite and satisfactory clues to everything; and these papers were available, though not to public knowledge, when Wilson left them behind him, without known instructions as to their disposition, when he fled Philadelphia to escape process servers in 1797. Colonel Mason, who took the oath with the others, also left his papers, without instructions, and when he died at least a third of the other members of the Convention survived him. Charles Pinckney and Gouverneur Morris were not so particular. In 1818 John Quincy Adams, then Secretary of State, requested that Pinckney transmit to the State Department, for preservation in the government archives, the original copy of his draft. Pinckney complied and when the paper went under the microscope the watermark was revealed to be "1797"; Madison noted, wistfully, that "the draft Mr. Pinckney sent was a little nearer the Constitution as adopted" than he had remembered it as being. Not to be set aside, three years later, in 1821, from the floor of Congress, where he was a representative, Charles Pinckney proudly asserted that he should know what a certain clause in the Constitution was—"Did I not write it myself?"—and finally Jameson (1902) felt obliged to note that "Charles Pinckney's place in the history of the constitution would be higher if he had not claimed so much for himself." Then there was Gouverneur Morris, who also took the oath of secrecy; he had been chosen by the Convention to head the Committee on Style, which worked on the final Wilson-Rutledge draft. When twenty years had passed Morris often referred (once on the floor of Congress) to "the Constitution as I wrote it." Doubtless William Pierce when he wrote his *Reliques,* containing excellent literary sketches of the various members of the Convention, did not think he was violating his oath; nor did Yates in his Notes, Few in his Autobiography, McHenry in his Diary, nor Martin in his *Information,* nor Hamilton, Robert Morris, Wolcott, Ellsworth, Read, Lee or Brearly in their letters and reminiscences. They were making revelations, however. They furnished the clues, while Mason in the Randolph-Rutledge draft and Wilson in the Wilson-Rutledge draft supply the fingerprints. Holding strictly to this source material, and ignoring all that came later, we can see the Federal Convention in the round; see it as the political story of the day; and, standing at the inside place that was JR's, understand the making of the Constitution.

VIII. MR. RUTLEDGE

Bibliography: Washington's writings as edited by Ford; the writings of Thomas Jefferson; the works of Alexander Hamilton; letters of Rufus King; lives of Washington by Woodward, Hughes, and Stevenson and Dunn; *The History of the Supreme Court* by Charles Warren; *Jefferson and Hamilton* by Bowers; *The Bulwark of the Republic* by Hendrick; *The Jay Treaty* by Bemis; histories of South Carolina by Ramsay, McCrady, and Wallace; lives of John Rutledge by Flanders, O'Neall, and Hartley; *Life of John Jay* by Patterson; Fraser's *Reminiscences;* and *The Life and Correspondence of James Iredell* by McRee. In official record there is the executive journal of the United States Senate, tenth session; records of the Supreme Courts of the United States and of South Carolina; and of the Court of Chancery, Southern District, S. C.

Mss.: Letters in possession of Mr. Arnoldus Vanderhorst of Charleston, S. C.; letters and documents in possession of the estate of Mrs. Edmund Felder; Rutledge family papers; the Pinckney papers; and holograph receipts in the United States Treasury.

Newspapers: *South Carolina Gazette; The National* (Pennsylvania) *Gazette; The Massachusetts Centinel; The New York Morning Post; The Virginia Independent Chronicle.*

It is not certain that JR's notification to Washington that he desired appointment as Chief Justice was unsolicited. His letter and Washington's response are recorded in Washington's writings. He wrote abruptly, as was his habit, with an extreme minimum of the customary courteous phrases, but some historians have inferred that he had been prompted earlier by Washington to make the application. A good explanation is offered by Dr. Archibald Henderson who says, "What more natural than that when Rutledge resigned as Associate Justice of the United States, explaining his preference for the place as Chief Justice of South Carolina, the President should say to him that if he ever changed his mind and wished to return to the national administration to let him know?" Such an understanding may have existed in some form, for it was not characteristic of Rutledge to project himself directly.

Because of the action taken by the Senate on December 15, 1795, along with the fact that JR was ill often in this period and compelled to remain in bed, the report spread that his nomination had been rejected because "his mind was unsound." This has been stated, without either full or sympathetic examination of the record, in numerous accounts of his life-work.

This writer has seen no historical account that contains the correct official record. Most printed versions of the Senate action either ignore the details, or assert that JR's nomination was rejected by the vote of 17 to 5, and this writer kept that figure in his notes during the period (1937–40) when the new Archives Building in Washington was being prepared to house its treasures, which made the original Senate record not readily available. Finally (in 1942), and merely as a final check, the Archives Building having been opened, the writer called on Mr. Solon Buck, Chief Archivist of the United States, and received through him access to the executive journal of the Senate for the tenth session (1795) and was astonished to learn the facts quoted in the text. Rutledge's nomination was rejected by the vote of *ten* to *fourteen.* That makes quite a different story than the one generally accepted for nearly one hundred and fifty years. A shift of three votes and he would have been confirmed. If this were a study of the times, and the vote on Rutledge's confirmation were being considered for what it was actually, a test of strength between two fiercely contesting parties, the proper deduction would be that Congress was nearly divided, the federalists holding the House by one vote and the Senate by three.

There is more in the record to indicate that the contest was very close. The yeas and nays were required. In other words, an attempt was made to rush the vote through by voice only. Evidently some of the senators who voted against Rutledge were not proud of their action. They were forced to come into the open by "one fifth of the senators present." One fifth of twenty-four (or even of twenty-two) amounts to five and that may be the source of the inaccurate accounts in many histories which state that Rutledge was "rejected by the Senate, seventeen to five." Among the ten senators whom the executive journal records as having voted for Rutledge's confirmation these names are readily familiar: Aaron Burr, Pierce Butler, George Mason, Luther Martin, and George Reed.

The question naturally arises: would Thomas Jefferson have endorsed for the chief justiceship a man of unsound mind, or would Aaron Burr, Pierce Butler, George Mason, Luther Martin, George Reed and five other senators have voted to confirm him? These responsible men must have known the facts.

The intensity of the Jefferson-Hamilton contest has persisted to this day, as witness two accounts in the present decade of JR's treatment by the Senate in 1795. Here is the Hamiltonian, Burton K. Hendrick, who, in his *Bulwark of the Republic* (1937), says, "The most grotesque of these early judges was John Rutledge, who, on Jay's resignation, solicited the office for himself. As he was an able and distinguished lawyer Washington acceded to his request, but news presently reached the administration that Rutledge was engaging in untempered denunciations of the treaty. . . . Another explanation is that Rutledge, hitherto a most dignified and learned judge, had suddenly gone mad; not unnaturally the senate refused to confirm his appointment."

Here is the Jeffersonian, Claude Bowers, in *Jefferson and Hamilton* (1937), "[There] rose a figure familiar to the generation of the Revolution, the then Chief Justice of the Supreme Court of the United States, John Rutledge. An able man was Rutledge, with a luminous career—he denounced the treaty as a betrayal of American interests and an insult to American manhood. . . . With celerity and eclat the senate threw down the gauntlet with rejection of the nomination of John Rutledge because of his hostility to the treaty. The motive was unescapable. He was an able jurist, an erudite lawyer, a pure patriot, with a superb record of high public services, but he had denounced the federalist treaty—that was enough. Jefferson viewed the incident from his hilltop with the vision of a prophet. 'A bold thing,' he thought, 'because they cannot pretend any objection to him but his disapprobation of the treaty.'" The latter is an extract from a letter, Jefferson to Giles.

The irony of it is that JR was neither Jeffersonian nor Hamiltonian.

BIBLIOGRAPHY

MANUSCRIPTS

Public Records

SOUTH CAROLINA: Admiralty Court Files, Charleston; Christ Church Parish documents, Mt. Pleasant; Court of Chancery Records, Southern District; Court of Ordinary Files, Charleston Court House (1732-1800); Journals of the Commons, Columbia; Memorials of Royal and Proprietary Governments, Columbia; Probate Court Files, Charleston; Real Estate Transfers, 1732 to 1800, Charleston (Register of Deeds); St. Michael's Church documents; Supreme Court Records.

NORTH CAROLINA: State and Colonial Records (Raleigh).

WASHINGTON: Supreme Court holograph documents; Treasury Department Receipts; United States Archives, including Executive Journal of the U. S. Senate, 10th session.

Collections of Letters

UNPUBLISHED: Bee, Thomas, Letters, Charleston Library Society; Barnwell, Joseph, Papers, Charleston Library Society; Cheves, Langdon, Papers, Charleston Library Society; Gadsden, Christopher, Papers, Library of Congress; Mason, George, Papers, Library of Congress; Pinckney Collection, Library of Congress, acquired in 1939 and never before available, 3500 items; Renne (Jones) Collections, Mss. section, University of Georgia, Athens, Georgia; Randolph, Edmund, Collection, Library of Congress; Rutledge, Edward, Letters—Charleston Library Society, Historical Society of Pennsylvania (to Joseph Read), and in the library of the University of Wisconsin; Rutledge Family Papers, Historical Society of Pennsylvania; Rutledge, John, Letters, Charleston Library Society, New York Historical Society (Gates Collection), the Historical Society of Pennsylvania (separately and in Wilson Collection), and in personal collections of Mrs. Edmund Felder and of Mr. Arnoldus Vanderhorst; Signers of the Constitution, documents and letters of, Pierpont Morgan Library, N. Y.

IN PART PUBLISHED: The Cornwallis-Clinton Collection in the Clements Library in Ann Arbor, Michigan; The Emmett Collections of Members of the Stamp Tax Congress and of Members of the Continental Congress in New York Public Library; The Laurens Papers in the Long

Island Historical Society; The Papers of Rawlins Lowndes, Library of Congress; McHenry Diary, in Mason Papers, Library of Congress; Collections of the North Carolina Historical Commission, Raleigh, N. C.; The Diary of John Rutledge, Jr.; The Collections of the South Carolina Historical and Genealogical Society; The Collections of the South Carolina Historical Society, including the Sumter Manuscripts, the Composite Origins of South Carolina, and the John Laurens Papers; The Southern Collection, University of North Carolina, Chapel Hill, N. C.; The Sumter Collections, in Summerville, South Carolina; The Wilson Collection, Historical Society of Pennsylvania.

NEWSPAPERS AND MAGAZINES

American History Magazine; American Historical Review; Annual Register or Review of History, Politics and Literature (London) for years 1780, 1781, 1782; Charleston City Year Books; Charleston Daily Journal of Commerce; Charleston News and Courier; Charleston Post; Confederate Veterans' Magazine; Constitution of the United States, Its Origins, etc., as set forth in the Collections of the Historical Society of Pennsylvania (pamphlet, 1937); D. A. R. Magazine; De Bowe's Review; English Historical Review; Federalist, The; Gentleman's Magazine; Georgia Historical Magazine; Green Bag; Journal of Southern History; Maryland Historical Magazine; Massachusetts Centinel; Mercury, New York; New England Magazine; New York Morning Post; New York Post Boy; New York Society Quarterly Bulletin; Niles Weekly Register (New York); North Carolina Booklet; Pennsylvania (National) Gazette; Political Science Quarterly; Raleigh News and Observer; Russell's Magazine; South Carolina Gazette, 1732-1775; South Carolina Gazette and Country Journal, 1765-1775; South Carolina and American General Gazette, 1758-1775; South Carolina Royal Gazette, 1780-1781; South Carolina Gazette and General Advertizer; Timothy's General Advertizer (these six are different names for practically the same newspaper published in Charles Town and Charleston almost continuously from 1732 to 1800); South Carolina Historical and Genealogical Magazine; Southern Historical Society Publications; Southern Review; United Service Magazine, September, 1881; Virginia Independent Chronicle; Virginia Quarterly.

PRINTED WORKS

Adams, John. *Works and Diary.*
Adams, John and Abigail. *Letters.*
Allaire, Lieutenant Anthony. *Journal.*
Amicus Reipublicae (pseud.). *Letters.*
Atwood, Harry Fuller. *The Constitution Explained—Back to the Republic.*
Austin, James. *The Life of Elbridge Gerry.*
Authentic Papers from America (London: Printed for T. Becket, 1775).
Avery, Elroy McKendree. *A History of the United States and Her People.*
Bailey, Rev. J. D. *Sketch of James Williams.*
Bancroft, George. *History of the American Revolution, History of the Formation of the Constitution of the United States of America, History of the United States.*
Ballagh, J. C. *Letters of Richard Henry Lee.*
Beard, Charles A. and Mary R. *Rise of American Civilization, Economic Interpretation of the Constitution.*
Beck, James Montgomery. *The Constitution of the United States.*
Bemis, Samuel Flagg. *Diplomacy of the American Revolution, The Pinckney Draft, The Jay Treaty.*
Benedick, Charles K. *The Law of the Constitution.*
Bethea, Andrew Jackson. *Contribution of Charles Pinckney to the Formation of the Constitution.*
Biddle, Charles. *Autobiography.*
Birney, Catherine H. *The Grimké Sisters.*
Bisset, George. *Life of George III.*
Book of America. Massachusetts Historical Society.
Botta, Charles. *History of the American War.*
Bowen, F. "Life of General Benjamin Lincoln" (in *Library of American Biography*).
Bowers, Claude. *Jefferson and Hamilton.*
Brearly, David. *Papers.*
British Library of Information.
Brotherhead, William. *Book of the Signers.*
Brown, William Garrett. *Life of Oliver Ellsworth.*
Bruce, David. *Materials for History.*
Bryce, James. *The American Commonwealth.*
Burnett, Edmund Cody. *Letters of the Members of Continental Congress, The Continental Congress.*
Burns, Edward McNall. *James Madison.*
Caldwell, Dr. Charles. *Life of Nathanael Greene.*

Campbell, Lady William (Sally Izard). *Diary.*

Carpenter, Hugh, *Kings Mountain.*

Carroll, Bartholomew Rivers. *Catechism of United States History.*

Carson, Hampton Lawrence. *Causes of the American Revolution and the Age of Washington, History of the Supreme Court of the United States.*

Chamberlain, W. H. *Government of South Carolina, Sketches of War History.*

Channing, Edward. *History of the United States.*

Charleston Historical Commission. *Report.*

Charleston State Rights Celebration, 1830.

Charleston Year Book, 1899.

Chesney, Alexander, *Journal.*

Chester, John. *Life of Sam Adams.*

Childs, St. Julian Ravenel. *Malaria and the Colonization in the Carolina Low Country.*

Clinton, Sir Henry. *Narrative of the Attack on Sullivan's Island.*

Clinton-Cornwallis Controversy (London).

Creecy, Richard Benbury. *Grandfather's Tales of North Carolina.*

Cruger, Henry. *A Journal of the First Congress of the First American Colonies.*

Cruger, Lewis. *Causes of the American Revolution, Catechism of the Constitution of the United States, Statesmen's Manual of the Constitution, Washington in his Relation to the National Idea.*

Cutler, Manasseh. *Life, Journal, and Correspondence.*

Dalcho, Frederick. *History of the Episcopal Church in South Carolina, History of St. Phillips Parish.*

Dale, Beulah May. *Controversies in Continental Congress.*

de Chastelleux, M. *Travels.*

de Puyster. *The Affair at Kings Mountain.*

de Tocqueville, Alexis. *Democracy in America.*

Documentary History of the Constitution.

Draper, Lyman Copeland. *Kings Mountain and Its Heroes.*

Drayton, John. *Memoirs of the American Revolution.*

Drayton, William Henry. *A Carolinian.*

Duane, William. *John Rutledge.*

Duyclinck, Evert Augustus. *National Portrait Gallery of Eminent Americans.*

Earle, Alice Morse. *Colonial Days in Old New York.*

Easterby, J. H. "Charles Pinckney" (*Dictionary of American Biography*), *History of the College of Charleston.*

Elliott's *Debates on the Constitution.*

Extracts from Votes in Continental Congress.

Fallows, Samuel. *Life of Samuel Adams.*

Farrand, Max. *Records of the Federal Convention, The Framing of the Constitution.*

Few, William. *Autobiography.*

Fiske, John. *Essays. Historical and Literary, History of the United States American Revolution, Critical Period of American History.*

Flanders, Henry. *The Lives of the Chief Justices of the United States* (John Rutledge, Volume I).

Force, Peter. *A Description of the Province of South Carolina.*

Ford, Paul Leicester. *Bibliography of the Constitution, Pelatiah Webster* (edited by), *Works of Thomas Jefferson* (edited by).

Ford, Worthington C. *Journals of the Continental Congress, Letters between Pinckney, Madison and Monroe, Washington's Writings* (edited by).

Franklin, Benjamin. *Works.*

Fraser, Charles. *Reminiscences of Charleston.*

Garden, Alexander. *Anecdotes of the Revolution.*

Gibbes, Robert W. *Documentary History of South Carolina.*

Gibbs, George. *Memories of the Administration of Washington and John Adams* (edited from the *Papers of Oliver Wolcott*).

Gordon's *History of the American Revolution.*

Gordon, W. "Count Pulaski" (*Georgia Historical Magazine*).

Graham, W. A. *General Joseph Graham and His Revolutionary Papers.*

Greene, Francis Vinton. *Revolutionary War, Life of Nathanael Greene.*

Greene, George W. *Life of Nathanael Greene.*

Gregorie, Anne K. "Andrew Williamson" (*Dictionary of American Biography*).

Grimké, John Faucheraud. *Order Book, Digest of Public Laws of South Carolina.*

Guedalla, Philip. *Fathers of the Revolution.*

Hamilton, Alexander. *Writings* (edited by Henry Cabot Lodge).

Hamilton, J. G. de Roulhac. *Best Letters of Thomas Jefferson*, "Notes on Diary of William Lenoir," "Notes on Isaac Shelby" (both in *Journal of Southern History*).

Hamilton, S. M. *James Monroe.*

Harlow, Ralph Volney. *Sam Adams.*

Harper, Roger Goodloe. *Letters.*

Harrison, Mrs. Burton. *History of the City of New York* (with Martha J. Lamb).

Hartley, Cecil B. *Heroes and Patriots of the South.*

Henderson, Archibald. *Conquest of the Old Southwest, History of North Carolina, Mecklenburg Declaration* (pamphlet), *Washington's Southern Tour, Life of James Wilson, Life of Isaac Shelby,* "Sketch of James Williams" (in *Raleigh News and Observer*).

Hendrick, Burton J. *Bulwark of the Republic.*

Hewatt, Rev. Alexander. *History of South Carolina and Georgia.*

Heyward, Duncan C. *Seed of Madagascar.*

Hicks, William. *On William Pitt's Speech.*

Hill, D. H. *Greene's Retreat* (North Carolina Booklet, Vol. I).

Hill, Colonel William. *Memoires* (edited by A. S. Salley, Jr.).

Hiltzeimer, Jacob. *Diary.*

Historical Record Survey, Columbia, South Carolina.

Hocket, Homer Cary. *Political and Social Growth of the American People.*

Hosmer, James K. *Life of Samuel Adams.*

House Journal of Continental Congress.

Howe, Dr. George. *History of the Presbyterian Church in North Carolina.*

Hoyt, William Henry. *Mecklenburg Declaration of Independence.*

Hudleston, F. J. *Gentleman Johnny Burgoyne.*

Huger, Alfred. *The Carolina Low Country* (with Thomas R. Waring and Herbert Ravenel Sass).

Hughes, Edward. "The English Stamp Duties" (*English Historical Review*).

Hughes, Rupert. *George Washington.*

Hunt, Gaillard. *The Constitution, Writings of James Madison* (edited by).

Hunter, Cyrus L. *Sketches of Western North Carolina.*

Irving, Washington. *Knickerbocker History of New York.*

James, Judge. *Life of Francis Marion.*

Jameson, John Franklin. *Studies in the History of the Federal Convention* (Annual Report of the American Historical Association, 1902), *American Historians' Raw Materials* (University of Michigan, 1923), *Dictionary of United States History.*

Jay, John. *Correspondence* (edited by H. P. Johnston).

Jefferson, Thomas. *Letters, Works* (edited by P. L. Ford, J. G. de R. Hamilton).

Jervey, Theodore. *The Slave Trade.*

Johnson, Joseph. *Traditions of the Revolution.*

Johnson, Hon. William. *Life of Nathanael Greene.*

Johnston, H. P. *Correspondence of John Jay* (edited by).

Jones, E. A. *American Members of the Inns of Court.*

Journal of the Commons, South Carolina (edited by A. S. Salley, Jr.).

Journal of the Continental Congress.

Journal of the First Congress of the American Colonies.

Journal of the General Assembly, South Carolina, 1776 (March and April) and 1778 (September and October).

Justinian (pseud.). *Letters.*

King, Rufus. *Correspondence.*

Knollenberg, Bernhard. *Washington, a Reappraisal.*

Konkle, Burton Alvah, *Address on James Wilson* (pamphlet, privately printed).

Landrum, John Belton O'Neall. *Colonial and Revolutionary History of Upper South Carolina.*

La Prade, W. T. "Stamp Act in British Politics" (*American Historical Review*).

Laurens Papers. Long Island Historical Society.

Lee, Henry. *Memoirs of the War of '76.*

Leiding, Harriette Kershaw. *Historical Houses of South Carolina.*

Lenoir, William. *Revolutionary Diary* (Notes by J. G. deRoulhac Hamilton).

Letters from Members of Continental Congress, Carnegie Institution.

Library of American Biography.

Library of Congress. *Original Sources.*

Lodge, Henry Cabot. *Writings.*

Logan, John H. *History of Upper South Carolina.*

Logan, John R. *Record of the Kings Mountain Baptist Association.*

Lossing, Benson J. *Pictorial Field Book of the Revolution.*

Madison, James. *Journal of the Constitutional Convention, Papers.*

Madison, James. *Writings* (edited by Gaillard Hunt).

Martin, Luther. *General Information.*

McCall, Major Hugh. *History of Georgia.*

McCrady; Edward. *History of South Carolina in the Revolution, South Carolina under Royal Government, St. Phillips Church.*

McKenzie, Lt. Rhoderick. *Strictures on Tarleton's History.*

McLaughlin, A. C. "James Wilson and the Constitution" (*Political Science Quarterly*).

McMaster, John B. *History of the United States, With the Fathers.*

McRee, Griffith John. *Life and Correspondence of James Iredell.*

Marshall, John. *Works.*

Massachusetts Historical Society. *Book of America.*

Meigs, William Montgomery. *The Growth of the Constitution in the Federal Convention.*

Meriwether, Robert Lee. "John Rutledge" (*Dictionary of American Biography*).

Mikhel's *Rumbling of the Chariot Wheels.*

Miller, John C. *Sam Adams.*

Mills, General Edward. *Letters.*

Monroe, James. *Writings* (edited by S. M. Hamilton).

Moore, Frank. *Diary of the American Revolution.*

Moore, M. A. *Life and Letters of Edward Lacey.*

Moravians of North Carolina, Records of, Vol. III.

Morgan, General Daniel. *Original Report on the Battle of Cowpens.*

Morris, Gouverneur. *Diaries and Letters.*

Morris, Robert. *Manuscripts* (edited by Henry A. Homes).

Moultrie Centennial. Charleston, 1876.

Moultrie, General William. *Memoirs of the Revolution.*

Murphey, Archibald D. *Papers* (North Carolina Historical Commission).

Nott, Charles C. *Mystery of the Pinckney Draft.*

O'Neall, John Belton. *Bench and Bar of South Carolina.*

Ordinances of the Provisional Government of South Carolina, 1776-1777.

Otis, James. *A Vindication of the American Colonies.*

Papers of General Staff of Washington and Marion.

Parrington, Vernon L. *The Colonial Mind.*

Patterson, S. M. *Life of Horatio Gates.*

Pennsylvania Portfolio.

Perry, B. F. *Biography of American Statesmen.*

Phillips, Ulrich. *Life and Labor in the Old South, Plantation and Frontier Documents, American Negro Slavery.*

Pickering, Timothy. *Observations.*

Pierce, William. *Reliques.*

Pinckney, Rev. Charles Cotesworth. *Life of Thomas Pinckney.*

Pitt, William. *Correspondence.*

Porcher, F. A. *Papers of Historical Society of South Carolina.*

Protest in Lords against Repeal of the Stamp Tax.

Quincy, Josiah. *Journal.*

Ramsay, David. *History of South Carolina, Memories, South Carolina in the Revolution.*

Ramsey, J. S. M. *Annals of Tennessee.*

Ravenel, Mrs. St. Julien. *Charleston; the Place and the People, Letters of Eliza Pinckney.*

Redpath, James. *History of the United States.*

Reed, Joseph. *Letters.*

Rhett, R. Goodwin. *Charleston, Epic of Carolina.*

Rice and Hart. *National Portrait Gallery of Eminent Americans.*

Rivers, William J. *Historical Sketch of South Carolina.*

Rives, W. Cabell. *Life and Times of Madison.*

Roberts, Owen J. *Pelatiah Webster.*

Roosevelt, Theodore. *Winning of the West.*

Rutledge, Archibald. *Plantation Lights and Shadows.*

Rutledge, Benjamin Huger. *American Memorial Day Address* (May 10, 1875).

Sabatini, Rafael. *The Carolinian.*

Salley, Alexander S., Jr. *Delegates to Continental Congress from South Carolina, History of Orangeburg County, Historical Papers of South Carolina, The Origin of Carolina.*

Sass, Herbert Ravenel. *The Carolina Low Country* (with Thomas R. Waring and Alfred Huger).

Schenck, David. *North Carolina in 1780-81* (Raleigh, 1889).

Schlesinger, Arthur Meier. *Colonial Merchants of the Revolution.*

Seabury, Samuel. *Conduct of Delegates to Continental Congress.*

Secret Journal of Continental Congress.

Sellers, Leila. *Commercial Transactions in Charleston on the Eve of the American Revolution.*

Shelby, Isaac. Letters.

Siege of Charleston.

Simms, William Gilmore, *The History of South Carolina, Eutaw, The Forayers, Life of Henry Laurens, Life of Francis Marion, Life of Nathanael Greene.*

Singleton, Esther. *Social New York under the Georges.*

Smith, Alice R. Huger and Dr. E. Huger. *Dwelling Houses in Old Charleston.*

Smith, Helen Evertson. *Colonial Days and Ways.*

Smith, W. Roy. *South Carolina as a Royal Province.*

Smyth, James Frederick Dalziel. *A Tour of the United States.*

Smythe, Augustine T. *The Carolina Low Country* (with Huger, Sass and Waring).

Snowden, Yates. *History of South Carolina.*

South, E. Albert. *Americans at Inns of Court.*

South Carolina. *Supreme Court Records.*

South Carolina. *Miscellaneous Publications of the State,* as edited by A. S. Salley, Jr., covering years 1780-81.

Southeron (pseud.). *South Carolina in the Revolution (being Diaries of persons in the Siege of Charleston).*

Sparks, Jared. *George Washington's Diplomatic Correspondence in the American Revolution* (edited by), *Life of Gouverneur Morris.*

Spencer, R. H. "Pulaski's Legion," (*Maryland Historical Magazine*).

Stamp Act Congress. *Journal.*

Steadman, C. *The Amercian War.*

Stevens, B. F. *Facsimiles of Mss. in European Archives Relative to America.*

Stevens, C. Ellis. *Sources of the Constitution of the United States.*

Stevenson and Dunne. *Life of George Washington.*

Stokes, I. N. Phelps. *Iconography of Manhattan Island.*

Sumter, Thomas. *Letters.*

Tarleton, Sir Banastre. *History of the Campaigns of 1780-81 in the Southern Province of North America.*

Taylor, Hannis. *Memorial in Behalf of the Architect of Our Federal Constitution, Origin and Growth of the Federal Constitution.*

Thomas, E. S. Contributor, Charleston newspapers.

Turnbull, James. *The Crisis.*

Uhlendorf, B. A., translator. *The Seige of Charleston in Diaries and Letters from Hessian Officers* (Von Junkkenn Papers, Clements Library).

Umbreit, Kenneth Bernard. *The Chief Justices.*

United States History of the Revolution: Military.

Van Doren, Carl. *Benjamin Franklin.*

Vaughn, L. B. *Life of Samuel Adams.*

Wallace, David Duncan. *Life of Henry Laurens, History of South Carolina.*

Waring, Thomas R. *The Carolina Low Country* (with Alfred Huger and Herbert Ravenel Sass).

Warren, Charles. *Congress, the Constitution and the Supreme Court, The Making of the Constitution, Supreme Court and Sovereign States, The Supreme Court in United States History.*

Washington, George. *Writings, Letters of G. W.* (edited by Jared Sparks, W. C. Ford).

Watson, John T. *Annals of Philadelphia in the Olden Time.*

Wauchope, G. A. *Literary South Carolina.*

Webber, Mabel L. "Descendants of Dr. John Rutledge," (*South Carolina Historical and Genealogical Magazine*).

Webster, Pelatiah. *A Dissertation on Political Union* (pamphlet).

Weems, Parson. *Life of Francis Marion.*

Welles, Edward L. *Charleston Light Dragoons.*

Wells, W. V. *Life of Samuel Adams.*

Wertenbaker, Thomas Jefferson. *The Old South, The Founding of American Civilization, The Golden Age of Colonial Culture.*
Wheeler, John H. *History of North Carolina.*
White, H. A. (in *South Carolina Historical and Genealogical Magazine*).
White, Katherine K. *The Kings Mountain Men.*
White's *Conspectus of American Biography.*
Whitefield, George. *Memoirs.*
Wilkin, Walter Harold. *Some British Soldiers in America.*
Wilkinson, Eliza. *Letters.*
Wilson, Rufus Rockwell. *New York, Old and New.*
Wilstach, Paul. *Patriots off their Pedestals.*
Winsor, Justin. *Narrative and Critical History of America* (War in the Southern Department).
Wolfe, John Harold. *Origins of Jefferson Democracy in South Carolina.*
Woodward, W. E. *George Washington; the Image and the Man, History of the United States.*
Yates, Robert. *Notes.*

INDEX

420 INDEX

Pennsylvania, Pennsylvanians, 110, 125, 160, 162, 179, 252, 271, 307, 309, 319, 320, 321, 327, 332, 334, 338, 352, 367
Peronneau, Duval, 61, 64, 65
Perroneaus, the, 27, 70
Peru 93
Philadelphia, Philadelphians, 16, 17, 21, 48, 113, 153, 154, 155, 156, 157, 162, 166, 168, 169, 170, 176, 182, 184, 186, 187, 188, 190, 197, 199, 220, 235, 239, 263, 271, 312, 314, 317, 318, 319, 320, 321, 323, 326, 328, 341, 353, 359
Phillips Plantation, 17, 28, 33, 35, 36, 41, 53
Pickens, 225, 282, 283, 293, 300
Pierce, William, 331
Pinckney, Chief Justice Charles, 22, 29, 52, 55
Pinckney, Charles Cotesworth, 21, 265, 303, 311, 313, 314, 324, 363
Pinckney, Charles, Jr., (The Charles; "Blackguard Charlie") appointed to Drayton's Council, 187; on constitutional committee (S. C.), 191; his father's departure, 220; relationship, 303; talks of new national constitution, 309; sketch of early career, 310-12; selected delegate to Federal Convention, 313; reads draft to associates, 313-14; his 'plan' discussed before convention, 318-19; his plan presented, 323; protagonist of South Carolina, 324; Hamilton perceives meaning of his floor leadership, 326-7; his plan before the Drafting Committee, 339; on judicial power, 349; his attitude on judicial power considered by Randolph, 350; on Jay Treaty, 355; gets his best expression through Rutledge, 371
Pinckney, Colonel Charles, Mr., 19, 20, 21, 23, 25, 29, 37, 38, 52, 64, 65, 66, 67, 69, 70, 75, 76, 79, 81, 82, 83, 87, 89, 90; confronts Chief Justice while in charge of hanging, 92, 93, 95, 98, 99, 100, 112, 124, 126, 128, 135, 143, 169, 170; heartsick with "Liberty", 174; instructs son to accord primacy to Rutledge, 175, 178, 184, 185, 200, 221, 246, 303
Pinckney Plan, the (Pinckney Draft), (South Carolina Plan), 309, 323

Pinckney, Mrs., 33, 83
Pinckney, Thomas, 20, 21, 303, 311, 313, 354
Pinckneys, the, 14, 27, 171, 220
Piragua, 15
Pitt, William, "The Great Commoner", 26, 94, 119, 120, 121, 122, 123, 124, 151
Pocatoligo Road, 291
Poinsett's Tavern, 83
Poland, King of, 200
Polish, 253, 254
Polish Legion, 252, 253
Pompey, 25, 48, 49, 55, 56, 69, 82, 158, 159, 163
Pontiac, 108
Poor Richard, see Franklin, 16
Pope, Mr., 12
Portugal, 93
Potomac, the, 307
"Powers of the President" clause, 341, 371
Presbyterian, Presbyterians, 112, 126, 145, 146, 226
President of the Continental Congress, 161, 181
President of the General Committee, 184
President of Pennsylvania, 321
President of the Provincial Congress, 184, 185
President, the (of the Republic of South Carolina), 186, 193, 195, 197, 202, 203, 221, 223, 224, 227, 233, 303
President of the United States, 341, 351, 352, 353, 356
Prévost, 241, 243, 249, 250, 253, 256, 257, 259, 260, 261
Prime Minister, British, 119, 120
Princeton, 274
Privy Council, 237, 240, 255, 260, 264, 265, 310
Providence (R. I.), 307
Provisional (Provincial) Congress of South Carolina, 171, 184, 185, 187, 189, 190, 191, 192
Prussia, King of, 246
Prussian, 274, 294
Pulaski, Count Casimir, 253-4, 255, 256, 260, 261, 262
Pulaski, Count Joseph, 252

seconds Washington's nomination, 181; persuades Virginia delegation to vote for Washington, 182; hears Drayton is Dictator, 182; returns to Charles Town, 183-4; secures recall of Drayton, 185; returns to Philadelphia, 186; plans to secure a more orderly government for S. C., 187-190; writes the constitution for S. C., 192-3; is elected President of the Republic of South Carolina, 193; prepares for war, 195-200; meets Charles Lee, 200; directs Moultrie in the first Battle of Charles Town, 201-217; gives sword to Jasper, 219; address to the Assembly on the Declaration of Independence, 220-21; directs the Cherokee War, 222-25; clemency, 225-26; Drayton's plot against, 226-30; vetos new constitution, 230-33; resigns as president, 234; is elected assemblyman and senator simultaneously and also appointed Privy Councillor, 237; decides for Lowndes, 240; elected Governor, 242; at Orangeburg makes his decision as to the military technique required to win the war, 243-48; plans with Lincoln, 249-51; in the second Battle of Charles Town, 252-62; conference on major strategy in 1775, 263; is declared Dictator with all power, including that over life, 264; proclamation to militia, 265; his dictatorship is modified and sharpened, 265-66; is challenged to a duel, 267-68; escapes from Charles Town, 269; his mother's opinion of him, 269-70; goes North for help, 272-4; sends Mathews to report on Greene, 274; finds deKalb in command, 275; Gates avoids him, 276; final phase of military career, 277-302; a "Dictator" in the form of a servant, 277-80; with Marion, 279-81; with Sumter and Pickens, 282-83; Hillsboro conference, 283, 285; with Williams, 283-5; his 'champion' at Kings Mountain, 287; his clemency adopted, 288; fight for political control of war-torn state, 289-91; makes indigo money, 291-2; asks for Greene, 292; meets Greene, 292; holds Greene in his mili-

tary technique, 293-6; loses control of Greene, 299; regains control of Greene, 300; final triumph of his military technique, 301-2; Chancellor, 303; reduced scale of living, 304-5; Rutledge Avenue not named for, 304; habit and reputation as judge, 305; his touch with outer world through the Exchange and with the local world through the Corner, 305-7; professional honor involved, 308; names child "States", 308-9; silently notes agitation for a federal constitution, 309-13; Junior supplies his deficiencies, 310; the Pinckney party resents his recognized leadership, 311-12; selected chief of delegation to constitutional convention, 313; receives colleagues at dinner, 313-4; hears Pinckney's plan, 314; sails for Philadelphia, 314; guest of James Wilson, 315; character contrasted with that of Wilson, 316-7; plans strategy of the convention with Wilson, 319-23; proposes "oath of secrecy", 321-2; seconds George Washington, 323; Franklin causes him to speak publicly, 324-5; analyzes components of the convention, 325-8; accepts from Wilson idea of copyright protection, 326; a conservative, 325-6 his position on property qualification for voters and office holders, 326; foresees the "money issue", 326, 330; perceiving his control Hamilton bolts the convention, 326-7; organization of the components of the convention come to him with Wilson and Sherman, 327; "sells" the slave trade to Roger Sherman, 328-32; his position on maritime trade acts, 330-2; on slavery, 328-9; as a race horse owner, 331; dinner for Roger Sherman, 331-2; calls Hugh Williamson to seal his pact with Sherman, 332; silent during discussion of slave trade, 332-3-4; faces the final crisis, 334; his soft speech on accommodation, 334-5; chosen Chairman of Drafting Committee, 338; reads Treaty of Five Nations, 339; becomes "the lens of the convention", 339-40; remarks on "foundation of great empire", 340; his "permanent view", 340; gives full mili-